Real Victory *for* Real Life

Volume 2

*365 Devotional Thoughts
in the Spirit of America's Keswick*

Dr. Bill Welte, General Editor

Unless otherwise noted, the majority of Scripture quoted is from the New King James Version. Scripture taken from the New King James Version®. Copyright © 1982 by Thomas Nelson, Inc. Used by permission. All rights reserved.

Scripture taken from the New Century Version® (NCV). Copyright © 2005 by Thomas Nelson, Inc. Used by permission. All rights reserved.

Scripture quotations marked (ESV) are from the *ESV® Bible (The Holy Bible, English Standard Version®)*, copyright © 2001 by Crossway Bibles, a publishing ministry of God News Publishers. Used by permission. All rights reserved.

Scripture quotations marked (HCSB) are taken from the Holman Christian Standard Bible®, copyright © 1999, 2000, 2002, 2003, 2009 by Holman Bible Publishers. Used by permission. Holman Christian Standard Bible®, Holman CSB®, and HCSB® are federally registered trademarks of Holman Bible Publishers.

King James Version (KJV), public domain.

Scripture taken from *The Message*. Copyright © 1993, 1994, 1995, 1996, 2000, 2001, 2002. Used by permission of NavPress Publishing Group.

Scripture taken from the NEW AMERICAN STANDARD BIBLE®, copyright © 1960,1962,1963,1968,1971,1972,1973,1975,1977,1995 by The Lockman Foundation. Used by permission. (www.Lockman.org)

Scripture quotations taken from the Amplified® Bible, copyright © 1954, 1958, 1962, 1965, 1987 by The Lockman Foundation. All rights reserved. Used by permission. (www.Lockman.org)

Scripture taken from the HOLY BIBLE, NEW INTERNATIONAL VERSION® (NIV). Copyright © 1973, 1978, 1984 Biblica. Used by permission of Zondervan. All rights reserved.

Dedicated to four godly influencers in my life who taught me the Victorious Christian Life message

Dr. Robert Alderman
Minister-at-Large, Shenandoah Baptist Church

Dr. Stephen F. Olford
Founder of Olford Ministries

Dr. William A. Raws
Grandson of the founder of America's Keswick

Dr. Roger Willmore
Senior Pastor, Deerfoot Baptist Church

Acknowledgements:

This book would not have been possible without the typing, proofreading and editing of Ruth Schmidt, Grace Bibik, Bill Bibik, Lynn Randall, Dianne Baergen, Jenn Lawrence, DeEtta Marsh, Cherri Freeman, Jane Holland and Nanci Duffy.

Introduction

I am addicted to books. I love to read books from all genres. But the books that mean the most to me are first of all, God's holy, precious and inspired Word and then the devotional books that I have collected over the years.

The Word of God continues to be my first delight and joy. My Bibles are filled with highlights, underlined and highlighted passages and notes in the margins that include dates, names and events that are tied to significant verses of Scripture.

I have been blessed to read so many of the classic devotional works: *Daily Light, Faith's Checkbook, My Utmost for His Highest, Streams in the Desert,* as well as some outstanding new devotionals: *Experiencing God – The Devotional* and *Jesus Calling.*

This second volume of Real Victory for Real Life contains 30 devotionals written by the late Dr. William A. Raws, the grandson of the founder of America's Keswick. Pastor Bill not only taught the Victorious Christian Life message – he lived it.

I am indebted to Dr. Robert Alderman (Shenandoah Baptist Church) and Dr. Roger Willmore (Deerfoot Baptist Church) for their significant contributions to this work. These giants of the faith have taught the victorious Christian life message around the world. I am privileged to not only have them as my mentors, but they are my friends.

I thank the Lord for the blessing of a godly wife, Jan Carol Toms, who has been my friend and wife for over three decades. God has blessed me with four wonderful children, Laura, Josh, Julie and Zach, three special "in-loves" – Jon, Jenny and Garrett, and ten precious grandkids: Tanner, Lindsay (in heaven), Case, Wyatt & Sydney Groen; Sam and Will Welte;

Emma, Ethan, & Weston Houston. They have all brought me such great joy.

I am also indebted to the Board of Trustees and staff of America's Keswick for the privilege to serve with them for this season of my life. They have enriched my life in so many ways.

May this devotional be instrumental in drawing you into a deeper relationship with the Lord. Allow Him to speak to your heart and transform your life.

Dr. Bill Welte
President & CEO
America's Keswick
2012

Contributors:

Dr. Bob Alderman – Minister-at-Large, Shenandoah Baptist Church, Roanoke, VA

Rev. Jeff Barbieri – Teaching Pastor, Grace Christian Church, Freehold, NJ

Allen Beltle – Chief Financial Officer, America's Keswick

Bernie Bostwick – Vice President, Ambassador Advisors, Lancaster, PA

Rev. John Bryant – Executive Director of Christ's Home, Warmister, PA; served on staff at America's Keswick from 1990-1996

Donna Connors – served on Guest Services staff at America's Keswick from June 2007-April 2010

Travis Dickinson – grandson of William A. Raws; Assistant Professor of Philosophy, The College at Southwestern, Fort Worth, TX

Rev. Neil Fichthorn – Fichthorn Associates, Gaynor Group

Jim Freed – Colony of Mercy Director, America's Keswick

Bevan Greiner – Director of Family Christian Inspiration, Inc.

Joyce Hayes – Artist-in-Residence, Women's Event Hostess, America's Keswick

Robert Hayes – Artist-in-Residence, Program Director, America's Keswick

Marilyn Heavilin – author, speaker, summer Counselor-in-Residence at America's Keswick

Carolyn Hibbard – pastor's wife, mother, grandmother, concert pianist

Rev. John Hibbard – teaching pastor at the Colony of Mercy Chapel; Keswick Board member

Rev. Chris S. Hodges – Founder and President of Abiding Above Ministries, Cordova, TN

Dr. Donald R. "Dick" Hubbard – former Pastor of Calvary Baptist Church, NYC

Joy Hubbard – wife of Dick Hubbard, ladies Bible teacher

Chris Hughes – Colony of Mercy graduate; Freedom Fighters contributor

Diane Hunt – Chief Development Officer & Director of Women's Ministries, America's Keswick

Bill Jahns – Colony of Mercy graduate; Housekeeping Director, America's Keswick

Dr. Lynne Jahns – Christian Counselor, America's Keswick

Dr. George Kelsey – retired missionary to Jordan

Mary Ann Kiernan – Colony of Mercy Intake Manager, America's Keswick

Jenn Lawrence – Guest Services Representative, America's Keswick

DeEtta Marsh – served on Keswick staff from 1995-2005, and 2008-2011

Chaplain Stan Marsh – Colony of Mercy Chaplain of Aftercare, America's Keswick

Dr. George L. Nichols, Jr. – Pastor of Faith Baptist Church, Wilmington, DE

Jack Noel – retired Colony of Mercy Chaplain

Dr. Joe Olachea – Pastor of Lakes Community Chapel, Medford Lakes, NJ; Keswick Board member

Stephanie Paul – Woman of Character Director, America's Keswick

Dr. Dino Pedrone – President of Davis College, Johnson City, NY

Chaplain Bill Pruitt – Colony of Mercy Chaplain, America's Keswick

Pastor Bill Raws – grandson of founder William Raws; served on staff for 58 years; with the Lord July 20, 2008

Rev. Robby Richardson – Executive Director of the Internet Evangelism Network; Northside Campus Pastor at Bridge Bible Church, Greater Grand Rapids, Michigan

Rob Russomano – Colony of Mercy graduate; Maintenance Assistant, America's Keswick

Midge Ruth – Keswick Board Member Emeritus

Glenna Salsbury – professional speaker, author and consultant

Ruth Schmidt – Administrative Assistant, America's Keswick

Rev. John Strain – Senior Pastor, First Baptist Church of Toms River, NJ

Rev. Chris Thompson – Colony of Mercy graduate; Pastor of Enderby Mission Church, Leicester, England

Dr. H. G. VanSandt – interim pastor, Christian counselor

Rev. Jason Walsh – Assistant Pastor for Youth Ministries, Whiting Bible Church, Whiting, NJ

Carl Washington – Colony of Mercy graduate; Food Service Department, America's Keswick

Ed Weiss – Colony of Mercy graduate; Director of Marketing & Guest Services, America's Keswick

Dr. Bill Welte – President & CEO, America's Keswick

Dr. Roger D. Willmore – Senior Pastor, Deerfoot Baptist Church, Trussville, Alabama; former Minister-at-Large for Stephen Olford Ministries International

Lynn Wilson – Guest Services Representative, America's Keswick

Kathy Withers – Development Associate, America's Keswick

Dr. John Woodward – Director of Education and Media, Grace Fellowship International, Pigeon Forge, TN

Foreword

Few things are more important to our spiritual and relational vitality than a regular time of communication with God through His Word. While we often do our devotions, the pursuit often gets crowded out by the busyness of our lives and our inability to know the best places to go in Scripture to help us navigate our lives through the day. This is where Bill Welte's compilation of outstanding daily devotionals comes to our rescue. You no longer need to do your time with the Lord alone. Every day you will find relevant thoughts to feed your soul from both internationally known Bible teachers as well as those who serve at America's Keswick. Best of all, their written words will be grounded in God's infallible Word and empowered by the Holy Spirit directly to you right where you live. Bravo to my friend Bill who has brought us this valuable resource.

~ Dr. Joseph M. Stowell, President,
Cornerstone University, Grand Rapids, Michigan

Genesis 1-3; Matthew 1   **January 1**

Worthy Goals for the New Year

And this I pray... (Philippians 1:9)

I do not know who originally compiled this list, but I have found it to be so helpful in reviewing the past year and looking forward to the new.

1. Love like the Philippians...Philippians 1:9-11 - *And this I pray, that your love may abound still more and more in knowledge and all discernment, that you may approve the things that are excellent, that you may be sincere and without offense till the day of Christ, being filled with the fruits of righteousness which are by Jesus Christ, to the glory and praise of God.*

2. Study like the Bereans...Acts 17:10-12 – *Then the brethren immediately sent Paul and Silas away by night to Berea. When they arrived, they went into the synagogue of the Jews. These were more fair-minded than those in Thessalonica, in that they received the word with all readiness, and searched the Scriptures daily to find out whether these things were so. Therefore many of them believed, and also not a few of the Greeks, prominent women as well as men.*

3. Pray like the Ephesians...Ephesians 6:18 – *Praying always with all prayer and supplication in the Spirit, being watchful to this end with all perseverance and supplication for all the saints.*

4. Witness like the Antiochans...Acts 11:19-21 – *Now those who were scattered after the persecution that arose over Stephen traveled as far as Phoenicia, Cyprus, and Antioch, preaching the word to no one but the Jews only. But some of them were men from Cyprus and Cyrene, who, when they had come to Antioch, spoke to the Hellenists, preaching the Lord Jesus. And the hand of the Lord was with them, and a great number believed and turned to the Lord.*

5. Give like the Macedonians...2 Corinthians 8:1, 4-5 – *Moreover, brethren, we make known to you the grace of God bestowed on the churches of Macedonia:...imploring us with* much urgency that we would receive the gift and the fellowship of the ministering to the saints. And not only as we had hoped, but they first gave themselves to the Lord, and then to us by the will of God.

6. Watch like the Thessalonians...1 Thessalonians 1:9-10 –
For they themselves declare concerning us what manner of entry we had to you, and how you turned to God from idols to serve the living and true God, and to wait for His Son from heaven, whom He raised from the dead, even Jesus who delivers us from the wrath to come.

Have a godly New Year!

Dr. Donald R. Hubbard

Genesis 4-6; Matthew 2   **January 2**

Redeem The Time

See then that you walk circumspectly, not as fools but as wise, redeeming the time, because the days are evil.
(Ephesians 5:15-16)

There are 1440 minutes in this 24 hour period.

»How many of those 1440 minutes will we spend thinking about ourselves?
»How many of those 1440 minutes will we spend thinking about money and bills?
»How many of those 1440 minutes will we spend thinking negative thoughts?
»How many of those 1440 minutes will we spend thinking about things we want but do not have?
»How many of those 1440 minutes will we spend worrying?
»How many of those 1440 minutes will we spend gossiping?
»How many of those 1440 minutes will we spend grumbling and complaining?
»How many of those 1440 minutes will we spend serving others?
»How many of those 1440 minutes will we spend loving others?

»How many of those 1440 minutes will we spend being kind to others?
»How many of those 1440 minutes will we spend being a doer of the word and not a hearer only?
»How many of those 1440 minutes will we spend obeying God?
»How many of those 1440 minutes will we spend walking by faith and not by sight?
»How many of those 1440 minutes will we spend believing God and taking Him at His word?
»How many of those 1440 minutes will we spend resting in the care of God?
»How many of those 1440 minutes will we spend living in Jesus Christ rather than in the world?
»How many of those 1440 minutes will we spend living in resurrection power?
»How many of those 1440 minutes will we spend meditating on the Word of God?
»How many of those 1440 minutes will we spend worshipping Jesus Christ?

At the end of the day will we have spent more time living for Jesus Christ or for self?

Diane Hunt

Genesis 7-9; Matthew 3　　　　　　　　　　**January 3**

How to Know God

"He who has My commandments and keeps them, it is he who loves Me. And he who loves Me will be loved by my Father, and I will love him and manifest Myself to him." (John 14:21)

We have before us a promise. Jesus said He would manifest (reveal, make known) Himself to the person who loves Him and keeps His commandments. This promise delights the heart of every true Christian. Who among us does not want to know the Lord Jesus more personally and intimately?

In verse 22, we read that Judas (not Iscariot) was brave enough to ask the question that many Christians may ask from time to time, *"Lord, how is it that You will manifest Yourself to us...?"*

God's promises are conditional. In order to receive what He promises we must meet the condition of the promise. Are you longing in your heart today to know Christ more fully and personally? There is a condition to fulfill and that condition is *obedience.* If someone asked me what I consider the most important word in the Christian vocabulary, I would say *obedience.* The Christian life matures in direct proportion to our obedience to the revealed word of God.

In this passage, John 14:1-24, Jesus reveals some important truths about *obedience.*

Jesus spoke of the <u>motive for our obedience</u>. He said, *"If you love Me, keep my commandments"* (v. 15). Motive is an important part of our Christian walk. Jesus makes it quite clear that our love for Him should be the primary motivation to obedience.

Jesus spoke of the <u>outward expression of our obedience</u>. He said, *"If anyone loves me he will keep my word"* (v.23). The apostle James reminds us that *faith without works is dead* (James 2:20). Obedience reveals itself in our active response to what Jesus tells us to do.

Jesus spoke of the <u>source of strength for obedience</u>. In verses 16 and 26 Jesus mentioned the *Helper,* the Holy Spirit, Who would divinely and supernaturally enable us to obey the word and will of God. God never requires something of His children without giving to them all that is necessary to do what He requires.

The key to knowing Jesus is: **Obedience.** Are you ready to obey?

Dr. Roger D. Willmore

Genesis 10-12; Matthew 4 **January 4**

Godly Living in an Ungodly Nation
Psalm 43 (Part 1)

This is the music of both a conflicted and a conquering heart. It is brief but to the point. It presents positive counsel as well as personal testimony. The situation is not unlike that which we face today throughout the nations.

Surrounded by an "ungodly nation" (v. 1), the child of God cries for God to take action on several matters. The cry is not the typical one we may expect. It is not primarily a cry to judge the nation, eliminate the evil and then punish the evil doers.

Interestingly enough, the psalmist's first request is that God may judge him. Now that is open boldness and powerful spiritual insight. Here God's child recognizes that the mess in his nation may at least in part be due to his own life. So he cries to the Lord, *Judge me* (v. 1).

He is being brutally honest about his own condition. He needs to know from the Master Judge that his own life is clean, that the problems within are not contributing to the problems without.

That desire to be personally judged by God is in full keeping with the request: *Search me, O God, and know my heart: try me, and know my thoughts: And see if there be any wicked way in me...* (Psalm 139:23-24 KJV).

Such openness is a manifestation of marvelous faith. It is faith to know that God will always do right when He deals with us, even and especially when we ask that He judge us for the purpose of protecting us in an ungodly nation.

There is more. *Plead my case against an ungodly nation* (v. 1). When the battle lines are drawn and a case is made against godliness, it is so very correct to invite God to present His case for godliness on our behalf. Godliness has a reason for existing and that case is best presented by God. The path to victorious living is marked clearly by the case He presents.

And there is more. *Deliver me from the deceitful and the unjust* (v. 1). Mark these three requests: Judge me, Plead for me and Deliver Me. There is nothing cheap or childish here. These are proper requests. Our willingness, even our desire for such, is key to a life of victory as we dwell in an ungodly nation.

Dr. Robert L. Alderman

Genesis 13-15; Matthew 5: 1-26   **January 5**

Godly Living in an Ungodly Nation
Psalm 43 (Part 2)

In Psalm 43 we are dealing with the heart cry for victory while living in an ungodly nation. In part one of these thoughts we looked at the first three requests made by the psalmist: Judge me, Plead my case and Deliver me.

There is more. The request is now made for God to send out His light and His truth (v. 3). Such light and truth are scarce in an ungodly nation. In fact, people and nations become ungodly by the simple act of rejecting God's light and God's truth. Little wonder then that a wise man will cry for such. If the nation will not cry for the same, then the individual is left, perhaps alone, to do so.

A further request is made. *Let them bring me to Your holy hill, and to Your tabernacle* (v. 3). It should be a shocking reminder that the striking reality of an ungodly nation is that it has first rejected the authority of the Word of God (light and truth), then it rejects the life of God (the holiness of God), and then it rejects the corporate worship of God (the tabernacles of God).

What happens when these are restored either to an individual or to a nation? Here is the answer of the psalmist, *Then will I go unto the altar of God* (v. 4). God gets our attention again. He gets it not in a form of mere religious ritual but in the form of meaningful altar worship. He gets our attention in the form of sacrificial devotion. That is what the altar means. We do not come to the altar of God in order to negotiate with God. We come there to abandon our negotiating rights and yield all to

Him. If that is not our intent then we need not go to the altar at all.

Not only do we go to the altar of God, we go there with the understanding that God is our *exceeding joy* (v. 4). We do not go to Him with a grudge or as a last resort. We go with the fullness of delight and utmost confidence. We go with the joy of knowing that He is approachable.

Then, with praise, I may say to my soul that it has no reason to be disquieted within me. And that is a major part of living victoriously in an ungodly nation.

Dr. Robert L. Alderman

Genesis 16-17; Matthew 5:27-48   **January 6**

"As I was with Moses ..."

No one will be able to stand against you all the days of your life. As I was with Moses, so I will be with you; I will never leave you nor forsake you. (Joshua 1:5 NIV)

Joshua 1 records for us the transition in leadership of the people of Israel from Moses to Joshua. Not only was Moses one of the greatest leaders in the brief (to that point) history of Israel, he is one of the greatest leaders the world has ever known. But the time for Moses' leadership was ending. Because of his disobedience (Deuteronomy 20), it would not be Moses, but another, Joshua, who would lead the nation across the Jordan River and into the Promised Land.

Joshua had served as Moses' second in command for a long time, but being a lieutenant is far different than being in charge. It would be very understandable for Joshua to have had reservations about his ability to carry out his new responsibilities.

God addresses Joshua and reassures him that he is indeed the one to lead the nation of Israel. There are a number of promises and guidelines that God gives in addressing Joshua, but the promise in verse 5 may have been the most powerful – ... *As I was with Moses, so I will be with you.*

Joshua had seen the mighty hand of God when Moses raised his staff and the waters of the Red Sea parted. When Moses went up Mt. Sinai to receive the Ten Commandments, it was Joshua who was on the side of the mountain. When Moses would meet with God in the "tent of meeting," Joshua was there, often lingering behind there after Moses left (Exodus 33:7-11). Joshua knew the reality and power of God's presence with Moses, and nothing could have meant more to him than the promise that God would be with him in a similar way.

God has also given us that same promise, that He will never leave us or forsake us. Would that we could know the power of that promise in the same way that Joshua did.

Rev. Robby Richardson

Genesis 18-19; Matthew 6:1-18   January 7

Passing the Faith Along

He said to the Israelites, "In the future when your descendants ask their parents, 'What do these stones mean?' tell them, 'Israel crossed the Jordan on dry ground.'" (Joshua 4:21-22 NIV)

Joshua chapter 3 records for us the miraculous crossing of the Jordan River that brings the children of Israel into the Promised Land and confirms, both for Joshua and for the nation of Israel, that God is honoring His promise to be with Joshua in the same way that He was with Moses.

Part of God's instruction to Joshua was to have twelve men, one from each tribe of Israel, choose a stone from the dry river bed and bring it over into their new home. Joshua had these twelve stones set up as a memorial at Gilgal, the place that was to serve as Israel's "base camp" for their conquest of the land of Canaan.

There were several purposes for these stones. They were to remind the people of what God had done and to keep them aware of the power of God. They were to serve as a message to those around *so that all the peoples of the earth might know that the hand of the LORD is powerful* (4:24). They were also to serve as a "teachable moment" for future generations, an historic touchpoint to God's faithfulness in the past and a pointer to God's faithfulness in the future.

What "memorial stones" are you building into your life and the life of your family? Where can your children look to see the reality of how God has worked in your life? If your faith is real and growing, it will show up in ways that will be visible to those around you. Let's make sure that we are passing along a vital faith with a living Savior, not a "philosophy of life" that is distant and ethereal.

Rev. Robby Richardson

Genesis 20-22; Matthew 6:19-34   **January 8**

Keeping It Fresh

Afterward, Joshua read all the words of the law—the blessings and the curses—just as it is written in the Book of the Law. There was not a word of all that Moses had commanded that Joshua did not read to the whole assembly of Israel, including the women and children, and the foreigners who lived among them. (Joshua 8:34-35 NIV)

Israel's entrance into the long-awaited Promised Land was accompanied by unmistakable evidences of God's presence and favor. The waters of the flood-swollen Jordan River were parted for the nation to pass across on dry ground. The seemingly impenetrable walls of Jericho were felled in a clear demonstration of God's power. Everything seemed to be going like clockwork for Joshua and the nation.

Then came the defeat at Ai and the subsequent revelation of Achan's sin. God dealt with the situation in a way that vividly communicated the seriousness of "sin in the camp." Then He gave renewed marching orders to Joshua, and the city of Ai was roundly defeated.

After the second battle of Ai, Joshua took the nation to the natural amphitheater that existed between Mount Ebal and Mount Gerizim, and there, as commanded by Moses in

Deuteronomy 27, *all the words of the law* were read aloud to the people of Israel. They were reminded again of the promises and the commandments that God had given to guide their lives and their relationship with Him.

God has graciously given us His Word as an historical record of His faithfulness, a revelation of His character and a guide for our daily lives. But unless we are regularly hearing and tasting of God's Word for ourselves, it can quickly fade from memory and often become no more than background noise in our lives. What are you doing to regularly keep His Word fresh in your life?

Rev. Robby Richardson

Genesis 23-24; Matthew 7   **January 9**

Why Bother God with the Small Stuff?

The Israelites sampled their provisions but did not inquire of the LORD. (Joshua 9:14 NIV)

After the bitter lesson of Ai and the sin of Achan that had brought on Israel's defeat, you would have thought that Joshua would have learned his lesson ... at least for the next couple of chapters. But Joshua 9 brings us the story of the Gibeonites and their deceptive treaty with the Israelites.

The Gibeonites played their roles perfectly: the moldy bread, the cracked wineskins, the worn out clothes. The Israelites saw the evidence with their own eyes. Their human reasoning convinced them of the truth of the Gibeonites' claim. I'm not sure if they forgot the ability to ask the Lord for guidance or if they just thought they'd save that step for a future time when things weren't quite as clear cut, but Scripture says clearly they *did not inquire of the LORD*.

I'm afraid that I often fall into the same behavior of which the Israelites were guilty. When it's obvious that divine guidance or intervention is needed, it's pretty safe to assume that I will ask the Lord for His help. But all too often, if I think I have a grasp of the situation on my own, I will neglect to bring it to Him. Why bother God with the small stuff?

But just like the Israelites in Joshua 9, I find that my self-perception of my own wisdom is far over-rated. God has given us the incredible opportunity of inquiring of Him. As James reminds us in the first chapter of his epistle: "If any of you lacks wisdom, you should ask God, who gives generously to all without finding fault, and it will be given to you."

Rev. Robby Richardson

Genesis 25-26; Matthew 8:1-17   January 10

Returning to Base Camp

Then Joshua returned with all Israel to the camp at Gilgal.
(Joshua 10:15 NIV)

Following the stories of Jericho and Ai, and the deception of the Gibeonites, the narrative pace of the conquest of the Promised Land as recorded in the book of Joshua picks up considerably. Chapter 10 records for us the decisive battle in finishing off the conquest of the southern half of Canaan, and chapter 11 summarizes the defeat of the northern half of the land. God had powerfully fulfilled his promise to Joshua in chapter 1 that no one would be able to stand against him.

In the middle of chapter 10, and again at the end of the chapter, we see these words, *Then Joshua returned with all Israel to the camp at Gilgal.* If you think about it, it makes a lot of sense. Gilgal was their "permanent" base camp. It was the staging area for their conquests. It was probably also home for the women and children of Israel while the men were carrying out the battle to conquer the land.

But Gilgal was also more than that. It was the place where Joshua had erected the memorial stones to remind the nation of God's intervention in crossing the Jordan River. It was the place where the nation had renewed their covenant with God, and He had renewed His covenant with them. This was a place where the nation did business with God.

Where is your Gilgal? Where do you take refuge from the rigors of battle to renew yourself both physically and spiritually? Where do you do business with God? There is nothing magical about an individual place. God is willing, and waiting, for us to come to Him wherever we are. But it is absolutely vital that we learn the discipline of returning on a regular basis to that place of deep communion with Him for replenishment, refreshment and new marching orders.

Rev. Robby Richardson

Genesis 27-28; Matthew 8:18-34   **January 11**

A Step Is Not a Walk

Therefore you shall keep the commandments of the LORD your God, to walk in His ways and to fear Him. (Deuteronomy 8:6)

This simple statement was made by Pastor Bill Raws one Sunday morning at chapel service: "a step is not a walk." Sometimes the simplest statements can have such profound meaning. A step is not a walk. If you have been a believer for any significant length of time you are probably familiar with the verses about our walk.

Therefore you shall keep the commandments of the LORD your God, to walk in His ways and to fear Him...But take careful heed to do the commandment and the law which Moses the servant of the LORD commanded you, to love the LORD your God, to walk in all His ways, to keep His commandments, to hold fast to Him, and to serve Him with all your heart and with all your soul...For the LORD God is a sun and shield; The LORD will give grace and glory; No good thing will He withhold from those who walk uprightly...Therefore we were buried with Him through baptism into death, that just as Christ was raised from the dead by the glory of the Father, even so we also should walk in newness of life...There is therefore now no condemnation to those who are in Christ Jesus, who do not walk according to the flesh, but according to the Spirit...For we walk by faith, not by sight...If we live in the Spirit, let us also walk in the Spirit

(Deuteronomy 8:6; Joshua 22:5; Psalm 84:11; Romans 6:4; Romans 8:1; 2 Corinthians 5:7; Galatians 5:25).

A step is not a walk. How we wish a single step constituted a walk. A single step in the right direction is just that, a single step. It isn't until we string a lot of steps together in the right direction that we could say we are walking in the right direction.

We often live as if a step is enough, but a step is not a walk.

Diane Hunt

Genesis 29-30; Matthew 9:1-17 January 12

A Soul Hungry for God

O God, You are my God; Early will I seek You; My soul thirsts for You; My flesh longs for You in a dry and thirsty land where there is no water. (Psalm 63:1)

I once heard Stuart Briscoe say that God meets man on the level of his desire; man can have as much of God as he wants.

If this statement is true, and I believe it is, then our level of desire to know God will affect the level of our intimate, personal knowledge of God. Do you desire to know God with all your heart? Or would you say that your pursuit of God is lukewarm?

Psalm 63 has been called the soul of the Psalms. It is packed with expressions of David's longing to know God, to serve God and to praise God.

The Psalm contains some practical guidelines to assist us in our pursuit of God.

First, we are to seek the Lord...*early will I seek You; my soul thirsts for You; my flesh longs for You*...(v.1). The psalmist is describing a seeking heart. Do you want to know God? Then seek after Him with your whole heart and soul.

Secondly, we are to remember the Lord...*when I remember You...I meditate on You...* (v.6). The psalmist is describing how God occupies his mind. This is a sign of the psalmist's love for the Lord. Is it not true that those we love are always on our mind?

Thirdly, we are to praise the Lord...*my lips will praise You*...(v.3). The psalmist praised the Lord not only for what He had done, but for Who He was. *And my mouth shall praise You with joyful lips* (v.5).

Do you long to know the Lord in a deeper, more intimate way?

And you will seek Me and find Me, when you search for Me with all your heart (Jeremiah 29:13).

Dr. Roger D. Willmore

Genesis 31-32; Matthew 9:18-38　　　　　　　　**January 13**

9 to 5

May the favor of the LORD our God rest upon us; establish the work of our hands for us – yes, establish the work of our hands.
(Psalm 90:17 NIV)

Have you ever wondered if your vocation really matters to God? Have you ever pondered the idea that maybe God wants to work through you and your vocation to reach those around you? Let me invite you to consider one of my favorite prayers in the Bible written by Moses, found in Psalm 90:17.

This verse follows immediately after a verse that implores the Lord to show His great deeds to His servants and their children. It would, therefore, seem to be a logical connection that one of "His deeds" is to bless "the work of our hands."

Sometimes we fall into the trap of compartmentalizing our lives – keeping our "spiritual life" separate from our "vocational life." These verses indicate that we should be careful to not make this distinction.

Remember that you have been uniquely gifted and wired by God to be who you are – so that He can work through you to touch the world in which you live - for His glory. This includes "the work of your hands" – or your vocation. Who you are and what you do is not a mistake. You are who you are and you do what you do by God's divine appointment and plan.

Therefore, keep in mind that God desires to bless your work. He desires to cause you to be a blessing at your work. Your work is a part of His "completing a good work in you" (Philippians 1:6). And He desires to impact your "work world" as you faithfully allow Him to work through you to reach others.

I'm reminded of Joseph in the Old Testament when he was sold into slavery in Egypt. As he lived faithfully before God, God blessed the work of his hands and all those around him. Consider these verses:

The LORD was with Joseph so that he prospered, and he lived in the house of his Egyptian master. When his master saw that the LORD was with him and that the LORD gave him success in everything he did, Joseph found favor in his eyes and became his attendant (Genesis 39:2-4 NIV).

So the warden put Joseph in charge of all those held in the prison, and he was made responsible for all that was done there. The warden paid no attention to anything under Joseph's care, because the Lord was with Joseph and gave him success in whatever he did (Genesis 39:22-23 NIV).

So, why not take a few moments right now to ask God to do for you what Moses asked Him to do – establish your work. Ask Him to bless your work that it would go well. Ask Him to help you be a contributor to the success of your work's endeavors and goals. Most of all, in establishing the work of your hands, ask Him to work through you so that His work of grace in your life may be clearly seen.

John Bryant

Genesis 33-35; Matthew 10:1-20   **January 14**

Bezalel and Aholiab Who?

Bezalel and Aholiab and every wisehearted man in whom the Lord has put wisdom and understanding to know how to do all the work for the service of the sanctuary shall work according to all that the Lord has commanded. (Exodus 36:1 Amplified Bible)

The past several days I have been in the book of Exodus and reading about the construction of the tabernacle and all the furnishings. Often we tend to gloss over this as it is a very detailed (especially if you are like most men as we hate reading instructions!) instruction manual on how God wanted the tabernacle and all the accessories built.

There's not a lot in Scripture about the guy Bezalel (what a name!), but he played a very pivotal role in doing the major part of the construction of the tabernacle and its furnishings.

Of this man, we read in Exodus 35 (Amplified Bible) that *God filled him with the Spirit of God, with ability and wisdom, with intelligence and understanding, and with a knowledge of all craftsmanship* (v. 31). It also said that *God has put in Bezalel's heart that he may teach, both he and Aholiab ... (v. 26). God filled them with wisdom of heart and the ability to do all the manner of craftsmanship, of the engraver, of the skillful workman, of the embroiderer in blue, purple, and scarlet, and in fine linen, and of the weaver, even of those who do or design any skilled work* (v. 34-35).

Read through the remaining chapters of Exodus and you will see the phrase "He made" 46 times (Amplified Bible). Bottom line, he did it all just the way God commanded Moses.

What has God called YOU to do? Does the job require that you follow His commands and instructions? Is it a job that seems "over your head?" One that seems to be above your pay-scale? Well, God will never call you to do something for Him unless He will be faithful to equip you to do the job.

Paul wrote to the body at Thessalonica: *Faithful is He who is calling you [to Himself] and utterly trustworthy, and He will also do it [fulfill His call by hallowing and keeping you]*
(1 Thessalonians 4:24 Amplified Bible).

If He has placed a call on your life – be obedient. Trust Him. And be amazed at what He will do in and through you!

Dr. Bill Welte

Genesis 36-38; Matthew 10:21-42 — January 15

Two Observations about Obedience

And Moses inspected all the work, and behold, they had done it; as the Lord commanded, so they had done it. And Moses blessed them. (Exodus 39:43 Amplified Bible)

Something jumped off the page this morning when I was reading the final chapters of Exodus (38-40). Yesterday I talked about Bezalel and Aholiab and I was even more impressed with them as I read the final chapters of this amazing book.

I would love to have these two guys on my team. They exhibited a trait that is very rare these days in that they did exactly what they were told. If that weren't something of importance, why did the writer of Exodus repeatedly say that they did "as the Lord commanded Moses." By the way – that phrase is used nine times – so obviously the Lord wants us to see something.

I have shared this quote from Pastor Tim Shorey on a number of occasions: "Obedience is doing everything you are told to do IN THE RIGHT WAY (with the right heart attitude inwardly), RIGHT AWAY (immediately) and ALL THE WAY (do a complete job.)"

That's exactly what Bezalel and Aholiab demonstrated. They could have tried to do it their way – but they were obedient and God blessed the work of their hands.

But something else to note: chapter 40, which closes out the book, showed that Moses modeled what he wanted others to do. Eight times it says, *Thus did Moses; according to all that the Lord commanded him, so he did!*

If we want those who follow us to get it, then we as leaders, fathers, supervisors, must model it for those who look up to us. Good reminder, Moses.

How about you today? As you look at Pastor Tim's definition of obedience, how are you doing? Take some time today to think about it!

Dr. Bill Welte

Genesis 39-40; Matthew 11   **January 16**

A Gift from God in These Last Days

And they were all filled with the Holy Spirit. (Acts 2:4a)

Some readers who are old enough remember where they were the day that President John F. Kennedy was shot by Lee Harvey Oswald. Most readers are old enough to remember where they were on 9/11.

My own experience on 9/11 was very surreal. Along with a group of educators and Christian leaders, I was about to enter the side door of the White House in Washington, D.C. for a briefing at about 9:30 a.m. Being at the front of a group of about 75 people brought me to within a few feet of the side entrance of the famous home of our presidents. The guard on duty seemed preoccupied. It was then that I sensed something was wrong. "There is a plane coming full throttle to the White House. Run to J Street!" he shouted! This is what I thought he said. Actually, he said run to G Street. I knew one thing very well... he said "Run!" Off I went and led the pack!

Without telling you my entire story, we all have a similar experience of remembering exactly where and when we heard the news that day. This experience would change our lives. It seemed to me to be surreal! This couldn't be happening. This date is simply called 9/11... everyone knows what it means.

The second chapter of Acts is a similar surreal moment in time. Jesus Christ had been crucified. The temple veil was torn from the top to the bottom. His followers were heartsick. He was gone! He told his followers many times that He would die, but they did not want to hear this! Then, just as He predicted, He arose from the grave. Many people saw Him alive and then He vanished out of their sight in the ascension. He was gone! He said He would return, but in the meantime there would be a gift given.

Just as Jesus is a gift and salvation is an unmerited gift, so there would be a gift given by God. That gift is the Holy Spirit.

It happened on the day of Pentecost. This gift was not given because people tarried or met certain conditions. Yes, the followers of Christ were praying. But this event occurred because it was the Day of Pentecost. The coming of the Holy Spirit was linked to the pattern of the feasts. There was the Passover, the Feast of Unleavened Bread, and then Pentecost which occurred fifty days after the first Sunday of Passover. And there was a noise like wind but it wasn't wind, a sight that resembled fire but wasn't fire. People from many areas heard the message of the truth in their own languages. This event seemed to be very surreal. The Holy Spirit had come in a new way! The Holy Spirit would now dwell in the believer's lives.

This blessed gift is available to all followers of Christ. When we trust Jesus Christ as our Savior, we are a part of the family of God. The Holy Spirit lives in each individual life. We need to listen to Him. He primarily speaks to us through the Word of God (Colossians 3:16). The command in Acts 2:4 is to be *filled with the Spirit*. As God's Word captivates and directs our minds, we are under the control of God's Holy Spirit.

C.S. Lewis wrote, "Our Lord finds our desires not too strong but too weak. We are half-hearted creatures, fooling about with drink and sex and ambition, when infinite joy is offered to us. Like an ignorant child who wants to make mud pies in the slum because he cannot imagine what is meant by holiday at sea, we are far too easily pleased."

Today enjoy the ministry of the Holy Spirit. He lives in you and this is a gift from God. He guides us and keeps us in the family of God.

Dr. Dino Pedrone

Genesis 41-42; Matthew 12:1-23 **January 17**

A Clear Conscience

This being so, I myself always strive to have a conscience without offense toward God and men. (Acts 24:16)

Have you noticed that you get an unsettled feeling deep down inside of you when you say or do something wrong? This is your conscience speaking to you when you sin. The Holy Spirit works through your conscience to direct you in matters of right and wrong. To enjoy unhindered communion with God, you must have a clear conscience.

A clear conscience gives you an inner freedom of spirit and soul that comes from knowing that you are right with God, and right with other people. Does your track record show that you are frequently in conflict with others? Do you subtly control others - manipulating friends and family members with your silence, withholding approval, making them perform to your expectations, and playing them one against the other? This is clear evidence of a soul that is sick and one who has a defiled conscience. These personal traits may seem to be for a lost person, but they can be true of a Christian, even someone in ministry faithfully ministering God's Word to others.

This is what Paul meant when he said, ... *I myself always strive to have a conscience without offense toward God and men.* This verse shows that a clear conscience involves being right with God. We must know in our heart that there is no sin between God and us. But it also involves being right with our fellow man. My friend, we must know that we have made things right with others. You simply cannot be right with God if you are in carnal conflict with anybody in the world.

Jesus said in Matthew 5:23-24, *Therefore if you bring your gift to the altar, and there remember that your brother has something against you, leave your gift there before the altar, and go your way. First be reconciled to your brother, and then come and offer your gift.*

If we want to have a clear conscience, we must allow the Holy Spirit to search our hearts and show us our offenses against others. When you have faithfully confessed your sins to God, and faithfully dealt with your sins against others, it will seem as though a great burden has been lifted from you. Maybe your new motto can be, "Stay close and clean."

Rev. Chris S. Hodges

Genesis 43-45; Matthew 12:24-50 **January 18**

A Generous Heart

So Moses gave command, and word was proclaimed throughout the camp, "Let no man or woman do anything more for the contribution for the sanctuary." So the people were restrained from bringing, for the material they had was sufficient to do all the work, and more. (Exodus 36:6-7 ESV)

The building of the tabernacle was an amazing feat. The exodus from Egypt has been compared to moving the population of Philadelphia. There were over 600,000 men 20 years or older, plus women and children, out in the desert and God asked them to build Him a tabernacle. The children of Israel are primarily known for their grumbling and complaining but they also showed they had very generous hearts. In Exodus 35, Moses asked them to give a contribution to the Lord: a free will offering of gold, silver, bronze, yarns, linen, animal skins, acacia wood, oil, spices, incense and precious stones.

This offering was truly a time of worship for the people. In verse 21 we see the phrase *everyone whose heart stirred him, and everyone whose spirit moved him...* In verse 22 we see *all who were of a willing heart...* In verse 29 we see again *whose heart moved them...* and once more in chapter 36 verse 2, *whose heart stirred him...* It is a beautiful thing when God's Spirit moves in His people. The end result of this outpouring of the Spirit is seen in 36:4-5, *...all the craftsmen who were doing every sort of task on the sanctuary came ... and said to Moses, "The people bring much more than enough for doing the work that the Lord has commanded us to do."* In 36:6 we see that the people were restrained from bringing anything more. We don't know all that was brought, but in chapter 38 we see that about 2,200 pounds of gold, 7,500 pounds of silver and 5,300 pounds of bronze were brought. At the beginning of 2010 their combined value was close to $37 million. The Israelites' giving was not limited to gold and silver but they also gave freely of all their possessions, their time and their abilities. In 36:2 we see *...every craftsman in whose mind the Lord had put skill, everyone whose heart stirred him up to come to do the work.* They not only gave their money but they gave of themselves.

All that we have is from God and should always be at His disposal. When God's Spirit stirs our hearts we need to respond not out of a feeling of obligation but out of our love for Him.

Allen E. Beltle

Genesis 46-48; Matthew 13:1-30   January 19

Gazing on Jesus

But we all, with unveiled face, beholding as in a mirror the glory of the Lord, are being transformed into the same image from glory to glory, just as by the Spirit of the Lord.
(2 Corinthians 3:18)

Do you remember the story of Moses standing on the mountain before the Lord? When he came down from the mountain, he had to wear a veil to cover his face because he radiated the glory of God (see Exodus 34). Moses' face was radiant from having been in the presence of God and experiencing His glory.

That's the idea Paul had in mind when he wrote 2 Corinthians 3:18: *But we all, with unveiled face, beholding as in a mirror the glory of the Lord, are being transformed into the same image from glory to glory, just as by the Spirit of the Lord.*

People may not know we've been in the presence of the Lord by the way we look, but the work God's Spirit does in transforming us makes us so much like Jesus that people will notice. The issue is being in Jesus' presence—beholding Him in all of His glory.

How do we do that? Several ways come to mind, and three seem most appropriate for "everyday Christians" who do not always sense great confidence in their walk with Jesus.

First, read the Gospels. They tell us about Jesus. We see Him gentle and powerful. We hear Him speak peace and judgment. We hear His teaching and watch His life. To consistently read the Gospels is to behold the glory of the Lord, allowing Him to transform our lives.

We can also use music that presents Jesus in all His glory. Music has power to move us and transform us. "What a Friend We Have in Jesus" lets us gaze on Jesus. "Mary, Did You Know?" takes us from His birth to His death and reminds us of His great power. The old Wesley hymn "And Can It Be" tells us the story of Jesus and His great work for us. Allowing the messages of good songs to settle in our souls is like gazing on Jesus repeatedly, each time we listen to or sing them.

Finally, we can "be with Jesus." The psalmist understood the importance of quiet reflection when he wrote, *Be still, and know that I am God.* We do not waste time by sitting quietly and intentionally in the presence of Jesus. It is life-changing! It is transforming!

Paul tells us that this transforming work in our lives happens by the Spirit of God working in us. How will you gaze on Jesus today? How will you give God's Spirit an opportunity to do some transforming work in your life today?

Rev. John Strain

Genesis 49-50; Matthew 13:31-58   **January 20**

A New Accounting System

...reckon yourselves to be dead indeed to sin, but alive to God in Christ Jesus our Lord. (Romans 6:11)

On the basis of God's declared truth regarding my position in Christ, I am instructed to put into operation a new accounting system. In the language of Paul's day, the work *reckon* (or consider), introducing our theme text, was used in accounting.

The thought was of one entering items into a ledger as an asset. The apostle applies this by commanding that believers are to carry two items forward on a continuing basis – their death to sin and their being alive to God.

The basis for this transaction is the truth of verses 1-10, our identification with Christ. The facts of the believer's relationship to Christ are clearly stated in a conclusive manner, but now there is to be an appropriation of them in the form of an entry in the ledger of our faith. God has credited to our account the death, burial and resurrection of Christ. He has made a direct deposit, but we are to act on His declaration and make a permanent entry by faith.

The implication of this transaction is that we no longer are obligated to sin as a dominating principle in our lives. We are free from that debt and are now alive to the new principle – life in Christ Jesus. Our identification with Him in His death makes it possible for us to be sharers in His life.

A little couplet of verse summarizes this transaction:
> "Reckon, Reckon, Reckon,
> Reckon when you cannot feel;
> If you will tend to the reckoning,
> God will make it real." – Source unknown

Rev. William A. Raws

Exodus 1-3; Matthew 14:1-21 **January 21**

Pleasing God

[Jesus said,] "...I always do those things that please Him."
(John 8:29)

As ones called "Christian," we should follow the teachings and the example of Christ. Holiness is pleasing God. But how do we go about doing that? Scripture reveals ways.

P - PRAY – (1 Timothy 2:1-3)
vs. 1, 8 – Prayer is presented as a command, not an option.

v. 3 – Praying is good and acceptable to God; when acceptable, then pleasing.

There are many Scriptures concerning prayer: David, Elijah, Daniel, Jesus, Paul. When we have a friend, we communicate with him or her. Is Jesus your friend today? He is? Then keep in touch with Him. Please Him and pray!

L - LEARN – (2 Timothy 2:15; 3:14-17)

v. 2:15 - Tells us to be diligent; to study. Why? This pleases God.

v. 3:14 - Then to continue in the things we have learned; what have you learned?

vs. 3:15, 16 – The Scriptures make you wise and are for instruction. "Learn" doesn't mean "to be taught!" Please Him by continuing to learn!

E - END sinning – (2 Timothy 2:4, 19)

v. 4 – A good soldier is not to be entangled with the world: home, relationships which can interfere with his military responsibilities.

v. 19 – The instruction is to depart from iniquity, turn away from wickedness.

In your walk with the Lord, sin interferes! Please Him; put an end to sinning!

A - ACT – (1 Timothy 4:12)

Be an example in your speech, conduct, love. An example of Christ? or….

How do you behave? How you act is being watched by all those around you.

The result is their opinion of to whom you belong. Act to please Him!

S - SERVE – (2 Timothy 2:2, 24)

v. 2 – "Commit" to faithful men the things you have heard. Tell them personally.

v. 24 – We should not quarrel, but be gentle, able to teach, be patient. In other words, these are ways to serve, by speaking to others and living before them. One of the key ways to please Him is to serve Him!

E - EVALUATE – (1 Timothy 4:15, 16)

    v. 15 – Meditate on these things.

    v. 16 – Take heed to yourself. That's right, evaluate yourself! Give yourself entirely to watching your life. How do you stack-up? Take inventory! Evaluate your life to please Him!

    Pleasing someone is based on love…and the desire to please the One we love.

Jack Noel

Exodus 4-6; Matthew 14:22-36   **January 22**

Cooperating with the Lord

If then you were raised with Christ, seek those things which are above, where Christ is, sitting at the right hand of God. Set your mind on things above, not on things on the earth. For you died, and your life is hidden with Christ in God. (Colossians 3:1-3)

    A.J. Gordon observed, "The method of grace is precisely the reverse of the method of legalism. The latter is holiness in order to (have) union with God; the former, union with God in order to (experience) holiness" (Victory in Christ, p. 11).

    How can we cooperate with God's grace so that the indwelling life of Christ may be manifested through us? Some key responsibilities include reckoning yourself alive to God in Christ Jesus (Romans 6:4-11), and living according to *the law of the Spirit of life in Christ Jesus* (Romans 8:2-4, 9-11)

    Charles Trumbull was editor of the Sunday School Times for about forty years. He summarized the basic conditions for fully cooperating with God's grace: "What are the two conditions of this victorious life? Only two, and they are very simple. Surrender and faith . . . Is there anything in your life this moment that you know you have been with-holding from the Lord? Won't you just tell Him you now turn over to Him, for time and eternity, all that you have and all that you are, for His complete mastery and use . .? Then you must remember that it at once becomes His responsibility, His -- I say it reverently -- duty to keep you from the power of sin. He pledges Himself to do so. *Sin shall not have dominion over you*, He says, *for you are not under law* (where your works have something to do with it) *but under grace* (Romans 6:14). So it is that our Lord has just been waiting for you, not to pray for victory, but to praise Him for victory" (<u>Victory in Christ</u>, p.14,15).

Rather than trying to operate <u>for</u> the Lord, let's learn to cooperate <u>with</u> Him.

Dr. John Woodward

Exodus 7-8; Matthew 15:1-20　　　　　　　　　　**January 23**

A God Who Forgives

*But this Man, after He had offered one sacrifice for sins forever, sat down at the right hand of God....*then He adds, *"Their sins and their lawless deeds I will remember no more."*
(Hebrews 10:12 and 17)

Have you ever stopped to ponder what it means to have your sins forgiven? Have you ever stopped to think about all that is involved in God's forgiveness of our sins?

The word **forgiven** is a strong word. It means to send away. This point is pictured graphically in Leviticus 16:7-10 where the sins of the people were confessed upon the scape goat and then the goat was taken far into the wilderness and left to die, never to return.

When God forgives our sins He sends them away. He forgives our sins and forgets our sins.

How can God be so gracious and kind to us? Well, God does not simply dispense forgiveness arbitrarily. Certain conditions have to be met before God's forgiveness can be received.

The writer of Hebrews reminds us that *it is impossible for the blood of bulls and goats to take away sins* (10:4). Then he reminds us that there is One who can take away our sins by the shedding of His blood. *But this Man, after He had offered one sacrifice for sins forever, sat down at the right hand of God* (10:12).

The forgiveness of our sins required the shedding of the blood of Jesus on the cross. Without the shedding of His blood, no one could experience forgiveness.

The great old hymn captures this truth, "What can wash away my sin? Nothing but the blood of Jesus. What can make me whole again? Nothing but the blood of Jesus. Oh! Precious is the flow that makes me white as snow; No other fount I know, nothing but the blood of Jesus." ("Nothing but the Blood," Robert Lowery, 1826-1899)

Did you know that there is enough power in the blood of Jesus to cleanse you of any sin you have ever committed? Yes, it is true. Our heavenly Father stands on the ground of the shed blood of His Son and pronounces repentant sinners forgiven of ALL sin. Amen.

Dr. Roger D. Willmore

Exodus 9-11; Matthew 15:21-39 **January 24**

A God Who Forgives and Forgets

This is the covenant that I will make with them after those days, says the Lord: "I will put My laws into their hearts, and in their minds I will write them," then He adds, *"Their sins and their lawless deeds I will remember no more."* (Hebrews 10:16-17)

The writer of Hebrews states that *it is not possible that the blood of bulls and goats could take away sin.* However, in Hebrews 9:13-14, the writer reminds us that blood is required for forgiveness of sins. He writes, *For if the blood of bulls and goats and the ashes of a heifer, sprinkling the unclean, sanctifies for the purifying of the flesh, how much more shall the blood of Christ, who through the eternal Spirit offered Himself without spot to God, purge your conscience from dead works to serve a living God.*

God cannot just arbitrarily say, **I forgive you**. His justice and righteousness and holiness demand that a price be paid for sin. That price was paid by God's own Son, the Lord Jesus

Christ. God stands upon the shed blood of Jesus to pronounce sinners forgiven.

The question before us now is **What sins can God forgive?** The answer is, **All sins and every sin.**

Sometimes someone will tell me he has committed a sin that is too horrible, too bad, and too great for God to forgive. I take great delight in telling that person that the blood of Jesus Christ has the power to cleanse a sinner of all sin and every sin.

You can also have assurance of forgiveness. Did you notice the words in Hebrews 10:17? *Their sins and their lawless deeds I will remember no more.* What God forgives, He forgets. You do not have to worry about God tapping you on the shoulder and reminding you of a past sin. If you have confessed that sin and repented of that sin, it is forgiven and forgotten.

Micah 7:19 says, *You will cast our sins into the depths of the sea.* Someone said that after God cast our sins into the depths of the sea, He put up a "No Fishing" sign.

The psalmist says, *As far as the east is from the west, So far has He removed our transgressions from us* (Psalm 103:12). Why did the psalmist say east to west rather than north to south? Because God has removed our sins from infinity to infinity, never to be found again.

Have you experienced the forgiveness of God?

Dr. Roger D. Willmore

Exodus 12-13; Matthew 16　　　　　　　　　　　**January 25**

God and Our Hearts

Blessed are those who keep His testimonies, Who seek Him with the whole heart. (Psalm 119:2)

The word "heart" occurs many times in the Bible. It is used physically and symbolically with spiritual applications. In its symbolic usage, the word "heart" refers to the innermost character of the individual, what he is really like on the inside, the deepest feeling, the seat of the emotions and the will, the center of the personality. It is the real person. And God has a great deal to say about Himself and our hearts. God speaks about the wicked heart (Jeremiah 17:9), the wandering heart (Hebrews 3:7-19) and the whole heart (Psalm119:2). Let's look at the whole heart.

When we place our trust in Jesus Christ personally for salvation, God gives us a "new heart." Salvation produces a sense of "wholeness" - the whole heart. God does not remove the old heart; nor does God take away the old nature. But God gives to the believer a new heart with a new nature, a nature that is whole, at peace with God and possessing amazing spiritual potential. "Wholeness" is produced by the divine act when saving faith in Jesus Christ is experienced by the believing person.

Jesus, then, becomes the center of our lives around Whom our decisions and choices are made. If He is not in His right place, then our choices may not be what they ought to be.

I recall when our children were small, we were visiting my husband's parents. Their grandfather had an old tent supported by a center pole. The children loved to play in it. But one day, as they were playing inside the tent, one of them hit the center pole, knocking it down and the tent collapsed on them amid many shouts. I have often reflected what a parable that was. When Jesus is not the center of our lives to give wholeness to our hearts, our lives can collapse. It is He Who gives life meaning and purpose.

As we make Jesus the center of our hearts in all of our choices and actions, He will guide and direct our steps. As Proverbs 3:5-6 reminds us, *Trust in the Lord with all your heart…and He shall direct your paths.*

Joy Hubbard

Exodus 14-15; Matthew 17 **January 26**

A Life of Encouragement

...That I may be encouraged together with you... (Romans 1:12)

Some people in life are unforgettable. One such person is a man I met during a Bible conference in the Albany, New York area. I was preaching a four-day meeting and on Tuesday the church had a meal in its basement. After the meal I was coming up the steps and an elderly man was struggling as he made his way. I took a few extra minutes to help him and tried to have an animated conversation with him. It went something like this.

"Is your wife here?"

"No, she is in heaven!"

"Oh, I'm sorry!" I replied.

"What are you sorry about?" he said, "She is in heaven!"

I asked him if he had any children. "Nope, they are all in heaven!"

Unfortunately, I said again, "I am sorry!" He laughed and said, "Like I asked before, why are you sorry? They are all in heaven!"

Did you ever have one of those conversations which seemed like it was going downhill and it didn't matter what you said? As we reached the top of the stairs I said to him, "Do you have any relatives anywhere?" Unbelievably he said, "They are all in heaven!" I did not say this time that I was sorry! He then proceeded to tell me that the church was really his home and with a big smile he said, "This church is my family. Every Sunday I pass out the bulletins and try to make everyone feel at home!" That man was a huge encouragement to me and probably never realized it!

If there is a word that described that gentleman, it is the word encourager. In the first chapter of Romans, the apostle is beginning the address on what many believe to be the greatest theological work in all of Scripture. He is about to write concerning the nature of sin that overwhelms every single person. Before he begins, he writes to the Roman Christians and states, *...that I may be encouraged with you by the mutual faith both of you and me.*

We need to encourage each other. There are people today with whom you will be in contact who need encouragement. So often we have our minds on our own problems and do not have any time or energy for encouragement. Perhaps you can join me and learn a lesson from my friend in Albany who lost all of his loved ones and yet found time to teach me about the art of encouragement.

Dr. Dino Pedrone

Exodus 16-18; Matthew 18:1-20   **January 27**

From a Heart of Stone

I will sprinkle clean water on you, and you shall be clean from all your uncleannesses, and from all your idols I will cleanse you. And I will give you a new heart, and a new spirit I will put within you. And I will remove the heart of stone from your flesh and give you a heart of flesh. And I will put my Spirit within you, and cause you to walk in my statutes and be careful to obey my rules.
(Ezekiel 36:25-27 ESV)

While living in Cozumel, Mexico I spent a good deal of time on the beaches. The beaches were covered with large grey stones full of holes and crevices. The intense sun would dry the stones out, making it difficult to see the dangerous holes. One day I stumbled across a heart-shaped hole filled with beautiful blue-green water. I photographed the heart, thinking that it too would dry up and disappear in the heat of the day. What I later realized was that this heart was always visible. The tide would come in each day and wash away the impurities, cleaning the heart out and filling it with fresh water. As the day became hotter, the color of the water in the heart would turn deeper and richer, making it even more pleasing than before.

This picture is tucked away in my Bible at Ezekiel 36 to remind me of the wonderful work that Jesus does in our hearts as we trust Him as our Lord. He washes away the impurities and idols of our heart. It is only because of His Holy Spirit in us that we desire to do His will. It is only because of His Spirit that we are capable of living true to His commands. As we walk with Him through our daily trials, through the heat of our day we grow into a deeper, richer and more beautiful relationship with Jesus Christ.

There is great reassurance of His sufficiency in these verses. It says, *I will sprinkle clean water on you..., I will cleanse you..., I will give you a new heart..., a new spirit I will put within you...,* He will even cause me to want to walk in His statutes. Not once does it say that I must do anything. Our job is to simply allow Him to do the work in us.

Lord, thank you for your cleansing and transforming power in my life. Create in me a clean heart, a pure heart. Lord, scrub me clean. I ask you to help me see the trials of my day as an opportunity to grow into a deeper, more beautiful relationship with You. Please give me the strength to allow You the proper place on the altar of my life bringing all glory and honor to You.

Chaplain Bill Pruitt

Exodus 19-20; Matthew 18:21-35   **January 28**

Avoiding Trials, Avoiding Maturity

Consider it pure joy, my brothers, whenever you face trials of many kinds, because you know that the testing of your faith develops perseverance. Perseverance must finish its work so that you may be mature and complete, not lacking anything.
(James 1:2-3 NIV)

Do you want to become mature in your Christian faith? Do you want to obey the Lord's command to "Grow in the grace and knowledge of our Lord and Savior Jesus Christ" (2 Peter 3:18a)? If so, then according to James you have just put in a request for trials of various kinds.

Some trials in life are unavoidable: a family member gets cancer, or a fire takes your home. These times are extremely stressful and can be accompanied by powerful emotions. I don't wish these circumstances on anyone. But God, in His goodness, works through these circumstances for our benefit, especially if we don't lose heart.

There is another category of trials, one in which we must choose between growth and comfort. This is no small matter in a country of comfortable Christians where people are fleeing testing more than they are fleeing temptation. Every day God presents us with tests that will help us progress on our road toward maturity (Christ-likeness). Seldom, however, are these growing opportunities mandatory—we are offered the test, but not forced into it.

This past summer I took a group of teenagers on a wilderness trip to Canada for seven days. Most were not the outdoorsy type and varying degrees of anxiety filled the van as we arrived at the point of no return. What moved them past the point of fear was the desire to grow. They knew there would be discomfort and circumstances beyond their control, but they chose growth over comfort. They didn't avoid the trial, they chose to trust that God would guide them <u>through</u> it.

Rev. Jason R. Walsh

Exodus 21-22; Matthew 19 **January 29**

God's Will for Us Is a Relationship

Abide in Me, and I in you... (John 15:4a)

If you want to fill the parking lot of your church, just advertise a seminar on "How to Know God's Will for Your Life." Speak to a new believer and he will often say, "I know God has a plan for my life, and I am praying that He will show it to me." While it is true that we were saved for a reason, and God has plans for us, plans for good and not for evil, His primary will is that we live in a relationship with Him. This has been the case from the beginning of time and will continue into eternity.

In the book of Genesis, God was reported to have walked with Adam and Eve. *And they heard the sound of the LORD God walking in the garden in the cool of the day, and Adam and his wife hid themselves from the presence of the LORD God among the trees of the garden* (Genesis 3:8). The purpose for which we were created is to glorify God by walking with Him. Even when man failed in this relationship, God's original intention didn't change. Rather than accusing man after he sinned, He asked Adam a question (Genesis 3:9), *Then the LORD God called to Adam and said to him, "Where are you?"* This, in essence, was an invitation to continue in their relationship.

The entire Bible is about God's plan to have a relationship with His people. Finally, in the book of Revelation, we find "the disciple who Jesus loved," the elderly apostle John, suffering on the Isle of Patmos. This book is no mere list of prophecies, but a love letter from Jesus Christ as the enthroned King. He is writing to His suffering servants to assure them that He is coming back to make everything in this world right. In the end of the book He assures them that, *"Behold, the tabernacle of God is with men, and He will dwell with them..."* (Revelation 21:3).

What that means to us today is that God loves us as His children and, as any parent, desires to be in a relationship with us. This is His will for our life!

Father, forgive me for missing the most crucial aspect of Your will. Help me to dwell in Your presence today.

Chaplain Jim Freed

Exodus 23-24; Matthew 20:1-16 **January 30**

Serving God in the Midst of Godlessness

Bind up the testimony, Seal the law among my disciples.
(Isaiah 8:16)

Isaiah served God at a most difficult time. The Lord revealed that, as a prophet, he would see his audience, outside of a small remnant, reject the word from God (6:10-13). Even so, Isaiah remained faithful, preaching the message of His God over several decades under different earthly kings. How does one remain so faithful to such a God-rejecting culture?

The key to remaining strong spiritually is found in verse 11 of our chapter, *For the LORD spoke thus to me with a strong hand, and instructed me that I should not walk in the way of this people...* To walk God's narrow way in opposition to the broad way of the surrounding culture demands the resolve to love and obey our God. In his obedience, Isaiah mentored others to walk the same path. As the Word from God had gone forth and been rejected by the majority, God's man determined that his mind would be stayed on the revelation of God and he declared further that he would go, *To the law and to the testimony! If they do not speak ac-cording to this word; it is because there is no light in them* (v. 20).

To walk godly in a godless culture requires unwavering faith in the revelation of God as the Truth to be accepted and acted upon each and every day. Isaiah was able to remain faithful in the face of great opposition because he had been allowed a glimpse of God which revealed his own sinful and needy condition (chapter 6). Such an ongoing revelation is necessary for the disciple to understand the need of total reliance upon God. Jesus would state it this way, *If anyone desires to come after Me, let him deny himself, and take up his cross daily, and follow Me* (Luke 9:23). Our revelation is God speaking to us through His Word. Our daily time in the Word and in prayer is our "conversation" with a God Who reveals His love to us in such a way that we grow in love toward Him. The outworking of this is a life of loving obedience lived out as light in the midst of the cultural darkness around us.

Dr. Joe Olachea

Exodus 25-26; Matthew 20:17-34 January 31

Marks of the True Christian

Let love be genuine. Abhor what is evil; hold fast to what is good. Love one another with brotherly affection. Outdo one another in showing honor. Do not be slothful in zeal, be fervent in spirit, serve the Lord. Rejoice in hope, be patient in tribulation, be constant in prayer. Contribute to the needs of the saints and seek to show hospitality. (Romans 12:9-13 ESV)

One of my favorite chapters in the New Testament is Romans 12. As a young Christian, I am constantly seeking instructions and Paul is not short of instructions in this passage. Not surprising that LOVE heads up the list Paul rattles off during this passage, right? The greatest gift God gave us is love.

But Paul expands. We are to hate what is evil. We are to love one another with *brotherly affection.* That's how we are supposed to act all the time. We are to outdo one another in showing honor. Be excited about serving the Lord. Pray all the time. Help one another and show hospitality.

Bless those who do you harm. This is tough for me, but this sounds like Jesus. In Matthew 5:44, Jesus says to love our enemies and pray for those who persecute us. Repay no one for evil; again, this is what Jesus taught. In Matthew 5:39, Jesus teaches to turn the other cheek. Vengeance is not ours, it's His.

We are to feed our enemies, we are to give them something to drink if they are thirsty. And we are to overcome evil by doing good. Doing good brings glory to God and shame to evil.

These are tall orders for us as Christians. Think about all that Paul says to do here in order to please God. Think about how this ties into all the teachings of Jesus in Matthew. Yet we fall short. We must strive to do better as His children.

I love the poster in my friend's office, a quote by St. Francis of Assisi. "Preach the Gospel at all times and, when necessary, USE WORDS."

Ed Weiss

Exodus 27-28; Matthew 21:1-22　　　　　　　　**February 1**

Keep Your Eyes on Jesus

For now we see in a mirror, dimly, but then face to face. Now I know in part, but then I shall know just as I am also known.
(1 Corinthians 13:12)

I had one of those very embarrassing moments. Some of my staff guys joined me for dinner and then we went to see the new "Three Musketeers" movie. (Don't write me letters, please!)

The movie was in 3D and, having seen the previews, I was excited to see the entire movie. When the movie started and we put on our 3D glasses, I was ticked because the movie was blurred. I turned to the guy next to me and asked him if he thought the movie was out of focus and he said it was a little bit.

Well, I was miffed that I paid for a 3D movie that was blurred so I went to the manager and asked if digital movies ever went out of focus. He said they did and he would adjust it. I came back to my seat and it wasn't any better. I was really getting ticked by now and asked the guy in front of me to look through my glasses. He did and said, "You got a bad pair of glasses, man!" I looked through his and the movie was perfectly clear.

I grabbed my glasses and my friends' glasses and went out to get them replaced. As I was looking at the three pairs of glasses, I realized that mine were different than the other two. The other two were clearly marked "3D" and mine were marked "polarized." Then I noticed the shape of mine was different.

Now with egg on my face, I realized that my 3D glasses were still in my pocket and I had put on my sunglasses that were on my head! With the right set of glasses, everything came into focus.

Right now some things may seem out of focus in your life. The trials and challenges you and I face may not make the slightest amount of sense right now. Someday we will understand and see the big picture. When we put on the right glasses, what was fuzzy and unclear will all make perfect sense.

We'll be able to see how it all worked out for our good and His glory (Romans 8:28).

For now – what we need to do is *fix our eyes on Jesus* (Hebrews 12:2).

Dr. Bill Welte

Exodus 29-30; Matthew 21:23-46 February 2

A Proud Heart in Motion

But He gives more grace. Therefore He says: "God resists the proud, But gives grace to the humble." (James 4:6)

Quite awhile ago I <u>had</u> to speak truth to someone. (At least that's what I told myself.) I remember thinking, "this is a good thing" because my friend <u>needs</u> to be shown this area of possible blindness in her life. It never occurred to me that the Lord wanted to show me a blind spot in my own heart as well.

Proverbs 15:33 (ESV) reads, *The fear of the Lord is instruction in wisdom, and humility comes before honor.* Our faithful God showed me a pride that was lurking right around the corner in my heart and because my focus was on someone else's pride, my own was seemingly out of sight and feeling pretty good about itself.

Do not offer the parts of your body to sin, as instruments of wickedness, but rather offer yourselves to God, as those who have been brought from death to life; and offer the parts of your body to Him as instruments of righteousness (Romans 6:13 NIV).

That morning I offered my tongue as an *instrument of righteousness* rather than for any form of wickedness. In speaking to my friend as I had, I may have done a <u>good thing</u>, but I didn't necessarily do the <u>better thing</u>.

I had weighed a deed done, judged it and spoken my thoughts concerning it. From Hannah's prayer in 1 Samuel 2:3 (NIV) I read, *"Do not keep talking so proudly or let your mouth speak such arrogance, for the LORD is a God who knows, and by him deeds are weighed.* Was it coincidence that all of this was in my morning devotions? I think not. Who am I to weigh the thoughts, deeds and heart of any other person? Only God has the power to know the thoughts and intents of my heart or yours and His call is for us to daily examine our lives for anything that exalts itself above the knowledge of Him.

My question for you: Do you see signs in your own life of a prideful heart? What is the fruit or lack of it that has been produced by it?

Stephanie D. Paul

Exodus 31-33; Matthew 22:1-22　　　　　　　　　**February 3**

"…straightway…"

And straightway he preached Christ in the synagogues, that he is the Son of God. (Acts 9:20)

After you have read the biography of Acts 9 you will recognize that this word "straightway" comes from the life of one who had just come to a life-changing encounter with the reality of Christ. The drama of his conversion is soon feeding a flood of information that will, through the years, present a clear path and a challenging stimulus to millions of others who desire a life of spiritual victory. A key part of that challenge is the word *straightway*. It means <u>immediately</u>.

S*traightway* is a challenging word. In a proper and forceful sense it challenges the nature of delay, defeat and disobedience. It challenges the timid, the uncertain, and the slothful. It can do that because s*traightway* describes the victory of that person who understands the victory of the can do, must do, will do response to the Will of God.

Straightway is often among the first few steps of the one who wants to walk the path of victory. If that victory is in gaining holy ground or being delivered from the unholy gutter, *straightway* (immediately) begins the journey.

Consider this part of Abram's life. God said to him:

Get you out of your country, and from your family, and from your father's house, unto a land that I will show you:...So Abram departed,... (Genesis 12:2,4).

And what about the missionary Paul who already had a great agenda of mission endeavor? Yet when he got a call to "come" over into Macedonia (Southern Europe), though he was a Jew living and working in Asia, the Bible said of him and his friends that <u>immediately</u> they endeavored to go.

In a very simple way the road to spiritual victory is not complicated. It is in large measure simply doing now what we know we need to do immediately. That may be throwing away the trash that has cluttered our life or adding the pearls that enliven it.

I must confront this question. In my path to victory, what must I now do *straightway*? How about you?

Dr. Robert L. Alderman

Exodus 34-35; Matthew 22:23-46   **February 4**

Biblical Restoration – A Step Beyond Our Expectations

"For behold, I create new heavens and a new earth; And the former shall not be remembered or come to mind."
(Isaiah 65:17)

Recently while surfing through the channels on my TV, I came to an auction where they were selling cars. These cars were more valuable than the ones listed for sale in the want ads for various reasons. Although some were rarer than others, much of their value came from the fact that they had been "restored." In human terms restoration means that they had been returned to their original showroom condition, the one that they were in when they came off the assembly line.

In working in an addiction recovery ministry, I often hear men say that they want to be who they were before they began their addiction. But experience has shown that God's intention goes beyond our expectations. The prophet Isaiah wrote, *"For My thoughts are not your thoughts, Nor are your ways My* ways," says the LORD. "For as the heavens are higher than the earth, So are My ways higher than your ways, And My thoughts than your thoughts" (Isaiah 55:8-9).

Such is the way I have seen God work in my own life and in the lives of many others. The secular world will tell you that addicts and alcoholics have an incurable disease and all we can do is treat the symptoms. God says, *Therefore, if anyone is in Christ, he is a new creation; old things have passed away; behold, all things have become new* (2 Corinthians 5:17). But what I have learned is that when God says new He means better than the original! The Scripture above states that the former things will not even be remembered.

When I first became sober and looked back at the train wreck that I had caused in my former life, all I could do was shudder. Today I don't have to do that anymore. I am a new creation. I have a new identity. I am not who I once was before I began drinking. I am a child of the Most High God. We need to be conscious of the fact that when we become born again, *old things have passed away...* and *all things* (including us) *have become new*!

Lord, thank you that your idea of restoration far exceeds ours.

Chaplain Jim Freed

Exodus 36-38; Matthew 23:1-22　　　　　　　**February 5**

A Symphony in the Father's House

... as he came and drew near to the house, he heard music and dancing. (Luke 15:25)

The parable of the prodigal son provides many lessons of encouragement to us as sons and daughters of the Father. We watch the earthly father run to welcome his son who is returning home from a life of sin. Never once does the father mention the son's sin and failure.

And, in addition, the father has ordered a celebration to be held in honor of the son. The fattened calf is killed and cooked.

The son is dressed in beautiful new clothes and given a ring on his hand, the symbol of authority. This, of course, is what our Heavenly Father does for us, His children whom He knew before the world began (John 17:6, 9; Ephesians 1:4). We are those who, like the son, were "dead" and "lost" in the world. We have been made alive by the Spirit and have been "found" by the Son (1 Corinthians 12:3; Luke 19:10). We have been clothed in Christ's robe of righteousness and given authority to reign as joint-heirs with Him in His kingdom.

And, as the elder son drew near to his father's house, he heard "music and dancing." The Greek word for *music* is *symphonia*. It is the basis for our word symphony, a sounding together in agreement, in harmony. What a thrilling truth lies hidden here for us! In the Father's house there is harmony, a unison of sound, voices of celebration, praising the Savior!

We read in Revelation 5:9-14 that the elders are singing a song at God's throne, in unison. And they are praising Christ for the privilege of reigning with Him on earth. Imagine the sound of that heavenly music!

Another important element for us to see is that those in the earthly father's house were all *in agreement* with what brought joy to the father. The one outside the house, in the field, was the elder son because he was not in agreement with the father.

The prophet Amos raised a rhetorical question, *Can two walk together, except they are agreed?* (Amos 3:3). And the apostle Paul raises similar questions, *And what concord hath Christ with Belial? Or what part hath he that believeth with an infidel? And what agreement hath the temple of God with idols?* (2 Corinthians 6:15-16a KJV). The Greek word for *concord* is *symphonesis*! No harmony can exist between the children of God and the children of the devil.

In the body of Christ we are gifted with the ability to harmonize together for the glory of God.

Lord, help us to be heavenly music-makers for your glory!

Glenna Salsbury

Exodus 39-40; Matthew 23:23-39   **February 6**

Stick Close!

Brethren, if a man is overtaken in any trespass, you who are spiritual restore such a one in a spirit of gentleness, considering yourself lest you also be tempted. Bear one another's burdens, and so fulfill the law of Christ. For if anyone thinks himself to be something, when he is nothing, he deceives himself.
(Galatians 6:1-3)

God has known from the beginning of humanity that no single human needs to live his or her life alone, in isolation. It is unhealthy, unwise and not what God intended for us.

Too often in Christianity as we know it today, people choose to live apart from the very people they most need. When we believe we can go it alone and do not need anyone else, we have believed the devil's lie, and we set ourselves up for failure. Motorcycle riders tell me there is a maxim among the riding fraternity: It is not a matter of <u>if</u> you will fall, but <u>when</u>. So it is with the isolationist crowd of Christians. Eventually, that isolation will do us harm.

Consider the words of Paul to the Galatian Christians. *Brethren, if a man is overtaken in any trespass, you who are spiritual restore such a one in a spirit of gentleness, considering yourself lest you also be tempted. Bear one another's burdens, and so fulfill the law of Christ. For if anyone thinks himself to be something, when he is nothing, he deceives himself.*

Look at the benefits of "sticking close." First, if you veer off course and find yourself caught in some kind of sin, you have brothers and sisters who love you and will gently draw you to restoration. They have your back!

You can look at this a different way, too. If you are "sticking close" to your brothers and sisters in Christ, you may have the opportunity to help someone who has veered off course. God may use you to help someone in desperate need. That cannot happen if you practice an isolated faith.

This "sticking close" has a beneficial mutuality to it. Paul tells us to *bear one another's burdens*. By doing that, we fulfill *the law of Christ.* Only when you choose to live in community with other believers can you *fulfill the law of Christ.* Isolation prevents you from living out God's calling upon your life.

Finally, living in community with other believers protects us from believing that which is not true about our own lives. We can think we are something really special when we live apart from those who love us. Engaging in community forces us to see clearly our struggles and the struggles of others.

All of us who follow Jesus need to stick close to our faith family. We need them, and they need us!

Rev. John Strain

Leviticus 1-3; Matthew 24:1-28　　　　　　　　February 7

...What We Once Were

Not that I have already attained, or am already perfected; but I press on, that I may lay hold of that for which Christ Jesus has also laid hold of me. (Philippians 3:12)

There are times we look at our lives and wonder if we are changing at all; but every so often, God gives us a glimpse of what we once were. It is usually when we look at our progress over years, not days or weeks, that we see the change God has accomplished in our lives. Progress often seems painfully slow or non-existent altogether. Yet, as months and even years pass, when we look back we see change has indeed occurred.

There are times we just have to take God at His word because we can't see it, feel it, taste it, or smell it. It's called faith. Trust He is at work!!

...being confident of this very thing, that He who has begun a good work in you will complete it until the day of Jesus Christ (Philippians 1:6).

Now may the God of peace Himself sanctify you completely; and may your whole spirit, soul, and body be preserved blameless at the coming of our Lord Jesus Christ. He who calls you is faithful, who also will do it (1 Thessalonians 5:23-24).

...work out your own salvation with fear and trembling; for it is God who works in you both to will and to do for His good pleasure (Philippians 2:12-13).

Diane Hunt

Leviticus 4-5; Matthew 24:29-51　　　　　　　　**February 8**

God Is Always Previous

It shall come to pass, that BEFORE they call, I will answer; and while they are yet speaking, I will hear.
(Isaiah 65:24, emphasis mine)

 Addison Raws, the son of our founder, William Raws, had a sermon that he regularly preached entitled "God is Always Previous." The gist of this message is that, as Christians, we spend so much time worrying and fretting rather than thanking God for the answers to prayer that are already on their way.

 This morning I was reading Spurgeon's <u>Faith's Checkbook</u> and his words echoed the words of Addison Raws. Let them burn into your heart today:

 "The Lord hears us BEFORE we call and often answers in the same speedy manner. Foreseeing our needs, and our prayers, He so arranges providence that BEFORE the need actually arises HE has supplied it, BEFORE the trial assails us HE has armed us against it. This is the promptitude of omniscience, and we have often seen it exercised. BEFORE we dreamed of the affliction which was coming, the strong consolation which was to sustain us under it had arrived. What a prayer-answering God we have!

 The second clause suggests the telephone! Though God be in heaven and we upon earth, yet HE makes our word, like His own word, to travel very swiftly. WHEN WE PRAY ARIGHT WE SPEAK INTO THE EAR OF GOD. Our gracious Mediator presents our petitions at once, and the great Father hears and smiles upon them. Grand praying this!

 Who would not be in much prayer when he KNOWS he has the ear of the King of kings? This day I will pray in faith, not only believing that I SHALL be heard, but that I AM heard; not only that I SHALL be answered, but that I HAVE THE ANSWER ALREADY! Holy Spirit, help me in this!"

I am very thankful today that God is ALWAYS previous. What a gigantic truth for today. My prayer is this: Holy Spirit, help me in this! How about you?

Dr. Bill Welte

Leviticus 6-7; Matthew 25:1-30   **February 9**

Anyone Who Believes

For I am not ashamed of the gospel of Christ, for it is the power of God to salvation for everyone who believes, for the Jew first and also for the Greek. (Romans 1:16)

Do we really believe the second part of this verse? Do we believe that the gospel of Jesus Christ is for anyone who believes? The word "power" is describing the regenerating, life-changing, transforming power that the Holy Spirit has in the life of a person who is saved, anyone with the faith to believe.

I talk to church leaders and pastors who doubt that God will change certain people or they will say that they have never seen anyone walk out of sin such as homosexuality. I think this might be where the first part of this verse needs to come into play, *For I am not ashamed of the gospel.* As Christians we need to claim the power that God says He has whether we have seen it or not. We need to stand firm in our faith - God's Word is true from cover to cover.

Now faith is the assurance of things hoped for, the conviction of things not seen (Hebrews 11:1 ESV).

The person in bondage to any life-dominating sin or addiction needs the hope, faith and even comfort that we can offer by standing on God's Word. I remember telling a friend of mine that I did not have the faith to do what God was asking me to do. His words to me were that he had never seen a situation too big for God, not even mine. He said that he had enough faith for both of us and that he would hold my hand and walk with me out of the darkness. I happen to know that my friend had not seen God bring someone out of the sin that I was living in, but that didn't shake his belief in the power of the gospel.

For the grace of God has appeared, bringing salvation for <u>all</u> people, training us to renounce ungodliness and worldly passions, and to live self-controlled, upright, and godly lives in the present age, waiting for our blessed hope, the appearing of the glory of our great God and Savior Jesus Christ, who gave himself for us to redeem us from all lawlessness and to purify for himself a people for his own possession who are zealous for good works. <u>Declare these things; exhort and rebuke with all authority. Let no one disregard you</u> (Titus 2:11-15 ESV, emphasis mine).

Chaplain Bill Pruitt

Leviticus 8-10; Matthew 25:31-46　　　　　　　　　**February 10**

In Quietness and Confidence

You will keep him in perfect peace, Whose mind is stayed on You, Because he trusts in You. (Isaiah 26:3)

These words come from Isaiah. As the Syrian invader loomed on the horizon, God wanted Israel to hear what He had to say. With human ability, Israel was figuring out what to do. Should they make a treaty with Egypt, because anything was worth it to maintain national independence? So ambassadors were dispatched to negotiate with the reigning Pharaoh.

But God's counsel was opposed to the politicians' reasoning. He said, *"...in returning and rest shall ye be saved; in quietness and confidence shall be your strength..."* (Isaiah 30:15). That is, "if you will wait for My deliverance, you will be rescued from your enemy."

Did you ever notice how, if a person is fearful, it is hard to accept this kind of counsel? It's hard to rest. It's hard to be quiet. We feel we have to do something. We plot and plan, scheme and sweat, all in an effort to get ourselves out of the problems we face, while at the same time we ignore God's words to us in the Bible. *Great peace have those who love Your law, and nothing causes them to stumble* (Psalm 119:165).

It is so easy to get upset with the problems around us and end up trusting ourselves. What we need, however, is a tranquil trust in God's Word. With that trust is a way into God's presence where there is peace and rest. We simply need God's counsel. In the words of the hymnwriter, "They who trust Him wholly, find Him wholly true."

Carolyn Hibbard

Leviticus 11-12; Matthew 26:1-25   **February 11**

A Sweet Smell

But thanks be to God, who always leads us in triumphal procession in Christ and through us spreads everywhere the fragrance of the knowledge of him. For we are to God the aroma of Christ among those who are being saved and those who are perishing. (2 Corinthians 2:14-15 NIV)

Did you know that God could smell? Genesis 8:21 tells us that He has the sense of smell. God specifically designed us to be able to smell for a reason. *If the whole body were an eye, where were the hearing? If the whole were hearing, where were the smelling?* (1 Corinthians 12:17 KJV).

Most of us can immediately sit back and think of both smells we have experienced that have been pleasant and those that we'd prefer to never smell again. Let me just name a few…

Comforting/pleasant smells:
- dinner in the oven
- chocolate chip cookies fresh from the oven
- freshly cut grass (unless you have allergies)
- spring flowers in bloom
- the fresh scent of the ocean
- your loved one's perfume
- a clean baby out of the tub
- the morning air after a peaceful rain

Could-do-without smells:
- trash on a hot summer day
- body odor
- dead animal
- rotten food
- refinery/plant burn off/pollution

I have always found it interesting that God calls us a sweet fragrance. Just like the different smells we can experience, our lives can be both sweet fragrances to God, as well as foul odors. Ecclesiastes 10:1 compares bad smells to folly. Our sins are compared with foul smells in Job 15, *He sees the flaws in the very heavens themselves, so how much less we humans, smelly and foul, who lap up evil like water?*

God wants us to be pleasing smells which represent Him before the world. In 2 Corinthians we are told that our fragrance as victorious Christians points others directly to Him. Our fragrance when we are walking in Christ is pleasing to God; it reminds Him of Christ. When He smells us – He smells His son. You know what that is like; perfumes often remind us of others and bring either pleasant memories, or not so pleasant, depending on of whom we are reminded. That's the same way we are to God… our lives can be both pleasing to God or can be as foul odors. I don't know about you… but I would like to be a pleasing fragrance.

When God gets a whiff of your perfume… what does He smell? Are you wearing Christ? Can others smell Christ through you? Paul himself knew what it was like to receive the sweet smell from others. *But I have all, and abound: I am full, having received of Epaphroditus the things which were sent from you, an odour of a sweet smell, a sacrifice acceptable, well pleasing to God* (Philippians 4:18 KJV).

Let us each daily give to God and others that sweet smell of Christ.

Dr. Lynne Jahns

Leviticus 13; Matthew 26:26-50   **February 12**

Build Your Life on a Solid Foundation

"Therefore whoever hears these sayings of Mine, and does them, I will liken him to a wise man who built his house on the rock: and the rain descended, the floods came, and the winds blew and beat upon that house; and it did not fall, for it was founded on the rock." (Matthew 7:24-25)

    Someone once said that life is the sum total of the choices we make. We are the product of our decisions. In this concluding section of the Sermon on the Mount, Jesus is pointing out that we have the option to make wise choices or foolish choices. He also made it very clear that our choices have consequences.

    Are you building on a solid foundation? Will your life withstand the storms and trials that will come your way?

    In the story before us, Jesus compared wise choices and foolish choices. The wise man built his house on rock. The foolish man built his house on sand. Each man had the opportunity to make a decision that would have a lasting effect upon his life. One man made a wise decision. One man made a foolish decision.

    What is a solid foundation? Jesus tells the answer to this question in verse 24, *"whoever hears these sayings of Mine, and does them, I will liken to a wise man who built his house on the rock."* In Luke 6:48a Jesus added, *He is like a man building a house, who dug down deep and laid the foundation on rock.* The foundation that will withstand the storms of life is a life that is lived in disciplined obedience to the revealed Word of God.

    The foundation of a building is not the most glamorous or attractive part of a building. It is usually hidden from view and rarely receives compliments, but it is the most important part of the building. The foundation determines the strength and durability of the building. And so it is with life, we tend to focus on appearance and style and convenience rather than the less popular fundamentals.

    If you desire a life that will withstand the trials and tests of time, then you must live a life of disciplined obedience to God's

Word. Jesus said any other choice will be classified as foolish, dull and sluggish. Or, as we would say today, the man who built his house on sand made a stupid decision.

Be a wise Christian; build your life on the Rock.

Dr. Roger D. Willmore

Leviticus 14; Matthew 26:51-75   February 13

Abiding Above

If then you were raised with Christ, seek those things which are above, where Christ is, sitting at the right hand of God. Set your mind on things above, not on things on the earth. For you died, and your life is hidden with Christ in God. (Colossians 3:1-3)

What does "Abiding Above" mean? "Abiding" means to remain, wait for, to be held, or kept. For the Christian, it speaks of resting in the Holy Spirit, Who lives inside of you, letting Him control you by living His life in you and through you.

As Dr. Stephen Olford used to say, "The Holy Spirit looks through your eyes, listens with your ears, loves others through your heart, serves others with your hands, and walks in your steps." This is abiding, my friend. Simply let go, and let God have all there is of you today. I promise you, on the authority of God's Word, that you will find rest for your soul when you choose to abide in Him Who is your life.

What does "Above" mean? "Above" speaks of the believer's heavenly position in Christ. Notice again what the apostle Paul said, ... *your life is hidden with Christ in God.* My friend, Paul is saying that when Christ died, you died, when He was buried, you were buried, and when He was raised from the dead, you were raised, and when He ascended to heaven, you ascended, and when He sat down at the right hand of the Father, you sat down with Him. When God the Father looks to His right hand, He sees Christ, and you in Him, clothed with His righteousness! This is your heavenly position.

Remember what Paul said, *If you were raised with Christ...* In order to be raised with Christ, you must have been crucified and buried with Him. You were baptized, or immersed into Christ, on the cross. Paul said in Romans 6:3, *Or do you not know that as many of us as were baptized into Christ Jesus were baptized into His death?*

This is what Paul means when He says, *Seek and set your mind above.* This is a profound truth that must be known and appropriated for a Christian to live a victorious and overcoming life. My friend, to enjoy a heavenly life on earth, you only need to "Abide Above."

Rev. Chris S. Hodges

Leviticus 15-16; Matthew 27:1-26   **February 14**

Love and Joy

... for the joy that was set before Him [He] endured the cross...
(Hebrews 12:2)

There is a significant connection between *love* and *joy*. The Scripture tells us that God so *loved* those who would come to believe that He sent His Son to die in our place. *For the wages of sin is death; but the gift of God is eternal life through Jesus Christ our Lord* (Romans 6:23 KJV).

Christ explained the connection between this love of the Father and our joy as believers. *As the Father hath loved Me, so have I loved you... These things have I spoken unto you, that My joy might remain in you, and that your joy might be full* (John 15:9, 11 KJV). Apparently, it is only when we grasp how *loved* we are, totally and unconditionally, that we can then walk in *joy*.

Christ says He wants *His* joy to remain in us. What is Christ's joy? We find that answer in Hebrews 12:2. *Looking unto Jesus, the author and finisher of our faith, who for the joy that was set before Him endured the cross....* You and *I* and all believers are Christ's joy. He loved us and therefore He experienced joy in saving us to an eternal love relationship with Him!

In His prayer to the Father, Christ reiterates this connection of *love* and *joy*. *Now I am coming to you. I have told them [the disciples] many things while I was with them ... so they would be filled with my joy* (John 17:13 NLT). Jesus had clearly told the disciples that He loved them as much as the Father loved Him, the Son! Again, it is in the anointed truth of Christ's unconditional love for us that we can experience joy.

The Holy Spirit's work in us also reveals the connection between love and joy. The Apostle Paul tells us that *the fruit of the Spirit is love, joy, peace, longsuffering, gentleness, goodness, faith...* (Galatians 5:22 KJV). Notice that the word *fruit* is singular. There are not *fruits* of the Spirit. Rather, the Spirit produces a *singular fruit*, the Fruit of the Vine! Christ is being formed in us. The manifestation of the character of God is being produced in us. And *love* is first in the *identification* of Christ's presence. And we know that *God is love* (1 John 4:8 KJV).

The *very next* identifying factor of the Lord's character manifested by the Spirit is *joy*. And *joy* flows out of *love*!

And, finally, the Lord is the Initiator of Love and the Sole Source of Authentic Love. *Herein is love, not that we loved God, but that He loved us...* (1 John 4:10a KJV).

> Open our eyes, Lord, to see that Your love is unconditional
> and nothing can separate us from Your love.
> Thus, we can walk in joy (Romans 8:39).

Glenna Salsbury

Leviticus 17-18; Matthew 27:27-50　　　　　　　　**February 15**

Achieving Righteousness

In the exercise of His will He brought us forth by the word of truth, so that we might be, as it were, the first fruits among His creatures. This you know, my beloved brethren. But let everyone be quick to hear, slow to speak and slow to anger; for the anger of man does not achieve the righteousness of God.
(James 1:18-20 NASB)

This text is often cited in reference to interpersonal communication. Stephen Covey famously stated that when we are talking with others, we should "seek first to understand, then to be understood." Similarly, it has been surmised that God gave us two ears and one mouth for a reason—we should listen twice as much as we talk. Yet if we carefully examine the context of this popular passage we will find a subtle connection with *the word of truth* (v. 18).

Every believer needs a constant connection with the Word of God. We are blessed when we meditate on it day and night (Psalm 1). When James wrote his book, the common way people received the Word was through speech. Indeed, preaching and teaching were vital means of learning the Word of God (Romans 10:14). But not everyone was happy about it in James' day, and the same holds true for us.

Have you ever gotten mad at your pastor for his message only to realize later that it was God you were really angry with? I have. The Word of truth cuts us when we are living falsely, and we don't like it. When the Scripture says, *The Word of God is living and active and sharper than any two-edged sword, and piercing as far as the division of soul and spirit* (Hebrews 4:12), we see the metaphor but know it often comes painfully close to a literal reality. Additionally, the Word of truth doesn't just prick us from the pulpit; it hits us during the week as well.

Have you ever broken off communication, or secretly resented someone for "calling you out" with a verse of Scripture? Yes, we know that people will have their opinions, but everything changes when we are confronted with chapter and verse! Today's Scripture admonishes us to be careful how we receive it, for the *anger of man does not achieve the righteousness of God.*

St. Augustine once got into a verbal spat with a man who said in anger, "Hear me, hear me." The theologian replied, "Neither let me hear thee, nor do thou hear me, but let us both hear the apostle." This is wise counsel that we would all do well to heed. Let us all hear the Word of God and receive it well.

Rev. Jason R. Walsh

Leviticus 19-20; Matthew 27:51-66   **February 16**

God's Guidance

Trust in the LORD with all your heart, and lean not on your own understanding; in all your ways acknowledge Him, and He shall direct your paths. (Proverbs 3:5-6)

Many Christians are confused over the question of how God guides us in our daily living. They want to do the will of God, but what bothers them is knowing what the will of God is in every decision they make and every situation in which they find themselves.

When anyone starts out with the determination to obey God in everything and to be led by the Holy Spirit, Satan begins to trouble them as to what the will of God is. This is one of the ways that Satan keeps Christians from being cheerful.

There is also the matter of the flesh or self that keeps God's children from seeing God's will and His guiding hand. The desire in us to have our own way directly inhibits our ability to perceive God's will. Also, damaged emotions that we all have because of problems in relationships with others can be obstacles to perceiving God's will and actions. The reason for this is that we sometimes view God as being like people we have known, not recognizing how very different He is. The true Christian life is the life of a trusting, glad, fear-free child; not controlled by rules, but by the personal guidance of the Holy Spirit who lives within him. Yes, there are many good rules to live by in life and the Bible is filled with godly principles for us to obey but the mature Christian knows that keeping rules does not make him righteous before God. My friend, only what Christ did for you on the cross gives you a right standing before your heavenly Father.

If you are a child of God, the Holy Spirit lives in you and is ready to lead you at every turn of life. A life surrendered to the control of the Holy Spirit is a life of joy, peace and freedom. There is no anxiety in such a life; there is no fear in the presence of God. Paul said in Romans 8:14, *For as many as are led by the Spirit of God, these are sons of God.*

Let go and let God lead you. Trust God and rejoice in His presence just as a child trusts his earthly father and rejoices in his presence and you will be guided by an unseen hand.

Rev. Chris S. Hodges

Leviticus 21-22; Matthew 28   **February 17**

The Story of Sister Asma

For my soul is full of troubles, and my life draws near to the grave...But to You I have cried out, O LORD, in the morning my prayer comes before You. (Psalm 88:3, 13)
Why are you cast down, O my soul? And why are you in turmoil within me? Hope in God, for I shall yet praise him, For the help of His countenance. (Psalm 42:5)

She was only nineteen when I asked her to help me start a school to teach Arabic to missionaries. Young people whom God had called from more than 25 countries to serve throughout the Arab world learned Arabic, Arabic culture and the power of love she showed. She displayed a gift of comforting and counseling. She became a mother and sister to countless missionaries. Rarely did anyone study with her whom she did not invite for a meal.

I helped her get engaged and dedicated her five children to the Lord in a little church that she, her husband and brother-in-law cared for. At 1:30 a.m. I received a call that her husband died suddenly at the age of 47. Her father died from a gunshot wound. Later, the younger of her two sons was killed in a car crash. A language school student from Georgia wanted to marry her second daughter, Mervat. I convinced her two uncles that it would be okay. We had a huge engagement party and then I performed the wedding in Amman, Jordan. I also took part in the wedding of the first son, Husam.

Mervat and her husband, Omar, ministered with a mission in Lebanon and Jordan, then went to Florida for further training. Through every trial it seemed that Asma, this young widow, faced so much. Yet after each tragedy she rebounded with tremendous faith, encouraging those who wanted to encourage her! I went over to Amman in May of 2009 to speak at the graduation ceremonies. The occasion also witnessed a great party for Asma's retirement after 45 years of helping missionaries become better communicators. I took a beautiful picture of Asma and her son Husam. Of course, I enjoyed a delicious Arabic meal in her home.

For the last several years she has been on pins and needles as word that Mervat's fourth child, Joseph, was suffering from leukemia. They were stressed out in Florida while Asma was stressed out in Amman. He has continued on and off for more than four years with chemo. Two years ago Mervat's husband was diagnosed with ALS. All of this has added to Asma's inner suffering. In March of 2010 another flood of waters overwhelmed her when Husam, her only remaining son, died suddenly. He was 41. Yes, her father, her husband, her youngest son, her grandson, her son-in-law and son all caused the waters to overwhelm her. Asma passed through those waters of turmoil in heart and soul as she shared with those suffering. In all of this she has remained strong and unbending in her faith in the Lord and trust in His sovereign will. She has shown that many waters cannot quench love or her faith in the Lord. Will my faith stand the tragedies of life as I call out to the Lord in faith? Our Jordanian teacher has something to teach each of us today. She could say, *Hope in God, for I shall yet praise Him.*

Dr. George Kelsey

Leviticus 23-24; Mark 1:1-22 **February 18**

Prayer and Action

Nevertheless we made our prayer to our God, and because of them we set a watch against them day and night. (Nehemiah 4:9)

Have you ever seen a team huddle for prayer before a big game? Have you ever prayed before taking a test? Most Americans pray at least occasionally, yet I come across few who seem to truly understand it. One of my Bible heroes is Nehemiah, a man who worked extremely hard and achieved great success, and always saw the results as ultimately coming from the hand of God.

In 445 BC, while in Babylon, Nehemiah received a report from those who had been to Jerusalem. The walls of the city were still in ruins and Nehemiah was very troubled by this. After much planning and prayer, he got up the nerve to approach the king and ask to be sent to personally oversee the rebuilding of the walls. He was a very trusted member of the king's court and the king granted his request.

Upon arrival in Jerusalem Nehemiah was greeted with opposition from the locals. He was mocked and ridiculed. He was threatened continually, but the work progressed. Here is a portion from chapter four:

So we rebuilt the wall till all of it reached half its height, for the people worked with all their heart. But when Sanballat, Tobiah, the Arabs, the Ammorites and the men of Ashdod heard that the repairs to Jerusalem's walls had gone ahead and that the gaps were being closed, they were very angry. They all plotted together to come and fight against Jerusalem and stir up trouble against it. But we prayed to our God and posted a guard day and night to meet this threat (v. 6-9 NIV).

Clearly Nehemiah was a man of action. He understood the relationship between prayer and hard work. But how many of us pray and then sit back and wait to see what God will do? Andrew Murray wisely stated that "Prayer is the power by which that comes to pass which otherwise would not take place." This is very true indeed. If you look through Scripture to find examples of God granting requests of the slothful, you will look in vain.

Let us therefore be people of earnest prayer, but not of the type that make prayer an excuse for laziness. Come, take up a sword in one hand and a trowel in the other. Together we shall be wall builders and, if the good hand of God is upon us (2:8), we shall succeed!

Rev. Jason Walsh

Leviticus 25; Mark 1:23-45 **February 19**

Red Sea/Jordan River

For you will cross over the Jordan and go in to possess the land which the LORD your God is giving you, and you will possess it and dwell in it. (Deuteronomy 11:31)

God delivers His children in various ways. When the Israelites were backed up against the Red Sea, Moses was told to raise his staff and the Red Sea opened up before the throng of people. Before the first person stepped foot into the sea it stood up on either side with walls of water, and they entered on dry ground. So even though it took great faith and trust to step into the rocky but dry seabed – God's work preceded their step of faith.

But lift up your rod, and stretch out your hand over the sea and divide it. And the children of Israel shall go on dry ground through the midst of the sea...Then Moses stretched out his hand over the sea; and the LORD caused the sea to go back by a strong east wind all that night, and made the sea into dry land, and the waters were divided. So the children of Israel went into the midst of the sea on the dry ground, and the waters were a wall to them on their right hand and on their left (Exodus 14:16, 21-22).

On the other hand, when the children of promise were blocked by the raging waters of the Jordan River at flood stage, instead of performing the miracle BEFORE they stepped out, God told them to step out FIRST.

So it was, when the people set out from their camp to cross over the Jordan, with the priests bearing the ark of the covenant before the people, and as those who bore the ark came to the Jordan, and the feet of the priests who bore the ark dipped in the edge of the water (for the Jordan overflows all its banks during the whole time of harvest), that the waters which came down from upstream stood still, and rose in a heap very far away at Adam, the city that is beside Zaretan. So the waters that went down into the Sea of the Arabah, the Salt Sea, failed, and were cut off; and the people crossed over opposite Jericho. Then the priests who bore the ark of the covenant of the LORD stood firm on dry ground in the midst of the Jordan; and all Israel crossed over on dry ground, until all the people had crossed completely over the Jordan (Joshua 3:14-17).

AFTER their toes got wet in the waters of the Jordan River, THEN God performed His miracle and divided the river, making a way to enter Jericho.

Are you resisting change in your life, refusing to surrender fully in an area of struggle or sin because you are waiting for a Red Sea miracle when God is sending you a Jordan River miracle? Are you waiting for God to do the miracle BEFORE you obey or are you willing to step out in faith and obey BEFORE you see the fulfillment of God's promise? If so, you may be sitting on the river bank a very long time. Don't be afraid to get your feet wet.

Diane Hunt

Leviticus 26-27: Mark 2   **February 20**

Claiming Holy Ground

Exodus 3:1-6 (Part 1)

The man Moses was on the forefront of an assignment and a responsibility that has not been matched by any other event in human history. You probably know most if not all of the story. As God was preparing Moses for the assignment, He introduced Moses to several aspects of understanding the holy. The Bible says that *the knowledge of the Holy One is understanding* (Proverbs 9:10). Moses would certainly need an abundance of understanding for the task before him.

Let the lessons begin. God attracted Moses to a bush that was burning but was not being consumed (Exodus 3:2). It was a miraculous appeal. As Moses approached the bush, God called him by name and instructed him not to come any closer because *the place where you [are] stand[ing] is holy ground.*

God never treats that which is holy with an unholy casualness. Care must be taken to understand and honor the distinctive nature of the sacred. Claiming holy ground is an honor beyond measure. It is a process for which no human writes the rules. There are more lessons to learn here.

Claiming holy ground is not dependent upon our position in life. At the time of this encounter with God Moses was keeping the flock of Jethro, his father-in-law. That is not a position of professional prestige. Moses did not even own the flock. Let this message be clear. Our opportunity to approach God, to approach "holy ground," is not a privilege reserved for human prestige. We must never put our self off limits for the call of God to occupy holy ground.

Claiming holy ground is often enhanced by our separation from the distractions of life. Moses was on "the backside of the desert." Life there was neither cluttered nor fast. The side-shows that often appeal to human lust were not competing for attention. The bleating noise of the tempters was scarce.

It is true that earth-bound humans can never fully escape the seduction of evil. However, there is often a remarkable opportunity in "the backside of the desert" to free ourselves from the constant bombardment of the evil seductions of an ungodly culture.

It was in such a setting that God got Moses' attention and directed him in the claiming of holy ground. Do you need a trip to the desert today?

Dr. Robert L. Alderman

Numbers 1-2; Mark 3:1-19   **February 21**

Claiming Holy Ground

Exodus 3:1-6 (Part 2)

As Moses looked with interest at the burning bush, (I hope you know the story from Exodus 3), God informed Moses that he was standing on holy ground. Holy ground is not to be taken casually. For that reason God instructed Moses to remove his shoes. It was a part of God's way of accenting the significance of the holy.

There are significant lessons here about holy ground. Two of those lessons were presented in Part 1 of these devotional thoughts.

Our third lesson comes from the simple statement in verse one that Moses came to *the mountain of God.*

Claiming holy ground means that I am willing to come as I am to where God is.

Approaching that mountain meant that Moses was putting aside the distractions of physical enticement and mental attitudes. This was God's mountain and God was in charge. Moses decided that was where he wanted to be.

For many of us it may be a terrifying thing to think of approaching such a place. We need time to contemplate what God will say. Will He have demands against my personal desires and habits? Will He allow a listening ear to a man in my position as a mere caretaker for another man's goats? Will it bother Him that I am not clothed in royal robes or that I am not in possession of parliamentary power? Will He notice the odor of goats and sheep? Should I take time to improve my physical appearance and plan my speech?

There is no indication that any of these matters caused Moses to delay his desire for a holy ground relationship with God.

As I face my own needs in life, especially my spiritual needs, I must often ask if I am ready to approach God as I am. Do I trust Him enough not to be afraid of His position, His person, His power and His plan for me?

Then I must ask if there has been a time in my life when I also have been willing to leave the world behind, to walk away from that which is familiar, and to approach that which is so different that it is miraculous and demanding.

Then I must ask if I am really being honest with my responses. Do I really desire that which is holy?

Dr. Robert L. Alderman

Numbers 3-4; Mark 3:20-35   **February 22**

Claiming Holy Ground
Exodus 3:1-6 (Part 3)

Since this is the third in a series on claiming holy ground, I trust that you have taken time to read the previous parts. In Part 2 we considered the fact that claiming **holy ground means that we are willing to come as we are to where God is.**

But there is more. Not only does *claiming holy ground mean that we are willing to come as we are to where God is,* it also means that **we are willing to come to a place where we are not looking for anything but God.**

We are told that Moses, in coming to *the mountain of God,* came *to Horeb* (v.1).

Horeb means desert, drought, desolate, waste, ruins. To put it simply, there were no natural and physical attractions on Horeb. Not anything for pleasure or entertainment. Nothing like the treasures in Egypt (Hebrews 11:24-26). Not even anything like the comfort of Jethro's home.

For many of us it may begin to appear that the price of claiming holy ground is a price we may not want to pay. We may get the idea that God is fine but God plus something else is better.

We may even begin to think that there is no reason to seek God if He is not going to provide all of the toys. After all, is that not the main reason people really seek God?

It is at this point that we must realize that those who sincerely seek holy ground need nothing else to attract them. That person is satisfied and content with God ONLY. The fact that Horeb offers nothing other than God is not a problem. He is all we need.

The faithful Jew put it this way: *In God is my salvation and my glory: the rock of my strength, and my refuge, is in God* (Psalm 62:7).

There was no thought like "God is my avenue to what I really need and what I really want." Not at all. The one who genuinely seeks holy ground seeks God ONLY. Christ had to confront the rich man with this very issue (Mark 10:17-22). That was the man who went away from Jesus "sad" because he had great possessions. In his thinking, Jesus without his possessions was not worth the price. That is sad.

I now ask this question concerning my own journey to holy ground, to the mountain of God: "Have I sincerely dealt with the Horeb issue?"

Dr. Robert L. Alderman

Numbers 5-6; Mark 4:1-20 February 23

Claiming Holy Ground
Exodus 3:1-6 (Part 4)

Amazing truths are revealed in the journey Moses experienced to his burning bush encounter with God. Some of those truths have formed the theme for this series of devotional thoughts on claiming holy ground.

Please recall that when Moses saw the bush that was burning without being consumed he said, *I will now turn aside, and see this great sight, why the bush is not burnt* (Exodus 3:3). When God saw what Moses was doing He announced to Moses that the place where he was standing was holy ground. That experience with holy ground changed the entire nature of this encounter. We are here considering some of the factors involved in claiming holy ground.

Claiming holy ground means that we are willing to be approached by a messenger of God.

This is what Moses needed to know at the outset. *And the Angel of the Lord appeared unto him (Moses) in a flame of fire from the midst of a bush* (v. 2).

At this point of the journey we do not know if Moses had even heard the description of "holy ground." But now he was soon to learn that claiming holy ground is not a self-directed tour. It is not a course for which we draw the map and make the rules. It is not a casual wandering in which we visit the points of personal interest and avoid those in which we have little or no interest.

We may not always know what the angel of the Lord is going to do – or say – or require. That in itself has proven to be frightening to some who are not sure they really want to finish this journey. Questions arise: How long is this journey? How difficult? Is the road narrow? Is holy ground a place of permanence? What happens if we become uncomfortable? Does God cut any slack with our desire for human diversity? Is God really narrow in His view of holiness? What does it mean that the angel appeared *in a flame of fire*? (More on that in Part 5.)

We have no record that Moses raised these questions. Perhaps he had witnessed enough in his life to know that there was a great need for an encounter with the supernatural. Perhaps he had witnessed enough of human depravity to investigate the unusual in what became known as *the mountain of God*.

Dr. Robert L. Alderman

Numbers 7-8; Mark 4:21-41 February 24

Claiming Holy Ground

Exodus 3:1-6 (Part 5)

We have just learned in verse one that Moses *came to the mountain of God*. As he, did an Angel (a messenger) of God appeared unto him in *a flame of fire* (v. 2). In Part 4 we considered some of the significance of being approached by a messenger of God. Now we consider the *flame of fire* aspect.

Claiming holy ground means that we will be willing to be approached by an angel of God in a flame of fire.

In our thought for today we look at the significance of fire. It is a fascinating and powerful matter. We all know that. Fire has many qualities and it does many things.

Fire changes the usefulness of things. It can change a field of golden grain into a field of scorched earth and it can change a bushel of golden grain into a loaf of warm bread. It can change a family's house into a pile of ashes and it can fill a family home with warmth, comfort and beauty.

Fire reveals. It uncovers the true nature of a thing.

Fire frightens as well as attracts. Fire has enough quality, power and purpose to get our attention.

Fire purifies the impure. It burns away the dross and the trash.

Please recall the story of the prophet Isaiah (Isaiah 6). The prophet had seen the Lord upon a throne, high and lifted up. He heard the angels saying to each other *"Holy, holy, holy, is the Lord of hosts;..."* At that Isaiah cries *"Woe is me"* and confesses that he is undone and that he is a man of unclean lips.

An angel is dispatched to Isaiah *having in his hand a live coal, which he had taken with the tongs from the altar*. The angel placed the live coal upon Isaiah's mouth and said, *this has touched your lips, and your iniquity is taken away, and your sin is purged.*

Fire is not always comfortable. It is often necessary. Holy ground is costly. Claiming it means that I am willing to be approached by and submissive to that messenger of God who has a job to do for me on God's behalf and on mine. I must now consider the significance of allowing such a messenger of God to approach me - especially for the purpose of purification. It is a part of the holy ground experience.

Dr. Robert L. Alderman

Numbers 9-11; Mark 5:1-20 　　　　　　　　　　**February 25**

Claiming Holy Ground

Exodus 3:1-6 (Part 6)

In the unfolding story of the man Moses standing on holy ground our next lesson comes from the reality that Moses was willing to approach both the unexplainable and the uncertain.

...and he looked, and, behold, the bush burned with fire, and the bush was not consumed. And Moses said, I will now turn aside, and see this great sight, why the bush is not burnt (v. 2-3 KJV).

Moses was attracted to the bush that burned and was not consumed. Such a sight and such an event were of an uncertain nature and surely were unexplainable by the natural mind.

Often things of such uncertainty frighten rather than attract. Such could frequently be said of a call to stand on holy ground. Questions arise. What will it cost me in the way of my personal agenda? Will this event embarrass me in the presence of my friends? Will it change my life? If so, what of my life will it change?

When we move toward God we must do so with abandon to all that God is – and to all that God will do. If we can't move toward God in that way – we are on a dead-end street and our path of advance is closed.

When we make our decision to move toward God's uncertain and unexplainable action – WE MUST REMEMBER THAT GOD HAS A WILL WHICH WE SHALL FOLLOW, NOT A NEGOTIATING TABLE AT WHICH WE WILL SIT.

As Moses looked for an explanation of that which was beyond his understanding, he found an assignment that was beyond his ability. What Moses learned in that encounter has been a blessing of victory to countless numbers of us, Jew and Gentile alike.

Many of us may avoid the holy ground relationship because we do not know what it will mean. We often want a full explanation of the uncertain before we move toward the attractiveness of God. If that is the case then it is possible that we may never claim holy ground. And what a loss that would be to us and to others.

Our willingness to claim holy ground never ends with just us. Others wait for the riches of our Lord to flow through us as we have received that flood of life and truth through those who have come before us in truth and devotion to Christ.

Dr. Robert L. Alderman

Numbers 12-14; Mark 5:21-43   February 26

Claiming Holy Ground
Exodus 3:1-6 (Part 7)

We come now to the seventh consideration of the willingness of the servant Moses to stand on holy ground.

Claiming holy ground means that I must be willing to go one-on-one with God.

When the LORD saw that he (Moses) turned aside to see, God called unto him out of the midst of the bush, and said, Moses, Moses. And he said, Here am I (v. 4).

There is no mention that Moses heard God call any other name. There was no reference to Abraham, or Isaac, or Elijah. There was no reference to any other name representing any other ethnicity or culture or geography.

There is no mention of Moses requesting that someone be allowed to accompany him, or that he be allowed to bring a counselor to stand by his side. There is no reference to poll takers being asked to advise Moses if his situation would be popular among peers and people.

There was no reference to searching the archives to examine the results of others who may have encountered God in such a personal way. There was no thought of an examination of the pragmatism of getting into such a relationship with God before being assured of material prosperity and social success.

There was none of that. There was obviously a desire to know the power that was at work. Perhaps we shall never know what encircled and penetrated Moses' thoughts in response to that significant summons.

But we do know the significance of an immediate and simple response - *Here am I*. It is a lesson we all should learn early in our pilgrimage with Christ. No delay or complexity is needed in a faithful response to the One we trust.

Neither should we stumble at the overwhelming nature of His assignments. Those assignments are in keeping with His great design for our victory. They are beyond our ability primarily because they are designed for victory that is experienced only in Christ.

The question is penetrating - Am I willing for such a one-on-one encounter with the God who stands on holy ground?

Dr. Robert L. Alderman

Numbers 15-16; Mark 6:1-29 February 27

Claiming Holy Ground

Exodus 3:1-6 (Part 8)

As Moses approached the bush that was burning but was not being consumed, God instructed him to remove his shoes from his feet for the place he was standing was holy ground (v. 5). We come now to another lesson Moses learned with reference to that holy ground experience.

Claiming holy ground means that I am willing to obey the limitations of God.

God further instructed Moses, *Draw not nigh hither* (v. 5, KJV). That means that Moses was restricted from coming any closer to the actual happening. That restriction may be questioned by some. It is obvious that God had done an unusual thing to get Moses' attention. And it did get his attention. And Moses responded properly. He approached, he obeyed and he learned as he did.

We may be justified in asking why God now instructs Moses not to come any closer. And of course there are reasons.

Holy ground must be honored with respect and reverence. It must not be abused with familiarity and casualness. God has always maintained a holy distinctiveness with reference to His holiness. He desires our nearness but not our casualness. Being able to share the presence of God is a favor He does for us, not one we do for Him.

Our worship must maintain respect not only for the presence of God but also for the very nature of His being. There is such a thing as a divine protocol in the court of the King. This was a lesson Moses was to learn, and one he was to teach, in his transition from the courts of Pharaoh to the courts of our Lord.

Our human tendency often causes us to think that grace allows us an unguarded protocol with the God of grace and holiness. Under such an attitude our worship may soon deteriorate into back slapping - a buddy, buddy relationship - rather than bending the knee - an honoring of majesty and respect.

God affirms such concerns and the reason behind them when He then reminds Moses of His identity – *"Moreover He said, I am the God of your father— the God of Abraham, the God of Isaac, and the God of Jacob..."* (v. 6).

Moses got the message and in respect and honor hid his face. for he was afraid to look upon God. Do I need to inspect my attitude for an improper casualness in the presence of His majesty?

Dr. Robert L. Alderman

Numbers 17-19; Mark 6:30-56   **February 28**

Claiming Holy Ground

I am the God of your father,... (Exodus 3:1-6) (Part 9)

As the man Moses moved toward the bush that was burning but was not being consumed he had every reason to believe that he was in for a most unusual encounter. Unusual encounters had not been a rare thing for Moses. Having been birthed to Hebrew parents and raised in the courts of the Egyptian Pharaoh, Moses could expect every day to produce something of the unusual.

What Moses could not have known at the time was the significant way his God was preparing him for the extreme encounters of his future. After the fact, we now know that Moses would soon be facing Egypt's Pharaoh with that unusual demand of God to let His people go from those years of cruel slavery. Moses did not know that at the time.

He would be facing Pharaoh's sarcastic denial of the authority of the God of the Hebrews. He would be facing the conflict with Pharaoh and the display of God's authority through the plagues visited upon Egypt. Moses did not know that at the time.

He would be facing the exodus and all of its challenges including the Red Sea experience, the murmuring of the Jews, and the reported impossibility of conquering the land of the giants (Numbers 13:29). Moses did not know that at the time.

But God knew what Moses needed to know in order to claim holy ground.

Claiming holy ground means that I am willing to affirm my encounter with the God of History.

Therefore, as Moses stood on holy ground in the presence of the Lord, he heard the Lord say to him, *"I am the God of your father— the God of Abraham, the God of Isaac, and the God of Jacob..."* (v. 6).

It was God's way of saying to Moses that He is the God who had already proven Himself faithful and powerful, that He was not a newly-revised god or a god fashioned by a new age or new circumstances. It was a great time for God to let Moses know that he (Moses) had encountered the God of History and the God of History had encountered him. Is it now time for me to affirm my encounter with the God of History?

Dr. Robert L. Alderman

February 29

Step To the Right Please

...and he will separate the people one from another as a shepherd separates the sheep from the goats.
(Matthew 25:32 NIV)

The Bible is divided into twos. Two sons; two animals; two plants; two men in a field; two women at a mill; two resurrections; ultimately, two destinies. Jesus died between two thieves. Either you know God, as He can only be known through Jesus, or you don't. Goats are just an illustration. It's not that

God hates goats. He said on day six that they were "good." I kind of like them, too. It's just an illustration, but I've looked into it. I'm no expert, and I know that this simple statement meant far more to Middle Eastern shepherds two thousand years ago than it does to us today, but even to folks like us, there are vast differences between sheep and goats. For instance, sheep (Ovis Aries) have 54 chromosomes, while goats (Capri Hircus) have 60.

Don't make a doctrine out of this, but here are three differences between sheep and goats. Sheep have very strong herding instincts, while goats tend to be very independent. Are you a person who is deeply devoted to unity? Would you be willing to surrender your point of view if it kept things moving forward? I'm not talking about compromising in sin or in any belief that makes us Christians in the first place. I'm just asking if fellowship means more to you than your own ego. Secondly, the tail of a sheep goes down, while the tail of a goat goes up. My point is that perhaps we could tell the sheep from the goats by what follows them? Like the priests of old who carried the Ark of the Covenant, are you a carrier of the mercy seat? When you walk into a room do people think, "Praise God, mercy's here!" Does the fragrance of Christ follow you or is it something, shall we say, "unpleasant" that you leave behind? Finally, sheep have a tear gland while goats do not. It's funny how we can cry at the end of a movie, but we can walk past overwhelming pain without batting an eye. We're told to rejoice with those who rejoice (that, too, is difficult for goats), but also to mourn with those who mourn. The only people who are really looking forward to the day when God wipes every tear from our eyes are people who have known what it was to cry over the things that break God's heart.

I know that because you're reading this that you are, or long to be, a sheep. That's great! The Good Shepherd has laid down His life for you. He faced the wolf and didn't run away. He knows your name. He will take you through the valley of the shadow of death. You will dwell in the house of the Lord forever; and even now you have heard and know His voice. We have a lot to praise God for! Let's put all we have into getting along together (herding), bringing joy into people's lives (humility), and allowing God to share His broken heart through us (tears). Let's live this day for our Lord Jesus, that great Shepherd of the sheep.

Rev. Chris Thompson

Numbers 20-22; Mark 7:1-13   **March 1**

Cleansing From All Sin

If we confess our sins, He is faithful and just to forgive us our sins and to cleanse us from all unrighteousness. (1 John 1:9)

    The verse before you is one of the most quoted verses in the Bible. Some people see it like a lifeboat and use it as license to sin. They say they can do what they want to do because all they have to do is claim 1 John 1:9. Lifeboats are not on ships so they can sink. Lifeboats are on ships in case they sink. This wonderful verse is not a license to sin. It is the promise of a loving Heavenly Father to assure cleansing and restoration when we do sin.

    This verse declares the certainty of God's forgiveness. It is an indisputable fact that God forgives sin. This certainty of God's forgiveness is based on the **faithfulness of God** and the **righteousness of God**. God is faithful and God is righteous.

    God is faithful. *Blessed be the Lord, who has given rest to His people Israel, according to all that He has promised. There has not failed one word of all His good promise, which He promised through His servant Moses* (1 Kings 8:56).

    God's faithfulness guarantees that He will never act inconsistent with Himself. God is His own standard. He is always true to Himself.

    This verse also declares that God is righteous. When Abraham was appealing to God on behalf of Sodom and Gomorrah, he said to God, ...*Shall not the Judge of all the earth do right?* (Genesis 18:25).

Jesus Christ died on the cross to meet God's demands upon Himself. Ponder the depths of this thought. God is true to Himself.

A.W. Tozer said, "All of God's reasons for doing what He does lie within Himself. That is to say that He can never contradict Himself."

This is the God who said, *If we confess our sins, He is faithful and just to forgive us our sins and to cleanse us from all unrighteousness.*

Dr. Roger D. Willmore

Numbers 23-25; Mark 7:14-37   **March 2**

Serving God in the Midst of Godlessness

Bind up the testimony, Seal the law among my disciples.
(Isaiah 8:16)

Isaiah served God at a most difficult time. The Lord revealed that, as a prophet, he would see his audience, outside of a small remnant, reject the word from God (6:10-13). Even so, Isaiah remained faithful, preaching the message of His God over several decades under different earthly kings. How does one remain so faithful to such a God-rejecting culture?

The key to remaining strong spiritually is found in verse 11 of our chapter, *For the LORD spoke thus to me with a strong hand, and instructed me that I should not walk in the way of this people...* To walk God's narrow way in opposition to the broad way of the surrounding culture demands the resolve to love and obey our God. In his obedience Isaiah was mentoring others to walk the same path as he states, *...among my disciples.* As the Word from God had gone forth and been rejected by the majority, God's man determined that his mind would be stayed on the revelation of God and he declared further that he would go, *To the law and to the testimony! If they do not speak according to this word; it is because there is no light in them* (v. 20).

To walk godly in a godless culture requires unwavering faith in the revelation of God as the Truth to be accepted and acted upon each and every day. Isaiah was able to remain faithful in the face of great opposition because he had been allowed a glimpse of God which revealed his own sinful and needy condition (chapter 6). Such an ongoing revelation is necessary for the disciple to understand the need of total reliance upon God. Jesus would state it this way, *If anyone desires to come after Me, let him deny himself, and take up his cross daily, and follow Me* (Luke 9:23). Our revelation is God speaking to us through His Word. Our daily time in the Word and in prayer is our "conversation" with a God Who reveals His love to us in such a way that we grow in love toward Him. The outworking of this is a life of loving obedience lived out as light in the midst of the cultural darkness around us.

Dr. Joe Olachea

Numbers 26-28; Mark 8　　　　　　　　　　　　**March 3**

Comfort Ye My People

Singing light songs to the heavyhearted is like pouring salt in their wounds. (Proverbs 25:20 The Message)

Have you ever been there? You are hurting and discouraged and someone comes along and tries to cheer you up. You know they mean well, but their insensitivity to where you are makes it hurt all the more.

Most of us can remember what that is like – so the question comes – how do I comfort without hurting people even more. I found this quote once and it is probably true of most of us… "I would like to help. I really would. But I just don't know what to say. I'm sure I say too much, and sometimes I think what I say hurts more than it helps. So, most of the time, I stay away and don't do anything at all" (source unknown).

I am in almost daily contact with hurting people, and most of you know people that are hurting. The questions that always seem to come up are… How do I help and how do I give comfort? Let me first suggest to you what comforting is not, then give ideas on what it might mean to be comforting.

Comforting is not having all the answers or being able to explain God's will. Only God knows what is going on and the purpose for situations and suffering in our lives. As friends, we can just remind them that God is on the throne and He knows. It is not about knowing the whys, but helping them walk through the pain (Isaiah 41:10, 43:2-3a).

Comforting is not fixing the problem. Many of us are fixers; we want people to be all better and we want to get them better. Sometimes we fix it by trying to make people look on the positive side or cheer them up. During times of pain and hurt, only time and God can truly heal the wounds. Our role is to listen, to allow them to cry, and to help in ways that are practical which allow them to focus on their healing process (Psalm 147:3).

Comfort is making yourself available. As I already alluded to, the best thing we can do for someone is be there (2 Corinthians 1:3-5). Maybe it's doing tasks that are now hard for them to do; possibly it is bringing in food or helping to drive them places. Often times we help by just being present – even without saying a word (James 1:19; Job 16:2).

Maybe you are a shoulder to lean on or a listening ear. We can listen with compassion. In John 11, Jesus allowed Martha to express feelings regarding the death of her brother Lazarus (vs. 21-22). He gave Mary the same courtesy (v. 32). He was Jesus; He knew exactly what was going on and what was going to happen, but He allowed them the freedom to express their heart. David expressed his feelings and thoughts often through his Psalms (Psalm 27:6 & 9; Psalm 34:6).

Comfort is letting them experience their pain. A key factor in moving on through our difficulties is to face them head on. In many ways we need to encourage others to feel the hurt, pain, and sorrow that is in their life at that point in time (Ecclesiastes 3:1-8). God has allowed it to happen for some reason, and in order for the pain to accomplish its work it is important for them to move with the pain, not away from the pain (Jeremiah 29:11-14).

Most of all... Turn to God for direction and POINT THEM TO CHRIST... Matthew 11:28-30, Psalm 32:8, Psalm 55:22. *Blessed are those who mourn, for they shall be comforted*, (Matthew 5:4).

May you and I learn to be Christ-like comforters, not salt pourers...

Dr. Lynne Jahns

Numbers 29-31; Mark 9:1-29   **March 4**

All Alone!

He is despised and rejected of men; a man of sorrows, and acquainted with grief: and we hid as it were our faces from him; he was despised, and we esteemed him not. (Isaiah 53:3)

The greatest suffering of Jesus on the cross was when He was forsaken by His God! If He had not experienced that (because of our sin on Him), then we would have to experience it when we face God with our sin. Have you ever been forsaken? It can be summed up in one word – ALONE: being entirely by oneself, apart from others. The following helps to describe it.

A – Abandoned: Leaving a person to the mercy of someone or something else; to give up with the intent of never again claiming one's rights or interest in. Jesus experienced being alone from the beginning, *the world knew Him not*; *His own received Him not* (John 1:10-11). Jesus became irredeemable, not acceptable, *He made Him to be sin for us* (2 Corinthians 5:21). Jesus went through abandonment for you.

L – Lonely: Solitary, feeling a lack of close companionship; longing for companionship. Being lonesome heightens the feelings of dreariness, dismalness. To be forlorn and desolate which bring a sharper sense of loneliness are all part of what Jesus felt – for you!

O – Oppressed: Anything between mere objection and intense hostility or warfare. Jesus was at war with Satan in the garden while He prayed. The enemy wanted Him to give up and take back His own will, but He did not….for your sake! Jesus, the man, knew that His God was against the sin which He bore. This brought a sense of oppression to Him.

N – Neglected: Jesus, being alone, had to feel a sense of neglect; a lack of sufficient attention; to be renounced; to be given up. The people, soldiers and a thief on a cross mocked and ridiculed Him. Jesus knew that God could help Him, but wouldn't! What a terrible feeling! Because of our sin He suffered neglect; because of His love He endured.

E – Excluded: This means keeping out what is already outside. To be deserted suggests that companionship was involved and no longer existed. *He bore our own sins in His body* (1 Peter 2:24). Therefore God had to exclude Jesus – because God is sinless, and Jesus on the tree was sin – your sin! You will never be excluded by God if you place your sin on Jesus and receive Him as your Savior. Thank Him for being excluded for you.

Whenever you feel alone, remember Jesus was forsaken for you, so you can be accepted.

Jack Noel

Numbers 32-34: Mark 9:30-50 March 5

Believing in God's Love

But God demonstrates His own love toward us, in that while we were still sinners, Christ died for us. (Romans 5:8)

Because of the effects of sin in our lives, we sometimes find it hard to believe that God really loves us. We somehow see God's love as based on our performance. Thus, we try to live up to unrealistic expectations that others set for us, or that we set for ourselves. All of this veils the biblical truth of God's unending love for us.

Not only do the effects of sin in our lives keep us from seeing God's love but our enemy, Satan, likes to confuse us and make us doubt God's love.

He puts thoughts like these into our minds: "God doesn't love you any more. You are such a failure. God could never love anyone like you."

My friend, God knew all about us when He saved us. He has seen us at our worst, and yet, He loved us enough to give the gift of His Son Jesus to die on a cross for us.

The Bible says, ... *in that while we were still sinners, Christ died for us.*

We are so unlike God in our daily relationships with others. While God forgives, we tend to keep score. This hinders our experiencing God's love.

If God loved us, sought us out, and brought us to Himself when we were rebellious and at enmity with Him, surely He will not stop loving us now that we belong to Him.

What each person must understand is this: God's love and acceptance is not dependent on me—what I am and what I do. I am loved and accepted "IN CHRIST." The Bible tells us that absolutely nothing in this world, or the next, can ever separate us from the love of God in Christ. Why God chose us out of all the millions of people in the world, and why He set His love upon us, we do not know. But God's Word tells us that He chose us "IN CHRIST" before the foundation of the world.

There will be times when we may feel that no one loves us, not even God. But feelings are not facts. We walk by faith in God's Word and not by our feelings. Let us simply choose to take God at His Word. He loves us!

Rev. Chris S. Hodges

Numbers 35-36; Mark 10:1-31   **March 6**

Today You Are in God's Hand

Summon your power, O God; show us Your strength...
(Psalm 68:28 NIV)

The Lord blessed me again yesterday with the timeliness of His Words at a time when I was anxious and discouraged. Let me share with you what He gave me from <u>Streams in the Desert</u> (Zondervan):

"The Lord imparts to me the underlying strength of character that gives me the necessary energy and decision-making ability in my life. He strengthens me "with power through the Spirit in my inner being" (Ephesians 3:16). And the strength He gives is continuous, for he is a source of power I cannot exhaust.

"Your strength will equal my days" *(Deuteronomy 33:25) my strength of will, affection, judgment, ideals, and achievement will last a lifetime.*

"The Lord is my strength" *(Exodus 15:2) to go on. He gives me the power to walk the long, straight, and level path, even when the monotonous way has no turns or curves offering pleasant surprises and when my spirit is depressed with the terrible drudgery.*

"The Lord is my strength" to go up. *He is my power to climb the straight and narrow path up the Hill of Difficulty, as Christian did in Pilgrim's Progress, and not be afraid.*

"The Lord is my strength" to go down. *It is often once I leave the invigorating heights, where the wind and sunlight have surrounded me, and begin to descend to the more confining, humid, and stifling heat of the valley below that my heart grows faint. In fact, I recently heard someone say, referring to his own increasing frailty, "It is coming down that tires me most!"*

"The Lord is my strength" to sit still. *And what a difficult accomplishment this is! I often say to others during those times when I am compelled to be still, "If only I could do something!" I feel like the mother who stands by her sick child but is powerless to heal. What a severe test! Yet to do nothing except to sit still and wait requires tremendous strength!*

"The Lord is my strength!" *Our competence comes from God" (2 Corinthians 3:5)."*

Thank You, Lord, for the reminder today that You, and You alone are my strength!

Dr. Bill Welte

Deuteronomy 1-3; Mark 10:32-52　　　　　　　　**March 7**

Assuming His Presence

...supposing Him to have been in the company, they went a day's journey... (Luke 2:44)

Jesus' parents had taken Him to Jerusalem for the Passover. They travelled homeward in the company of a large crowd of pilgrims returning to Galilee. Assuming that Jesus was somewhere in the crowd, they went a day's journey before they discovered His absence. When they failed to find Him among their relatives and friends, they returned to Jerusalem.

Several lessons and applications can be drawn from this incident. First, there is a danger in assuming that He is walking with us in fellowship. It is true that He has promised His presence to be with us always, but the realization of His presence is conditional – *if we walk in the light* (1 John 1:7).

Second, it is possible for Him to be obscured by the crowd. There were instances in His ministry when needy persons could not see Him for the crowd. Zacchaeus, because he was short of stature, was prevented by the crowd from seeing Jesus. He overcame the problem by climbing a tree for a better view. In a different situation, a paralytic in need of the Master Healer was prevented from getting to Jesus because of the crowd in the house. His enterprising friends solved the problem by removing roof tiles and placing the man directly before the Lord. Crowds and popular opinion can deter people from finding Jesus.

Third, Jesus was found in the place where His parents had left Him. When we have turned away from the Lord and assumed that He would follow us on a way that we have chosen, we can only be restored by returning to the place of departure. In this account, it was the place chosen by the Heavenly Father for His business to be carried on (Luke 2:49).

Instead of merely assuming that He is with us, we must learn to practice His presence. Don't lose Him through the influence of the crowd. Before the day's journey begins, be sure you're in the fellowship of His presence.

Rev. William A. Raws

Deuteronomy 4-6; Mark 11:1-18　　　　　　　　**March 8**

Brokenness

For we who live are always delivered to death for Jesus' sake, that the life of Jesus also may be manifested in our mortal flesh.
(2 Corinthians 4:11)

    The word sends a chill up our spine. Brokenness. We shudder at the thought. In fact, most of us will do whatever it takes to avoid the vulnerability, the lack of control, and the humbling that accompanies brokenness.

    We tend to think of brokenness as something that requires healing; but let's consider brokenness in a different light. Steve McVey's definition of brokenness is, "A condition which exists when a person has given up all confidence in his own ability to manage life." [1] Using this definition, brokenness is not something we attain and move on from or from which we get healed. Rather it is a condition we want Christ to maintain in us. The moment we move beyond brokenness we have moved back into self-sufficiency, self-effort, living in our own strength and the flesh. "To walk after the flesh really just means living out of our own abilities. Another way to describe it is self-sufficiency. Flesh refers to those techniques that I depend on when I try to get my needs met or manage my own life apart from Jesus Christ." [2]

    If brokenness is giving up all confidence in our own abilities to make life work, then it is a condition we want to settle into, seeking moment by moment to rejoice in our brokenness.

    Why would we want to be broken and to live broken lives? Because it is in our brokenness that full surrender comes allowing the life of Jesus Christ to flow in and through us.

    Are you broken before the Lord?

Diane Hunt

---

[1] Steve McVey - <u>The Grace Walk Experience</u>
[2] IBID

Deuteronomy 7-9; Mark 11:19-33   **March 9**

Do You Have a Discouraged Heart?

I call on you, O God, for you will answer me; give ear to me and hear my prayer. (Psalm 17:6 NIV)

"How are you feeling today?" can be one of the worst questions someone can ask us, at least if we want to be honest with them. We are taught to have the joy of the Lord and to rise and shine as Christians and never be down or discouraged as believers. I am not sure about you, but this seems like a tall order to complete some days. Our strength does come from the Lord (Nehemiah 8:10), but there are still days when life seems to grip our hearts and lives and we become discouraged.

I have a saying that I use over and over in my life: "I NEED A POSTCARD." To me a little postcard in the mail from a friend can be such a blessing. It can tell me how they are doing, that they are on vacation or maybe they just send a friendly hello with a verse of Scripture to encourage me. A postcard always brings a smile to my face and brings a little joy.

When life gets me down and discouraged and my heart is heavy, I find myself asking the Lord to send me a postcard of hope, encouragement, direction or whatever I think I need for that day. Sometimes I have asked for a certified letter instead when things are really discouraging.

Is your heart discouraged today? Do you need a postcard? We need to be in the Word daily to read and hear His words for us and we need to be in prayer daily to share our hearts with Him. You might say that this is too basic and yes, we already know to do this ... but are we doing it? Sometimes when our heart is discouraged, we have stepped away from the Word and prayer without realizing how far we have gone.

I call on you, O God, for you will answer me; give ear to me and hear my prayer (Psalm 17:6 NIV). When I pray and then ask for a postcard, it is exciting to know that I will get one from the heavenly postal system. It is always awesome to see the notes that He sends my way.

God is always moving in our lives. We do not always see it at the time and of course hindsight is 20/20. We need to keep moving forward, and if we hit a road block of discouragement, ask for a postcard of direction, yell out for help and wait for the heavenly mail system to deliver just what we need.

Lynn A. Wilson

Deuteronomy 10-12; Mark 12:1-27　　　　　　　　　　**March 10**

Do Not Forget the Comforts

In the multitude of my anxieties within me,
Your comforts delight my soul. (Psalm 94:19)

My wife, Bobbie, had a stroke after our morning church service on October 6, 2002. It happened at church, and when I got to her, I wasn't sure she was alive. She regained consciousness, and the paramedics got her to the hospital. While I was standing beside her gurney in the ER, she spoke these words to me: *In the multitude of my anxieties within me, Your comforts delight my soul* (Psalm 94:19).

I didn't recognize it as a verse of Scripture, and I asked her about it. She told me the reference and said she had run across it in her Bible reading just a week or two back and had memorized it. Even though she does not remember the conversation, that verse of Scripture got us through a month of hospital stay and her doing the hard work of learning to walk again.

All of us, eventually, experience multitudes of anxieties. Job knew what he was talking about when he said, *"Man who is born of woman is of few days and full of trouble"* (Job 14:1). The psalmist also knew what he was talking about. When those *full of trouble* days come our way, we have a way to get through them.

Your comforts delight my soul provides the way through the dark days. Do not forget the ways God brings comfort to your soul. Maybe a particular song gives you strength when you struggle. Perhaps a favorite verse of Scripture comes to mind when life is hard. A good friend may have just the right word when it seems like the *multitude of ...anxieties* is about to overwhelm you. Do not forget those comforts!

You can hold onto them by doing two or three simple things. You can share them with others when you recognize them. Talking about them will settle them in your mind, and God's Spirit will bring them back when you need them. You can also hold onto them by writing them down. Journaling has many benefits, but helping us remember God's work in our lives is one of the best. You have a way to go back and review the last month, the last year, the last several years. Finally, choosing to thank God for those comforts will help fix them in your heart and mind.

All of us need God's comforts. They sustain us during the *full of trouble* days. Let God's comforts delight your soul when anxieties try to rob you of your peace in Jesus.

Rev. John Strain

Deuteronomy 13-15; Mark 12:28-44 **March 11**

Complete Access

Who shall ascend the hill of the LORD? And who shall stand in his holy place? He who has clean hands and a pure heart.
(Psalm 24:3-4a ESV)

Have you ever stopped to consider just how approachable our great God is? Scripture tells us that He is so holy we cannot look upon Him and live. It says that He dwells in unapproachable light. He is devastatingly holy and righteous. How can fallen and cursed sinners dare to look to Him and expect favor? And yet, He Himself tells us to draw near, to seek Him, to call upon Him, to walk with Him, to call Him Father.

The goodness of God does not end with the invitation. He does not uselessly invite unjustified men into His presence, but He makes a way for them to come near to Him. With our sins in the way, we cannot stand before Him, and He cannot tolerate us. The psalmist says that the one who can stand in His holy place is *he who has clean hands and a pure heart"* That description can only be fully true of one Man – our Savior Jesus Christ. The Father provided a way for us to draw near through Jesus. On our behalf, Jesus fulfilled the law that we broke and bore the wrath that we earned. After conquering death, Jesus ascended to the Father, where He perfectly intercedes for us in the presence of God.

Because Jesus made us righteous and acceptable to God, we can now approach God with confidence. The writer to the Hebrews put it this way, *Therefore, brothers, since we have confidence to enter the holy places by the blood of Jesus, by the new and living way that he opened for us through the curtain, that is, through his flesh, and since we have a great priest over the house of God, let us draw near with a true heart in full assurance of faith, with our hearts sprinkled clean from an evil conscience and our bodies washed with pure water* (Hebrews 10:19-22 ESV).

God's plan from eternity past was for His people to be with Him. He assured us of His intentions from the first pages of Scripture, and He made it possible through Jesus Christ. He said that the pure and the clean can enter His presence, and then He provided a way for us to be made pure and clean. We are justified and declared righteous in Jesus. Through our Savior, although we are still sinners and do not in any way merit God's approval, we have total and complete access to God. As if it couldn't get better, the Holy Spirit assures us of our adoption and gives us the freedom to call God Father, just as He told us to. His graciousness is worthy of our adoration.

Jenn Lawrence

Deuteronomy 16-18; Mark 13:1-20   **March 12**

Caring Without Quitting on the Path to Victory

And they come unto Him, bringing one sick of the palsy, which was borne of four. (Mark 2:3-12 KJV)

The path to victory is not always easy and often it is not well-marked. Neither are the obstacles in that path clearly identified.

Consider the story of these *four* who were determined to get the *one* with palsy to Jesus. They had a noble and unselfish objective. They soon learned that the path to that victory would not be easy. In fact, they soon learned that the obstacles would come from different sources, different attitudes and different situations. That is why I often refer to this story as the story of those who care and will not quit. It is the story of experiencing victory in our pursuit of it. It is the story of simply not quitting on the Path To Victory. Here are some significant lessons for us all as we take that journey.

The four cared and they did not quit because the job was too small. They came to Christ *bringing one*. They were dealing with only *one*. Yet they did not turn from the small opportunity in order to demand a more prestigious responsibility.

Neither did they quit because the need was so great. This *one* had palsy. That is no easy problem with which to deal.

They did not quit when they encountered the obstacle of the uncaring. The crowd of the curious had no understanding of the compassion of the caring. They cluttered the path to victory.

They did not quit when they encountered the obstacle of physical barriers. The door may have been blocked but they saw that the roof was available. You know the story. When the *four* could not get the *one* to Jesus because the crowd blocked the door, they *uncovered the roof.* That is just one explanation of why victory belongs to those who see beyond the obstacles and focus on the opportunities.

Neither did the four quit when they encountered the criticism of the uncaring. They were *sitting there* (v. 6). Criticism generally comes from those who *sit*. Victory comes for those who know how to handle the path to it.

And Jesus clearly identified the path to such victory when *He saw their faith* (v. 5).

... And this is the victory that has overcome the world— our faith
(1 John 5:4b).

Dr. Robert L. Alderman

Deuteronomy 19-21; Mark 13:21-37   **March 13**

The God of All Comfort

...clearly you are an epistle of Christ, ministered by us, written not with ink but by the Spirit of the living God, not on tablets of stone but on tablets of flesh, that is, of the heart. And we have such trust through Christ toward God. Not that we are sufficient of ourselves to think of anything as being from ourselves, but our sufficiency is from God, who also made us sufficient as ministers of the new covenant, not of the letter but of the Spirit; for the letter kills, but the Spirit gives life. (2 Corinthians 3:3-7)

    A number of years ago I was at a Youth for Christ teen activity held at Camp Sunrise Mountain in western Pennsylvania. It was winter and the kids were tubing in the snow on a hill behind the cabins. We were having a blast until a number of teens grabbed me and put me on an inner tube to send me down the hill. They didn't realize that they got me off course and that I was headed toward a pile of snow-covered logs. They tried to warn me but when you are tubing you have your back to where you are going and you can't see any danger! Well, I wiped out on the pile with my tube going one way and me the other. I bounced off the tube and suffered a hematoma on my back which hospitalized me for a week.

    I had never been in a hospital as a patient. I had visited many parishioners in hospitals but this was new to me. As a result of the accident, I suffered a ruptured disc in the area of my cervical spine which required surgery. In this surgery I had to literally have my throat cut. The doctor went in from the front part of the neck. Having never faced surgery and finding my first to be one of this nature was a little unnerving to me. That night, as I was praying, God brought this passage to my mind. Literally God said to me, "I am the God of comfort. Trust me!" He gave me an overwhelming peace. I also found that He called me to experience what others had gone through. I believe that as a result this experience made me a better pastor. I can empathize with those who are going through trials.

As you meditate on this passage, realize that God will comfort you in your trial. Through that trial He will help you in your ministry to others. "He is the God of all comfort, Who comforts us in all our tribulation, that we may be able to comfort others."

Dr. George L. Nichols, Jr.

Deuteronomy 22-24; Mark 14:1-26   **March 14**

Limiting God

And the LORD said to Moses, "Is the LORD's hand shortened? Now you shall see whether my word will come true for you or not." (Numbers 11:23 ESV)

God's way is certainly not our way. Our God is the God of the impossible and He delights in continually proving that nothing is too hard for Him. He chose Israel, the fewest of all people (Deuteronomy 7:7). He chose David to be king of Israel, the youngest and least likely of Jesse's sons (1 Samuel 16:11 & 12). Jesus was born in Bethlehem, too little to be among the clans of Judah (Micah 5:2). In each of these instances God chose to use something that would be easily overlooked as a way to show His great power. Similarly, He will continually bring us into difficult trials as a way of building our faith and trust in Him.

Oswald Chambers said, "Living a life of faith means never knowing where you are being led. But it does mean loving and knowing the One who is leading." Faith is the key to our walk with God. Everything we go through is meant to strengthen us and ultimately conform us to the image of Jesus Christ. We are brought into situations that overwhelm us so that we will look to God and not our own abilities to find the solution. *Now to Him who is able to do exceedingly abundantly above all that we ask or think, according to the power that works in us, to Him be glory in the church by Christ Jesus to all generations, forever and ever* (Ephesians 3:20-21). The three key words are *exceedingly*, *abundantly* and *all*. All is totally inclusive; there is nothing that we can ask of God that He cannot do exceedingly abundantly more than what we ask. This is so that we will trust Him and that others will see that it is God and He will receive the glory.

There are always people watching us. God wants to bring us to the point that when people see us, they actually see God. This only happens when we yield every aspect of our lives to Him and follow Him with complete trust, keeping our eyes securely on the One who is leading and not watching the things that are going on around us. When we reach this point we know that all that comes our way is based on God's perfect love for us and He will carry us through.

Allen E. Beltle

Deuteronomy 25-27; Mark 14:27-53 **March 15**

Back to Basics

Now the people came up from the Jordan...and they camped in Gilgal... And those twelve stones which they took out of the Jordan, Joshua set up in Gilgal...Then the Lord said to Joshua, "This day I have rolled away the reproach of Egypt from you."
(Joshua 4:19-20; 5:9)

Divinely-given illustrations concerning the Christian life are recorded for us in the history of Israel. Deliverance from Egypt on the basis of the blood of a lamb reminds us of the redemption purchased for us through the blood of Christ. Their miraculous passage through the Red Sea forms a picture of deliverance from the bondage of sin. Their wandering years in the wilderness teach us that despite the deliverance from bondage to sin we may still be defeated by the flesh nature. Passing over Jordan depicts the entrance by faith into the promised victory of the Lord.

As Israel landed on the western shore of the river, they camped at a place that was later named Gilgal. Several symbolic things took place there. An altar of river stones was set up as a monument to the Lord's provided entrance to the promised land. Also there was the act of circumcision of the men. Then they were able to celebrate the Passover, which they hadn't done in the wilderness. Finally, they ate the produce of the land and the heaven-sent manna ceased. The site became known as Gilgal (rolling away) in remembrance that the reproach of Egypt was now rolled away.

This is not the end of Israel's visits to this site. After several of the battles in the land, they returned to Gilgal. This was the place of the foundation of their future victories. When they experienced defeat in battle, they returned to this place for renewed cleansing.

Have we a spiritual counterpart in our lives? When sin occurs or we are defeated by temptation, we need to get back to basics at Gilgal. Here is where confession, cleansing and commitment are renewed. That which takes place at our personal Gilgal becomes the basis for renewed victory. Are you overdue for a return visit?

Rev. William A. Raws

Deuteronomy 28-29; Mark 14:54-72　　　　　　　　**March 16**

Purpose

Now it came to pass, when the time had come for Him to be received up, that He steadfastly set His face to go to Jerusalem...
(Luke 9:51)

Long ago, William Law had this to say about purpose and the child of God, "I am a being that has no other business in this universe God created, than to be that which God requires me to be; to have no desires, to seek no self-ends, but to fill that place and act that part which the Divine pleasure has ordained. To think that you are your own, or at your own disposal, is as absurd as to think that you created yourself."

The only example we have in Scripture of someone who perfectly walked in God's purpose for His life was the Son of God. He once said, *"My food is to do the will of Him who sent Me, and to finish His work..."* (John 4:34).

My friend, when we became children of God we lost all of our rights. We must remember we have been bought with a price. Our purpose should be to walk in God's pure intention for us. We see in Scripture how completely Jesus submitted to the Father's will, *"Who committed no sin, nor was deceit found in His mouth"; who, when He was reviled, did not revile in return; when He suffered, He did not threaten, but committed Himself to Him who judges righteously...* (1 Peter 2:22-23).

To think this way is so foreign to us in these days in which we are living. "Lovers of selves" characterizes us completely. With our own selfishness we dismantle the character of others through subtle and inciting words, we are argumentative, and we jealously covet the success of others. We need to take an assessment of our lives and ask ourselves these questions, "Am I living as if there were no tomorrow?" "Am I living as though I am God?" "What are the guiding factors of my life, the world's philosophy or God's Holy Word?"

My friend, I encourage you from this day onward to make God's purpose for your life primary, and everything else secondary. Maybe you need to get alone somewhere to be quiet for a season and have a time of real heart-to-heart with your Creator. You may be surprised at what God is just about to reveal to you. Choose to begin living life on the highest plane!

Rev. Chris S. Hodges

Deuteronomy 30-31; Mark 15:1-25 **March 17**

Waters Cover the Sea, Patrick of Ireland

For the earth will be filled with the knowledge of the glory of the LORD as the waters cover the sea. (Habakkuk 2:14)

Answering God's call is costly. God has seraphs. Why then did He choose Isaiah? Because He chose him! That's God's way. Angels can't preach like repentant, redeemed men and women. How often do we hear someone say today, "Send me! Use me!"? Full surrender will cry, "Take me as I am; use me as You will." One who said that was born in Scotland in 390 AD.

Various denominations had just begun and had not yet developed opposing ideologies as appeared later in the church. So today both Protestants and Roman Catholics celebrate the birth of this remarkable person: Patrick.

One day while alone in his home in Scotland a loud cry was heard, "Pirates!" Red-bearded men speaking a strange language tied him up and stuffed him, with thousands of others, into the holds of ships. Soon he found himself a slave tending sheep. He thought, "One day I'll get the hated Irish for this cruelty." After six years as a slave while Patrick watched his sheep, the Holy Spirit touched his hate-filled heart. He wrote, "I turned my whole heart to the Lord." Bitterness and hatred melted away. In a dream he heard, "Return to your country; your ship is ready." That night he slipped away and fled 200 miles to the seaport. The captain of the ship rebuffed him, calling him a slave and shouted, "Scram!" However, a sailor signaled to him to come quickly.

Some time after returning to his beloved Scotland, he had another vision, "Come walk among us again." Patrick took some other believers in Jesus and returned to Ireland. He challenged his team with these words, "Fish well, for the Lord has called us to be fishers of men."

With his writings and preaching of the Gospel, Patrick shook the foundation of slave trading. The coming of thousands to Jesus Christ threatened the idolatrous Druid religion. Patrick started a work that for two centuries sent missionaries from Ireland to evangelize across Europe. The power of heathenism was shattered in Ireland and across the continent. Patrick was known for a clear statement of faith. He demonstrated a missionary heart. He focused on Jesus Christ.

Today we have many wearing medals but few with the scars of battle with heathendom. Patrick had the scars. The Druids robbed him, beat him, imprisoned him and tortured him. They nearly killed him twelve times. At the end of his life Patrick said, "The greatest gift in my life has been to know the love of God; to serve Him is my highest joy."

God used Patrick to partially fulfill that great prophecy of Habakkuk as he spread the Gospel of Jesus as water covers the sea. I ask myself if I am ready with Paul of Tarsus and Patrick of Ireland to spend and be spent to see the continued miraculous spread of this life giving message. Pray with me, "Send me, Lord, use me, Lord!"

Dr. George Kelsey

Deuteronomy 32-34; Mark 15:26-47   March 18

Magnify Christ in Your Body

...according to my earnest expectation and hope that in nothing I shall be ashamed, but with all boldness, as always, so now also Christ will be magnified in my body, whether by life or by death.
(Philippians 1:20)

I beseech you therefore, brethren, by the mercies of God, that you present your bodies a living sacrifice, holy, acceptable to God, which is your reasonable service. (Romans 12:1)

Paul's goal was to magnify and exalt the Lord Jesus Christ. Magnify is an interesting word. There are two kinds of magnification. There is the magnification of the microscope and the magnification of the telescope. The microscope makes little things look big. The telescope makes big things look larger.

Warren Wiersbe says, "Magnifying Christ means being a lens that makes a small Christ look very big and a distant Christ look very close."

Paul's desire was that people see Jesus in all His grandeur and glory.

How can you magnify Christ?

- o Magnify Him with your lips as you testify of Him.
- o Magnify Him with your hands as you happily serve Him.
- o Magnify Him with your feet as you walk with Him and march to His orders.
- o Magnify Him with your knees as you pray for others.

- Magnify Him with your shoulders as you carry a brother's burden.

I beseech you therefore, brethren....magnify Christ in your body!

Dr. Roger D. Willmore

Joshua 1-3; Mark 16   **March 19**

Body Language

I waited patiently for the Lord, and He <u>inclined</u> to me, and heard my cry. (Psalm 40:1)

Body language is an interesting study. We tell someone by how we stand or what we do with our hands whether we are interested in them. "Body language is an important part of communication which can constitute 50% or more of what we are communicating.[3]"

I find it interesting to watch a political debate and then the media coverage following the debate. Every body movement is analyzed to see if the candidates are telling the truth and can be trusted. Their body language can tell us if they are nervous or confident.

I was visiting a counselor and during my session he looked at his watch. All I could think was, I'm pouring my heart out, sharing my deepest feelings, and you are not interested; you are getting paid to be interested!

My husband and I were making conversation with another couple and I was telling a story. Before I finished my story, the people lost interest and it was obvious by their body language. I looked at my husband and finished the story so that it ended without anyone noticing how ridiculous I felt. I didn't want to just quit mid-sentence. My husband had heard the story and knew how awkward I felt. It was all we could do to keep from cracking up laughing.

---

[3] http://changingminds.org/techniques/body/body_language.htm

Body language gives an indication of our attitudes and feelings towards others. "We angle toward people we find attractive, friendly and interesting and angle ourselves away from those we don't, it's that simple."[4] In Psalm 40:1, the psalmist says that God uses body language, too. When I call on Him, He not only listens to me, He leans in to hear what I have to say. He finds me interesting, and He never stops listening!

Joyce Hayes

Joshua 4-6; Luke 1:1-20   **March 20**

Making Right Choices

...choose this day whom you will serve... (Joshua 24:15 ESV)

Billy Sunday, evangelist of yesteryear, wrote, "One reason sin flourishes is that it is treated like a cream puff, instead of a rattlesnake." Does not that statement still pertain today in the 21st century?

What once was considered, in my childhood, a particular sin, is now to be enjoyed, even embraced. And I'm thinking of the freedom of the homosexual community to practice – whatever!

What once was considered a private sin is now considered a "cream puff" to be enjoyed. And I'm thinking of sexual indulgence outside of one's marriage and of sexual indulgence if single.

What once was considered a particularly egregious sin against a family member, a friend, a neighbor, is not now so considered. And I'm thinking of the widely accepted practice of lying.

Today everything is relative. What may be true for you is not true for me. What may be sin for me is not sin for you. It depends on the circumstances.

With God, however, there is no middle ground, no relativity regarding morals, no equivocating regarding sin. Even Paul,

---

[4] http://www.selfgrowth.com/articles/Phipps3.html

God's specially chosen messenger, struggled from time to time with making correct choices. He wrote, *I do not do the good things I want to do, but I do the bad things I do not want to do* (Romans 7:19 NCV). Can you identify?

What a miserable man I am! (v. 24a) continued Paul, wondering how to get victory over this temptation to sin. In the end, however, Paul realized the ability to gain victory came from outside himself, and he gratefully exclaimed, *...thanks be to God, who gives us the victory through our Lord Jesus Christ* (1 Corinthians 15:57).

The Holy Spirit, who resides within the Christian's heart, gives divine help to overcome temptation to sin. It is comforting, it is strengthening, to be able to acknowledge that the ever-present help we need is "closer than hands or feet." Again, thanks be to God!

No two images are more disparate than that of a delicious *cream puff* and that of a dangerous *rattlesnake*. Do not be caught in mistaking one for the other! And you won't, if you keep yourself close to the Lord, your sure Defense against making wrong choices.

Midge Ruth

Joshua 7-9; Luke 1:21-38 **March 21**

Brother Demas, Where Art Thou?

Be diligent to come to me quickly, for Demas has forsaken me, having loved this present world, (2 Timothy 4:9-10)

Having loved the present world. It doesn't really sound that bad. You could say that there are a great many things in the present world that are worthy of love. I can give a list of earthly things, right off the top of my head, that are worthy of my love. My wife, my children, a steak done just right and a good cup of Starbucks© coffee are just a few. But when Paul penned this statement he did not have these worldly things in mind. Demas just up and bolted out of Rome and headed for Thessalonica while Paul was preparing for a date with an executioner's axe.

Now to be fair, Demas wasn't the only one who left. Crescens had gone to Galatia, Titus went to Dalmatia but Paul does not write that these men had forsaken him, only Demas gets that denoted to him for the rest of biblical history. I tried really hard to find something else written about Demas in all the resources I have at my disposal. I even paged through the Complete Works of Flavius Josephus to see if there was something more historical on the man than what Paul described of him. But like Yukon Cornelius, I toss my pick ax into the air and pull it from the snow…. "Nothin'!!"

I feel badly for Demas. He couldn't take the heat and he got out of the kitchen. Paul was being poured out as a drink offering for keeping the faith and Demas must not have wanted to go the distance that should call all of us heavenward in Christ Jesus. But I feel badly for myself in the role of being like Demas. I, too, am guilty of being weary of going that kind of distance. We are told there is no greater love than to lay down one's life for their brother or sister but aren't we selective for whom we are willing to do this?

There were other moments when Demas got an honorable mention. He is acknowledged, ahead of Luke, as a fellow laborer in Philemon, gives a greeting in Colossians, but nothing compares to *for Demas has forsaken me*. Forsaken is a strong word to describe the action that Demas took against Paul. I guess the other two at least told Paul they were leaving. But it sounds like Demas turned his back on Paul. This had to hurt "The Way" during a time when the Roman Empire could have used a better way. History tells the ugly tale of The Roman Empire, doesn't it?

So do we want to be part of the ugly tale? Do we want to clothe ourselves in "Demas" when the going gets tough? I guess it might be understandable if the thought just crosses our minds but Jesus gives us strength to overcome the moment, if we diligently seek Him when we know, outright, that we are having a weak moment. I pray that this day we see it to the end.

Chris Hughes

Joshua 10-12; Luke 1:39-56   **March 22**

Faithful To The End

Nevertheless, when the Son of Man comes, will He really find faith on the earth? (Luke 18:8b)

My friend, are you living a life of faith? Are you simply trusting the Lord Jesus Christ in your daily walk to provide all that you need?

We cannot see into the future but we know Who holds the future. We are His sheep; we belong to Him. A wise old minister once said, *"The Lord is our Shepherd, and nothing can get to the sheep unless it comes through the Shepherd."*

As we think of the soon return of Jesus Christ, will He find His children faithful? A dear friend of my family, Mrs. Carolyn Alsip, wrote this poem entitled:

Will He Really Find Faith?

In times like these will He really find faith?
In the homes of America, in churches that sing "Amazing Grace."
Blinded by self and steeped in sin, we doubt our salvation and blame it on Him.
Our pews are half empty with pulpits to fill; we do not pray, we do not read, we do not die to our own selfish will.
No power to witness, no longer we see, as we sit, we soak, we sour, and blame on others our own ugly deeds.
Yes, time is at hand, no signs we can miss.
Will He really find faith in a life such as this?

These are sobering words, my friend. Let's take them to heart and ask ourselves these questions, "Am I making the most of this life God has given me?" "Am I choosing to walk in His Spirit, allowing Him to live His life through me unhindered?"

Today, determine in your heart that when the Son of Man returns He will find you faithful, doing what He left all of His children to do, going and making disciples wherever you are. This is living a true life of faith. There will be those who will not understand you. Expect it and keep moving. There will be times when you will feel you have accomplished little.

Remember, when you are faithful, little is much in the hands of God. Simply by faith, turn and do the duty that lies nearest.

Rev. Chris S. Hodges

Joshua 13-15; Luke 1:57-80 March 23

Don't Take It Easy

Now godliness with contentment is great gain. (1 Timothy 6:6)

We live in a day when training and discipline are unpopular. But the apostle Paul said to Timothy, *...and exercise (train) yourself toward godliness. For bodily exercise profits a little; but godliness is profitable for all things, having promise of the life that now is and of that which is to come* (1 Timothy 4:7b-8). Why do we need to train to be godly?

In thinking about that question, I would suggest three reasons. The first is to be prepared for life. Why do you think football players put in hours of practice for 60 minutes of play in a given game? They practice in order to be prepared to do their best and win! There must be preparation.

"Bear" Bryant, former coach of the University of Alabama football team, said, "You can't live soft all week and play tough on Saturday!" This is what Paul means when he says, "training yourself in godliness." Do it every day to be prepared for what's ahead. Jeremiah 12:5a (NIV) states, *If you have raced with men on foot and they have worn you out, how can you compete with horses...?*

The second reason is to endure. Some things are hard to take. If there is a failure or a loss, we must learn not to let up, but rather to endure. We need believers, those who have come to know Jesus Christ by accepting Him into their lives, who endure...believers who keep on with their exercise of godliness and don't slack off day after day.

The third reason is to be whole or complete. God wants each one who knows Him to be that way. Paul says we are to keep our bodies in shape, but we need the mind and spirit to be exercised as well.

Bodily exercise or training is limited to the body and this life, while godliness is of value in every way because it holds promise for the present life and also for the life to come.

How do you exercise yourself to godliness? By association with God on a daily basis, not just your day of worship or holidays. It is taking time to read His Word, the Bible, and talking to Him in prayer. And then we are to live by what we have learned.

It is up to us! We are to train ourselves. It is up to us to be obedient. Begin now; don't take it easy. We must exercise ourselves to be prepared, to endure, to be complete.

Rev. John Hibbard

Joshua 16-18; Luke 2:1-24   **March 24**

Don't Lose Heart

I would have lost heart, unless I had believed that I would see the goodness of the Lord in the land of the living. (Psalm 27:13)

We are living in troubled times. The economy is bad, unemployment is high, and people are hurting severely. Just this week I became aware of several attempted and completed suicides. Obviously people see no way out and little hope for change.

As Christians we do have the answer. Do you believe that? Not long ago I arrived at my speaking destination only to discover that my books had not arrived…a speaker without a book table is like someone sitting in a boat without a paddle in the middle of a lake. I sputtered, fumed, called my publisher and ranted and raved until I was exhausted. When I had let off enough steam, it dawned on me that I had done everything except *PRAY*! I often laughingly say, **When all else fails, pray!** So I prayed, "Dear Lord, I'm in a mess. I am hundreds of miles away from home. I am supposed to speak about my story tonight, but I have no books to sell…my book table will be empty. Please tell me what to do." I heard the Lord speak very clearly in my mind, *"You are my child. Now act like it!"*

Now that message wasn't hard to understand, was it? My instruction was I am a child of the King, and I needed to act like it; so I did, and I made it through the evening. People even signed up to order the books which were arriving the next day, and the staff of the sponsoring group arranged to deliver the books to those who had ordered them.

Today look around to see the goodness of the Lord. Write down what you see. Has He been faithful to you? Has He provided your needs? Take good notes. He is always faithful. Remember the ways He has answered your prayers. He doesn't always answer according to our schedule, but He is always on time and never late.

DON'T LOSE HEART! BELIEVE! LOOK AROUND YOU AND PAY ATTENTION. YOU CAN SEE THE GOODNESS OF THE LORD IN EVERY SITUATION.

Marilyn Willett Heavilin

Joshua 19-21; Luke 2:25-52   **March 25**

It's All about Him

You may say to yourself, "My power and the strength of my hands have produced this wealth for me." But remember the LORD your God, for it is he who gives you the ability to produce wealth, and so confirms his covenant, which he swore to your forefathers, as it is today. (Deuteronomy 8:17-20 NIV)

As the Israelites were preparing to cross over the Jordon to the "promised land, a land flowing with milk and honey," Moses urged them not to forget that it was God that had provided them with everything they had. He exhorted them to observe the commands of the Lord their God, walk in His ways, (Deuteronomy 8:6), and praise Him for the good land He was giving them (v.10). Don't forget God; observe His commands, laws and decrees (v.11). Moses reminded them that it was God who led, protected and provided for them the whole time they were in the desert, and it was He who gave them the ability to produce wealth (v. 18). It ended with a strong warning, though. If they ever forgot the Lord and followed other gods and worshiped and bowed down to them, they would not be unlike other nations before them that He destroyed (vs. 19-20).

For many, personal reflection is warranted when Moses warns the Israelites not to forget to observe the Lord's commands after achieving great wealth and power, because their hearts will become proud and then they will forget the Lord (v.14). I say this because too often I've followed the same pattern as the Israelites. I get busy, focus on my work (don't spend as much time in God's Word), unknowingly follow other gods (success, money, security), then give myself credit for what "I've achieved." Then, because of His great love for me and desire to have my devotion, it is taken away. Then I get it! So, the big question is how do I stop this pattern? I have found that spending time in God's Word is a great start. Having accountability partners (spouse, friend, group of friends) is another great way to help keep on track. Talking to God everyday in prayer, praising Him for all He does and asking for His continual intervention into our lives is important. Most importantly, increase doing all of this during times of great success and prosperity rather than waiting for things to get bad. We must always remember it is Satan who wants to steal away peace and joy, while God wants to give it abundantly. All He is looking for is our devotion to Him. It's all about Him!

Bernie Bostwick

Joshua 22-24; Luke 3 March 26

Hope for the Struggle

For I know that in me (that is, in my flesh) nothing good dwells; for to will is present with me, but how to perform what is good I do not find. (Romans 7:18)

Every believer has known some kind of failure during his walk with Jesus. We anticipate life without sin when we enter the presence of Jesus, but while we're here on the earth, we share Paul's struggle. *For the good that I will to do, I do not do; but the evil I will not to do, that I practice* (Romans 7:19).

Paul's transparency is beneficial. As we read his words, we come to understand that the struggle is part of the human condition, even the born-again human. We live in a broken world that presses against us. We live in a fallen body, and that flesh can raise its ugly head at the most unexpected times. And, do not forget the enemy of our souls. The devil and his subversive minions work 24/7 to take us down.

The apostle knew all those negative forces at work in his life. They prompted him to say, *O wretched man that I am! Who will deliver me from this body of death?* (Romans 7:24). Many of us feel the hopelessness we hear in Paul's expression of despair. We have known the frustration of wanting to do right but choosing to do wrong.

The struggle is destructive if we look only at the situation. Our enemy wants nothing more than to keep us focused on our condition and our inability to win the battle. If he can convince us that the struggle is ours alone and that we can't win, then we are stuck in the despair Paul voiced.

Paul, however, got past the despair, and so can we. Hope rests in his understanding that our victory over the struggle rests in who Jesus is and what He does for us. When we resist the deceptions of the wicked one and set our eyes on Jesus, we can affirm Paul's statement of hope. *There is therefore now no condemnation to those who are in Christ Jesus, who do not walk according to the flesh, but according to the Spirit* (Romans 8:1).

We do have a struggle. We know that without a doubt. The struggle does not have to overcome us or defeat us. In Christ, we have hope, confidence and power to claim victory. While we have responsibility to resist the devil, we do so knowing that our effort is successful when we do it in the power of Christ who is our life.

Rev. John Strain

Judges 1-3; Luke 4:1-30   **March 27**

Lord, Open My Eyes

Then Elisha prayed, Lord, I pray You, open his eyes that he may see. And the Lord opened the young man's eyes, and he saw, and behold, the mountain was full of horses and chariots of fire round about Elisha. (2 Kings 6:17 Amplified Bible)

Maybe it is because I have had to have two rounds of laser surgery – both eyes. When I went to the retina specialist, I asked him what was causing my problem. His response was not what I wanted to hear: "Your eyes have lived long enough!"

In both eyes the retina separated from the gel in my eye, creating huge floaters. It wasn't that I couldn't see – they just clouded my vision from being really clear. Thankfully, the laser surgeries were successful, and most of the floaters are gone. I can see much more clearly now.

I love this story in 2 Kings 6 when Elisha is standing there with a young man who has become overwhelmed and fearful about his circumstances. From his human eyes, the battle raging all around him was so intense that there didn't seem to be any way out.

Elisha saw life from a totally different perspective. His intense and intentional walk with the Lord helped him to see that God was at work all around him, and that even when he couldn't necessarily see EVERYTHING – He placed his trust in the one who sees ALL.

I love Elisha's prayer – *Lord, open his eyes that he may see*! Not a long drawn out prayer. Not a prayer filled with tons of "Christian-ese." Simple. Direct. Right to the point.

And God heard Elisha and answered his prayer of faith. The Lord pulled back the curtain and allowed this young man to SEE with eyes of faith that all around him were a host of horses and chariots of fire! Wow!

I find myself praying just about every day, "Lord, open my eyes that I may see You at work all around me." I don't want to miss Him at work. He's there. He is working out His plans and purposes. Sometimes I get to see BIG-picture stuff. Sometimes I get to see Him at work in little ways that I might miss because of a floater passing by, the floater of busyness or the floater of my agenda.

I keep writing these things in my journal because I don't want to forget them. They are reminders that HE can be trusted and that HE IS ALWAYS AT WORK ALL AROUND ME.

Don't knock it. Try it first, then write me and tell me I am a whacko. Are you bold enough? Daring enough – to ask God to open your eyes to see Him at work all around you? I dare you! In fact, I double-dog dare you.

Dr. Bill Welte

Judges 4-6; Luke 4:31-44　　　　　　　　　　　　　**March 28**

More Than Conquerors

... in all these things we are more than conquerors through him that loved us. (Romans 8:37 KJV)

Sometimes we hear familiar Scripture verses and we fail to really meditate on what the Spirit is actually saying. In this verse Paul tells us that we are more than conquerors *in all these things.* In all *what* things? And *what* does it mean to be *more* than a conqueror?" And <u>how</u> is it that Christ's love is the *means* by which we are "more than conquerors"?

If we go back to Romans 8:35, Paul describes seven specific "things" that believers experience that would seem to be *negative* "things." They are: tribulation, distress, persecution, famine, nakedness, peril and sword. Can you or I relate to any of these in our own current life situations?

The Greek word for *tribulation*, for example, is *thlipsis* and means to be in *anguish*, to be *afflicted*, to be *troubled* or to be *burdened*. Are you *troubled* about some things in your life? Paul is reminding us that whatever may be *troubling* us has already been handled. We are already, even now before we see the resolution of what is troubling us, victorious over it.

And *why* is that? Because those of us who are *in Christ* have been *in Him* since before the world began! (Ephesians 1:4) We have been loved by Him from eternity past, even before we ourselves knew of His love (Galatians 1:15; Jeremiah 1:5). And, because He has loved us from the beginning of time, He alone has determined our circumstances and designed them for *our good* (Romans 8:28). Therefore, we are free to walk in the knowledge of our *victory* in Christ rather than focusing on our *troubles*!

The Greek word for *distress* refers to *calamity*. Most of us can relate to having experienced a calamity or two in our lives. *Persecution* refers to being mistreated or being misunderstood by those who are offended by our faith in Jesus Christ. This is often inflicted upon us by family members or even by those in the organized church who claim to be Christians. Most of us have not yet faced famine or nakedness or "the sword," though many believers around the world have faced these conditions or are facing them at this very moment. The Greek word for *peril* is a reference to *extreme danger* which could be life threatening. Severe illness would be a *peril*; serving one's country in battle is *perilous*.

Each of these seven words describes situations or circumstances that can produce fear, worry, lack of faith or a frantic desire to "fix things" or "escape." Yet Paul tells us that we are to be fearless, at peace, knowing we are "more than conquerors," already victorious over these circumstances. The Greek word for this phrase, *more than conquerors*, is *hupernikao*. It literally means to be *abundantly, exceedingly victorious and triumphant*. And *why* is this true for us, no matter where we find ourselves? Because we are secure in Christ Who has conquered all the negative elements that might ever touch the lives of His sheep.

We are called as saints to live in the awareness of the Lord's sovereign reign of love over all the challenges in our lives.

Lord, give us grace to see that You are the Victor and, therefore, we can live victoriously because we are hidden in You.

Glenna Salsbury

Judges 7-8; Luke 5:1-16   **March 29**

Beware of Barnacles

...let us throw off everything that hinders and the sin that so easily entangles. (Hebrews 12:1 NIV)

    An advertisement for the Copper Development Association of New York pictures the hulls of two shrimp trawlers, identical in every way except for one thing: ship number one has a copper-nickel hull, while ship number two has a hull of steel.

    In the case of the first ship, the Copper Mariner, after two years of constant shrimping, the hull remains clean and free of barnacles. During this time the hull has never been scraped, not even once.

    The second ship, on the other hand, the Matagalpa, has to be scraped and painted every six months.

    Without the barnacle drag of a steel hull, the Copper Mariner is faster and, after a 26-month test, results show a 25% saving on fuel. Without the regular scraping and painting required by steel hulls, maintenance costs run lower and the ship is available for work more days.

    So reads the advertisement.

    If I can compare the Christian life to a sea journey, then one of life's dangers is to be slowed by "barnacles." Luke 8:14 indicates some of these life barnacles to be ...*cares, riches, and pleasures of life.* Such things may not be regarded as immoral but they can hold us back from progress.

    If barnacles get on boats and ships, we are told they can also make steering most difficult. Perhaps this is one reason why some of us have trouble getting into the current of God's will.

    Hebrews 12:1 says, *let us throw off everything that hinders and the sin that so easily entangles.* Let's get rid of the barnacles of life in order that we may be able to better please the Lord.

Rev. John Hibbard

Judges 9-10; Luke 5:17-39 **March 30**

Resurrection Power

For if we have been united together in the likeness of His death, certainly we also shall be in the likeness of His resurrection. (Romans 6:5)

Are you living in resurrection power? As long as we avoid obeying God in "that" area, actually in any area, we are not living in resurrection power. As long as we refuse to obey God in any area of our lives, we are not living in resurrection power.

To live in resurrection power, we must first die. Only that which is dead needs to be resurrected. The dying is the sacrifice necessary to obey. We have to die to our self-will, and our self-centered, proud, rebellious choice to continue in our sin.

2 Corinthians 4:10-11, *...always carrying about in the body the dying of the Lord Jesus, that the life of Jesus also will be manifested in our body. For we who live are always being delivered to death for Jesus' sake, that the life of Jesus also may be manifested in our mortal flesh.*

2 Corinthians 5:15, *and He died for all, that those who died should live no longer for themselves, but for Him who died for them and rose again.*

2 Corinthians 13:4, *For though He was crucified in weakness, yet He lives by the power of God...*

And further: Ephesians 1:19-20, *and what is the exceeding greatness of His power toward us who believe, according to the working of His mighty power which He worked in Christ when He raised Him from the dead and seated Him at His right hand in the heavenly places.*

Philippians 3:10, *that I may know Him and the power of His resurrection...*

Are we ready to obey all that God shows us? Will we be doers of the Word and not hearers only? Are we living in resurrection power?

Diane Hunt

Judges 11-12; Luke 6:1-26   **March 31**

Complacency

It happened in the spring of the year, at the time when kings go out to battle, that David sent Joab and his servants with him, ... Then it happened one evening that David arose from his bed
(2 Samuel 11:1-2)

    By this point David had come through some rough times as he was the up-and-coming king set to rule over Israel. In the previous chapters we see David's conquest of Jerusalem and his defeat of Philistia. People lost their lives while David was transporting the Ark of the Covenant due to his disobedience to the law. In chapter 8 we see him defeat Moab and the son of the King of Jobah and kill 22,000 men of Syria before going on to rule Israel. So, we have arrived at another spring, when the king is normally preparing his troops for battle. This happened each spring, since the roads and terrain were thawed and passable for troops to march on and go to battle, yet David wakes up in the late afternoon. Instead of going himself he sent his chief commander, Joab, and his servants into battle to destroy the people of Ammon. What I see here is David showing all of the signs of complacency in his life. He has the "I got it made" or "life is comfortable" attitude. Maybe he is even thinking "I deserve a break." It appears David is thinking that he doesn't need to follow God's direction in his life right now.

    The attitude of complacency results in what takes place next, as Bathsheba shows up bathing on a rooftop in David's view. The passage tells us that she was beautiful. What followed was adultery, pregnancy out of wedlock, and a cover-up attempt that led to the murder of a good commander. It was the same commander who fought hard to help David gain all that he had accomplished. All of this happened because David chose to stay back from battle and get up late; in other words, all this happened because David let down his spiritual guard.

    This, my friend, is the very mindset that Satan looks for to pick off God's people. We let down our guard and we become complacent. Our morning devotions or evening devotions have lost their priority in our lives. Reading and studying God's Word takes a back seat to reading books about being a Christian or maybe living a Christian life. Maybe even going to church or attending Bible studies are starting to lag in your life along with the fellowship that accompanies them. Possibly all of this has been replaced by TV, sports and other leisure activities. These are sure signs of complacency. God's Word states in Proverbs 1:32, *For the waywardness of the simple will kill them, and the complacency of fools will destroy them.* Are you becoming a David? Or are you already a David and are living the complacent Christian life? Beware; it is at this point that sin can enter your life and cause much destruction. Don't be like David... stay in the Word and continue to be prepared to go to battle for God.

Bill Jahns

Judges 13-15; Luke 6:27-49   **April 1**

Have You Established Your Heart?

...Establish your hearts, for the coming of the Lord is at hand.
(James 5:8)

My friends have a sign at their front door with their family name stating, "Established in 1985." This reflects the year they decided to establish a new family. In life we try and establish many things for ourselves. We establish a family, a home, a business, a type of lifestyle and so on.

In the dictionary it says that the word "establish" means... "to institute, build, or bring into being on a firm or stable basis." Establishing something is important and it can bring stability and focus in one's life. When we have established something or focus in on something we then have a goal to try to reach.

In James we see that it asks us to establish our hearts. The Bible talks about the heart 743 times. The Lord wants us to love Him with all our heart. The Bible talks about...blessed are the pure in heart ... a thankful heart ... the desires of your heart ... a humble heart ... God looks on the heart ... and to establish your heart.

Where is your heart today? Many times when we are weary, or things don't seem right in our life, we hear the expression... "It is a heart thing." Have you established your heart to be focused on things of the Lord? In the world we live in, it is easy to give our heart away to things of this world. It is easy to have the desires of our heart turn away from things of the Lord. It is easy to work on establishing the things we "think" are important like careers, a bank account, a status in the community and even in our church. But our heart is what needs to be established first in our life in order for the rest of our life to fall into place.

"...love the LORD your God with all your heart, with all your soul, and with all your mind" (Matthew 22:37). Establish your heart on loving the things of the Lord.

James not only tells us to establish our heart but that the coming of the Lord is at hand. Join me in establishing our hearts for the right things with the expectancy of HIS return.

Lynn A. Wilson

Judges 16-18; Luke 7:1-30　　　　　　　　　　April 2
God's Forgiveness

If we confess our sins, he is faithful and just to forgive us our sins and to cleanse us from all unrighteousness. (1 John 1:9 KJV)

1 John 1:9 is among the most quoted verses in the Bible. This verse has been a source of strength and encouragement to Christians through the ages. However, there are some who take advantage of the verse and use it to excuse habitual sin. This wonderful promise of God's forgiveness is not a license for us to go on sinning.

Someone said that a cruise ship does not carry lifeboats in order that it might sink. The ship carries lifeboats in case it does sink. In the same way 1 John 1:9 is given for the times we do sin...not in order that we may sin.

1 John 1:9 gives us three wonderful truths about God's forgiveness.

First, we see the certainty of God's forgiveness. How can God forgive sins? On what grounds can He pronounce forgiveness of sins? Look at what the verse says about God. It tells us that God is *faithful* and *just*.

In 1 Kings 8:56, King Solomon said, *Blessed be the LORD, who has given rest to His people Israel, according to all that He promised. There has not failed one word of all His good promise, which He promised through His servant Moses.*

God is faithful, but He is also just. In Genesis 18:25, Abraham said, *Shall not the Judge of all the earth do right?* This statement was made by Moses in full awareness that God is a just God.

Secondly, we see the completeness of God's forgiveness. The promise is made to forgive our sins and to cleanse us of all unrighteousness.

How complete is God's forgiveness? Let's allow the Word of God to answer this question.

God removes our sins *as far as the east is from the west* (Psalm 103:12 KJV). This to say that God removes our sins from infinity to infinity…from vanishing point to vanishing point.

The prophet Micah (7:19) tells us that God puts our sins into the depths of the sea. Stephen Olford used to add, "…and He puts up a No Fishing sign."

Thirdly, we see the condition of God's forgiveness. We must confess our sins! The word confess means to agree with God.

Admit your sins to God…agree with Him and experience His wonderful forgiveness.

Dr. Roger D. Willmore

Judges 19-21; Luke 7:31-50 **April 3**

The Completeness of God's Forgiveness

If we confess our sins, He is faithful and just to forgive us our sins and to cleanse us of all unrighteousness. (1 John 1:9)

Dr. Stephen Olford was my friend and mentor for more than thirty-five years, before he went to be with the Lord. He was my favorite preacher. I loved to hear him open the Scriptures. He would often say, when talking about our sins and God's forgiveness, that Jesus Christ came to clean up the mess we have made.

This wonderful verse before you describes how thoroughly God cleans up the mess you have made. He forgives and He cleanses.

In Leviticus chapter sixteen we read that on the Day of Atonement two goats were selected. One was offered as a sacrifice. The second goat became what was known as the scapegoat. Aaron laid his hands upon the goat and confessed the sins of the children of Israel. Then a suitable man was chosen. A strong man was chosen to take the goat into the wilderness, far into the wilderness, to assure that it would never return. That goat never returned. It eventually died in the desert. This is a graphic picture of Jesus Christ taking our sins upon Himself and taking those sins far away from us.

The writer of Hebrews wrote, *...their sins and lawless deeds I will remember no more* (Hebrews 8:12).

God removes our sins from us completely. He remembers them no more. I know what you are thinking. Somebody remembers them because someone is constantly reminding you of them. You can be assured that it is not God who reminds you. You remind yourself, your family may remind you, your friends may remind you, your enemies will certainly remind you and the devil will remind you. But God will never remind you of forgiven sins. They are gone, never to return.

God not only forgives our sins, He cleans up the mess we made with our sins. What a Savior.

Dr. Roger D. Willmore

Ruth 1-4; Luke 8:1-25   **April 4**

His Saving Grace

...not pilfering, but showing all good fidelity, that they may adorn the doctrine of God our Savior in all things... teaching us that, denying ungodliness and worldly lusts, we should live soberly, righteously, and godly in the present age.
(Titus 2:10, 12)

When I put aside Christian living, I allowed the enemy to enter into my life. This brought me to my need of surrender.

Knowing and growing up in Christ my Savior – the God of the universe, the Alpha and Omega – I knew the truth. In all honesty, I saw that there was work that must be done and not just by me alone.

When God created the heavens and earth, He filled them with stars, clouds, animals and man. He intended that we would be trustworthy with faithfulness, that others would desire the teaching of God through our conduct. And we, having the full knowledge of the truth (the triune God), are saved by grace.

The grace of God is actually God Himself in Christ, who is everything to us. God supplies man with grace; it is to meet what God demands. No man can partake of God through the law, but grace enables man to enjoy God. Reality is God realized by man, and grace is God enjoyed by man. With saving grace God called us to a holy calling, not according to our works but according to His own purpose. This is so we might share His life and position. Then also we may be His testimony.

So the most important role of God's salvation in our life includes forgiveness, justification, reconciliation, redemption, regeneration, sanctification, transformation and conformation, to redeem us back. This reunites us with God for the fulfillment of His eternal purpose.

However, we must be Christ-like, expressing God in all things. Ungodliness is the absence of God's expression, and worldly lust is the expression of the flesh. We must deny them both that we may live a God-expressing and flesh-restricting life. Living soberly for God has not given us a spirit of cowardice, but of power and of love and of a sound mind. Living for the kingdom of God brings righteousness and peace and joy in the Holy Spirit. To be godly we must accept persecution, knowing that it is a part of His godliness in this present age. It is because of the fight, the good fight of faith, laying hold of the eternal life, that we are called. Proclaiming the good confession before many witnesses, gives God the VICTORY, saving us by His grace! For His divine power has given to us all things that pertain to life and godliness through the knowledge of Him who called us by His glory and virtue.

Carl Washington

1 Samuel 1-3; Luke 8:26-56   **April 5**

My Ole '67 Pontiac

Then He who sat on the throne said, "Behold, I make all things new." And He said to me, "Write, for these words are true and faithful." (Revelation 21:5)

Once when I was struggling through life, as I often did before Jesus came along, I needed a car to transport my family. A so-called friend gave me a 1967 blue Pontiac Catalina. It was a classic that looked and ran great, for about fifteen minutes. Then it would stop running completely! Since that was the only problem and I prided myself in my skills as a shade tree mechanic, I set out to fix it. For the next three months that car drove me absolutely crazy. I flushed out the fuel lines, rebuilt the carburetor and even installed an electric fuel pump to keep the fuel system from vapor locking. Nothing worked. I finally took someone else's advice to keep the oil and change the car!

That's kind of how our flesh is. No matter how hard we attempt to fix it and make it better, we fail. We become totally frustrated and end up reverting even deeper into destructive behaviors. The addict knows this all too well, but then again so do those of us who have tried to diet repeatedly. Most of us have at least some clothes in our closets for when we lose that temporary ten pounds that we are carrying around.

If you go into a bookstore, probably the most prominent display is the one offering "Self Help" books. In reality, as Christians we ought to categorize self help books as Fiction. Because there is no such thing as "Self Help." Paul says, *For I know that nothing good dwells in me, that is, in my flesh. For I have the desire to do what is right, but not the ability to carry it out* (Romans 7:18 ESV). So biblically speaking there is no help for self. We will have as much success fixing ourselves as I did fixing that old Pontiac.

And wisely, God doesn't try either. He knows what is needed. He states simply at the end of His book about mankind, *Behold, I am making all things new.*

Father, forgive me for even attempting to fix my old fallen flesh. Help me please to yield myself completely to You, that You may make me new today. Amen

Chaplain Jim Freed

1 Samuel 4-6; Luke 9:1-17   **April 6**

We're All God's Children

Jesus said, "Let the little children come to me, and do not hinder them, for the kingdom of heaven belongs to such as these."
(Matthew 19:14 NIV)

I do children's clubs every week, partly because kids need to know that they're loved, and I fit right in there – but mostly because it keeps me close to God's heart. Here is a month's worth of quotes.

Adele (age 7), **"Chris, do you know what brain freeze is?"** When I said that it was when you suck a slushy too fast she said in amazement, **"How did you know that?"** Jonathan (age 6) went home in my son's sneakers. They were two sizes bigger than his own. When I asked him later if he had even noticed he said, "Yes, but I didn't think about it." *Jamie (age 10),* "Don't ever put your finger on the cigarette lighter in your car when the coils are red. See." *Ellie (age 6) was sitting next to me one night when she whispered,* "I think you're the best looking 'Monday Club' leader." *Jonathan (age 6),* "You can pray to God anytime, even when you're shaving." *Jonah (age 7) when asked in an interview what his favorite Bible story was said,* "David and Goliath," *and then when asked what lesson we could learn from it said,* "If you see a giant, kill him."

But maybe the best of all is this conversation with a slightly strange kid called George. Someone else was doing the talk, and while they were at it I was just praying. It was only in my head, but my lips must have been moving because George looked up at me and said, *"What are you doing?"* I said, "Praying." George: *"What for?"* "For you, George." *"Why?"* "Because I want you to know Jesus." *"Why?"* "So that you can go to heaven." *"Do you think I'm funny?"* "Yeah George, I think you're hilarious."

I think it's great how all George wanted to know was what was going on – and that I thought that he was OK. Isn't that what we all want? We want to know what's going on. Why do things happen? But then that's never enough. Mostly we just want to know that we're lovable. We want to know if we're accepted. What we really want is to know that everything is going to be OK. And sooner or later, we all need that from God.

Take comfort today in that you are God's child. Did you get that? GOD'S CHILD. And He loves everything about you. And He thinks that you're lovable. And accepted. And He wants you to know that everything is going to be OK. That He would kill for you. Actually, He already has. Please take a little time today to just think about how much love God has for you. You are His little child, and you always will be. His Son prays for you all the time because He wants to bring you to heaven, and He even thinks you're funny.

Rev. Chris Thompson

1 Samuel 7-9; Luke 9:18-36   **April 7**

Called By His Name

Then all the peoples of the earth shall see that you are called by the name of the Lord... (Deuteronomy 28:10)

These words were spoken by Moses to Israel in preparation for their entrance into the land of promise. Assurance was given them that they would strike fear in the hearts of the residents of the land because they were called by the name of the Lord. His name was the source of *authority* for possessing the land. It was also the guarantee of **sufficiency** and enablement to meet the opposition that lay ahead.

Just as Moses spoke this message during his final days as leader of Israel, so Jesus, when He was about to leave His disciples, prayed that they might be kept in the name of the Father (John 17:11). Being called by His name provided **security** for the disciples in a world of people rebellious against God. The security was not in terms of immunity from rejection and persecution but of being kept in the Father's hand.

Another significance of being called by His name is in the area of **identity**. In other words, it means that God was identifying Himself with His people Israel. They were to be recognized as God's own people. He would be among them, leading them and fighting for them.

For many of us, it is an honor to be called by the name of our earthly father. There is a degree of prestige in some cases and a healthy form of pride. We attempt to live up to that name and do not want to bring shame and disgrace upon it. Being called by our heavenly Father's name calls for a holy life – free from compromise and sin. Just as for His people Israel, being called by His name carried authority over the enemy, sufficiency to meet life's challenges, and security from the attacks of the enemy, so believers today can experience these benefits through being called by His name.

Rev. William A. Raws

1 Samuel 10-12; Luke 9:37-62   **April 8**

God's Word - a Lamp unto My Feet

Your word is a lamp to my feet and a light for my path.
(Psalm 119:105 NIV)

    Back in the Old Testament days God communicated with man in various ways. To Moses, in Exodus 3, it was a burning bush that God used to get his attention so He could communicate with him. For young Samuel, in 1 Samuel 3:1-11, God spoke at night in a voice that Samuel thought was old Eli, the priest, calling him. God told Noah, in Genesis 6:11-14, to build an ark because it was going to rain and flood the earth. No one knew what rain was because it had never rained before. We are told that Noah believed and walked with God. An angel of the Lord spoke to Mary and Joseph before Jesus was born. Today we have God's written Word, the Bible. God communicates with us every time we open our Bibles and read. God does not speak audibly to us today but through His Word, the Bible.

    Communication is a two-way street. It takes more than one person to complete a communication network. If our Bibles just sit on the desk, table, or in the book case, we are not seeking to hear from God. When our phone rings or plays music, or whatever alert is programmed in, we must activate it in order to communicate with the person on the other end. When the e-mail alert signal sounds it means someone is trying to communicate with us. Unless we take some positive action, no communication will take place. Another way God communicates His Word to us is through other people who expound the truths of God from His Word, the Bible. We must listen and follow along with them as they use the Bible to make clear the message of God recorded there for us.

    Let's check out what God's Word says about God's Word.

    And the words of the LORD are flawless, like silver refined in a furnace of clay, purified seven times (Psalm 12:6 NIV).

    Your word, O LORD, is eternal: it stands firm in the heavens (Psalm 119:89 NIV).

For the word of God is living and active. Sharper than any double-edged sword, it penetrates even to dividing soul and spirit, joints and marrow; it judges the thoughts and attitudes of the heart (Hebrews 4:12 NIV).

I am not ashamed of the gospel, because it is the power of God for the salvation of everyone who believes: first to the Jew, then for the Gentile (Romans 1:16 NIV).

How can a young man keep his way pure? By living according to your word (Psalm 119:9 NIV).

How does this purification take place? By obeying John 3:16 and asking Jesus into your heart and life to forgive you of your sins.

We are told to search the Scriptures (God's Word) and hide them in our hearts. *I have hidden your word in my heart that I might not sin against you* (Psalm 119:11 NIV).

Victory in Jesus is waiting for you. Do you hear God speaking through His Word, the Bible?

Chaplain Stan Marsh

1 Samuel 13-14; Luke 10:1-24　　　　　　　　　　　**April 9**

Taste Test

Oh, <u>taste</u> and <u>see</u> that the Lord is good; Blessed is the man who trusts in Him! (Psalm 34:8)

　　I don't know about you, but I love to taste food. Food can look really good, but the litmus test is how does it taste? After you taste it then you will really know if it is truly good. In the very same way God wants us to "taste" Him.

　　What does that mean? Well, I think of it this way… many people say they know God and are Christians, but they have not "tasted" Him. What I mean is… they have not taken what He has to offer and applied it in their lives. We can hear all about Him, read all about Him, but we need to take Him in – put what He has to offer us to use - then we will know how good He really is – not how good we hear He is.

We are told in Proverbs that honey is sweet to the taste (24:13); in Psalm 119:103 we are told that His word is sweeter than honey to the mouth. God gave us our sense of taste so that we can fully appreciate food and enjoy the bounty of food offered to us. When we are struggling and down or even rejoicing - we often use food to comfort and celebrate. God wants us to taste Him, to use Him when we are struggling or when we are celebrating the blessings of life – just like we taste food for satisfaction.

As I write this the staff has just made some kettle corn. I can tell you it smells good – but until I get up and go get some and taste it, I will not know for myself what it is truly like. We cannot experience God's fullness just by hearing it or smelling it or listening to others' opinions – we need to try Him for ourselves and when we do that, then we will know that He is good.

Maybe right now, instead of making some sweet treat or some comfort food, you need to get alone with God and "taste" what He has to offer you at this time. What He has is far greater than the temporary experience of food. In Song of Solomon 2:3b, we read, *I sat down in his shade with great delight, and his fruit was sweet to my taste.* Have you sat down under His tree and savored His flavor?

Once you have tasted Him and put your trust in Him it will become evident in your life that His fruit is sweeter than anything you have tasted from a human perspective. I don't know about you, but I have tasted some pretty fine foods, and they don't compare to the pleasure we can find in Him.

Next time you are enjoying a fine meal or treat and you are thinking… my, how good this tastes… remember that God tells us that He is even better. Savor HIM!! Join me at His banquet table.

Dr. Lynne Jahns

1 Samuel 15-16; Luke 10:25-42   **April 10**

That I May Know Him…

That I may know Him, and the power of His resurrection, and the fellowship of His sufferings, being made conformed to his death. (Philippians 3:10)

    As part of my Inner Renewal Time I am studying <u>Going Deeper</u>, a book by one of my dad's favorite authors, J. Sidlow Baxter. This book is so old (1959) that the price on the cover is $1.95. The exciting thing is that books about God's Word are never outdated if they present the eternal truth of God's Word. I now realize why Baxter was one of my dad's favorite writers. Over 80 pages of this book are a commentary on one verse, Philippians 3:10, *That I may know Him, and the power of His resurrection, and the fellowship of His sufferings, being made conformed to his death.*

    Those of us who have a prayer life (and all of us should) have probably asked for the power of God in our lives. But what's interesting in this text is that the *power of His resurrection* is tied directly to *His suffering*. We may desire the power, but are we willing to suffer? Much of our suffering is the general suffering of life. Christ's suffering was that of suffering for doing righteousness. The apostle Peter wrote, *"But even if you should suffer for righteousness' sake, you are blessed…For it is better, if it is the will of God, to suffer for doing good than for doing evil"* (1 Peter 3:14 & 17).

    It is also interesting to note that this is directly tied in with discipleship, for in Philippians 3:17 (KJV) we read, *Brethren, be followers together of me.* All believers have been called to discipleship. The Great Commission of Matthew 28:16-20 is a reminder that we are to be discipling others even as we are discipled by others. This is to be done intentionally.

    Baxter writes, "In this Philippian verse Paul is not thinking of the order in which we savingly *appropriate* Christ at the *beginning* of our Christian life, but of the way in which we *subsequently* learn to know Him in a heart-to-heart sympathy" (italics the author's, p. 74). This discipleship is, ultimately, the personal application of what we learn as we dig deeper and deeper into God's Word. Are you applying what you know of the Scriptures? Do you live it out?

Dr. Joe Olachea

1 Samuel 17-18; Luke 11:1-28 April 11

Tempted by the Ultimate

*The thief comes only to steal and kill and destroy;
I have come that they may have life, and have it to the full.*
(John 10:10 NIV)

Many people think of Christianity as a restrictive worldview. After all, we have the ten commandments and hundreds of other Old Testament commands, not to mention many commands that came from the mouth of Jesus and his apostles. Our individualistic culture is dominated by the idea that one needs to do whatever is in one's heart. "Be true to oneself" is the defining mantra. So, let's grant that it is restrictive but ask what's so bad about being restrictive? I suppose the thought is that if we strive to live by the prescriptions of Christianity, then our lives will be rigid and constrained. We would lose our freedom to live the way we want to live and nothing is worth the loss of freedom.

However, Jesus said that He came to give us life to the full, life *more abundant*. How could restriction ever lead to abundance? To see this, let's think about the decision that faces every professional athlete at some point in his career. There is no doubt that for an athlete to be successful there has to be enormous sacrifice. The athlete must *restrict* his or her life from the normal activity of others to practice his or her athletic craft. But my guess is the athlete does not think that his or her life is rigid and constrained when he or she achieves success in his or her respective sport. In fact, the athlete has gotten to do things that only a few others get to do. There is a sense in which the restricted life has produced a greater freedom and along with this freedom comes greater pleasure. C.S. Lewis once said: "Indeed, if we consider the unblushing promises of reward and the staggering nature of the rewards promised in the Gospels, it would seem that Our Lord finds our desires, not too strong, but too weak. We are half-hearted creatures, fooling about with drink and sex and ambition when infinite joy is offered us, like an ignorant child who wants to go on making mud pies in a slum because he cannot imagine what is meant by the offer of a holiday at the sea. We are far too easily pleased." (<u>The Weight of Glory</u>)

All would agree that living an upright life is difficult and it is filled with temptations. Today, be tempted by the Ultimate. Don't settle for the mud pies.

Travis Dickinson

1 Samuel 19-21; Luke 11:29-54   **April 12**

The Heavens Declare

The heavens declare the glory of God; and the firmament shows and proclaims His handiwork. (Psalm 19:1 Amplified Bible)

Here's a description of the heavens and the glory of God that should blow your mind:

A scientist once suggested an interesting analogy. Imagine, he said, a perfectly smooth glass pavement on which the finest speck can be seen. Then shrink our sun from 865,000 miles in diameter to 2 feet, and place this gilt ball on the pavement to represent the sun.

Step off 82 paces of about 2 feet each, and to proportionately represent the first planet, Mercury, put down a mustard seed.

Take 60 steps more, each about two feet, and for Venus, put down an ordinary shot the size of a BB.

Mark 78 steps more, and for our earth, put down a pea.

Step 108 paces from there, and for Mars, put down a pinhead.

Sprinkle some fine dust for the asteroids, take 788 steps more, and for Jupiter, put down an orange.

Take 934 steps, and for Saturn, put down a golf ball.

Mark 2,086 steps more, and for Uranus, put down a marble.

Step off 2,322 steps from there, and for Neptune, but down a cherry. This will take 2 ½ miles, and we haven't discussed Pluto. If we swing completely around, we have a smooth glass surface 5 miles in diameter representing our system, just a tiny fraction of the heavens. On this surface, 5 miles across, we have only one mustard seed, BB, pea, pinhead, dust, orange, golf ball, marble, and cherry.

And we should have to go 6,720 miles, not feet, on the same scale before we could put down another two-foot ball to represent the nearest star!!!

He created all of this and holds it all together by the word of His power! And He created you and me! What an amazing God we serve.

Dr. Bill Welte

1 Samuel 22-24; Luke 12:1-31 April 13

The Trees of the Forest Will Sing for Joy

Let the heavens rejoice, and let the earth be glad; Let the sea roar, and all its fullness; Let the field be joyful, and all that is in it. Then all the trees of the woods will rejoice before the LORD. For He is coming, for He is coming to judge the earth. He shall judge the world with righteousness, And the peoples with His truth. (Psalm 96:11-13)

The writers of the Psalms strike us with their dramatic use of symbols. The Semitic mind uses concrete concepts, not abstract and intangible expressions. These symbolic expressions reveal non-tangibles of the heart. This phrase and a similar one in I Chronicles 16:33 shows in symbolic form that people rejoice with exuberance when they realize that the "Lord reigns."

I experienced this truth during my forty-five years in the Arabic Kingdom of Jordan. When people came to the Lord they sang, and how they could sing! In poverty, perplexity and persecution with many degrees of suffering, when they encountered Jesus Christ, they sang as the trees in the forest.

They incarnated the principles of Christ in their walk. No other belief system has ever produced the richness and variety of joyful music as has the Christian faith. In the New Testament period people began singing Psalms, hymns and spiritual songs.

Happiness and joy don't imply you won't hurt getting a root canal. Amy Carmichael said, in <u>Edges of His Ways</u>: "Settle this in your minds…there is no promise of ease… We are told to expect this sort of thing." This joy shows the difference in the lives of those living in the light and those in the deadening darkness of unbelief.

A dear friend of mine in Jordan was injured when an army truck overturned. Nineteen of the men were Muslims; he the only nominal Christian. Although he had no faith he felt his being from a traditional "Christian" tribe should have kept him safe. Suffering with a broken back, confined to a wheelchair for the rest of his life, he let loose on everything including God. But after some real believers visited him a number of times he opened his heart to Jesus. The anger and bitterness disappeared. It was a joy to visit with him and discuss God's Word. When he found Jesus his life was dramatically changed. He now was among the trees of the forest singing with joy. Among the nations, including the Arab nations, the Lord reigns and many trees of the forest are singing with joy.

Dr. George Kelsey

1 Samuel 25-26; Luke 12:32-59   **April 14**

The Happy Man Is Like a Tree

He shall be like a tree Planted by the rivers of water, That brings forth its fruit in its season, Whose leaf also shall not wither; And whatever he does shall prosper. (Psalm 1:3)

Blessed is the man who trusts in the LORD, And whose hope is the LORD. For he shall be like a tree planted by the waters, Which spreads out its roots by the river, And will not fear when heat comes; But its leaf will be green, And will not be anxious in the year of drought, Nor will cease from yielding fruit.
(Jeremiah 17:7-8)

Stand in the mall and look at the faces of people hurrying along. Those faces reflect distraught, tired, frustrated, frenzied, even frantic hearts. One could never say "I saw a lot of happy smiling faces!" Both the Psalmist and Jeremiah reveal the secret to happiness. They speak of a blessed man. One could translate the Hebrew word for blessed as "O, how happy is the man!"

That happy man is like a tree! He walks the walk. He is planted by a source of life-giving water. This nameless tree is firmly rooted, sending out roots to the water. His behavior is characterized by not walking, standing or sitting with those choosing evil over goodness. He who has learned to live principally in line with God's Word and has cultivated a life of reliance on the Lord always will enjoy indescribable happiness and tranquility.

But individuals, tribes and nations who reject godly principles and trustful reliance on the Lord always descend into darkness, brutality and joyless living. Because they do not trust God they can't trust each other. Joyful contentment is the reward God gives those who consistently live a godly life of obedience and trust.

Happy people exude a contagious joy that encourages and lifts up others. How often while living in Jordan did I find comfort and protection under scarce trees in the desert whose leaves remained green when all the fields had turned to brown dust. Those trees remained green in the harshness of the desert winds and heat. People who put their roots down to the living water that Jesus gives, even in barren societies, bring fruitful blessings to unhappy people. The harsh winds of the desert do not uproot a tree planted near a source of water. Neither will the harsh currents of modern godless societies uproot the believer whose roots go deep.

Are you one of those fruitful trees giving shade to those living in the harsh climate of modern society? Are you producing soul-satisfying joy for anxious hearts? May you be like a tree planted by streams of water!

Dr. George Kelsey

1 Samuel 27-29; Luke 13:1-22   April 15

The Olive Tree and You

But I am like an olive tree flourishing in the house of God; I trust in God's unfailing love for ever and ever. (Psalm 52:8 NIV)

    I consider the olive tree one of the most beautiful of all the trees in Palestine. In the extreme heat of the summer the leaves shine a silvery green. Hebrew poetry is characterized by its rich use of symbols. Here the singer of Israel likens himself to a green olive tree in the house of God.

    They grow so slowly. In the Arabic Language School in Jordan we used to use a fourth- grade reader. One story told of a grandfather taking his young grandson to the field to plant some tiny olive trees. The child said, "Grandpa, why are you planting these little trees? They take so long to produce olives; you'll never get to taste them!" Grandpa wisely answered, "Others have planted and I ate; I plant and others will eat." I have pictures of olive trees in Jordan over a thousand years old. He was teaching the value of a legacy for future generations.

    Why an olive tree? From ancient days the olive was used for food. With some olives and a few pieces of bread a Bedouin could survive many days in the desert. Jesus prayed under the olive trees. In the days of Moses they used olive oil to anoint Aaron the priest and later kings of Israel. The taste of olive oil on a salad reminds me of anointing in the life of a child of God. When they built the tabernacle, they used fine oil to light its lamps. People carried clay lamps burning olive oil. This reminds the believer that he is to be a source of light to those living in darkness. It is a light that guides our feet and leads us along the way.

    When a certain man winding down a tortuous road to Jericho was waylaid and left half-dead, a despised Samaritan stopped while others passed by. That Samaritan we consider good as he reached out and anointed the wounds of that wretched victim with oil. Until recent times people used oil as medicine for healing. People around us may smile but are often hiding the hurts and scars deep within. We as olive trees in God's house need to be ready with that healing oil of our loving concern.

May we strive to become olive trees bringing food to the hungry, receiving an anointing from the Spirit of God in our lives, showing the way as lights in darkness and bringing healing to sin-stricken hearts. Stand as an olive tree today!

Dr. George Kelsey

1 Samuel 30-31; Luke 13:23-35 April 16

A Palm Tree

The righteous shall flourish like a palm tree... (Psalm 92:12-15)

Standing on the roof of a home in Basra, Iraq, I could see in the distance thousands of date trees. They stand so tall and straight. While the olive tree has a massive knotty trunk and does not grow very tall, the date palm is tall, erect and dignified. The wind might blow them but they bounce back as straight as ever.

The verse here is followed by the idea that *those who are planted in the house of the LORD shall flourish in the courts of our God.* That challenges the believer to consider that as he represents Jesus Christ he must stand straight without any twists and turns in his life. He must reveal Christian grace in relationships.

I also loved the taste of the dates from the world's largest exporter of that sweet fruit. That continues to test me to see whether in my relationships there is something that brings sweetness to others. When I returned from that preaching trip in southern Iraq, I brought with me a suitcase nearly full of dates. Some we ate, but others we shared with friends in Amman. I would be pleased if I could always share something of sweetness in a world filled with anxiety, suspicion and bitterness.

The verses end this section of the Psalm with the encouraging word that those who live as a date tree in the house of the Lord will bear fruit in old age. Old age doesn't make a date tree fruitless nor should it make the believer of Christ barren of blessings for others.

I met a dear Christian lady in 1954. She and her family had been living in a cave, having fled from Turkey. Our co-workers let her live with her husband and children in a shack that we used as a church. She never learned to read yet continued to bring blessing to others. She was a true date tree living fruitfully for the Lord. I visited her in May of 1999 and she was full of vigor and blessing. She lived through many horrors, wars, persecutions and displacements but always praised the Lord and lifted the spirits of others. She died on Christmas day, 1999, a ninety-five-year-old true date tree in the courts of the Lord. What can you do to share sweetness with others?

Dr. George Kelsey

2 Samuel 1-2; Luke 14:1-24　　　　　　　　　　　　**April 17**

A Cedar of Lebanon

The righteous ... grow like a cedar in Lebanon. (Psalm 92:12)

In ancient times the mountains of Lebanon were covered with forests of majestic cedars. This tree has become the symbol on the Lebanese flag. I took my family high into the 3000 foot high mountains of Lebanon to see the cedars. My wife and children holding hands could not stretch around the girth of the tree trunk. Spreading branches and ninety foot high trees fill one with awe! And we should grow like them!

Due to the popularity of cedar wood, the many forests have diminished to a few hundred trees. One can never forget the fragrance of the cedar. From early times people were glad that this wood is insect-resistant. We know that King Hiram agreed with King Solomon to bring great quantities of the cedar wood to the hills of Jerusalem to build the temple (1 Kings 2). The Bible speaks of the great height and strength of the trees. Amos said the might of the Amorites was like the height of the cedars. Ezekiel compared the powerful cruelty of the Assyrians to a strong cedar of Lebanon.

As worshippers journeyed from far away lands to Jerusalem, the beautiful fragrance of the cedars caused them to lift their hearts in joyful worship. The aroma triggered a sense of awe in the presence of God in His temple. High in the mountains, in spite of extremely violent windstorms and the effects of freezing ice and snow, the cedars stand strong! Some of those trees are more than 3000 years old.

The Psalmist reveals the fact that righteous people grow like a cedar. Whenever people entered that cedar-lined temple they had a sensory experience of that fragrance enhancing their worship. That happy righteous man of Psalm 1 is shown to have the strength to withstand every kind of violent storm in life. His joy and steadfastness will challenge and encourage others. His godly life will bring people to see our God in a new way. God will spread through us the aroma of Christ among those who are being saved…and the fragrance of life (see 2 Corinthians 2:14-15). The fragrance of your knowledge of God will touch the lives of others in life-changing ways. But most of all your godly, joyful living enables people to savor the fragrance of the presence of God as an undeniable reality.

Dr. George Kelsey

2 Samuel 3-5; Luke 14:25-35   **April 18**

Is God Trustworthy?

For all the promises of God in him are yea, and in him Amen, unto the glory of God by us. (2 Corinthians 1:20 KJV)

During a particularly challenging season in my life, I watched as what I thought were many constants went into chaos. Unfortunately, my first instinct was to run to friends, family, even books. My inner storm continued until I willingly yielded to the only One who can truly restore peace – my Lord and Savior, Jesus Christ.

Once I submitted to Him, He reminded me that only He is unchanging, immovable and sovereign. These and so many other attributes and characteristics about God are useful in my everyday life and especially when I find myself in internal chaos.

I must train my mind and my heart to run to Him first, instead of to other people or things.

One tool I use is to rehearse things that are ALWAYS true. These phrases and the corresponding Bible verses are not dependent on my current circumstances. The list is personal but not exhaustive or comprehensive. I use the list to review and remember what God promises to me, what He has done for me, and what is always true. Here's part of my list:

- God loves me and never stops loving me (1 John 4:7-11).
- God is sovereign (Ephesians 1:3-6).
- God is all-knowing (John 16:29-30).
- God is all-powerful (Nahum 1:3).
- God offered me salvation through the death and resurrection of Jesus (Romans 6:23).
- Salvation is forever (John 10:29).
- I accepted the offer of salvation and am a daughter of the King (Romans 5:8-10, Romans 8:15-16).
- God pursues me (Luke 15:1-10).
- God hates sin (Psalm 97:10).
- There is forgiveness from sin for the asking (1 John 1:9).
- All things in my life are for His glory and my good (1 Peter 5:6-11).
- God is good – all the time (Matthew 19:17).
- God allows difficult times to increase our faith and trust in Him (James 1:2-4).
- All God's promises are "Yes" in Him (2 Corinthians 1:20).
- God desires to hear the wishes of my heart – even though He already knows them (Psalm 37:3-5).
- God is always listening (Psalm 121:3-4).
- God is my protector (Psalm 18:1-2).

Pray about creating your own list. Your list may be different. God will give you things that meet you where you are. Feel free to use some of the same entries, or start from scratch. I pray it will be profitable as you continue on your journey with the Lord.

Donna Connors

2 Samuel 6-8; Luke 15:1-10   April 19

God's Solution for a Longing Heart

"Eye has not seen, nor ear heard, nor have entered into the heart of man the things which God has prepared for those who love Him." (1 Corinthians 2:9)

Many people admit they have not experienced what they thought they would when they first became a Christian. The cry of their heart seems to be, *"I must know something I don't know."* Well, has the kingdom of God been over-advertised or is it only that it has been under-believed? Has the Lord Jesus Christ been over-estimated or has He only been under-trusted? I firmly believe that the kingdom of God could not possibly be over-advertised nor the Lord Jesus Christ over-estimated.

My friend, all the difficulty and the doubt of what God has told us in His Word arises from the fact that we have under-believed and under-trusted. This causes that spiritual and emotional distance we can feel deep down inside of us. The Holy Spirit uses this to set us searching God's Word to find the solution for a longing heart.

You see, in the Lord Jesus Christ, there is a deep and lasting peace and comfort of soul which nothing earthly can disturb. It belongs to those who by faith embrace what has already been provided for them in Christ. Let me ask you this question: are you this day truly resting in Him Who is your all-in-all? Take a moment to reflect on this statement, "You are in Christ and Christ is in you." The Bible says this is true of a born-again child of God. If this is true, you have need of nothing. All of your needs have been met in Him.

Blessed be the God and Father of our Lord Jesus Christ, who has blessed us with every spiritual blessing in the heavenly places in Christ... (Ephesians 1:3).

The key to this is appropriation. You must exercise child-like faith in what God has already provided for you in Christ Jesus. Keep your eyes on Jesus, my friend, not on the things of the earth. Remember, when Jesus died for you He also died with you. This means at the cross you were immersed or baptized into

Christ. If you are in Christ and He is everything, what do you really need? Christ and Christ alone is all that you need.

Rev. Chris S. Hodges

2 Samuel 9-11; Luke 15:11-32 **April 20**

How Can I Know There Is a God?

The heavens declare the glory of God;... (Psalm 19:1a)

    When I first accepted the presidency of Davis College in Binghamton, New York, I continued as the Senior Pastor of New Testament Baptist Church in South Florida. On Sunday mornings I would lead the services and then fly to the college. Usually I was placed in a first class seat because of the many frequent flier miles I accumulated.

    On one occasion a student from Temple University sat next to me. I love being around college students and immediately we hit it off. We began chatting and I asked him how such a young man could afford to sit in first class. He laughed and explained to me that his father had purchased the ticket. When he found out that I was a president of a Bible college he asked me a penetrating question. "How do you know there is a God?" For two hours we had a delightful conversation. I took him to Psalm 19. There are three evidences about how we can know there is a God. I shared these thoughts with my new friend.

    The first is found in the first six verses of Psalm 19. God is seen in the wonders above. We have in this passage the argument for God. The psalmist simply declares that "the heavens declare" God's marvelous glory. In theology we learn that there are arguments for God. There is the cosmological argument which tells us there is a cause behind the universe. There is the teleological argument which speaks to order. The anthropological argument for God speaks to morality; mankind is different from the animal world. The ontological argument addresses there must be a perfect being Who is in charge of all things. The amazing universe proclaims that God simply is!

The second part of this psalm reminds us that God is seen in the Word. In verses 7–11 there are six comparative statements reminding us of the way in which the Word of God develops in our lives. God's Word is the tremendous source of the truth and it guides our steps in life.

The third part of the psalm speaks about God's workers who are close to Him. Those who walk with God confess sin and meditate on His Word. They become the greatest examples by confirming to people that God is real!

As I shared these wonderful principles with this young man I asked him if he would like to trust Christ as his Savior. He thought a moment and then said "no." I asked him if he understood and he assured me he did. He said that his father did not believe in God and he loved and trusted his father and would not want to disappoint him.

Every time I reflect on this brief encounter it reminds me that the greatest way people will come to know the Lord is through the life and witness of someone they trust. My encouragement to you, dear reader, is to live out your faith, and your life will be a testimony that makes it clear to others that God is real! Perhaps our lives speak louder than we realize!

Dr. Dino Pedrone

2 Samuel 12-13; Luke 16   **April 21**

Sufficiency for the Insufficient

And He said to me, "My grace is sufficient for you, for My strength is made perfect in weakness." (2 Corinthians 12:9a)

There are times when we, like the apostle Paul, plead with God to change the circumstances. It may be a persistent health problem, unemployment, financial limitation, an unsaved loved one, etc. Or perhaps it is the apparent call from God to serve Him in some way that seems impossible, and you pray for Him to release you from this obligation. God's answer to you and me is likely to be the one He gave to the apostle Paul in today's theme verse.

Three times Paul had offered a pleading prayer that an unnamed thorn in the flesh might be removed. God answered him, but not in the way he hoped. He said, *My grace is sufficient for you.* He did not remove the condition, but He pointed to His provision of enabling grace.

The key word in God's answer seems to me to be "is." Christians tend to pray "make your grace sufficient for this situation," or "make your grace available to me in my time of need." God longs for us to claim the "is." He has already made His grace both adequate and available for every Christian in every situation. It becomes a matter of unbelief if we pray for what is already available.

Dr. A. W. Tozer declared, "God is always previous." He has made provision prior to our petition. One day during the construction of the main building at Keswick, my father was approached by the electrical contractor. He said, "Mr. Raws, this is Friday, the day I pay my men. I'll need a check for $3,000 to deposit by noon so I can write their pay checks." Dad knew that the Keswick account was near zero, and as he stood by his desk, he told the Lord how impossible the situation was from the human standpoint. He said, "Lord, only you can do something about this." He picked up the first letter from the pile of morning mail. As he unfolded its contents, he discovered a check for $3,000. The attorney writing the letter apologized for having taken so long to settle the estate of a man who had died three years before. International complications had delayed the payment until this time. God's timing was perfect. He had made provision for the need three years in advance.

Rev. William A. Raws

2 Samuel 14-15; Luke 17   April 22

What Do You Crave?

As the deer pants for streams of water, so *my soul pants for you, O God.* (Psalm 42:1 NIV)

I have recently been challenged with this question. Now, if I was honest I would tell you that I crave coffee every morning. But, that's not exactly what I am asking myself with this question.

Scripture tells us that as the deer pants for water, so we should pant for God. Psalm 42:1 tells us that, *As the deer pants for streams of water,* so *my soul pants for you, O God.* Whenever my husband (because I don't do it very often) takes our dogs for a walk they immediately come in seeking water, and often if we find a puddle or walk by the lake they will attempt to drink from it. Based on that observation and the above Scripture, I have to ask myself – do I seek out God like my dogs seek out water after a walk? In the summer, if I am working outside or in the heat – I understand the craving for water or liquid refreshment. Do I apply that understanding to my need for God?

At Keswick, we deal with men who are struggling to overcome different addictions in their lives. It is probably appropriate to say that they once craved a substance or something in a powerful way. My husband craved heroin in his past to a point that all he thought about was when and how he could get it.

Do I crave God like that? I hate to say it, but probably not. There are definitely times I am drawn to God and I am looking forward to spending time with Him, but certainly not in the way that people crave drugs, sex, alcohol, gambling or food. It is even safe to say that I do not crave God to the point that I crave food. Have you been around a hungry baby? Do you desire God or a spiritual connection with God like a baby desires his bottle? 1 Peter 2:2 (NIV) states that: *Like newborn babies, crave pure spiritual milk, so that by it you may grow up in your salvation...*

Based on this question I am attempting to spend time with God before each meal and before I go to bed at night. Not a lot of time, just some reading or praying in addition to my regular times of devotion and study. Maybe for you it might be that you need to spend time with God before a certain TV show that you just can't miss, or before you read a book – or go shopping. Whichever it is… Do you seek to spend time with God as much as you feel the need to do other things in your life?

Dr. Lynne Jahns

2 Samuel 16-18; Luke 18   April 23

Saving Faith

What use is it, my brethren, if someone says he has faith, but he has no works? Can that faith save him? (James 2:14)

    One of the distinctives of classic Evangelicalism is a firm belief in the concept of *sola fide*, which is Latin for "faith alone." Martin Luther said, "This doctrine is the head and the cornerstone…and without it the church of God cannot exist for one hour."[5] John Calvin echoed that sentiment saying, "Wherever the knowledge of it is taken away, the glory of Christ is extinguished, religion abolished, the Church destroyed, and the hope of salvation utterly overthrown."[6]

    If the doctrine of faith without works is so fundamental to the Gospel, then what do we make of James 2:14? Martin Luther reportedly thought the book of James unworthy to be in the canon because of its "weak" stance on the doctrine of *sola fide*.

    However, a close inspection reveals that James is not contradicting Paul. He is dealing with the gravely mistaken notion that all one really needs to garner salvation is to give a

---

[5] Ewald M. Plass, comp., *What Luther Says: An Anthology,* 3 vols. (St. Louis: Concordia Publishing House, 1959), 2:703-4, 715,718.
[6] John Dillenberger, *John Calvin: Selections from His Writings* (n.p.:Anchor Books, 1971), 95

casual acknowledgement of the facts about Christ while doing anything about it remains optional.

Let us be clear; works do not save, no matter what quantity or what quality. But the kind of faith that does save (the kind James is referring to) is the kind that *naturally* produces the "fruit of righteousness" (Philippians 1:11). There is a simple cause and effect relationship here, and any other way of producing fruit would be like stapling fruit to a dead tree.

So, what does your life say about your faith? Is it alive? Is it genuine? There is always evidence in the life of a true believer. Beware though, it is easy to be fooled. Jesus said, *Many will say to me in that day, "Lord, Lord, have we not prophesied in Your name, cast out demons in Your name, and done many wonders in Your name?"* (Matthew 7:22). They will not enter heaven because they expected salvation resulting from their own self-righteousness. Just because someone talks like a Christian and faithfully slides into a pew at 11:00 on Sunday morning doesn't mean they're saved. Appearances can be deceiving. Genuine faith is characterized by repentance, humility and dependence upon God. They are attitudes—along with the fruit of the Spirit—that become "the sweet aroma of Christ" to the Father (2 Corinthians 2:15).

Rev. Jason R. Walsh

2 Samuel 19-20; Luke 19   **April 24**

Roots and Weeds

Pursue peace with all people, and holiness, without which no one will see the Lord: looking carefully lest anyone fall short of the grace of God; lest any root of bitterness springing up cause trouble, and by this many become defiled. (Hebrews 12:14-15)

I was visiting a friend recently and admiring the garden and landscape work she and her husband had done in front of their home. She pointed out to me a tree that has yet to be removed, and what a bother the roots from it have been as they've tried to put in new plants. It reminded me of a bush I dug out of my yard back in the early summer. It was constantly sending out shoots that I was pulling up to keep them from spreading through the whole yard. It wasn't a particularly pretty bush, or anything special, so I finally cut it down, dug it up and threw it away.

But the funny thing is, every time I go out and wander in the yard, I still find shoots from that bush that need to be pulled out. There are roots under the ground that keep trying to start a new bush.

As I was telling my friend about this, it reminded me of the verse about not letting any root of bitterness take hold in our lives. It is so easy to let those little thoughts of hurt and resentment take root, and before long, you've got little shoots of bitterness springing up all over the place. And if we don't keep up with the weed pulling, before long there's a full-grown plant that has taken over – springing up to cause trouble.

Pursuing peace with all people is not an easy task. People will disappoint us. Let's face it. We all fall short of the grace of God and need a daily, fresh supply to keep our hearts soft and make those roots easy to pull out. I'm going to use my gardening time as an opportunity for the Lord to keep my heart free of the weeds and roots of bitterness. How about you? Need to do some gardening?

Ruth Schmidt

2 Samuel 21-22; Luke 20:1-19 **April 25**

Do You Know Where You're Going?

Jesus answered, "I am the way and the truth and the life. No one comes to the Father except through me." (John 14:16 NIV)

Before you skip this reading and assume it's not for you because "I am already saved," have a look. Normally this is a good question to ask someone who may not know Christ as Savior. You have probably experienced a moment when the Lord opened the door to witness to someone, and if we took a survey this is probably the #1 question.

Recently my mother died. It was the end of an up and down battle with cancer; she was 84. About a year and a half ago I had the opportunity to lead her to Jesus as He used cancer to draw her to Himself. She was given over to hospice and the next few days were not looking good. Kneeling at her bedside, in a fatigued, beaten down condition, the question I asked was "Mom, do you know where you're going?" The typical answer was given, "I hope so, after all I was a good person…" You know the "lost's lingo." She accepted Jesus as Savior.

From that day on my mom began a recovery for which no one had an answer. She got back her independence and was up and going. She often called me with a prayer request to relay to the men of the Colony who, by the way, were prayer warriors God used to get her to this point.

I wish I could say my mom spent the next year and a half reading God's Word and fellowshipping with believers. She still had a love for life and the things of this world.

Last week, on her death bed, I began to usher her into the arms of the Savior, letting her know it was OK to go. It was a little disturbing to see the resistance to let go; I mean, who wouldn't want to see Jesus?

My wife and I love to travel, each year going to a new place. We always read everything we can so when we get there we "know where we're going." Well, that night I realized that although mom had a ticket to heaven, she never read the "brochure" on where she was going.

So my question remains, "Do you know where you're going?" Have you read the Bible (brochure), the greatest love story ever about a God desiring to have fellowship and spend eternity with you? We are reminded over and over, "This is not our home…," "I go to prepare a place…," "Where I am you will be…," "let not your heart be troubled…," etc.

I hope when my time comes I'm ready and willing; how about you?

Rob Russomano

2 Samuel 23-24; Luke 20-20-26   **April 26**

Thought Control

Casting down imaginations, and every high thing that exalteth itself against the knowledge of God, and bringing into captivity every thought to the obedience of Christ.
(2 Corinthians 10:5 KJV)

But we see Jesus, who was made a little lower than the angels, for the suffering of death crowned with glory and honor, that He, by the grace of God, might taste death for everyone.
(Hebrews 2:9)

Have you ever wondered why God blessed/cursed us with our imagination? I have. When I read Hebrews 2:9 I thought that it was a hyperbole but I now realize that it is a proper use of a saint's imagination.

When you pray do you ever take the time to imagine where Christ is and what He is doing that He should stop to listen and to do what you desire? He does, you know. The passage sees Jesus enthroned with His "servants" who are ready to do His bidding so:

"Take your burdens to the Lord and leave them there," wrote the hymnist.

When we struggle with temptation we need to *bring every thought into captivity.*

Temptation only exists as long as our thoughts feed it. Use the thoughts that Paul mentions in Philippians 4:8 . You cannot ***not think****! You can, however, use good thoughts to replace evil ones (2 Corinthians 10:5).*

To stop unwanted negative thought you must ignore the negative by concentrating on the positive. The feelings that we have that come from our thoughts will change almost immediately.

I remember my first boot leave in San Diego. I was alone in front of a night club. There was no one there to report my actions but Jesus was very real to me. I said to Him. "You can wait here and I will run in and come right back out. I just want to see what it is like."

I felt that the Lord said, "No, that's alright, I will just go with you." At that point I said, "No forget about it. I just won't go."

When Christ is that real, temptation loses its power.

Dr. H. G. VanSandt

1 Kings 1-2; Luke 20:27-40 April 27

What Are You Meditating On?

For as he [a man] thinketh in his heart, so is he.
(Proverbs 23:7 KJV)

Someone has said, "You are what you think!" or "What you think about determines who you are!" From time to time it is important to take an inventory of what we think about – what we think about during the day that consumes the free moments. What do you think about at night when you are lying in bed and can't sleep? What do you think about when you are driving, walking, running?

Puritan preacher, George Swinnock, suggests that we take those thinking moments and turn them into times of meditating on spiritual things. Here are his suggestions which I think are timeless:

"Meditation prepares the heart for prayer.

Meditate on your sins, and hunt them out of their lurking holes; this helps in our confession.

Meditate on your needs, for God is fully able to supply them. Consider what you need – pardoning mercy, strength for victory, power against sin – that you may entreat God to give them to you.

Meditate upon His mercies to you from birth. Look at the dangers you have been delivered from, the journeys you have been protected in, the seasonable help he has sent to you, the suitable support he has afforded you in distress, the counsel he has given you in doubts, and the comforts he has provided you in sorrow and darkness. Every breath in your life is a gift of mercy.

Do not forget the former favors bestowed on you and your family.

Meditate on your present mercies. How many do you enjoy – your house, family, body, and soul are full of blessings! Think of them particularly. Spread them out like jewels to your view.

Meditate on how freely they are bestowed, on their fullness and their greatness. But, O, your soul's mercies – the image of God, the blood of Christ, eternal life, and seasons of grace! Your whole life is a bundle of mercies. These stir us up to bless the Giver.

Meditate on God to whom we pray. O how we are ashamed of our drops when we stand by this ocean!

Meditate on His mercy and goodness. These like Moses' strokes will fetch water out of a rock. God delights to be sought and found. He delights to see men joyful in the house of prayer. God will not send you away sad.

When you have by meditation put the wood upon the altar, you may by prayer set fire to it and offer up a sacrifice of sweet smelling savour." – Adapted from Voices from the Past; Banner of Truth.

Great stuff! Take that list and begin to meditate on the RIGHT things. You are what you think!

Dr. Bill Welte

1 Kings 3-5; Luke 20:41-47   **April 28**

A Work in Progress

To all who are in Rome, beloved of God, called to be saints:...
(Romans 1:7)

The wording of the Spirit-inspired Scriptures is very important. God has chosen to give us a library of 66 books in one book – the Bible. Even so, much concerning this life and spiritual things is left unsaid. God has chosen to give His message for us as we have it.

In the Gospels and Acts we find the word most often used of believers is from the root for disciple (*mathētēs*). It is used over

265 times in Matthew through Acts. In the book of Acts the word disciple is interchangeable with the word believer. "Christian" in singular or plural form is used only three times in the whole of the New Testament.

When we come to the remainder of the New Testament, Romans to Revelation, a new word appears for the believer, the word saint. Several of the books open with the words "To the saints of…" and then reference the location of the recipients. God is revealing what we are positionally as His followers. However, practically we are not there yet as this will take place only when we are in His presence.

A disciple can be defined as "a disciplined one." This description used most often of believers carries with it the idea of one who practices the biblical spiritual disciplines. As disciples we are in the process of moving from where we are practically - disciples, toward what we are positionally - saints. Spiritual transformation is moving toward sainthood as we have been admonished to …*exercise yourself toward godliness* (1 Timothy 4:7). The word "exercise" has also been translated as "train" in some of our English versions.

So often I hear believers say, "I try to live the Christian life" or "I try to do what is right." Scripture admonishes us that we don't just try to be Christlike, we must train to be so! The apostle Paul reminds us that the transformation in our lives is directly related to our contemplation of "…the face of Jesus Christ" (2 Corinthians 3:18 – 4:6). This is only accomplished through the implementation of the spiritual disciplines in our lives as a result of our love for Him.

Dr. Joe Olachea

1 Kings 6-7; Luke 21:1-19   April 29

Bread Alone….

*But He answered and said, "It is written, 'Man shall not live by bread alone, but by **every word** that proceeds out of the mouth of God.'"* (Matthew 4:4)

Here's what I'm thinking… I've begun to look at the word "bread" not just as earthly food, but more as those spiritual things I do. In our Christian life we "do church," we "do Christian literature," we "do devotions," and we "do Christian conferences and seminars," just to name a few. Yet, here's the big question… How much do we "do the Word of God"? Let's look at the verse again; note that it says **EVERY** word that proceeds out of the mouth of God.

Now to me that is where I struggle – **EVERY** word. I have read the Bible through once in my life and that was a requirement for college, so I bet I didn't read EVERY word. I am convicted – I know Scripture, yes, and I can teach Scripture, but I believe I am often failing myself and my God by not knowing and using **ALL** of Scripture.

All of Scripture teaches… *For the word of God is quick, and powerful, and sharper than any twoedged sword, piercing even to the dividing asunder of soul and spirit, and of the joints and marrow, and is a discerner of the thoughts and intents of the heart* (Hebrews 4:12 KJV).

All of Scripture has the power to transform and lead me in victory… *For this cause also thank we God without ceasing, because, when ye received the word of God which ye heard of us, ye received it not as the word of men, but as it is in truth, the word of God, which effectually worketh also in you that believe* (1 Thessalonians 2:13 KJV).

I have written unto you, fathers, because ye have known him that is from the beginning. I have written unto you, young men, because ye are strong, and the word of God abideth in you, and ye have overcome the wicked one (1 John 2:14 KJV).

All Scripture can help me through life and lasts forever...
And have tasted the good word of God, and the powers of the world to come (Hebrews 6:5 KJV).

Being born again, not of corruptible seed, but of incorruptible, by the word of God, which liveth and abideth for ever (1 Peter 1:23 KJV).

All those things we "do" are great, but I challenge you to "do" the whole Word of God. I have learned something that works for me... I listen to the Word in order, but I read the books in any order. It really isn't the HOW that matters, it's "EVERY WORD" that matters.

Dr. Lynne Jahns

1 Kings 8-9; Luke 21:20-38   April 30

Seek the Lord

But from there you will seek the LORD your God and you will find him, if you search after him with all your heart and with all your soul. (Deuteronomy 4:29 ESV)

With **all** your **heart**? With **all** your **soul**? I have read these words in Scripture many, many times over the years. However, it has only been in the last few years that I have begun to seriously ponder them. And it's only been in the past few months that I have scratched the surface toward more deeply, more fully understanding the profound impact that "seeking with all your heart and all your soul" has on my spirit. Without question I am closely acquainted with how thirsty and dry the spirit becomes when seeking is neglected. But what of this seeking and searching with the whole heart and soul? **Who** does that? **How** does one do that?

I've heard the word soul defined as "mind, will and emotions." Webster's dictionary defines soul as "the central or integral part; the vital core." From the same resource, the heart is defined as "the vital center and source of one's being, emotions and sensibilities."

So, in essence, anyone, anywhere, anytime can and will find God if, if, **if** we do what we are being encouraged to do over and over and over and over again in the Word of our Lord. If and when **I** commit myself to seeking, locating, obtaining or reaching God, with all my mind, will and emotions, **and** with all that is the source of my being, I am **promised** to find Him.

My question for you today: When is the last time you sought and found God? When was the last time that you knew, that you knew, **that you knew**, that God was, present tense, with you?

When you call on me, when you come and pray to me, I'll listen. When you come looking for me, you'll find me. Yes, when you get serious about finding me and want it more than anything else, I'll make sure you won't be disappointed,... (Jeremiah 29:12-14 The Message).

Stephanie D. Paul

1 Kings 10-11; Luke 22:1-23 May 1

Appropriating Truth

Likewise you also, reckon yourselves to be dead indeed to sin, but alive to God in Christ Jesus our Lord. (Romans 6:11)

Reckon: "to accept something as certain."[7]

Personalize this verse, together with faith, and experience great power that halts temptation to sin and refocuses the heart and mind towards obedience and truth. It is by no means a magic formula but as you embrace and live out truth, God is glorified and you experience victory. Perhaps you will find one of these helpful. If not, fill in the blank to fit your situation.

I am dead to the sin of worry, but alive to God to seek first His kingdom and His righteousness, in Christ Jesus my Lord (Matthew 6:31-33).

I am dead to the sin of anxiety, but alive to God in trust, peace and faith, in Christ Jesus my Lord (Proverbs 3:5-6; Philippians 4:6-7; Matthew 17:20).

---

[7] www.merriamwebster.com

I am dead to the sin of lying, stretching the truth, exaggerating, misleading and deceiving, but alive to God by speaking the truth, offering my mouth as an instrument of righteousness, in Christ Jesus my Lord (Proverbs 8:7, 12:17, Ephesians 4:25; Romans 6:13).

I am dead to the sin of overeating, gluttony, anorexia, bulimia and emotional eating, but alive to God by honoring God with my body and treating it as a temple of the Holy Spirit, in Christ Jesus my Lord (1 Corinthians 6:19-20).

I am dead to the sin of pride, arrogance, self-righteousness and superiority, but alive to God, in humility and sober judgment, in Christ Jesus my Lord (James 4:10; Romans 12:3).

I am dead to the sin of gossip, but alive to God, in edifying speech, in Christ Jesus my Lord (Proverbs 12:18, 15:4; Ephesians 4:29).

I am dead to the sin of believing error and lies, but alive to God, in truth and healing, in Christ Jesus my Lord (John 8:32).

I am dead to the sin of lust, but alive to God, in purity and holiness, in Christ Jesus my Lord (1 Timothy 4:12, 5:2).

I am dead to the sin of laziness and procrastination, but alive to God, in diligence, work and obedience, in Christ Jesus my Lord (Proverbs 12:27, 18:9; 1 Corinthians 10:31).

What is it for you? What do you need to reckon yourself dead to and then alive to God?

I am dead to the sin of _____, but alive to God, in _____ in Christ Jesus my Lord.

Diane Hunt

1 Kings 12-13; Luke 22:24-30　　　　　　　　　　**May 2**

All My Ducks in a Row

Your word have I hidden in my heart, that I may not sin against You. (Psalm 119:11)

On a rare day we can find that everything lines up just right. They are few and far between but it is wonderful when it happens. We can look at these times as God's hand works out all of our circumstances to our advantage. But we need to be careful when everything is coming together so nicely. King David found himself in a situation where everything lined up to his advantage. 1 Samuel 24:1-5 tells us how David's circumstances lined up like ducks in a row. David was seeking refuge in a cave because Saul sought his life. Saul needed to take a "break" and just so happened to walk right into the same cave where David and his men were hiding. David's men advised him to take Saul's life while he had the chance. He was so close he could have killed him easily. It all lined up so perfectly. Even though all the circumstances lined up, David only snipped a piece from Saul's robe. It would seem that God was arranging these events so perfectly and yet David did not follow through on this golden opportunity. Why not? Beyond his circumstances, David knew the principles of God. *"The Lord forbid that I should do this thing to my master, the Lord's anointed."* David knew that killing Saul was not what God would have him do. God's commands were greater than his circumstances. He chose God's Word and principles rather than taking an easy way out.

God may be lining up all your ducks in a row. Things look good. But what will drive your decisions today? Will it be your circumstances or godly principles from the Word of God?

Kathy Withers

1 Kings 14-15; Luke 22:31-46 May 3

The Invitation

"Come now, let us reason together," says the LORD. "Though your sins are like scarlet, they shall be as white as snow; though they are red as crimson, they shall be like wool."
(Isaiah 1:18 NIV)

An invitation arrives in the mail and it invites you to "come." Most of the time when one arrives there is anticipation and excitement…who is it from? What is it for? We tear open the envelope and it invites us to come to...a wedding, a baby shower, a party, a fellowship night at the church or a hundred other occasions. I've noticed the Lord just loves sending out invitations to "come" as well. You know, He just loves us so much that He keeps sending out those invitations to "come" even though too often the invitation is turned down.

In Isaiah 1:18 (NIV) God gives an invitation for personal cleansing...come. *"Come now, let us reason together," says the LORD. "Though your sins are like scarlet, they shall be as white as snow; though they are red as crimson, they shall be like wool."*

What an invitation this is! All we have to do is "come" and the Lord promises to bleach our "dirty laundry" (sins) whiter than snow, just as if they never were!

In Isaiah 55:1, 3 (NIV) God promises to supply and satisfy...come. *"Come, all you who are thirsty, come to the waters; and you who have no money, come, buy and eat! Come, buy wine and milk without money...Give ear and come to me; hear me, that your soul may live."*

Now this is some invitation! God says "Come" and leave your wallets and credit cards at home because the price has been paid by God. These are top of the line, premium goods! There isn't even a price tag that could be placed on it....it's priceless, a picture of His grace!

In Matthew 11:28 (NIV), Jesus promises rest for the weary soul...come. *"Come to me, all you who are weary and burdened, and I will give you rest."* Many of us tend to overload ourselves with worries, anxieties, things that we don't have to carry but do...and there is Jesus, the perfect gentleman, offering to carry all that baggage and all we have to do is answer the call to "come."

In Revelation 22:17 (NIV), the Bible even ends with one final invitation...come. *The Spirit and the bride say, "Come!" And let him who hears say, "Come!" Whoever is thirsty, let him come; and whoever wishes, let him take the free gift of the water of life.*

God doesn't wish for any to perish and through the apostle John makes this final appeal to "come." God continually calls to the lost "come" and He does so over and over in His Word.

    The Lord's door is always open and the invitation stands…come.
    He is ready to receive any…come.
    The Lord accepts all who respond to His invitation…come.
    You hold His invitation in <u>your</u> hand…come.
    What will you do?
    Come.

Mary Ann Kiernan

1 Kings 16-18; Luke 22:47-71   **May 4**

Christian Emotional Activity Syndrome Experiences

Therefore, my beloved, as you have always obeyed, not as in my presence only, but now much more in my absence, work out your own salvation with fear and trembling; for it is God who works in you both to will and to do for His good pleasure.
(Philippians 2:12-13)

    Have you ever had a Christian Emotional Activity Syndrome Experience (CEASE)? This is a condition many believers have after attending or participating in a special meeting, conference, weekend retreat, short-term mission trip or some other highly moving, motivating gathering. You were challenged to some higher form of commitment, dedication or Christian involvement, left determined to make significant changes in your life, and forgot about it within a week! Then, lo and behold, another similar experience took place and you went through the same routine.

    There is a wonderful gospel song we seldom hear: "I'm So Tired of Being Stirred But Not Being Changed." Does that describe your experience?

    I'm thinking of a young lady who responded to so many different invitations at a conference center that it seemed odd if she was not at the altar! As I view her life today I see no visible evidence of follow-through on any of them.

I'm thinking of a young family man who was blind-sided by an invitation to which he responded. He didn't even intend to be in the room where the meeting was held and only heard the last five minutes of the devotional. But he followed through and today heads an organization which has world-wide involvement directly related to that challenge.

Two extremes? Perhaps. But how about you? Why not cease from CEASE?

Paul says in Philippians 2:12-13 (NLT), *Dear friends, you always followed my instructions when I was with you. And now that I am away, it is even more important. Work hard to show the results of your salvation, obeying God with deep reverence and fear. For God is working in you, giving you the desire and the power to do what pleases Him.*

Please note that God placed that desire in you and He also gives the power to do what pleases Him. Our lives are not determined by our good intentions but by the choices we make. Choose today to tap into the power He placed within you to follow through on the promptings of the Spirit you experienced when you were so deeply moved.

By the way, don't check with your Christian psychologist about CEASE. I just made that up!!!!

Rev. Neil Fichthorn

1 Kings 19-20; Luke 23:1-25   May 5

Divine Real Estate

...do you not know that your body is the temple of the Holy Spirit ... and you are not your own? (1 Corinthians 6:19)

Much is said in the Old Testament about the temple in Jerusalem. In different periods of history, it had varying degrees of splendor. Initially, when Solomon built the original structure, it was incomparable in its beauty. In subsequent years, it fell into disrepair, reflecting the spiritual condition of the people of Israel.

In the New Testament, Herod's temple must have been an impressive structure. However, it was destroyed by military forces. But prophetic writers assure us that there will be a new temple built during the millennium. It will undoubtedly be a magnificent structure suitable for the worship of the Messiah, the reigning world monarch – the King of kings.

Since there is no divinely-appointed temple at this time, where is God's presence to be centered? The apostle Paul answers that question in the words of our theme verse. God's presence is not primarily found in a building, even church buildings. In the person of the Holy Spirit, He has chosen to dwell in the bodies of believers. This is an amazing fact – God is resident in me.

Considering my body as the temple of God results in certain conclusions. First, I don't own it any longer. It has been purchased. Second, I'm merely a temporary manager with responsibility for its internal and external maintenance (v. 20). Third, all of its functions are to be to the glory of God (v. 20).

How will these truths impact and regulate our performance today?

Rev. William A. Raws

1 Kings 21-22; Luke 23:26-56 May 6

Growing Used to the Presence of God

Now it came to pass, as Aaron spoke to the whole congregation of the children of Israel, that they looked toward the wilderness, and behold, the glory of the LORD appeared in the cloud.
(Exodus 16:10)

The gracious provision of our Lord for His people can be seen in His revelation of Himself upon freeing them from the hardships and slavery of Egypt. In Exodus 13:21-22 we find that, as soon as the Hebrews had left the travelled road for the open barrenness of the wilderness, God wonderfully revealed Himself in the form of a cloud that went before them. The cloud was not just sent by Him but was the manifestation of His presence with them. The cloud by day provided cover from the oppressive heat (Psalm 105:39; Isaiah 4:5-6) and the fire by night provided light for comfort and illumination wherever God might lead them. In Exodus 14:19-20 we find that the cloud moved between the Hebrew camp and the advancing Egyptian army becoming light to God's people for crossing the sea as well as darkness to the army so as to conceal that crossing. The cloud further revealed God's presence when Moses would enter the tent of meeting and the cloud would descend to the door of the tent (Numbers 12:5). What a comfort it must have been for the freed slaves to see and know His presence!

However, just a few weeks later we come to our text in Exodus 16. After the miraculous crossing of the sea, the drowning of the Egyptian army, and the bitter water made sweet, the people now complain that God didn't let them die in Egypt where the food was plentiful. The Lord revealed to Moses that He would miraculously provide manna and meat for the people. Moses then commanded the people to gather and, as Aaron spoke to them, *...behold, the glory of the LORD appeared in the cloud*. The people had grown so used to the miraculous presence of God in the cloud that He had to reveal Himself further to them.

How often, as God's people, do we grow accustomed to the miracle of the presence of God in our lives? How is it that we can go through parts of our day acting on our own will and wisdom and ignore His presence and power? We need to be reminded of this miracle that He has provided for us! Our daily time in the spiritual disciplines of study and prayer is a reminder of how we must surrender to Him by taking up our cross daily to follow Him (Luke 9:23).

God graciously responded to His people with just the provision that they needed. In His grace He will do the same for us as we turn to Him for our needs. What a wonderful God we serve!

Dr. Joe Olachea

2 Kings 1-3; Luke 24:1-35   **May 7**

Open Your Mouth

Open your mouth for the mute, for the rights of all who are destitute. Open your mouth, judge righteously, defend the rights of the poor and the needy. (Proverbs 31:3-5 ESV)

    I try to travel through Proverbs every month. It's been a good exercise for me through the years, and I invite you to consider reading through each month; it only requires one chapter a day. It's one of the best ways I know to gain godly wisdom for living life as God designed it.

    These lines from the last chapter speak to an issue mentioned several times throughout Proverbs, which is the way God's people treat the poor and the needy. I don't know that I've lived in a time when people were so divided over how to speak for those in genuine need. Without getting into the controversy about who deserves help or who doesn't, I think we can all agree that too many people in our country, and in our world, are in need of a voice.

    Twice in these lines from Proverbs 31 the writer instructs us to *open your mouth.* The clear intent of his words is that those who can speak will speak for those who cannot. Those who have power, influence and the courage to speak to those in authority will speak for those who have no power and no influence.

    The county I live in has a huge homeless problem. Our government wants nothing to do with them. We're the only county in the state of New Jersey that has no homeless shelter, but we're spending millions of dollars for new animal shelters. Through the Proverbs writer, God calls people like me and the people of my church to "open [our] mouth."

    Those people who are poor and needy may be senior adults. They may be children. In many of our communities, they are people of color who may not even speak our language. Across our country, men and women who were employed, owned homes, and lived well are now the poor and needy. God says, *Open your mouth.*

    I confess to you that I often don't know what to say nor to

whom I should speak. I'm still instructed to speak; these verses won't let me off the hook. If we choose to follow Jesus and live by His Word, we'll care for the needy. We'll show mercy. We'll be Jesus' voice in our world, sharing His love, offering His hope, caring for those for whom He cares.

He has told you, O man, what is good; and what does the Lord require of you but to do justice, and to love kindness and to walk humbly with your God? (Micah 6:8 ESV)

Rev. John Strain

2 Kings 4-6; Luke 24:36-53 May 8

Shine as Lights

[Jesus] said, "I am the light of the world. Whoever follows me will never walk in darkness, but will have the light of life."
(John 8:12 NIV)

As I was doing my exercises, I began to see sparkling lights on the wall and ceiling. Trying to discern what was causing them, I realized that as I moved my arms and hands my rings were catching the sunlight coming through the window. As I watched the colorful display, I thought about the fact that without the sun hitting them they did not transmit the beauty that I was seeing. This made me think of my life - does it transmit the beauty of the Son within, shining forth to attract others to want to know what the cause is? The reflection of the sun on my rings got my attention. I pondered, "does His reflection in my day to day activities draw attention to Him?" Jesus said in Matthew 5:14,16 (NIV), *You are the light of the world...let your light shine before men, that they may see your good deeds and praise your Father in heaven.* And also Paul reminds us in Philippians 2:14-16, *Do all things without complaining and disputing, that you may become blameless and harmless, children of God without fault in the midst of a crooked and perverse generation, among whom you shine as lights in the world, holding fast the word of life...* We do not have to do this in our own strength though, *...for it is God who works in you both to will and to do for His good pleasure* (vs. 13). Jesus said, *"I am the light of the world. Whoever follows me will never walk in darkness, but will have the light of life"* (John 8:12). As He lives within us and His "light of life" is reflected by us in and through our lives, we will bring glory to God the Father and the Son.

Consider the following Scriptures and be challenged and encouraged to keep on "shining" and "reflecting" Him - for Him, by Him, through Him:

2 Corinthians 4:5-7 (NIV) *For we do not preach ourselves, but Jesus Christ as Lord, and ourselves as your servants for Jesus' sake. For God, who said, "Let light shine out of darkness," made his light shine in our hearts to give us the light of the knowledge of the glory of God in the face of Christ. But we have this treasure in jars of clay to show that this all-surpassing power is from God and not from us.*

2 Corinthians 3:18 (NIV) *And we, who with unveiled faces all reflect the Lord's glory, are being transformed into his likeness with ever-increasing glory, which comes from the Lord, who is the Spirit.*

Lord, let it be so. Amen.

DeEtta Marsh

2 Kings 7-9; John 1:1-28 May 9

That New Song

Sing unto him a new song; (Psalm 33:3a KJV)

The Psalmist spoke about it on several occasions. So did the prophet Isaiah who expressed it this way - *Sing unto the LORD a new song, and His praise from the ends of the earth,* (Isaiah 42:10a KJV).

That is the inspiration of anticipation. We may not know all of the reasons we experience the desire for that new song but we do know that there are times when the heart and the soul yearn for such a refreshing experience.

Such a desire is prompted by our LORD'S declaration. Isaiah passed it to us in these words, *Thus saith God the LORD, he that created the heavens, and stretched them out; he that spread forth the earth... I the LORD have called thee in righteousness, and will hold your hand, and will keep thee, and give thee for a covenant of the people, for a light of the Gentiles; To open the blind eyes, to bring out the prisoners from the prison, and them that sit in darkness out of the prison house....* **Sing unto the LORD a new song**, *and his praise from the end of the earth,...* (Isaiah 42:5-10 KJV, emphasis mine).

News like that should prompt a new song and it often does in the hearts of the weary and depressed, the lost and the heavy laden, the burdened and the bruised.

It is a song of security; *I...will hold thine hand, and will keep you.* It is a missionary song; *I will give thee ...for a light for the Gentiles*. It is a song of purpose; *... to open the blind eyes.* It is a song of emancipation; *...to bring out the prisoners from the prison, and them that sit in darkness out of the prison house.*

But our greater anticipation is that which we see in the great exaltation of our Lord Jesus. It breaks with splendor upon the scene of eternal praise and is known as The Song of the Redeemed; ***And they sung a new song***, *saying, Thou art worthy to take the book, and to open the seals thereof: for thou wast slain, and hast redeemed us to God by thy blood out of every kindred, and tongue, and people...* (Revelation 5:9 KJV, emphasis mine).

Just perhaps, are you now ready for The New Song? Are you at that time of life where you need the reality of that which is new - and eternal?

Dr. Robert L. Alderman

2 Kings 10-12; John 1:29-51 May 10

Garage Sale God

Ahh, spring time. So many things are specific to spring time. Yes, that includes a slew of garage sales, yard sales, flea markets, etc... Some of us at Keswick hold a sale early in the summer, and I live next to Keswick's perpetual yard sale – the thrift shop.

I see things come and go and often wonder, "Why in the world did they bring us that?" Or, "Who's going to want that?" It is amazing to watch people find treasures at the thrift shop. I see junk while others see potential and possibilities. Yes, I admit I sometimes find my own treasures at the thrift shop much to the dismay of my dear husband.

God has taught me another lesson as I continually watch this thrift shop process ... my God is a God of Garage Sales. Hang in there with me - while we see things as being trash, or without value... He sees the potential and the treasure in it all. This time though I'm not talking about material items - I'm talking about people. I don't know about you but I am so moved when I realize that in us He only sees our potential and our value.

Your value in Christ...to name a very few:

- You are a saint (Ephesians 1:1)
- You are God's workmanship (Ephesians 2:10)
- You are a fellow citizen in God's family (Ephesians 2:19)
- You are Christ's friend (John 15:15)
- You are a joint heir with Christ, sharing in His inheritance (Romans 8:17)
- You are righteous and holy (Ephesians 4:24)
- You are one of God's living stones, being built up in Christ as a spiritual house (1 Peter 2:5)
- You have been given the mind of Christ (1 Corinthians 2:16)
- You have been blessed with every spiritual blessing (Ephesians 1:3)
- You are Christ's home (Colossians 1:27)

He has a plan and purpose for us even when we think of ourselves as a potential garage sale item. God has no plan of selling you at a garage sale, but He will purchase you and give you value, hope and purpose.

Jeremiah 29:11, *For I know the thoughts that I think toward you, says the Lord, thoughts of peace and not of evil, to give you a future and a hope.*

Dr. Lynne Jahns

2 Kings 13-14; John 2   **May 11**

Doing It Right: The Power of Praise in the Trial of Faith

...Position yourselves, stand still and see the salvation of the LORD... (2 Chronicles 20:17)

These simple words spoken to Jehoshaphat laid out God's sure plan for victory in a time of trial. On a previous occasion, Jehoshaphat's alliance with wicked King Ahab had almost proved disastrous for this good king of Judah who should have known better than to join hands with those who hate the Lord. He had faltered miserably during a time of testing. But God in His grace mercifully brought him through that unfortunate but necessary episode to reinforce important lessons in the school of faith (2 Chronicles 18). The incident was not without rebuke from Jehu, whose words helped to reestablish the king in his walk with the Lord (2 Chronicles 19:1-4).

Now another test loomed on the horizon. This time the enemy was threefold and it came without Jehoshaphat's compromising concessions (2 Chronicles 20). Some of our problems are self-induced; others come unexpectedly and without our provocation. When Jehoshaphat received the report that his enemies were gathered against him, he set himself to seek the Lord, a good strategy when we are faced with overwhelming circumstances. Soliciting prayer support from others, Jehoshaphat strengthened himself by recalling God's faithfulness in the past, v. 7. The situation looked bleak and so the prayer went up: *...neither know we what to do, but our eyes are upon You* (v. 12).

Here is the best position for the child of God—full dependence on the Lord and reliance on His Word. To aid Jehoshaphat, the Spirit of God sent Jahaziel to encourage him as he headed into battle. The timely words must have been reassuring: *the battle is not yours, but God's* (v. 15). How gracious of God to send His faithful servants to encourage us in our time of need!

As he headed into battle, Jehoshaphat placed out front those who would praise the Lord for His mercy. The result was a sound defeat of the enemy without lifting sword or spear. The nation was enriched as Jehoshaphat led them back to Jerusalem in full praise of the victory that God had wrought and the rest that ensued. And so it is for us—praise leading to victory, victory leading to rest—the fruit of allowing the Lord to work for us to His glory.

Mark Kolchin

2 Kings 15-16; John 3:1-18 May 12

From Victim to Victory

"Come to me, all you who are weary and burdened, and I will give you rest. Take my yoke upon you and learn from me, for I am gentle and humble in heart, and you will find rest for your souls. For my yoke is easy and my burden is light."
(Matthew 11:28-30 NIV)

It is so easy for us to remain stuck in a "victim mentality" rather than live in victory through Christ. Each one of us has sinned against someone and we have been sinned against. Some hurts are so deep that we walk around ready to rip open the bandage and expose our wounds to anyone who will look so that they can know of our pain and perhaps comfort or sympathize with us. We walk around with a "placard" that says, "I've been betrayed, abandoned, cheated against, abused (physically or emotionally) or…" well, you can fill in the blank. Our tendency is to first take our hurts to our family or friends and eventually to God.

I imagine our heavenly Father with His arms opened wide waiting for us to bring all our wounds to Him. He wants to comfort and give us His strength.

God is the only One who will listen anytime night or day. He is the only One who can truly comfort us. He's the One who stands ready to take us from victim to victory. We don't discount our pain or what has happened, but God takes our pain, hurts and suffering and transforms them to treasure for His glory. We can claim victory through Christ! Our pain will no longer define who we are. It is included in the fabric of our life to make us who we are.

I remember, ever so clearly, before I was a Christian walking around, downcast all the time, saying to just about everyone, "Why me? Poor me." My teen sons were spiraling out of control in the drug world; I was in pain, miserable and hurt. I beat myself up for being a bad mom and wife. But after I gave my heart to Jesus, I began to continually cry out to Him and surrender it all to Him daily. I admit I took it back a few times. I came to know He was the only One who could give me or my family victory.

Romans 8:28 (NIV) became my reality. *And we know that in all things God works for the good of those who love him, who have been called according to his purpose.* God is in the business of transforming lives as they are surrendered to Him. Not only has my victim status been transformed to victory, but He has transformed my pain for His glory. Who but God!

Mary Ann Kiernan

2 Kings 17-18; John 3:19-36   **May 13**

Need Directions?

Blessed is the man who walks not in the counsel of the ungodly...
(Psalm 1:1a)

The other day I was in the check-out line in a store and overheard an interesting conversation. Two women were making plans to do something the next day together. One of the women said, "I wish I could say 'yes,' but I'll have to read my horoscope."

I thought, "There is a woman who wants direction in her life." If a newspaper column said it would be a good or a bad day, then she would give her "yes" or "no" to plan accordingly. I am amazed how people become addicted to this kind of thing, trying to find what their future holds and whether, through the "stars" in their daily newspaper or by other means, they should do this or that.

You should do what I did the other day. I took two different newspapers and looked at the horoscopes they ran. Do you know what I found? I read two completely contradictory horoscopes for the same sign. It might be wise for those who are "hooked" on reading horoscopes to do the same thing.

But there is a better choice. As those who have come to know Jesus Christ as our personal Savior, we have God as our guide. Who needs to walk in the counsel of the ungodly?

In Psalm 32:8, God promises, *I will instruct you and teach you in the way you should go; I will guide you with My eye.* In Psalm 1:6 we are told that the Lord *knows the way of the righteous.*

In a real sense we sin and slap God in the face when we choose to seek the horoscope of the day. Our todays and tomorrows are in God's hands; He knows the way.

Look to Him, believer, for His direction!

Rev. John Hibbard

2 Kings 19-21; John 4:1-30   **May 14**

Shout to the World, "He Lives"

"You are the light of the world. A city that is set on a hill cannot be hidden." (Matthew 5:14)

The knowledge that Jesus Christ is alive and lives in me produces a sense of peace that passes all understanding, especially in times of challenges and trouble. I look back over my life and see how He has taken me through difficult times and carried my burdens, made my yoke light and protected me. Without this knowledge made known to me by and through Christ, my life would be meaningless, almost unbearable at times. I can't think of anything better to know in my life! It is a gift that I wouldn't have today if not shared by someone else. The question I must ask myself is this, "Am I doing my part in sharing this gift of peace with others?"

When I was in the Air Force, a young Lieutenant enthusiastically shared this knowledge with me. Afterwards I wanted to tell all those around me. I joined a local church to grow in my knowledge of the Word of God, became involved in activities at church and Bible studies, made new friends and spent less time with the old group of friends. Outside of church and work, I didn't make time to do anything else. I steadily became critical of my old friends and the choices they made. The tragedy of all of this was that I stopped sharing my faith with those around me. In time, I began reflecting on Christ's great commission in Matthew 28. He didn't say to go and hang with the disciples, but instead go and make disciples! God made me realize that as much as I need to be refreshed in His Word, so did others and they weren't going to automatically come to Him. I needed to take it to them.

Am I approachable to those who don't know Christ and are searching for answers? Do people feel comfortable sharing their burdens with me with no judgment? Do I make myself available to those outside my group of friends at church? Is my heart broken for those lost, who live in this world without the same peace that dwells within us, whose eternal salvation is hopeless without Christ?

Church is important, a place for enrichment and growth. It is very special to Christ; it is His bride and He loves it. Does the world know this? Or do we keep the light of the truth hidden?

Bernie Bostwick

2 Kings 22-23; John 4:31-54 **May 15**

The Faith Life

...the life which I now live in the flesh, I live by faith in the Son of God, who loved me and gave Himself for me. (Galatians 2:20)

Following a statement of what has been called "The Exchanged Life," the apostle Paul testifies to the fact that this life, which is actually His life in me, must be worked out on my daily path. If I were to claim the doctrinal truth of the previous part of the verse without translating it into the practice declared in the second, it would be a mere intellectual exercise. The principle which brings reality is faith. I live by faith in the One who lives in me. The recognition of the facts of my death in His death and my spiritual life found in His life can only become reality on the basis of faith.

The faith we're talking about is more than a formal statement of a doctrinal position. It is a functional commitment of trust in the indwelling Person to live out His life in us. The sequence moves us from mere recognition of our position to the realization of His indwelling presence and then to reliance on His power.

It should be noted that faith is not to be placed in oneself, one's closest friend, one's church, etc. It is to be faith in the Son of God. People often say, "My faith is not that strong," or "I wish I had your faith." That's because they are thinking of faith as the object rather than the instrument. We are never told in Scripture to have faith in our faith. The effectiveness of faith depends on its object. It is possible to have strong faith in a wrong object and be terribly disappointed. But we shall never be disappointed if our faith is in the Son of God.

If we believe that the victorious Christ lives in us, we must also believe that He wants to live His life through us. For this to become a reality, we must yield ourselves to Him for the expression of His victorious power through us (Romans 6:13b). This must become a constant process rather than a single act. Such a life of faith and yieldedness does not release me from responsibility for an active obedience to His commands. Letting go and letting God must be accompanied by the disciplined performance of His will.

Rev. William A. Raws

2 Kings 24-25; John 5:1-24 May 16

God's Provision

And my God shall supply all your need according to His riches in glory by Christ Jesus. (Philippians 4:19)

God wants us to learn how to face life with joy and confidence. Now, you may be thinking, "How is this possible when trials, troubles and heartaches come our way?" My friend, we must learn to be content in all circumstances in this life.

Here is a great truth that I pray God will fix in your heart and mind for the rest of your life. The truth is this, "God alone, and what God provides for me is all that I need." Right now, in your mind, I want you to picture a circle, and let this circle represent God. When you became a child of God, He placed you in Christ. Picture yourself in Christ. Name one thing that God needs. He needs nothing. You are in Him, and all that He has is yours. Paul said in 1 Corinthians 1:30, *But of Him you are in Christ Jesus...* He also said this in Ephesians 1:3, *Blessed be the God and Father of our Lord Jesus Christ, who has blessed us with every spiritual blessing in the heavenly places in Christ....*

When this truth is not known, we have a wrong belief that we need something other than God, and what God has provided for us. This causes thoughts like these: "I must have this person's love to meet my needs;" " I must punish myself for my past sins;" "God is not able to take care of me."

How can you experience this great truth? You must remember, God alone and what God provides for you is all that you need. My friend, I want to encourage you this day to begin to think this way. Proverbs 23:7 says, *For as he thinks in his heart, so is he.* This is the biblical way to think, which we know is God's way for us to think and live our lives. It may take you some time to adjust yourself to this simple truth, but I promise this is the way to live life at its very best. This is the roadmap for you to live life on a higher plane. Choose to walk in this truth with simple childlike faith, until you walk in this truth by faith without choosing. Being mindful of God's provision brings genuine joy and confidence.

Rev. Chris S. Hodges

1 Chronicles 1-3; John 5:25-47   **May 17**

How Much Do You Love Me?

For God so loved the world that He gave His only begotten Son, that whoever believes in Him should not perish but have everlasting life. (John 3:16)

After my husband tells me he loves me I have gotten into the habit of asking him, "How much?" I just want him to come up with creative ways to tell me! Usually he rolls his eyes not knowing how to answer me differently than he already has. Malachi 1:2 says, *"I have loved you," says the Lord, "Yet you say 'In what way have You loved us?'"* I can ask God the same question. When trials have come into my life I don't always feel, see or trust that God loves me. "How much can You love me and let _____ happen?" If You loved me so much You would _____." Maybe hearing "Jesus loves you" has become so familiar we don't even hear it anymore. Perhaps we have lost the awe of God's love for us.

While working on a Bible study I was led to read John 3:16. I was ready to skip over the verse. I know this one by heart. I have read it so many times. Did I really need to even look at it again? I turned to the passage half-heartedly but God showed me again just how much He loves me. He showed me that He is love, the giver of love. He is a Redeemer, Savior and Provider of eternal life. In this very familiar verse He showed me again how much He loves me and how that was proven by Jesus Christ's death and resurrection. I just needed to come to that familiar verse willing to hear Him tell me again just how much He loves me.

Let me encourage you to read a verse or two about God's

love. Don't just read it but ask Him, "How much do You love me?" He never gets tired of telling you and He can be very creative with His answers!

Kathy Withers

1 Chronicles 4-6; John 6:1-21   **May 18**

The Danger of Secret Sin

So the Lord said to Joshua: "Get up! Why do you lie thus on your face? Israel has sinned, and they have also transgressed My covenant which I commanded them. For they have even taken some of the accursed things, and have both stolen and deceived; and they have also put it among their own stuff."
(Joshua 7:10-11)

    Have you ever committed a sin and then tried to hide the thing you have done? I think it would be safe to say that most Christians have a *Watergate* in their lives.

    The text before us reveals a sobering lesson about the danger of trying to hide our sins from God. Joshua, the great military leader of Israel, had just experienced a remarkable, supernatural victory at Jericho (6:1-27). In chapter seven Joshua apparently felt that he did not need God for the smaller battles so he went in his own strength to Ai and experienced a brutal defeat. (There is a lesson to be learned here.) It was the public humiliation of the defeat at Ai that brought Joshua to his knees and it was while he was praying that God instructed him get up, stop praying and deal with the sin in the camp. There was a hidden sin that caused the defeat.

    In Joshua 6:26, the Lord instructed Joshua that nothing was to be taken from the rubble of the destroyed city of Jericho. However, a man named Achan wandered into the city and took gold, silver and an expensive Babylonian garments and hid these things in his tent. Achan thought he had committed the perfect crime. He thought no one would ever know. Isn't this the way we are with our sins? We think no one will ever know. But God always knows our thoughts and our actions.

Over the years I have observed that the family and friends of someone who is living in sin actually sees the results of his sin before he does. A wife sees her husband's sins. A child sees his parent's sins. An employer sees the employee's sin.

Achan's sin was exposed in three different ways. Your sins will reveal themselves in similar ways.

1. Sin brings defeat. The defeat at Ai was a result of hidden sin.

2. Sin hinders prayer. God told Joshua to stop praying. There was no need to pray until sin had been confessed.

3. Sin hurts others. The entire nation suffered as a result of Achan's sin.

Spiritual *Watergates* never work. Come clean with God.

Dr. Roger D. Willmore

1 Chronicles 7-9; John 6:22-44　　　　　　　　　　**May 19**

The Dangerous Progression of Sin

And Achan answered Joshua and said, "Indeed I have sinned against the LORD God of Israel, and this is what I have done: When I saw among the spoils a beautiful Babylonian garment, two hundred shekels of silver, and a wedge of gold weighing fifty shekels, I coveted them and took them. And there they are, hidden in the earth in the midst of my tent, with the silver under it." (Joshua 7:20-21)

Achan stands before us a real life example of the dangerous progression of sin. His actions reveal where sin begins and ends.

Where does sin begin? It always begins in the heart. Many years ago I heard Dr. James Dobson on his radio program, Focus on the Family, say, "Sin is always consented to in the private recesses of the heart before it is acted upon in deed."

Notice what Achan said when he confessed his sin to Joshua.

1. *When I saw among the spoils…*(v.21). He is acknowledging the role his eyes played in his sinful actions. It is

true that our eyes are the gateway to our soul. The devil knows this quite well and he has led many to perfect the trade of appealing to the eye. Jesus drove this point home very powerfully in the Sermon on the Mount when He said, *But I say to you that whoever looks at a woman to lust for her has already committed adultery with her in his heart* (Matthew 5:28).

2. *I coveted them…*(v.21). This was Achan's second confession. What had gone into his eye had now moved down to his heart and had stirred up covetousness.

3. *I took them…*(v.21.). Achan admits that he saw, he coveted and he took the things from Jericho. What went through the eye to the heart found its way to his hand. Now Achan's hand accommodates his heart by taking the forbidden thing.

4. *I hid them in the earth…*(v.21). Achan now hides what he has done, just as Adam and Eve covered their nakedness with leaves and hid in the bushes. Man's instinct is to hide his sin, but it cannot be hidden.

Beware of the dangerous progression of sin.

Dr. Roger D. Willmore

1 Chronicles 10-12; John 6:45-71   **May 20**

Master the Flesh

So I find this law at work: When I want to do good, evil is right there with me. For in my inner being I delight in God's law; but I see another law at work in the members of my body, waging war against the law of my mind and making me a prisoner of the law of sin at work within my members. What a wretched man I am! Who will rescue me from this body of death? Thanks be to God – through Jesus Christ our Lord! (Romans 7:21-25 NIV)

If we are all honest, we understand totally what Paul is saying, don't we? Most of us really want to do the right things, live the right way – BUT – there is this thing called the FLESH that keeps getting in the way.

Part of the battle is that for most of us, we are TRYING to live the Christian life in our own strength. Well as Pastor Bill

Raws always said, "It is absolutely impossible to live the Christian life apart from Jesus Christ living His perfect life in and through me." That is the message of Galatians 2:20.

A friend recently showed me the verse in The Message: *...I have been crucified with Christ. My ego is no longer central. It is no longer important that I APPEAR righteous before you or have your good opinion, and I am no longer driven to impress God. Christ lives in me. The life you see me living is not "mine," but it is lived by the faith in the Son of God, who loved me and gave Himself for me...* (Galatians 2:20).

The problem is that we haven't figured out three things about the flesh: 1) It can control us, 2) It isn't something we can play with, 3) We need to put it to death.

Our flesh was already crucified with Christ on the cross. It no longer needs to master us. We get ourselves into trouble because we want to keep it alive rather than put it to death. Christ has come to give us victory over the flesh! More about this tomorrow. The good news is that JESUS CHRIST has come to give you and me VICTORY!

Dr. Bill Welte

1 Chronicles 13-15; John 7:1-27   **May 21**

Paul's Words on the Flesh

Yesterday we talked about the flesh. I want to share with you today what Paul wrote about the flesh. It doesn't take a rocket scientist to figure out what God wants us to know about the flesh. The Scripture makes it quite clear:

Romans 6:17-20: *But God be thanked that though you were slaves of sin, yet you obeyed from the heart that form of doctrine to which you were delivered. And having been set free from sin, you became slaves of righteousness. I speak in human terms because of the weakness of your flesh. For just as you presented your members as slaves of uncleanness, and of lawlessness leading to more lawlessness, so now present your members as slaves of righteousness for holiness. For when you were slaves of sin, you were free in regard to righteousness.*

Romans 8:5: *For those who live according to the flesh set their minds on the things of the flesh, but those who live according to the Spirit, the things of the Spirit.*

Romans 8:8: *So then, those who are in the flesh cannot please God.*

Romans 8:13: *For if you live according to the flesh you will die; but if by the Spirit you put to death the deeds of the body, you will live.*

Romans 13:14: *But put on the Lord Jesus Christ, and make no provision for the flesh, to fulfill its lust.*

2 Corinthians 7:1: *Therefore, having these promises, beloved, let us cleanse ourselves from all filthiness of the flesh and spirit, perfecting holiness in the fear of God.*

Galatians 5:24: *I say then: Walk in the Spirit, and you shall not fulfill the lust of the flesh.*

I don't think I could make it any clearer than that for you. Allow the Holy Spirit to speak to your heart as you read over the above verses. Might be good for us to memorize them as well. I appreciate you, my friends, and thank you for being on the journey with me.

Dr. Bill Welte

1 Chronicles 16-18; John 7:28-53   **May 22**

The Land of Good Intentions

But be doers of the word, and not hearers only... (James 1:22)

Some years ago at a meeting at Keswick, I heard a message on Romans 12:1 (ESV). *I appeal to you therefore, brothers, by the mercies of God, to present your bodies as a living sacrifice, holy and acceptable to God, which is your spiritual worship.* Developing that verse, the speaker went on to say, "The problem with a living sacrifice is that it can crawl off the altar."

"How clever!" I said to myself. And then the embarrassing truth of that statement hit me! Years before, I had embraced the challenge of offering myself as a living sacrifice to God, and I was quite comfortable with my good Christian intention. Now, however, I had to do some serious rethinking. Had I crawled off the altar?

I realized I frequently lived in "the land of good intentions." Sometimes that is my comfort zone. I satisfy my pricking conscience by saying, "Yes, I must do so and so, but not just now!" So there I go again, crawling in the wrong direction! What does that cavalier attitude do to my relationship with the Lord?

It does not please Him, I'm sure. Will I go too far someday? Will I crawl off the altar one time too many? Will my propensity to intend to do something good and then not do it cause me to experience no longer His continued lovingkindness and blessings?

As I pondered those questions that pertain to my well-being as a Christian, to my dedication to keep my promise to give my life as a sacrifice to Him, I suddenly remembered reading *"My Spirit will not always strive with man."* (Genesis 6:3) That's the Truth! Therefore, I need to forsake "the land of good intentions." I need to get back on the altar, and I need to be careful to give the Lord preeminence in my life so once again I can bring Him pleasure and joy. And once again, I can receive the benefits of His lovingkindness, His grace, and His amazing love!

> Dear Father God, accept me back on your altar.
> And farewell to the land of good intentions.

Midge Ruth

1 Chronicles 19-21; John 8:1-27   May 23

Can You Pass the Tests?

Now it happened as they journeyed on the road, that someone said to Him, "Lord, I will follow You wherever You go." And Jesus said to him, "Foxes have holes and birds of the air have nests, but the Son of Man has nowhere to lay His head." Then He said to another, "Follow Me." But he said, "Lord, let me first go and bury my father." Jesus said to him, "Let the dead bury their own dead, but you go and preach the kingdom of God." And another also said, "Lord, I will follow You, but let me first go and bid them farewell who are at my house." But Jesus said to him, "No one, having put his hand to the plow, and looking back, is fit for the kingdom of God." (Luke 9:57-62)

One of the common threads in this story is that each of the men addressed Jesus as Lord. They used the word that means master, owner or boss. They indicated in their words that they were submissive servants to their Lord and Master; however, they also made statements that contradicted their use of the word Lord.

Jesus gave each of the men a test to reveal to him that he did not fully understand the claims he had made. If you call Jesus Lord of your life, then you need to be ready to take the tests that will either verify or negate your claims.

What if every Christian had to take a test to validate the authenticity of his claim? Well, in reality every Christian does need to pass the tests Jesus gives.

The first test is the test of poverty. When Jesus said, *"Foxes have holes and the birds of the air have nests, but the Son of Man has nowhere to lay His head,"* He was telling the man that sacrifice was required of those who follow Him. This sacrifice includes the Christian's time, talent and treasure.

The second test is a test of urgency. When Jesus said, *"Let the dead bury their own dead,"* He was not being cruel or callous. The man's father was not dead at that moment. He was actually asking for permission to go home and wait until his father passed away and his inheritance was in hand. The inheritance would be his "safety net" in case serving Jesus did not work out. He had no concept of the urgency of serving Christ. Dr. Stephen Olford used to say, "Delayed obedience is disobedience."

The third test is a test of sovereignty. When Jesus said, *"No one, having put his hand to the plow, and looking back, is fit for the kingdom of God,"* He was saying Lordship excludes other pre-occupations. It requires singular focus.

Did you pass the tests? It is a serious matter to call Jesus Christ Lord.

Dr. Roger D. Willmore

1 Chronicles 22-24; John 8:28-41   **May 24**

Are You Grieved?

Therefore we do not lose heart...for our light affliction, which is but for a moment, is working for us a far more exceeding and eternal weight of glory. (2 Corinthians 4:16a, 17)

Friend, are you grieving over something in your life? Do you feel weighed down by a trial, a hardship, a failure, an affliction, the loss of a loved one?

The apostle Peter offers rich insight for the child of God as to how to respond. In 1 Peter 1:6 we read: *In this you greatly rejoice, though now for a little while, if need be, you have been grieved by various trials.* In our grief, Peter exhorts: *greatly rejoice.* I dare say that is the least of our proclivities in the midst of our various trials! And yet, he goes on to repeat once more in verse 8: *you rejoice with joy inexpressible and full of glory.* Our response to grief is to rejoice.

Let's go back to the verses which precede *In this you greatly rejoice,* and we will discover in WHAT we are to rejoice. In Peter's text, *In this* refers not to the cancer, the job loss, the heartache, the failure, etc ... (although we are to be thankful and rejoice that <u>through</u> our trials, God is working all things together for our good). Peter is exhorting us to rejoice in our God and Savior! Here Peter is articulating exactly what will most tip the scales of our hearts and enable us to rejoice and help offset the weight of grief.

Peter is saying rejoice in His mercy upon us! Rejoice that we have been born again! Rejoice that our Savior is risen! (v. 3) Rejoice in our incorruptible inheritance which will not fade away! Rejoice that we are kept and secure through our faith in Him! (v.4)

Dear friend, as we focus on these realities, we will enjoy a heightened capacity to rejoice in and through each and every trial. Through our trial, we will see the treasure. Through our testing, we will see the triumph. Through our problem, we will see the promise. Through our pain, we will see the prospect. Through our burden, we will see the Bearer. And through the suffering, we will see the Savior! *In THIS you greatly rejoice!*

Bevan Greiner

1 Chronicles 25-27; John 8:42-59 May 25

Broken Unto Usefulness

The sacrifices of God are a broken spirit, A broken and a contrite heart— These, O God, You will not despise.
(Psalm 51:17)

There appears to be an inconsistency in the biblical instruction concerning the subject of brokenness. Much devotional writing and pulpit preaching focuses on spiritual brokenness as related to holiness and service. The thought expressed is that the Christian must come to the place of being emptied of self seeking and be submitted to the will of God. One of the biblical illustrations of this may be found in the account of Mary's breaking the alabaster flask and anointing Jesus with its contents of costly oil (Mark 13:2). The use of the contents required breaking its container. Apart from the breaking there would be no blessing.

Essentially, brokenness is brought about in the life of a Christian through the conviction of the Spirit, His ownership claim seen in the Word of God, and the pressure of circumstances. In some instances suffering and sorrow might be used as agents.

Some years ago Keswick was given a riding horse which had been on the open range for many months. He hadn't been saddled or ridden. It fell to my lot to be the one to "break" this animal so that he could be useful. It didn't take me long to realize that this horse had a mind of his own. His will had to become broken to mine. Following some rough encounters, he gave up the struggle and became useable. On each subsequent occasion the horse recalled who was in charge.

Perhaps the experience of a believer may be likened to Jacob's wrestling with the Lord until submission took place (Genesis 32:24-32). For him, a physical affliction became the continuing reminder that he was not in charge.

What might appear as an inconsistency is the requirement for a sacrificial offering in the Old Testament. God demanded wholeness and an unblemished condition for these. Why was brokenness not permitted in this case? The answer is that these sacrifices portrayed Christ – the perfect offering. He fully satisfied the demands of the law as an unblemished sacrifice. Not a bone of His was broken. Since He came to do the will of the Father and performed it perfectly, He needed no crisis of brokenness. Even as He prayed in Gethsemane on the night of His betrayal, His repeated declaration was, "Not as I will, but as You will."

Rev. William A. Raws

1 Chronicles 28-29; John 9   **May 26**

God's Delight

Delight yourself in the LORD, and he will give you the desires of your heart. (Psalm 37:4 ESV)

Because of our sin nature many of us will focus on the last part of this verse and only think about the desires of our heart. But this is not a blank check; rather it is the result of what when we delight in the Lord. We will never delight in the Lord if we are only thinking about our desires.

Our sin nature keeps us from naturally delighting in the Lord. As we grow in our relationship with God we will learn how to delight in Him; it is part of our walk of faith. Our walk with God is not a religion but a relationship. A religion would make things much easier as it would be based on what we do, such as praying a set number of times each day or reading a certain number of chapters in the Bible. The relationship starts with the confession of the fact that there is nothing that we can do that will make us righteous before the Lord, and the acceptance of the sacrifice of Jesus that does make us righteous before Him. This is the first step of faith in our journey to spend eternity with Him.

As we walk by faith, we delight in the Lord by trusting in Him as we go through what each day brings. Proverbs 3:5 (ESV) tells us, *Trust in the LORD with all your heart, and do not lean on your own understanding.* Our natural tendency is to need to understand. But how can we understand a God whose ways are so far above anything we can understand? We need to trust in the Lord based on His promises: to protect us, to keep our paths straight, to work all things together for good, to discipline in love. He will bring us into situations that all of our human logic will tell us that we can never get out of, and then He will get us out in such a way that there is no doubt that He did it. Lessons like this increase our faith in Him and our delight.

Our walk of faith brings us to the place that we start to see that delight is a two-way street: God also delights in us. We know the basic fact *Jesus loves me*, but as our faith deepens we start to see that the love of God for us holds no limitations and He truly delights in us as a loving Father.

Allen E. Beltle

2 Chronicles 1-3; John 10:1-21   May 27

Show Forth the Beauty of the Lord

And let the beauty of the LORD our God be upon us, and establish the work of our hands for us; Yes, establish the work of our hands. (Psalm 90:17)

The beauty of the Lord should not abide only on nature and other created life. The beauty of the Lord should abide upon those of us who know the Lord Jesus Christ as our personal Savior. We should join the psalmist in his prayer, *...let the beauty of the Lord our God be upon us.*

The beauty of the Lord's kindness, compassion, mercy, grace and love should be upon us. We should show forth this beauty in the practical aspects of life. We should reflect the beauty of the Lord in the course of daily routine.

The psalmist reminds us that the beauty of the Lord can be lost. Just as a moth eats away silently and secretly, destroying a beautiful garment, sin can eat away the beauty of the Lord from our lives. *When with rebukes You correct man for iniquity, You make his beauty melt away like a moth; surely every man is vapor* (Psalm 39:11).

If you have lost the beauty of the Lord, take courage, it can be found and restored. The Lord says that He will...*console those who mourn in Zion, to give them beauty for ashes...* (Isaiah 61:3).

The beauty of the Lord comes upon the repentant person. If you desire to have the beauty of the Lord upon your life, then you must turn away from the things that destroy the beauty of the Lord. Have you ever seen beautiful gossip? Have you ever seen a beautiful mean spirit? Have you ever seen a beautiful spirit of jealousy? Have you ever seen a beautiful bad temper? No, the beauty of the Lord cannot be found in such things.

Today you have the opportunity to reveal the beauty of the Lord that is waiting and watching. Ask the Lord to bestow His beauty upon you.

Dr. Roger D. Willmore

2 Chronicles 4-6; John 10:22-42   **May 28**

Rejoice in the Lord Always

Rejoice in the Lord always. Again I will say, rejoice! Let your gentleness be known to all men. The Lord is at hand. Be anxious for nothing, but in everything by prayer and supplication, with thanksgiving, let your requests be made known to God; and the peace of God, which surpasses all understanding, will guard your hearts and minds through Christ Jesus. Finally, brethren, whatever things are true, whatever things are noble, whatever things are just, whatever things are pure, whatever things are lovely, whatever things are of good report, if there is any virtue and if there is anything praiseworthy—meditate on these things. The things which you learned and received and heard and saw in me, these do, and the God of peace will be with you.
(Philippians 4:4-9)

    Some commands are easy to obey, but sometimes the command "rejoice in the Lord always" is difficult to obey. It is easy to rejoice when everything is going great but quite another thing to rejoice when we are facing trials. When I was a student at Philadelphia College of Bible (PCB), I spent my summers working at Sandy Cove Bible Conference. In fact, I had the privilege of singing in the very first Choraliers directed by Chuck Pugh. I also worked in the bookstore with Horace Perkins.

    Horace was a unique man. He ran the bookstore and played either the organ or piano for every service at Sandy Cove. I never heard him complain with all he had to do. He was an absolute joy to be around. I especially remember one occasion when he went to the Baltimore/Washington International Airport to pick up his mother-in-law. There was a hard driving rain that day and on the way back from the airport Horace had a flat tire! I can still see him out there in the rain changing a tire and singing a hymn. I wonder what most of us would do if we were in the same situation.

    Years later, I was on my way from the church in western Pennsylvania, where I was then pastor, to Philadelphia in order to participate in an Alumni Council Meeting at PCB. It was pouring down rain and I was the one with a flat tire! This brought back the memory of Horace in the rain singing a hymn. For Horace, the joy of the Lord definitely was his strength and he truly rejoiced.

Another admonition is *In everything give thanks; for this is the will of God in Christ Jesus concerning you* (1 Thessalonians 5:18). Verse 16 simply says, *Rejoice evermore.* This is what I saw in Horace that day, thanks and rejoicing. Is this difficult? Yes, but it is the will of God and we will be blessed as we obey this command of the Lord.

Dr. George L. Nichols, Jr.

2 Chronicles 7-9; John 11:1-29   **May 29**

Broken To Be Given

Then He commanded the multitudes to sit on the grass. And He took the five loaves and the two fish, and looking up to heaven, He blessed and broke and gave the loaves to the disciples; and the disciples to the multitudes. (Matthew 14:19)

On Sunday morning, July 26, 2009, I stood in the pulpit at the Colony of Mercy Chapel at America's Keswick with my Bible opened to Matthew 14:13-21 and a bottle of Pepto Bismol® in my hand. I can remember the morning as though it were yesterday, because I knew most of the people in the audience that day could identify with what I was about to say. I read the passage of Scripture and then I held up the well-known bottle of pink medicine and read from the label, **Shake well before using**.

The stage is set! Herod had just murdered John the Baptist. Jesus was grieving the death of His cousin, friend and forerunner. In His grief, Jesus withdrew to a place of solitude and rest. However, He found Himself surrounded by 5000 (when women and children were added to the number, since only the men were counted, the number could have been around 20,000 people).

The disciples wanted to send the people home. Jesus instructed the disciples to give the people something to eat. The disciples informed Jesus that they did not have the resources to feed so many people.

Do you ever feel that the demands upon your life surpass your ability to meet those demands? Two facts faced the disciples: 1) They were overwhelmed by the enormity of the need. Almost 20,000 hungry people stood before them waiting to be fed. 2) They were overwhelmed by the inadequacy on their part to meet the need.

In John 6:9, we learn that Andrew found a lad in the crowd who had five loaves and two fish. However, what good was this small portion when so many needed to be fed?

The miracle occurred in verse 19, when Jesus *broke and gave*. A great lesson is taught here. It is not our strength that the Lord needs, it is our brokenness.

A.W. Tozer once said, "It is doubtful that God will use a man greatly, until He has hurt him deeply."

Shake well before using. Are you ready to be broken in order to be used by the Master?

Dr. Roger D. Willmore

2 Chronicles 10-12; John 11:30-57   May 30

My God

But as for me, I trust in You, O LORD; I say, "You are my God."
(Psalm 31:14)

My God. Those two simple words are strikingly profound. Meditating on them almost creates a conflict in our minds.

God, Creator, Sustainer of all things. He is all mighty and powerful. He is all knowing and all wise. He is equally everywhere all the time. He is Alpha and Omega, Beginning and End. He is the Great I AM. He is our environment. In Him we live and breathe and have our being. He is the giver and taker of life. He is sovereignly in control of all things. He is the redeemer of His people. He calls the stars into place each by name. He is love and truth. He is Holy and pure. He is righteous and just. There is none like Him; there is no other.

To say He is my God takes all those things and more that faintly describe the One True God and says He is not just a God, nor that He is the God, nor that He is God, but that He is MY God, personally and intimately known by my finite heart and mind.

Meditate on this simple thought today -- MY GOD -- and feel your heart swell with the reality of this truth. Hallelujah!!

Diane Hunt

2 Chronicles 13-14; John 12:1-26 May 31

Recall What God Remembers

...Thus says the LORD, "I remember you, the kindness of your youth..." (Jeremiah 2:2)

Have you ever noticed that we tend to remember what we should forget, and forget what we should remember? Well here are some questions and thoughts from the pen of Oswald Chambers (My Utmost For His Highest) that are worth our consideration today:

"1. Am I as spontaneously kind to God as I used to be, or am I only expecting God to be kind to me?

2. Does everything in my life fill His heart with gladness, or do I constantly complain because things don't seem to be going my way? A person who has forgotten what God treasures will not be filled with joy. It is wonderful to remember that Jesus Christ has needs which we can meet— "Give Me a drink" (John 4:7).

3. How much kindness have I shown Him in the past week?

4. Has my life been a good reflection on His reputation? God is saying to His people, "You are not in love with Me now, but I remember a time when you were." He says, "I remember . . . the love of your betrothal . . ." (Jeremiah 2:2).

5. Am I as filled to overflowing with love for Jesus Christ as I was in the beginning, when I went out of my way to prove my devotion to Him?

6. Does He ever find me pondering the time when I cared only for Him?

7. Is that where I am now, or have I chosen man's wisdom over true love for Him?

8. Am I so in love with Him that I take no thought for where He might lead me?

9. Or am I watching to see how much respect I get as I measure how much service I should give Him?

As I recall what God remembers about me, I may also begin to realize that He is not what He used to be to me. When this happens, I should allow the shame and humiliation it creates in my life, because it will bring godly sorrow, and "godly sorrow produces repentance . . ." (2 Corinthians 7:10)."

Take some time to work through these questions today. Recall today what GOD remembers.

Dr. Bill Welte

---

2 Chronicles 15-16; John 12:27-50　　　　　　　　**June 1**

Fast Food or Gourmet?

They who wait for the Lord... (Isaiah 40:31 ESV)

Today I want to share two possible examples of waiting. One I'll call <u>fast food</u> and the other <u>gourmet</u>. I choose this illustration because it quickly brings a picture to mind that makes a clear distinction between these two types of meals.

As someone who enjoys eating, I can tell you without hesitation that I get pleasure from both fast food <u>and</u> gourmet. However, you don't have to be a rocket scientist to know that one is definitely better than the other.

Fast food is just that, <u>fast</u>. We rush in, inhale it quickly to fill the void, and just as quickly get back to the busyness of our day. Our tummies are full, our appetites momentarily satiated and our desire for food is no longer pressing in on us.

<u>Gourmet</u>, on the other hand, requires lots of time. Ingredients must be gathered and prepared. Each course having

its own steps, details all fixed on the presentation of delightful flavors and an experience our palate won't soon forget.

There is no rushing. Focused attention to each course is essential for the end result and the final presentation. Whether it's a three, five or seven-course meal, you sit for the full length of time required, savoring each delectable bite, allowing the senses to be aroused. You rarely, if ever, rush away from gourmet.

Why? You're usually so satisfied that all you want is to sit still and marvel over its goodness. When you <u>do</u> get up, it isn't to rush away and get busy, but rather to sit in a comfortable chair and revel.

Now take a leap and imagine the difference it would make in our everyday lives if our time with God was more often than not <u>gourmet</u>. Believe me, I am fully aware of the arguments that can be made for time. Gourmet requires time, and fast food, is after all, still food and most definitely meets the need.

My question for you is simple: does it really meet the deepest need your soul and spirit have for the Father, the One who is the Lover of your soul?

I, for one, know from first-hand experience that in the natural and in the spiritual, fast food is not enough to keep you healthy and strong.

May we choose today to plan, prepare and enjoy a gourmet meal with *Him who was and is and is to come.*

I have not departed from the commandment of His lips; I have treasured the words of His mouth more than my necessary food.
As the deer pants for the water brooks,
so pants my soul for You, O God. (Job 23:12, Psalm 42:1)

Stephanie D. Paul

2 Chronicles 17-18; John 13:1-20   **June 2**

God Never Gives You More Than You Can Bear...

Years ago I believed this came from Scripture...or at least that it was a biblical truth. I said it many times, and tried to find comfort in that statement for myself. And yet, it seemed as if what I observed all around me was the exact opposite. So what is the truth?

My eyes were opened during a Bible study called <u>The Grace Walk Experience</u> by Dr. Steve McVey. We were asked to examine 2 Corinthians 1:8-9 (NIV), *We do not want you to be uninformed, brothers, about the hardships we suffered in the province of Asia. We were under great pressure, <u>far beyond our ability to endure</u>, so that we despaired even of life. Indeed, in our hearts we felt the sentence of death. But this happened that we might <u>not rely on ourselves but on God</u>, who raises the dead* (emphasis mine).

It's all in there...the truth about the trials and suffering that comes into our lives. I would never compare the hardships or trials in my life to that which the Apostle Paul endured but I've had some hard times that have taken me into the pit. In these verses, Paul tells us the hardships that he and his companions went through were just <u>too</u> much for them to handle...it went far beyond what they could physically, mentally and emotionally endure. They couldn't bear the strain and the pain. It was so bad that they really just wanted to die so that they would escape the unbearable circumstances. But why would God allow them to get to this unbearable state?

Paul came to realize it was <u>all</u> in the hands of God. Their <u>very lives</u> had to be surrendered into God's hands. There wasn't a thing they could do to save themselves or ease their suffering. And <u>that</u> was where God wanted them to be...the place where they would give up their *self* sufficiency and rest in *His* sufficiency.

God tries to get our attention. As I look back on my trials, I see He was trying to get my attention but I kept trying to control and handle everything on my own. It was only when I came to the end of my *self* sufficiency that I was able to see that is was all about God's sufficiency and not about mine.

No, I don't believe the statement "God never gives you more than you can bear" any more. It's a bit scary, I have to admit. But I have seen in my own life that...I can't...but He can. Instead of relying on my self sufficiency (really non-existent) I need to rely totally on His sufficiency.

MaryAnn Kiernan

2 Chronicles19-20; John 13:21-38   **June 3**

Come To Me and Rest

Come unto me, all ye that labour and are heavy laden, and I will give you rest. (Matthew 11:28 KJV)

One of the devotional tools I have been using the past two years is Spurgeon's Chequebook of the Bank of Faith. I am addicted to leather-bound devotionals, and while you can get this in paperback from Amazon or CBD, Christian Heritage Publications has a nice little leather-bound edition.

Spurgeon's January 14th devotional really spoke to my heart and I wanted to share it with you:

"We who are saved find rest in Jesus. Those who are not saved will receive rest if they come to Him, for here He promises to "give" it. Nothing can be freer than a gift; let us gladly accept what He gladly gives. You are not to buy it, nor to borrow it, but to receive it as a gift.

You labor under the lash of ambition, covetousness, lust, or anxiety: He will set you free from this iron bondage and give you rest. You are "laden," yes, "heavy laden" with sin, fear, care, remorse, fear of death; but if you come to Him He will unload you.

He carried the crushing mass of our sin that we might no longer carry it. He made Himself the great Burden-bearer, that every laden one might cease from bowing down under the enormous pressure.

Jesus gives rest. It is so. Will you believe it? Will you put it to the test? Will you do so at once? Come to Jesus by quitting every other hope, by thinking of Him, believing God's testimony about Him, and entrusting everything to Him. If you thus come to Him the rest which He will give you will be deep, safe, holy, and everlasting. He gives a rest which develops into heaven, and He gives it this day to all who come to Him"

What are you doing battle with today? He wants you to come to HIM and rest!

Dr. Bill Welte

2 Chronicles 21-22; John 14 June 4

Daily Reminders of the Gospel

For I delivered to you as of first importance what I also received: that Christ died for our sins in accordance with the Scriptures, that he was buried, that he was raised on the third day in accordance with the Scriptures...
(1 Corinthians 15:3-4 ESV)

Why did Paul label the Gospel as of *first importance*? What relevance does that have for 21st century believers? Once a person is regenerated, born-again, saved, redeemed what relevance does the Gospel have in everyday life?

In a culture in which entitlement is more the norm than the exception, it is a valuable reminder that we did not get what we deserve (hell), and we did get what we don't deserve (heaven). To keep life in proper perspective, we need daily reminders of what Christ accomplished on the cross on our behalf:

I deserve death, but You gave me life. John 5:24
I deserve hell, but You gave me heaven. John 14:1-3
I deserve bondage, but You gave me freedom. Galatians 5:1
I deserve anxiety, but You gave me peace. Philippians 4:6-7
I deserve judgment, but You gave me justification. Romans 3:24
I deserve punishment, but You punished Another in my place.
   1 John 2:2

I deserve separation, but You gave me unity. John 17:23
I deserve isolation, but You gave me fellowship.
   1 Corinthians 1:9
I deserve the law, but You gave me grace. Romans 6:14
I deserve darkness, but You gave me light. Ephesians 5:8
I deserve despair, but You gave me hope. Romans 12:12
I deserve to be an orphan, but You adopted me. John 14:18,
   Romans 8:15
I deserve to wander, but You guide me. Psalm 31:3
I deserve to be lost, but You direct my path. Proverbs 3:5-6
I deserve condemnation, but You redeemed me. Romans 8:1,
   Titus 2:13-14
I deserve blindness, but You gave me sight. Luke 7:22
I deserve poverty, but You gave me riches. 2 Corinthians 6:10
I deserve sadness, but You gave me joy. Romans 14:17
I deserve fear, but You gave me perfect love. 1 John 4:18
I deserve filthy rags, but You gave me robes of righteousness.
   Revelation 7:14
I deserve hunger, but You gave me the Bread of Life. John 6:35
I deserve to be overlooked, but You chose me. Ephesians 1:4
I deserve to labor and to be heavy laden, but You gave me rest.
   Matthew 11:28
I deserve to be alone, but You gave me family. Matthew 12:50

And the list goes on and on. Daily we need to be reminded that because of the Gospel, we did not get what we deserve.

Diane Hunt

2 Chronicles 23-24; John 15   **June 5**

Deserted Dwellings

For we know that if our earthly house, this tent, is destroyed, we have a building from God, a house not made with hands, eternal in the heavens. For in this we groan, earnestly desiring to be clothed with our habitation which is from heaven.
(2 Corinthians 5:1-2)

I received a magazine yesterday that has a picture on the front of a deserted house. Our country is in the grips of a mortgage crisis and many families are losing their homes. There are housing developments that resemble the ghost towns of the old west springing up all across the USA. And while it is sad, the loss of a house made of wood and stone is dwarfed by the loss or deterioration of a human body. Many people suffer the loss of their health due to old age or sickness resulting from man's fall from grace in the Garden of Eden.

Many people are quick to blame God when tragedy comes upon them in any shape or form, whether financial or physical. But the truth is that our Father God never intended us to be in this predicament. It was only when we separated ourselves from God by sinning that we got into trouble. We are fortunate that our God didn't give up on us, but has a plan for our redemption.

We all have the opportunity to return to God by receiving the forgiveness offered to us by Jesus Christ our Redeemer. The good news is that as we do this we gain the hope of knowing our future is brighter. According to the verses above, our ailing physical bodies, called tents because of their temporary nature, will be deserted and we will inhabit buildings instead. Imagine a house made by God that will last for eternity!

I don't know about you but my tent is breaking down, as are the tents of some of the people that I love. But I have hope in Christ my Redeemer. Romans 8:23 is a promise from God, *Not only that, but we also who have the firstfruits of the Spirit, even we ourselves groan within ourselves, eagerly waiting for the adoption, the redemption of our body.* The day is coming when this tent will be deserted but I will be in my new home with Jesus!

Thank you, Lord, for the hope I have in You.

Chaplain Jim Freed

2 Chronicles 25-27; John 16   **June 6**

Letting Go of Peanuts

Do not love the world nor the things in the world. If anyone loves the world, the love of the Father is not in him. For all that is in the world, the lust of the flesh and the lust of the eyes and the boastful pride of life, is not from the Father, but is from the world. (1 John 2:15-16 NASB)

    It has been a challenge for me to hold loosely to the things of this world. I look at my hands and see how tightly my fists are clenched. And what are they holding onto so tightly? I hold on to my family, my house and all my "stuff." Jesus is asking me to give it all to Him.

    I shared with a friend how I was struggling to loosen my grip. She shared with me this illustration: We hold our peanuts in our fists. Jesus wants to give us more than peanuts but like little children we grip our peanuts tighter, refusing to let them go. Jesus asks, "May I have your peanuts?" We reply, "No, thank you. I like my peanuts!" Jesus again offers us something greater if we will let go of our peanuts. Again we say "No, they are MY peanuts!" We really don't trust God with our peanuts, and we don't believe He would take better care of them.

    What is in your hands? Are you willing to relinquish all to Christ?

Kathy Withers

2 Chronicles 28-29; John 17   **June 7**

Preconceived Conclusions

But sanctify the Lord God in your hearts, and always be ready to give a defense to everyone who asks you a reason for the hope that is in you, with meekness and fear; having a good conscience, that when they defame you as evildoers, those who revile your good conduct in Christ may be ashamed. (1 Peter 3:15-16)

I live in a seniors' community. Everyone who knows me knows I am a Christ-follower. This leads to some interesting conversations. I have a friend who is an atheist. I have a number of friends who believe the Bible is a good book and contains truth but cannot be taken literally. They have preconceived notions which lead to strange conclusions. Facts are superfluous.

A minister decided that a visual demonstration would add emphasis to his Sunday sermon so he placed four worms into four separate jars. The first worm was put into a container of alcohol, the second into a container of cigarette smoke, the third into a container of chocolate syrup and the fourth into a container of good, clean soil. At the conclusion of the sermon, the minister reported the results as follows: the first worm in alcohol: dead. The second worm in cigarette smoke, dead. The third worm in chocolate syrup: dead. The fourth worm in good soil: alive. So the minister asked his congregation what they learned from the demonstration. A lady in the back raised her hand and said, "As long as you drink, smoke and eat chocolate, you won't have worms!"

Since I am a slow learner, it has taken me a couple of years to learn not to try to argue these people into the kingdom. Now I am trying to live the truth of the gospel so that when they ask why I do what I do or don't do what I don't do, or why I believe a certain thing, I am able to give a well-conceived answer: a reason for the hope that is in me.

These are great times to be speaking about the accuracy and veracity of the Bible. World events, the alignment of nations, the hatred of the Jews, the rise of Islam, the frequency of earthquakes, the expansion of knowledge, the wickedness of our culture and many more issues speak to the accuracy of the Bible. Some people simply don't want to hear the truth. In fact, one of the men in our community said he stopped reading his Bible because it is so accurate and it scares him!

I admit. I have a preconceived notion. Jesus is coming. My task in my community is to get people over their preconceived notions and bring them to Jesus while there is still time.

Rev. Neil Fichthorn

2 Chronicles 30-31; John 18:1-18   **June 8**

Feelings of Inferiority

For the Lord does not see as man sees; for man looks at the outward appearance, but the Lord looks at the heart.
(1 Samuel 16:7b)

    There is a certain problem which almost everyone faces at some point in his or her life. It's the feeling that you are not as good as other people. It's the feeling that you are a failure. What you're experiencing in those moments are feelings of inferiority.

    These feelings come from accepting the wrong values of the world. The Bible tells us that Satan is the ruler of this present age (John 12:31). Because of this, the world thinks the way Satan thinks, and puts its highest value on three things, physical attractiveness: intelligence, and money.

    What's the answer to these feelings of inferiority? The answer, my friend, is to change the way you think. True wisdom is seeing things as God sees them. In order to change the way we feel about ourselves, we must change the way we think about ourselves. When we choose to open God's Holy Word and learn from His Holy Spirit, the truth about God and His Son, our minds begin to be renewed. This affects our actions, and also those feelings of inferiority. We must see ourselves as God sees us. We learn to do this as we see God's principles, and apply them in daily living.

    Remember, Jesus died for us. Because of this, God sees us now, and forever, in Christ Jesus. We see this in Galatians 2:20 where Paul says, *I have been crucified with Christ; it is no longer I who live, but Christ lives in me; and the life which I now live in the flesh I live by faith in the Son of God, who loved me and gave Himself for me.*

    So, see yourself the way God sees you, perfect in Christ Jesus! This is not true of you because of anything you have done; it is because of what Jesus has done for you, and with you on the cross.

    God's love does not depend on how we look, what we are or what we have. My friend, you will be able to overcome the feelings of inferiority if you understand that accepting the values of the world leads to those feelings, but accepting God's values, learned in His Holy Word, takes away the feelings of inferiority.

Rev. Chris S. Hodges

2 Chronicles 32-33; John 18:19-40 June 9

Do We Really Pray?

Let my prayer come before You; Incline Your ear to my cry.
(Psalm 88:2)

    Not long ago I read an advertisement from Canada. It was for a "talking prayer doll." This caught my eye! The ad went on to say that the doll "kneels and says her bedtime prayers." There was nothing to wind nor strings to pull. Whenever the user wanted, the doll would say:

    "Now, I lay me down to sleep
    I pray Thee, Lord, my soul to keep.
    Guide me safely through the night,
    Wake me with the morning light.
    God bless Mommy…and Daddy
    And make me a good girl. Amen."

"Just press her tummy," said the ad, and "Patty recites the entire children's bedtime prayer, in her precious childlike voice. Operates on a single penlight battery. Available also in French."

    How easy it is to allow our prayers to become mechanical! We crank out petitions and intercessions, but with no real life! They may be biblically correct and theologically sound, but if there is no reality to them, God does not hear our prayers.

    To the people of Israel who were offering mechanical prayers to God, He said, *When you spread out your hands, I will hide My eyes from you; Even though you make many prayers, I will not hear* (Isaiah 1:15). This points out to me that not all prayers are heard in heaven. Some prayers never get higher than the ceiling. The following seems to capture the whole point:

    "I often say my prayers, but do I really pray?

And do the wishes of my heart go with the words I say?
I may as well kneel down and worship gods of stone
As offer to the living God a prayer of words alone.
For words without the heart the Lord will never hear;
Nor will He to those lips attend whose prayers are not sincere."

May our prayers be a delight and not a duty as we sincerely and lovingly meet with our Lord each day. Psalm 145:18, *The Lord is near unto all those who call upon Him, to all who call upon Him in truth.*

Carolyn Hibbard

2 Chronicles 34-36; John 19:1-22   **June 10**

Just Do It

Ask, and it will be given to you; seek and you will find; knock, and the door will be opened to you. For everyone who asks receives; he who seeks finds; and to him who knocks, the door will be opened. (Matthew 7:7-8 NIV)

I have found myself frustrated over the years thinking and verbalizing this: "Why is prayer such hard work?" Why have I been so frustrated in my prayer life?

I have collected and read dozens of books on prayer. I've looked for the right model, the right formula, the right method, so that I can pray effectively. The bottom line is that I can have the largest collection of books on how to pray – but in the words of Nike© – I need to JUST DO IT!

Rather than get so hung up on the right and wrong way to pray, figuring out the right position and posture for prayer, and trying to make sure I say the right things and not say the wrong things, God wants me to come to Him in childlike faith and just pray.

It's really not as complicated as I make it. It isn't about saying a prayer that will impress the Lord. Who am I kidding? He knows the real me. He knows when I am using "vain repetitions" or praying things I don't really mean.

I am new on this journey – but I have made a commitment to myself – to move from reading and learning about prayer – to become a man who prays. I will make mistakes, I'm sure. But at the end of the day, it matters more to Him that I love Him enough that I want to spend time with Him at the throne of grace.

Lord, help me to keep it simple – JUST DO IT! Pray!

Dr. Bill Welte

Ezra 1-2; John 19:23-42   **June 11**

Seek First

But seek ye first the kingdom of God, and his righteousness; and all these things shall be added unto you. (Matthew 6:33 KJV)

One of the first verses of Scripture I learned as a boy in Sunday School was Matthew 6:33, *Seek ye first the kingdom of God.* I always thought that the kingdom of God meant heaven. Through the years of reading and hearing about many verses describing the kingdom, none of them seemed to be describing heaven, but rather ways of living here and now. Then one time while studying this verse I discovered a whole new concept. The Lord showed me what "kingdom" really meant; I'd like to share it with you.

In the Greek, the word kingdom is "basileia," and in the New Testament this is synonymous with reign. The word denotes not only territories of a king but royal power and dominion, or the rank, state, or attributes of a king, and also royal authority. Rather than a place, it refers more to the living subjects of the king.

Let's read the verse like this: "Seek first His reign/the reign of God," or "seek first the royal authority of God." When you do this, you put yourself under the authority and rule of the Lord God, thus giving up to the Lord's reign of your life.

So, of what is the kingdom composed? What is involved in His kingdom? Romans 14:17 (NIV), *the kingdom of God* (the "reign" of God) *is not a matter of eating and drinking, but of righteousness, peace and joy in the Holy Spirit.*

Righteousness – His way of doing and being right; what He requires; the state which makes one acceptable to God, pleasing to Him. We are made righteous in God's sight through Christ (2 Corinthians 5:21). Righteousness is seen in our relationship to God.

Peace – heart-peace; peace with our neighbors; in concord with our brethren. *Let the peace of Christ rule in your hearts* (Colossians 3:15). This brings peace in your heart and with others. Peace is seen in your relationship with your neighbors.

Joy – that which comes from within; not as pleasure which comes from without. Jesus speaks about keeping His commandments so that your joy may be full (John 15:11). Do you joy at the presence of the Holy Spirit – when He convicts? When He allows trials? Is your joy evident to others? Joy is seen in our relationship with ourselves.

Today, seek His kingdom – a lifestyle of righteousness, peace and joy.

Jack Noel

Ezra 3-5; John 20　　　　　　　　　　　　　　　　　　**June 12**

Show Me Your Glory

And he said, "Please, show me Your glory." (Exodus 33:18)

Many years ago, while attending a Christian Life Convention, I heard Stuart Briscoe make a statement that I have never forgotten and that remains a significant influence on my life. He said, "God meets man on the level of his desire; man can have as much of God as he wants."

I was a college student, over 40 years ago, when I heard that statement and I am continually inspired by it. God will meet me on the level of my desire for Him and I can have as much of God as I want. This is an incredible thought.

Desire is a very important part of our Christian life. It is possible to counterfeit many aspects of the Christian life. But, it is impossible to counterfeit desire. You cannot pretend to have desire.

The Lord told Jeremiah, *...And you will seek Me and find Me, when you search for Me with all your heart* (Jeremiah 29:13).

Look at this incredible expression of desire for God in the heart of the psalmist, *My soul longs, yes, even faints for the courts of the LORD; My heart and my flesh cry out for the living God* (Psalm 84:2).

Look at this picture of a man's desire for God, *As the deer pants for the water brooks, so pants my soul for You, O God. My soul thirsts for God, for the living God* (Psalm 42:1-2).

Moses cried out to God, *Show me your glory!* What an incredible request. Moses longed with all of his heart to see the true nature, character, weight and value of God. He wanted to see God's glory.

Beware of substitutes for God's glory. Moses had just dealt with the Israelites and their hand-made substitute for God, a golden calf. We also must guard against the thing that could become a substitute for God. It is possible that our pursuit of knowledge about God can be a substitute for knowing God. It is possible to substitute busyness in church work for true service to God.

Ron Owens writes in his book, <u>Return to Worship</u>, "The measure in which we know God is the measure in which we will be able to worship Him. The way we get to know God is through the Scriptures. In the Scriptures we have the revelation of God's nature—His ways and who He is." Show me Your Glory!

Dr. Roger D. Willmore

Ezra 6-8; John 21   **June 13**

Efforts Which Fail to Please

So then, those who are in the flesh cannot please God.
(Romans 8:8)

One expression often heard in family counseling sessions is: "Nothing I do seems to please him (her, them)." These words are filled with stress. The perception they reflect is difficult to counteract. Sometimes perceptions can be superficial or outright deceptive.

Let's apply the expression to the realm of the spiritual – mankind's effort to do things pleasing to God. It's an impossible undertaking. In the context of our theme text, the apostle Paul discusses two types of mindsets: the flesh-dominated mind vs. the Spirit-renewed mind. The conclusion drawn is that the flesh-dominated person cannot please God. In that state he/she closely resembles an unsaved person and cannot please God (1 Corinthians 3:3).

When Christians attempt to please God by self-effort, they are attempting the impossible. They may be sincere but sincerely wrong. Many believers live lives of frustration through their attempts to gain God's approval. The only way any believer can please God is by following God's way. Hebrews 11:6 gives the correct way to please Him: *But without faith it is impossible to please Him...* Stating it positively, *...he who comes to God must believe that He is, and that He is a rewarder of those who diligently seek Him.*

By nature we are programmed to introduce self-effort into any of the programs of God. However, God's Word provides correction when It declares that our salvation is gained *not by works of righteousness which we have done, but according to His mercy He saved us...* (Titus 3:5). We are further instructed concerning our continued progress in the Christian life: *As you have therefore received Christ Jesus the Lord, so walk in Him* (Colossians 2:6). We received Him by faith and are to continue to walk on the same basis. It is through our reliance upon Him that we are most pleasing to Him.

We must also understand that faith is to be coupled with obedience. As the hymn writer put it, "Trust and obey, for there's no other way to be happy in Jesus, but to trust and obey." We might paraphrase it to say, "there's no other way to please Him but to trust and obey."

Rev. William A. Raws

Ezra 9-10; Acts 1 — June 14

Sensing Spiritual Moments

You will show me the path of life; In Your presence is fullness of joy; At Your right hand are pleasures forevermore.
(Psalm 16:11)

Sometimes we find ourselves in a moment where everything around us seems to shout the presence of God. They may come often for some but as rarely as a comet for others. I'm in one as I write this out in my backyard by the fire on perhaps the most beautiful evening of the year. The kids are in bed, and I've dimmed my screen to avoid spoiling the starlit sky.

Sensing spiritual moments requires something intangible of us, and in my experience, they come when I least expect them. We cannot manufacture them and they cannot be scheduled in our planners, although we can plan time to be alone in nature with His Word, or in communion with close, believing friends.

I was reminded by our missions trip teens (on a recent Sunday evening) about a memory forged en route from New Mexico to New Jersey. We were returning from two weeks of ministry and travel and were experiencing the tension of events beyond our control. We became aggravated by our slow progress at rest stops, which was compounded by vehicle trouble and allowed an open door for Satan to stir up strife. One of our students recognized the danger and soon Bible verses were beating back the darkness and we fought frustration with worship music.

I am certainly not known as a mystic, but I cannot explain to those who were not there how intense this season of praise became. The Spirit of God descended on that van like at Sinai and we all spoke about it afterward. Perhaps you have experienced this, too?

Sound theology reminds us that God is always with us. But, if we are honest, we spend the majority of our days thirsting for a sense of the divine that seems just out of reach. I think Paul knew what I meant when he wrote, *now we see in a mirror dimly*. Our spiritual senses are not near what they ought to be; they are dull to the point of regularly missing our Father's omnipresence.

Is there anything we can do to cure this deficiency? I mostly encounter these "spiritual moments" when I sense that I have been a part of something that God is or has been doing. When we are battling darkness and clinging to the Lord, or when He comes through for us in power, these are the times of spiritual exhilaration. For a biblical example, consider Miriam's dance and song after being delivered from Pharaoh's death chase in Exodus 15.

Rev. Jason Walsh

Nehemiah 1-3; Acts 2:1-21   **June 15**

Are You Free in Theory or Indeed?

Therefore if the Son makes you free, you shall be free indeed.
(John 8:36)

Sometimes I think that we read the Word of God too fast. When I read the Bible in a year I prefer an easy-read translation, but I believe that God desires us to mull over the words of Scripture at times to stimulate our minds. In fact I have heard it suggested by a pastor that the reason that the Bible is not more definitive, or "black and white" on certain subjects is that He wants to join us in the process of wrestling through difficult passages. If it were too easy we wouldn't need to involve Him!

It was during a time of writing that the word "indeed" came to my attention. What a curious addition to a statement of fact. Just what does it mean? Webster's Dictionary defines the word "indeed" as an adverb meaning: "in reality; in truth; in fact." With that in mind, let's ponder over the Scripture, *Therefore if the Son makes you free, you shall be free indeed.*

One of the challenges that we face in ministering the Gospel to persons involved in life-dominating sin or addiction is the question, "How can I be saved and still be in bondage?" While the first obligation as a counselor is to examine the validity of a person's salvation, we need to accept the fact that not all who are saved are walking in victory. A good example of this was the church in Corinth. While many were caught up in sin, Paul never admonished the members of the body to get saved.

Many come into our addiction recovery ministry as (what I affectionately refer to as) "Bible Scholars." They impress newer believers, but indeed their superior intellectual knowledge has gotten them into the same predicament as those with little or no knowledge of God's Word. What most of them lack is experiential knowledge of the person of Jesus Christ through an intimate personal relationship with Him. Jesus Himself taught that ... *this is eternal life, that they may know You, the only true God, and Jesus Christ whom You have sent* (John 17:3). It is only through personal, intimate, experiential knowledge that the Son will make you free "indeed!"

Lord, may I never be satisfied until I am free indeed.

Chaplain Jim Freed

Nehemiah 4-6; Acts 2:22-47   **June 16**

Focus

If then were raised with Christ, seek those things which are above, where Christ is, sitting at the right hand of God. Set your mind on things above, not on things on the earth. For you died, and your life is hidden with Christ in God. (Colossians 3:1-3)

I have had more than a few traffic accidents in my more than forty years of driving. Some were my fault, others were not. None have been serious, and I'm thankful for that. Those accidents that were my fault occurred for the same reason—I was not paying attention. Something caught my eye and took my focus from the road. Anyone with a cell phone knows the dangerous combination of driving and phones. Focus is important!

So it is in our walk with Jesus. Life seems good. We are walking down the journey of life with Jesus and all is well. The next thing we know, we're in the ditch! Usually the lack of focus is what put us in the ditch.

The apostle Paul understood the need for focus. Without ever using the exact word, he talks often in his letters about the need to keep our minds clear and focused. Consider his words to the Colossian church: *If then you were raised with Christ, seek those things which are above, where Christ is, sitting at the right hand of God. Set your mind on things above, not on things on earth. For you died, and your life is hidden with Christ in God* (Colossians 3:1-3).

All of us who have experienced new life in Christ have a responsibility. The instruction is simple. Keep yourself focused! The songwriter had it right in an old gospel song, "This world is not my home; I'm just a passin' through. My treasures are laid up somewhere beyond the blue." Keeping our focus on that which has eternal value keeps us out of the ditch! It is just that simple, even if it is not that easy.

Scripture offers believers a number of spiritual disciplines that help us stay focused. If we choose to obey the instruction of Colossians, we will use the disciplines of the Spirit that are available to us. Regular time in God's Word helps us stay focused. Consistent conversation with God (talking <u>and</u> listening) keeps us aware of that which is important. Silence, solitude and fasting can sharpen our focus and help us put away the things of earth that can distract us.

God tells us to stay focused on heaven and that which is of eternal value. It is our responsibility. He gives us His spirit and the tools we need. Let's get to work!

Rev. John Strain

Nehemiah 7-9; Acts 3   **June 17**

Harmony with God

And the world is passing away, and the lust of it; but he who does the will of God abides forever. (1 John 2:17)

    Have you ever noticed all but the will of man obeys God? If you look right through history, you will find this to be true. In the beginning *God said, "Let there be light"; and there was light.* Then God continued His creation work and said, *"Let the waters bring forth"* (KJV) and the waters brought forth abundantly. God spoke only once and He was obeyed immediately. One of the proofs we use from the Bible that Jesus Christ is God is that He spoke to nature and nature obeyed Him. Remember the time when He traveled with His disciples in a boat on a stormy day and they were afraid. He did what only God can do. He spoke to the sea, and the sea recognized and obeyed Him and became calm. At a later time, He spoke to a fig tree and instantly it withered and died. All these instances involved nature, which obeyed God literally and at once. In the spirit world, He spoke to devils, and the devils fled. He spoke to the grave, and the grave obeyed Him and gave back the dead. But, when He speaks to man, man will not obey Him. This is why man is out of harmony with God.

    God desires obedience, and the only way man can have harmony with God is to have a personal relationship with Him, and live a life desiring to obey Him.

Satan and those who are in rebellion against God rule this present world-system. In James 4:4 we read, ...*Do you not know that friendship with the world is enmity with God? Whoever therefore wants to be a friend of the world makes himself an enemy of God.*

    My friend, God has purposely left us here to share the simple gospel with every person and to encourage spiritual growth in every believer, by the power of the Holy Spirit, and for His own glory. This can never happen if our love for God is secondary to our love for this world, and if God's desire for immediate obedience is not met. Let's remember, obedience is positive, not negative. When we are abiding in Him, we are obeying Him, and we have harmony with God.

Rev. Chris S. Hodges

Nehemiah 10-11; Acts 4:1-22 June 18

Seventh Inning Stretch

Children, obey your parents in the Lord, for this is right. "Honor your father and mother"(this is the first commandment with a promise), "that it may go well with you and that you may live long in the land." Fathers, do not provoke your children to anger, but bring them up in the discipline and instruction of the Lord. (Ephesians 6:1-4 ESV)

Sometimes there are just too many days that are dedicated to the honoring or acknowledging of an event or a person and, at times, I think it is just a scam in order to sell cards, candy and flowers. Now Mother's Day is a given and should not even be questioned but Father's Day is a bit different. It is looked at as a great excuse for Dad to eat BBQ or receive a new tool.

My Dad was an easy buy. If you went to a Phillies game, get him a hat. If you went near a Home Depot, get him a tool. If you had gone fishing…well, you get the idea. My Dad was real cool about Father's Day. Even if you just called him, he was fine with it. But I'm a Dad now and my children have done through their short lives abundantly more than I could have ever hoped for. Just that it is Father's Day is gift enough. But there is a bit more.

You see, to me Mother's and Father's Day are things to be viewed biblically. We are told to honor our parents straight from the tablets God forged for Moses to take to the nation of Israel. I tell my children that all they have to do is do it for God first and I'll be honored by it. Then it is up to me to keep up the encouragement. I have to do that by living out the words of encouragement that I say to them. If I tell them to PRAY FIRST before they do, … they had better see me do it. If I tell them not to be ashamed of the Gospel I had better pray for the meal when we go out to eat, even if it is McDonald's, and, if necessary, wear my America's Keswick T-shirts in public and not just on the grounds when I am spending time there.

Our children need to see us, as men, honoring our Heavenly Father. They need to hear us cry out "ABBA" when we are at our weakest so they know what to do when they are at their weakest. And if you can say it like you mean it, raise your voice and shout "SANTO" when you have been blessed. In all things show your children that "Our Father who art in heaven" matters in your everyday coming and going.

Chris Hughes

Nehemiah 12-13; Acts 4:23-37 June 19

Nothing We Do for God is Pointless

As the rain and the snow come down from heaven, and do not return to it without watering the earth... so is my word that goes out from my mouth: It will not return to me empty...
(Isaiah 55:10-11 NIV)

As a pastor in England, I've been doing high school assemblies for twenty years. The religious education teacher sets a theme for each week. The whole school gathers at the start of each day. After a bunch of notices, someone does sort of a "pep talk" on that theme. Twelve times each year that person is me. It isn't a Christian school. Evolution and all other religions are taught. The students are as full of sin as most teens are. Less than 1% of people in Europe attend any church at all. It's just that some traditions run very deep and because the school was founded centuries ago by the Church of England, some things stay in place.

So basically I get to preach for 8 minutes to hundreds of students and teachers who are nowhere near Christian. It's a bit daunting, but I love it. I try to make it fun, but in the end, I want them to know Jesus and I make the Gospel very clear. I have dozens of great testimonies. There's the funeral I did for a man who died of alcohol-related illness. His son was impressed with me and asked his mom if she would get me to do the funeral. There's the young man who stopped me in a shop to tell me that he had become a Christian and that it was my talks that had opened his eyes years ago. There's the teacher named Rose who started coming to our church, got saved, and is still with us. And there are works in progress. One teacher that I always felt didn't like me, maybe because she's gay, or maybe because I'm always holding up the Bible, was crying. I asked her if she was all right. She said that she had something in her eye. I told her that I would pray for her eye, and as I was walking away she said, "OK, your assemblies always get to me."

Preparing these talks or standing very alone with the Word of God in your hands and on your lips isn't an easy thing to do, but I am committed to doing it because God has promised that it will never be a "void" thing. It will never be "pointless." God has His reasons. Would you be prepared to do the same today? I don't expect you to have the same kind of opportunities that I do. But I know that God loves every soul that He's ever created and that His desire is that no one would perish but that all would come to repentance. He wants all men to be saved and to come to the knowledge of the truth. And I know that today someone will cross your path, and you'll have an opportunity to say one simple thing. It may be as easy as "God bless you." Or as profound as an invitation to heaven. Just remember that it's the goodness of God that leads us to repentance and that we love God because we came to understand that He first loved us. His Word will not return to Him empty. Think of it as rain. And of how God is going to use it to water the earth.

Rev. Chris Thompson

Esther 1-2; Acts 5:1-21   **June 20**

Appearances

Abstain from all appearance of evil.
(1 Thessalonians 5:22 KJV)

    This seems like such a simple verse to live by, but recently I have been challenged more and more on what it really means.

    There have been many instances in my past of having to sort out "what really happened" while dealing with students involved in disciplinary proceedings. It was always difficult when you only have two distinctive sides to a story and no witnesses. I have also found that even if you have witnesses they often distort what really happened because they begin to interpret happenings from what they think they saw happening rather than just what happened. I remember distinctly a time when I was placed in the awkward position of having to observe the goings on at the home of one of my "clients." We had suspected some activity for some time and had received rumored reports but had nothing factual to go on. Now, I can tell you what I saw, and then I can tell you what I started thinking might be going on. It was at that point that the reality of this verse came through loud and clear. From what I saw, I could have made all kinds of judgments regarding their behavior, which went from innocent to very guilty. In this case the appearance of evil really did make a difference in the conclusions that were drawn.

    It is the same way in my life; what I do and how it "may" look to others can really distort their view of my faith and me. I came away from that evening being ever so mindful that even if what I am doing is innocent, if I am not aware of how others may view my actions I could be accused of being very guilty by those watching me.

    I also became vividly aware of John 7:24 (NIV) that reminds me to *Stop judging by mere appearances, and make a right judgment*. As much as I do not want people to make judgments about me by what they think they see, I need to make sure I don't do the same.

How are you living? Are you living so that others cannot misconstrue your actions to be something they are not? Are you making sure that before you come to conclusions about others you find out the truth? May we all take a good look at ourselves and make sure we are only displaying godliness through our lives.

Dr. Lynne Jahns

Esther 3-5; Acts 5:22-42   **June 21**

Hearing….Listening….Obeying

I will hear what God the LORD will speak, For He will speak peace to His people and to His saints,… (Psalm 85:8)

While preparing to go to an early morning breakfast and long day of meetings, after laying out my clothes, I headed from the bedroom to the kitchen for my tea and time with the Lord. I was stopped in my tracks at the door, hearing, "Get dressed first today." "But Lord, I'm going to have my time with You." Going back I made sure my shoes were out and everything ready to get dressed quickly later and started to the kitchen again, but turned back to do a couple of other things. I repeated this for the third time, not willing to obey, questioning "Why?"

Finally getting to the kitchen, I started my tea and said to my husband Stan, "I didn't know what to do first, get dressed or come out to read." I had thought on my way, "if he tells me to get dressed first, then I will." No response. While my tea was brewing, I was still discussing this with the Lord asking, "Why?" Very clearly I heard the answer in my head and heart, "You always wanted *your* children to obey you without questioning. And you always wanted *your* class in school to obey whatever you told them to do. If for no other reason than that you should obey Me." So I covered my cup of tea, thinking it would be cold when I got back, and said to Stan, "I need to go and get dressed first." He replied, "That's what I would have told you, but you usually do the opposite of what I think, so I didn't say anything." "But I wanted you to say it this time."

So obediently, trustingly, I went and got dressed first, coming back 20-25 minutes later. I was amazed that my tea was still hot!! I went to my time with the Lord knowing all was well. That was God's grace and love poured out to my heart, as He taught me more about not only hearing but listening and obeying! (And not questioning the "whys" of His ways.)

"For My thoughts are not your thoughts, Nor are your ways My ways," says the LORD. "For as the heavens are higher than the earth, So are My ways higher than your ways, and My thoughts than your thoughts" (Isaiah 55:8-9).

A man's heart plans his way, But the LORD directs his steps (Proverbs 16:9).

DeEtta Marsh

Esther 6-8; Acts 6 **June 22**

The Care of Your Feet

He will keep the feet of His saints… (1 Samuel 2:9a KJV)

When I was growing up, my grandmother would often say, "Me feet and legs ache so bad it kills me." It always made me laugh.

Now that I am older, and do battle from time to time with sore feet, I realize how important my feet are and how thankful I am for the two feet God has given me.

I recently read this about the care of my feet in Spurgeon's book, Checquebook of the Bank of Faith:

"The way is slippery and our feet are feeble, but the Lord will keep our feet. If we give ourselves up by obedient faith to be His holy ones, He will Himself be our guardian. Not only will He charge His angels to keep us, but He Himself will preserve our goings.

He will keep our feet from falling so that we do not defile our garments, wound our souls, and cause the enemy to blaspheme.

He will keep our feet from wandering so that we do not go into paths of error, or ways of folly, or courses of the world's custom.

He will keep our feet from swelling through weariness, or blistering because of the roughness and length of the way.

He will keep our feet from wounding: our shoes shall be iron and brass so that even though we tread on the edge of the sword, or on deadly serpents, we shall not bleed or be poisoned.

He will also pluck our feet out of the net. We shall not be entangled by the deceit of our malicious and crafty foes. With such a promise as this, let us run without weariness and walk without fear.

He who keeps our feet will do it effectually." Are you thankful today for your feet? For His care of your feet? I am!

Dr. Bill Welte

Esther 9-10; Acts 7:1-21   **June 23**

How God Encourages Us to Enter into Our Possessions

"Therefore understand today that the LORD your God is He who goes over before you as a consuming fire. He will destroy them and bring them down before you; so you shall drive them out and destroy them and bring them down before you; so you shall drive them out and destroy them quickly, as the LORD has said to you." (Deuteronomy 9:3)

"For the LORD your God is bringing you into a good land, a land of brooks of water, of fountains and springs, that flow out of the valleys and hills; a land of wheat and barley, of vines and fig trees and pomegranates, a land of olive oil and honey; a land in which you will eat without scarcity, in which you will lack nothing; a land whose stones are iron and out of whose hills you can dig copper." (Deuteronomy 8:7-9)

The Old Testament story of God's promise to His children of a land that flows with milk and honey, a land in which the children of God eat bread without scarcity, is one of the most dramatic pictures of the Christian life in the whole of the Bible. I have often said that if I had only one message to preach to the church, it would be this message: <u>Enter into your possessions.</u>

The old Keswick preachers used to emphasize the much more of the Christian life. I am concerned that we currently live in the much less of the Christian life.

Dear ones, the Lord encourages you to enter into fullness of life in Christ. He knows that you must face barriers and He knows there will be *battles,* but He has assured you that He will see you through on your journey into your promised possessions. Notice how the Lord encourages His people.

He promised His presence. He said, *Therefore understand today that the LORD your God is He who goes before you as a consuming fire...*(v. 3). You are not alone in your journey. You are not alone when you encounter your barriers and battles. He is with you.

Remember these comforting and encouraging words, *...I will fear no evil; For you are with me; Your rod and Your staff, they comfort me* (Psalm 23:4).

He promised His protection. He said, *He would destroy them and bring them down before you; so you shall drive them out and destroy them quickly, as the LORD has said to you* (v. 3).

He promised His provision. Reflect again on the verses above (8:7-9), and think about the bountiful provisions of God.

Here is the encouragement you need for this day. Now, enter into your possessions.

Dr. Roger D. Willmore

Job 1-2; Acts 7:22-43　　　　　　　　　　　　　　**June 24**

Hindrances to Entering into Our Possessions

"Hear O Israel: You are to cross over the Jordan today, and go in to dispossess nations greater and mightier than yourself, cities great and fortified up to heaven, a people great and tall, the descendants of the Anakim, whom you, and of whom you heard it said, 'Who can stand again before the descendants of Anak?'"
(Deuteronomy 9:1-2)

The Old Testament story of the children of Israel standing before the promised land and eventually going into the promised land is a beautiful Old Testament picture of a glorious New Testament truth.

This picture reveals God's plan for us to enter into fullness of life in Jesus Christ. Jesus said in John 10:10...*I have come that they may have life, and they may have it more abundantly.*

However, this promised life does not come to us easily or without conflict. This promised life has enemies. The devil does not want you to know the blessings of the Lord. Satan's purpose is to rob you of God's blessings and to block the way of you experiencing God.

The passage before us describes some of the hindrances faced by the people of Israel. These conflicts represent the same hindrances you and I face today.

The children of Israel faced cities fortified up to heaven. This means the promised land was occupied by enemy who lived behind walled cities and fortresses. These walled cities were potential barriers to the children of God occupying the land. What barriers do you face today? Some people encounter barriers in their home life where the circumstances make life difficult. Others encounter barriers in their workplace or in a classroom. We all face these barriers in a culture that is anti-God and anti-Christian.

Barriers will always be present in this life. However, we have been given a promise that we can penetrate the barriers and enter into our promised possessions in Christ.

The children of Israel also encountered battles with giants, the people of Anakim. The people of Anak were large, towering and intimidating people. They fought against the people of God. There are giants in our lives today who have declared war against us.

God promised His children that the land was theirs. He did not say it would be easy to occupy the land, but He did promise that they could and would occupy the land.

Have you overcome the hindrances to your Christian life? You can, through the strength and power of Jesus Christ.

Dr. Roger D. Willmore

Job 3-4; Acts 7:44-60   June 25

In His Steps

To this you were called, because Christ suffered for you, leaving you an example, that you should follow in his steps.
(1 Peter 2:21 NIV)

    In the early 20th century, Charles Sheldon wrote a book, In His Steps. It is considered a classic and continues to be a best-seller. The story involves a pastor and some of his people who decide to ask the question "What would Jesus do?" They then made the commitment to walk "in His steps" for a full year.

    Charles Sheldon drew inspiration for his novel from 1 Peter 2:21, *To this you were called, because Christ suffered for you, leaving you an example, that you should follow in His steps.* He understood that the Lord Jesus Christ is our example and that our calling as Christians is to walk as He walked.

    In May, 2010, I had the privilege of making my first trip to Israel. During the trip our group visited Bethsaida, an archeological site undergoing continued excavation. One section of the excavation offered us the opportunity to walk a stone pathway certified as first century. It sits right at the opening of the gate to the city, meaning that anyone who entered the city had to walk this path. Both archeologists and biblical scholars agree that Jesus certainly would have walked on the stones our group encountered. I literally walked in Jesus' steps!

    That experience is unforgettable. In fact, I use a picture of those stones as the wallpaper for my computer. They are the first things I see when I turn on my computer each day. Another experience is even more unforgettable. In July, 1962, I received Jesus Christ as my Savior. I became His follower, and I received the instruction to "walk in His steps." The steps I am to follow are not stones in Bethsaida. Rather, they are the teachings He gives us in the gospels. I am to live as He lived in obedience to His Father.

    All of us who follow Jesus have the same responsibility. We are to love God and love our neighbors as ourselves. We are to live out the simple instructions of the Sermon on the Mount, no matter how difficult doing so may seem. By the transforming work of God's Spirit, Jesus calls us to live out His character, to love as He loved. Peter had it right! Jesus left us the example, and we're to follow "in His steps."

Rev. John Strain

Job 5-7; Acts 8:1-25   **June 26**

How The Son of Man Lived

Then Jesus answered and said to them, "Most assuredly, I say to you, the Son can do nothing of Himself, but what He sees the Father do; for whatever He does, the Son also does in like manner." (John 5:19)

Our Lord Jesus not only exemplified the ideal standards of motive, words and deeds; He also exemplified the *method* God intends for His people to live.

Notice three principles regarding the dynamic of Christ's earthly life:

1. Christ's perfect human life was a testimony of God the Father expressing Himself *through* His Son by the power of the Holy Spirit.

Jesus said, *"Do you not believe that I am in the Father, and the Father in Me? The words that I speak to you I do not speak on My own authority; but the Father who dwells in Me does the works"* (John 14:10).

2. Christ modeled full surrender to the Father's will.

Hebrews 10:7 speaks of Christ's surrender: *"Then I said, 'Behold, I have come– In the volume of the book it is written of Me– To do Your will, O God.'"* And Christ testified, *"And He who sent Me is with Me. The Father has not left Me alone, for I always do those things that please Him"* (John 8:29).

3. Christ modeled complete dependence on the Father through the Holy Spirit.

In John 8:28, Christ declared, *"When you lift up the Son of Man, then you will know that I am He, and that I do nothing of Myself; but as My Father taught Me, I speak these things."*

Ian Thomas has noted, "Now if it is true that the Lord Jesus Christ will live His life through you on earth today, as He lived His life in His own body on earth more than nineteen hundred years ago, it is both interesting and necessary to discover *how* He lived *then*, so that you may know *how* He will live through you *now*." (The Saving Life of Christ, p.16).

The true Christian life requires this surrender and faith so that divine life can be expressed through our mortal vessels.

Dr. John Woodward

Job 8-10; Acts 8:26-40   **June 27**

Judging Others

Judge not, that you be not judged. (Matthew 7:1 ESV)

That's how it reads in the English Standard Version of God's Word. In The Message paraphrase, it reads like this: *Don't pick on people, jump on their failures, criticize their faults—unless, of course, you want the same treatment.*

I love to read My Utmost for His Highest, a devotional book by Oswald Chambers, compiled by his wife after his death and in continuous print since 1935. As I sat reading it a few years ago, the message for the day was about being critical of others. He wrote, "The average Christian is one of the most piercingly critical individuals known." He went on to say, "Criticism serves to make you harsh, vindictive, and cruel, and leaves you with the soothing and flattering idea that you are somehow superior to others." (My Utmost for His Highest, June 17th)

When I read those words I cried and cried. My conscience was pricked by those stinging words and it hurt a lot. At that time I was being especially critical and judgmental towards certain people and God used those famously penned words to bring rebuke, correction, conviction, confession, repentance and change - change that is in constant ebb and flow as I grow in the knowledge of Him.

Please don't think this task was by any means easy, because it wasn't and isn't. If I don't draw near and press in to God, my natural bent is toward being critical of myself and others. As a Christian, this simply will not do.

Jesus' words to the people ready to stone the woman caught in adultery are words that come often to my mind in the midst of critical thinking. *"He who is without sin among you, let him throw a stone at her first"* (John 8:7b).

While I pursue blameless living, I am far from sinless. Who am I to look at the faults and failures of others and be critical? *Search me, O God, and know my heart! Try me and know my thoughts! And see if there be any grievous way in me, and lead me in the way everlasting!* (Psalm 139:23-24 ESV).

My challenge for you: If you find you can relate in any way to what I've shared today, go to God now, confess and allow His Spirit to transform your heart in this area. You'll be so glad you did!

Stephanie D. Paul

Job 11-13; Acts 9:1-21 **June 28**

Makeover

Therefore, if anyone is in Christ, the new creation has come: The old has gone, the new is here! (2 Corinthians 5:17 NIV)

Have you noticed how many "makeover" shows there are on television lately? There are home makeovers, body makeovers, style makeovers, child discipline makeovers…it seems that everyone is trying to take what they have and have someone else make it better or make it totally new. Everyone is searching for the perfect makeover to make their life complete or perfect. I'm just wondering how long it takes after the makeover is complete and the cameras are no longer rolling when the realization comes that the new look may have made a more attractive appearance or a more comfortable life but that it is all just the " "façade" that has been altered. The hole is still there and dissatisfaction with self or circumstances still exists even if the outside package looks prettier. The heart is still empty. There is a longing for true change from the inside out…the kind of true change that only comes from a heart transformed by Jesus Christ.

    Don't get me wrong… I'm not against makeovers per se, but if it is only the outside that is changed, then what is rotten on the inside will eventually make its way back to the outside.

    Jesus rebuked the Pharisees because they were so concerned about outward appearances. And from that perspective, on the outside they looked great. Jesus was much more concerned with what was on the inside.

    Matthew 23:25-26 (NIV), *Woe to you, teachers of the law and Pharisees, you hypocrites! You clean the outside of the cup and dish, but inside they are full of greed and self-indulgence. Blind Pharisee! First clean the inside of the cup and dish, and then the outside also will be clean.*

    Jesus could see the "inside." He could see their hearts and from that perspective it was pretty ugly in there. All Jesus could see was self-centeredness and greed. All they could think about was "self" and how they could get more of whatever their hearts desired. Jesus had the answer for making the inside beautiful, clean and satisfied. I remember all too well how I used to be only concerned with the "outside," with the appearance of things, yet my insides were so disgusting….until I invited Jesus in to occupy my heart. Therein is the true "makeover," the only "makeover" that really matters. This "makeover" is not a temporary fix or window dressing but a change from the inside that lasts for eternity.

MaryAnn Kiernan

Job 14-16; Acts 9:22-43 — June 29

No Vacancy After Victory

...to know the love of Christ which passes knowledge; that you may be filled with all the fullness of God. (Ephesians 3:19)

These words were taken from a devotional article written by W. Glyn Evans, a college friend of mine. His thesis was that when God drives out a spiritual enemy from our lives, we must be sure that there is a positive replacement. To proclaim the need for emptying ourselves of flesh domination without presenting the need for the Spirit's filling is folly and futility. I tilled a plot of ground in our yard but didn't get around to planting anything in it. It looked neat and orderly at first, but it became filled with weeds that thrived on the newly turned soil.

Jesus used a parallel illustration when He told of the tragedy of a life that was emptied of an unclean spirit but left vacant. *When an unclean spirit goes out of a man, he goes through dry places, seeking rest, and finds none. Then he says, "I will return to my house from which I came." And when he comes, he finds it empty, swept, and put in order. Then he goes and takes with him seven other spirits more wicked than himself, and they enter and dwell there; and the last state of that man is worse than the first* (Matthew 12:43-45).

For years America's Keswick has been declaring to those seeking to be rid of life-dominating sins that they are not only to be reckoning themselves dead to sin but alive to God through Jesus Christ (Romans 6:11). They must no longer present themselves as instruments of unrighteousness unto sin but to present themselves to God (v. 13). The negative act of renunciation must be followed by the positive renewing of the Holy Spirit.

Mary Maxwell, in a hymn often sung at past Keswick conferences – "Channels Only" – declares, "Emptied that Thou shouldest fill me, A clean vessel in Thine hand; With no power but as Thou givest Graciously with each command." In her final stanza she says, "Jesus, fill now with Thy Spirit Hearts that full surrender know, That the streams of living water From our inner man may flow."

Let's not short circuit God's purpose by settling for evicting the old occupant without enthroning the new.

Rev. William A. Raws

Job 17-19; Acts 10:1-23   **June 30**

Oil in the Lamp

Let your light so shine before men, that they may see your good works and glorify your Father in heaven. (Matthew 5:16)

Not so long ago I took a side trip from my planned itinerary. I drove out to a very remote area to see an old monastery called The Abbey of Gethsemani. It is a place where men who feel called to a solitary life go and live until they die. We know them as monks. While there, I visited the gift shop where they sell items made by the hands of these men in residence. I purchased two clay oil lamps and gave them to friends.

I received a note of thanks with these insightful words, *"As I look at the clay lamp I can't help but think of spiritual things. How the clay lamp was made by a potter and had nothing to do or say with how it was made or for what purpose. As I think about the oil in the lamp, I think of how the Holy Spirit fills me and that in order to be full, the inside of the lamp has to be empty first. What a picture of 'Be ye filled with the Spirit.' I also was amazed when you told me I would never have to buy another wick because if this one was set just right, only the oil would burn, and the wick would act as a conduit so that what is inside the lamp can come out. This is so symbolic of the Christ Life."*

My friend, this is very true. As we yield to the Holy Spirit we are His empty vessels filled with His Spirit and instruments of righteousness. People will see the beauty of Jesus in us and this influence will be like a light that will expose the darkness and encourage all those around. Let me encourage you to be that man or woman, boy or girl who lives in immediate control of God's Spirit. Be that light that God uses in a special way wherever He has planted you in this life. As you choose to live this way, you can know that your life is bringing glory to the One Who created you. This is the chief aim for man and this is God's perfect will for you. So friend, shine, let Him shine!

Rev. Chris S. Hodges

Job 20-21; Acts 10:24-48 July 1

Simple Stuff

He has shown you, O man, what is good; And what does the LORD require of you but to do justly, to love mercy, and to walk humbly with your God? (Micah 6:8)

We make Christianity far too complicated. The account of the early church in the book of Acts makes us long for the simplicity our first brothers and sisters experienced. Almost every pastor I know wishes for a new simplicity in church ministry. We often wonder how Christianity got so complicated.

The problem is more than just the complications. All those complications make it difficult for Christians to figure out the "rules." Even with our commitment to Scripture, the "rules" seem to change from church to church. New Christians, especially, can't always find their way through the maze of expectations and layers of organization that plague most of our churches.

How do we avoid the complication quagmire and get back to simplicity in our churches and in our Christian lives? Several different pieces of Scripture hint at the desired simplicity, but no single verse nails it down as clearly as the words written by the prophet Micah. *He has shown you, O man, what is good; And what does the LORD require of you but to do justly, to love mercy, and to walk humbly with your God?*

Micah gives us three simple principles that will revolutionize our lives and our churches if we let them lead us out of the forest of complicated rules and rituals.

First, he tells us to do right. That's what "do justly" means: do the right thing. Outback Steakhouse has a motto that resonates with this simple principle, "No rules, just right!" A regular reading of Scripture will help you understand "right" well enough to remove most of the complications. Doing right speaks to our relationship with God.

In the pursuit of doing right, we're also to love mercy, or compassion. Our hearts are to beat with the needs and cares of those around us. We do not live for ourselves, but for those whom God brings into our lives. Loving mercy speaks to our relationship with others.

Finally, Micah tells us to walk humbly with God. If the evangelical church in America has an "acceptable sin," it may be pride. We work our way through the complications we build into our Christian faith, and doing that often causes us to become proud of our accomplishments. Walking humbly with God speaks to our relationship with ourselves.

Many of us long for simplicity. We will only discover it when we take charge of our lives, remove clutter that complicates them, and seek to do right, love mercy, and walk humbly.

Rev. John Strain

Job 22-24; Acts 11　　　　　　　　　　　　　　　　　　　**July 2**

Spiritual Heritage

Unless the LORD builds the house, they labor in vain who build it. (Psalm 127:1)

Reading through Psalm 100 recently, I was overwhelmed with the goodness of the Lord in our lives as I meditated on the final words, *His faithfulness endures to all generations.* It brought to mind Stan's grandmother, Mom Mom, and the time when she taught this psalm to our daughter (who was probably between 2 and 3 years old) while she was visiting Mom Mom for a few days. Michele came home reciting the whole Psalm. As I recalled this, it stirred my memory about the rich spiritual heritage both Stan and I have through our parents, grandparents and great-grandparents. How grateful we are for the examples of godly living and the prayers of those who have gone before us for not only ourselves, but for our children and grandchildren. Mom Mom was a woman of prayer and impacted many lives, including our family, through her times of doing "God's work," as she called it, before the Lord in prayer.

Perhaps you are thinking that you have not had this kind of heritage in the family you come from, but I would like to encourage you to believe that today can be the beginning of a new heritage in your home and family. As you put your faith and trust in Christ and choose to follow the Scriptures claiming, *...as for me and my house, we will serve the LORD* (Joshua 24:15); and *Unless the LORD builds the house, they labor in vain who build it* (Psalm 127:1). God will be faithful to do what only He can do in your family for generations to come. *Your kingdom is an everlasting kingdom, and your dominion endures through all generations. The LORD is faithful to all his promises and loving toward all he has made* (Psalm 145:13 NIV).

As I sat thanking the Lord for His sovereignty and grace in the lives of the generations of our families, I also contemplated the ongoing impact of our lives on the future generations as we trust Him and live out His faithfulness in our daily lives. Each of us has the opportunity to have a part in the far-reaching effect of the gospel in the lives of those God has placed in our family – our children, their spouses, our grandchildren and eventually their spouses, and then great-grandchildren, and on and on until the Lord returns. It's been said that the only thing we can take to heaven with us is our children.

Thinking on these blessings and promises of the past, for the present, and even the future, causes me to pray that all those whose lives we impact will know God's abundant faithfulness day by day. And that we will be found faithful and obedient, living by His grace.

What a privilege, opportunity and responsibility is ours!!

Be encouraged and take heart, we do not have to attempt this great task by ourselves in our own strength, for *He who calls you is faithful, who also will do it* (1 Thessalonians 5:24). Trust in Him!

DeEtta Marsh

Job 25-27; Acts 12   **July 3**

What's in a Name?

To the church of God which is at Corinth, to those who are sanctified in Christ Jesus, called to be saints, with all who in every place call on the name of Jesus Christ our Lord, both theirs and ours. (1 Corinthians 1:2)

    Christian, Believer, Disciple -- are all titles that speak of those who have put their faith in Jesus as Savior. However, the title that is used the most in the New Testament is that of "Saint."
    The title "saint" comes from the Greek word meaning holy, sacred, set apart. In 1 Corinthians 1:2, Paul defines a saint as anyone who calls on the name of the Lord Jesus. In 2 Thessalonians 1:10, Paul further clarifies the definition of a saint as *all who have believed*. So, any believer in Jesus is defined as a saint by God, one who is set apart and holy. Ephesians 1:4 helps us to further understand how God sees you as a saint. In your relationship with Christ you have been chosen by God to be *...holy and without blame before Him in love.* Your designation as a saint does not have anything to do with how good you are. You are set apart as a saint, holy and blameless in love before God, because God sees you covered in Jesus' righteousness (Romans 3:22).
    In spite of the biblical truth that believers are called saints over 60 times in the New Testament, it is still common for believers to refer to themselves as sinners. The title "sinner" appears in the New Testament 42 times. In 41 of those occurrences the title relates to a person who is not a believer. Only James 4:8 appears to use "sinner" to address a believer. That is a 60-1 ratio! Even a casual reading of these references demonstrates that God's primary title for believers is that of "saint." Thus, God refers to believers not based on what they do

(their imperfect behavior) but rather on who they are in Jesus Christ.

So, what is in a name? Well, if you see yourself as a sinner whom God just tolerates, will you trust Him? Will you love Him? Will you serve Him with joy? Probably not! But if you see yourself as a saint, as one set apart, holy, blameless and loved, you will trust God, you will joyfully submit to Him who accepts you. So, instead of seeing yourself as a sinner saved by grace, see yourself as a saint who sometimes sins, who is already seen by God as holy, blameless and loved. Live in light of who God says that you are!

Rev. Jeff Barbieri

Job 28-29; Acts 13:1-25 July 4

Being Where God Wants You

Then the word of the Lord came to him saying, "Get away from here and turn eastward, and hide by the Brook Cherith, which flows into the Jordan. And it will be that you shall drink from the brook and I have commanded the ravens to feed you there."
(1 Kings 17:2-4)

God has certain requirements that we are to meet before He can use us as effectively as He desires to use us. One of the important requirements God places upon us is for us to be in the right place. I often use a word, I may have coined it, but I know what it means and I believe you will also. The word is <u>thereness</u>. I like to say that there is a <u>thereness</u> to the Christian life.

There is a place where God will do things to us and say things to us that we will not receive anywhere else. If we are not there, in His appointed place, we can miss much of what He had in store for us.

Are you in God's appointed place for your life? God instructed Elijah to go to the Brook Cherith. Then, after the brook dried up and everyone was coping with the effects of the drought, God told Elijah to go to a widow's house in Zarephath.

Then God told Elijah to go show himself to Ahab, the king who had placed a bounty on Elijah's head. Each of these commands to Elijah to be in a certain place at a certain time seemed humanly irrational. However, Elijah knew the importance of being where God told him to be.

Are you in God's appointed place for your life? The Brook Cherith was a couple of hundred feet down in a ravine. There he was isolated and alone. There he was removed from the sounds and the busyness of the world. Day after day he sat, watching the brook slowly dry up and eating the food that was delivered to him. There he was, all alone with God. There he was, just where God wanted him.

The problem with many Christians in the modern world is that they are not where God wants them to be. They are busy. They are active. They are doing good things. Nevertheless, they are not in the place where God has their undivided attention. They have not discovered the <u>thereness</u> of the Christian life.

Are you in God's appointed place for your life? God will reveal Himself *THERE* in ways that He will not reveal Himself anywhere else.

Make haste, get to God's appointed place in your life.

Dr. Roger D. Willmore

Job 30-31; Acts 13:26-52   July 5

Choosing a GPS

There is a way that seems right to a man, but its end is the way to death. (Proverbs 16:25 ESV)

The growing popularity of Global Positioning Systems is amazing. A GPS system will provide accurate time and location information in all weather, day and night, anywhere in the world. In order for this system to work you need a satellite orbiting the earth, a control and monitoring station on earth, and a receiver. With all three of these components working properly you can enter an address into your receiver and it will give you step-by-step directions to get from your present location to that address.

But all of this information will not benefit us unless we take a step of faith and trust the receiver's directions. The receiver is only as reliable as the information that has been programmed into it. Some of us have learned the hard way that the receivers have their flaws and the directions do not always take us where we want to go.

A less popular GPS is God's Positioning System. He also will lead us in all weather, day and night, anywhere in the world, but the primary difference is that God enters the destination and we follow His directions. We don't always know the destination but we do know that His directions are perfect; there are no flaws in His programming. God will lead us on a course that does not make sense to us in order to build our faith in Him and to test our faith in Him. In our flesh we feel much safer when we feel in control, but twice in Proverbs, in verses 14:12 and 16:25, we are told: *There is a way that seems right to a man, but its end is the way to death.*

Jesus told us to *"Enter by the narrow gate. For the gate is wide and the way is easy that leads to destruction, and those who enter by it are many. For the gate is narrow and the way is hard that leads to life, and those who find it are few"* (Matthew 7:13-14 ESV). Many times God's way just does not make sense. Naaman was told in 2 Kings 5 to wash in the Jordan River seven times to be cured of leprosy. In John 9 Jesus put mud on the eyes of a blind man to heal him. God's directions don't make sense but they do show us that our journey is a walk of faith and those who are faithful will hear Him say, *"Well done, good and faithful servant"* when we reach the end (Matthew 25:21 ESV).

Allen E. Beltle

Job 32-33; Acts 14   July 6

God's Call

"Everyone who calls on the name of the Lord will be saved."
(Romans 10:13 NIV)

    What is a call? It is an action to alert us. Life is filled with calls. In sporting events it is the whistle of the referee to call attention to an infraction of the rules; the phone rings because someone is calling us; at the Colony of Mercy the bell in the morning is the wake-up call; e-mails are another way to call people; a call can be made to redeem stocks or bonds; sometimes we call attention to ourselves; or there may be a call to a vocation, trade, profession or occupation. The call I want to focus on is "God's Call." Has He called you to be a pastor, teacher, counselor, missionary, chaplain or youth group leader? Of course, there are other calls God may be directing your way. Only you can answer that for yourself.

    The important issue of life is – what does the Bible instruct us about "Our Call." Here are a few. First is our divine call to salvation. There are two choices we can make in answer to this call: accept or reject God's divine call. In Proverbs 1:24-32, we read what we can expect if we refuse God's divine call. In verse 33 we are told what we can expect if we obey: *But whoever listens to me will live in safety and be at ease without fear of harm* (NIV). In 2 Corinthians 5:17-21, it is our divine call to be reconciled to God through salvation. In John 3:16, *"For God so loved the world that he gave his one and only Son, that whoever believes in him shall not perish but have eternal life"* (NIV). And in Romans 10:13 ... *"Everyone who calls on the name of the Lord will be saved"* (NIV). To be able to answer God's divine call we must hear Him calling and listen to what He is telling us, through His Word, prayer and Christian fellowship. Then we must obey His call and be in a right relationship with Him. As we experience drawing nearer to Him we will also hear His call to rest and be secure in Him (Matthew 11:28-30). Once we have developed this desire to be closer to God we will be sensitive to hearing Him call us to: 1) Spiritual leadership in our homes to our families, in our church, para-church ministries and in all areas of our lives as we impact others for Christ. 2) Service - in Galatians 5:13b ...*serve one another in love* (NIV). Matthew 6:24 warns us about whom or what we serve, and Romans 12:1-2 instructs us to ...*present your bodies a living and holy sacrifice, acceptable to God, which is your spiritual service of worship* (NASB). 3) Behavior - in Galatians 5:16-21, we are told what we are not called to do and in verses 22-25 we read what we are called to do.

By keeping these instructions in front of us daily we will be able to hear God's call to us and live victoriously in Him and His strength.

Chaplain Stan Marsh

Job 34-35; Acts 15:1-21   **July 7**

How Others May Know that You Are a Christian

Now when they saw the boldness of Peter and John, and perceived that they were uneducated and untrained men, they marveled. And they realized that they had been with Jesus.
(Acts 4:13)

The question before us is a searching one. Can people see that you have been with Jesus?

Let us ponder some ways that others can know that we have been with Jesus.

Our attitude toward sin will reveal that we have been with Jesus. *Whoever has been born of God does not (practice) sin, for His seed remains in him; and he cannot (habitually) sin, because he has been born of God* (1 John 3:9). A person who has been to Jesus and received salvation cannot and will not live habitually in sin.

The things that bring satisfaction to our lives will reveal that we have been with Jesus. *"But God said to him, 'You fool! This night your soul will be required of you; then whose will those things be which you have provided?' So is he who lays up treasure for himself and is not rich toward God"* (Luke 12:20-

21). Are you obsessed with the things of the world? A true Christian will invest in eternity by giving his time, talent and treasure to the work of the Lord. His delight is not in the things of this world but in the things of God.

Others can know that we are a Christian by our attitude toward other people. *"By this all will know that you are My disciples, if you have love for one another"* (John 13:35). When Jesus gave that dramatic description of judgment when He would separate Christians from non-Christians (Matthew 25:31-46), He spoke about those who had given food to the hungry, water to the thirsty, clothes to the naked and comfort to the sick and lonely.

These are some definite and practical ways that others can see that you have been with Jesus.

Dr. Roger D. Willmore

Job 36-37; Acts 15:22-41　　　　　　　　　　　　　　　**July 8**

Marching

*Teach me Your way, O LORD; I will walk in Your truth;
Unite my heart to fear Your name.* (Psalm 86.11)

Ephesians 4 describes ways we are to "walk" worthy of the Lord. That word "walk" has been changed to "live a life" which is what it means. But I always remember Pastor Bill Raws saying that he always liked the word "walk" because it gives the picture of taking one step after another, which is how to "live your life." What a great lesson!

2 Timothy 2:3 instructs us to *endure hardship as a good soldier.* One of the hardships of a soldier is "walking." The military terms for walking are what we are looking at today.

M – March: marching is walking. Scripture teaches us to walk uprightly, in the light, humbly, by faith, honestly, in the Spirit, circumspectly, worthy of the Lord, after the commandments. Walking is progressing; progressing through life. A good soldier is to *march* well, be a good and worthwhile soldier. As a Christian we are to *walk* well, be a good and worthwhile Christian. How are you *marching* today?

A – About Face: while marching, sometimes it's necessary to reverse the direction. In life, it is necessary to reverse the direction you are going. There may be an obstacle that will not allow you to continue forward, and God is leading you to turn around. When Jesus is saying *you must be born again* (John 3:7), this means an *about face* is necessary in your life. When Romans 3:23 tells you that sin causes you to *fall short of the glory of God*, it's time for an *about face* in your lifestyle. Do not ignore this important part of your *marching* today.

R – Right Face: this involves a different direction or path to take. What way is right? Proverbs 14:12 (NIV) says, *there is a way that seems right…, but… it leads to death*. There are many decisions to be made, but without the proper commander we may not make the correct turns in order to avoid disaster. *The ways of the LORD are right* (Hosea 14:9). Many times you can't move forward; a *right face* may be needed in your marching.

C – Command: always involved in marching; it is necessary to obey or suffer the consequences (no option). For the Christian it is the same; we must listen and be alert for the commands. John 14:15 (NIV), *If you love Me, keep my commands*. There are many commands in *walking* through this life, but they are given to us in His Word, so we are without excuse. How are you doing in following the commands in your *marching*?

H – Halt: when necessary. Sometimes you must just "stop!" Where are you going? It may be in the wrong direction. 1 Corinthians 10:31 tells us to *do all to the glory of God*. If you're not doing that, then *halt*! Are you letting your light shine (Matthew 5:16)? No? Then you must *halt*. This is important to do in your *marching*.

Jack Noel

Job 38-40; Acts 16:1-21   July 9

Guest or Host?

...that Christ may dwell in your hearts through faith...
(Ephesians 3:17)

There is a great difference between being a guest or a host in a home. As a guest, proper etiquette demands conformity to the will and desires of the host. One waits to be invited to the meal table, to use the TV, to take things from the refrigerator, and to utilize the bathroom facilities. The articles of furniture remain where the host placed them and rearrangement would be totally improper.

On the other hand, the host or homeowner would determine the time and place to be seated at the meal table, or would offer the use of the TV or access to the refrigerator. The owner has the right to occupy the lounge chair in the TV room, kick off his shoes, and use the remote to choose his programs.

These obvious differences have their parallel with the role we assign to Christ in our hearts. Our theme text uses the word "dwell" to translate a Greek word meaning to settle down. It contains the thought of feeling at home. Paul was praying for the believers in Ephesus. In his prayer he included the petition that Christ would be at home in their hearts. He would have the freedom of the heart-home just like the host. He would make changes that would be in keeping with His will. He would set the standard for the household functions. It would be His responsibility to determine acceptable conduct and entertainment. In a sense we would be like the guest in the home rather than the homeowner (1 Corinthians 6:19).

Parents go through a transition from being able to set the house rules for their children until the children are grown, married and homeowners. Now they visit as guests. Spiritually speaking, believers must determine whether they are going to treat Jesus as a temporary guest or the owner of their lives.

Is Jesus Christ at home in your heart today?

Rev. William A. Raws

Job 41-42; Acts 16:22-40   July 10

Open Your Mouth Wide

I am the LORD your God, Who brought you out of the land of Egypt; Open your mouth wide, and I will fill it. (Psalm 81:10)

When I think of this invitation, I picture a young bird eagerly responding to its mother's feeding in the nest. That imagery was impressed upon me when a baby blackbird ended up sitting helplessly in our front yard. It would incessantly chirp and open its little beak skyward, urgently wanting its feeding. The mother wasn't coming around, so we carefully fed it a small worm. Unfortunately, this episode concluded with a funeral service.

We need to abide in God's "nest," feeding on His gracious Word: *It is written, "Man shall not live by bread alone, but by every word that proceeds from the mouth of God"* (Matthew 4:4). In the beginning, God created our first human parents with ultimate needs that are unique to mankind--those made in the image of God (Genesis 1:28). These include the need for love, acceptance, significance, security, and belonging. In the Garden, Adam and Eve initially had complete fulfillment as they enjoyed full fellowship with God and each other. Alas, after the Fall, everyone has been on a quest to get these ultimate needs fulfilled. Most people try to get these needs met through relationships but end up disappointed by mild or severe rejection. Thankfully, God has made provision for healing and abundant life through Christ's redemption and indwelling presence (Ephesians 1:3, 6; 2:4-10).

Like a young bird we should "open our mouth wide" to feed upon God's love and grace. Jesus said, *If you abide in My word, you are My disciples indeed...* (John 8:31). Our God yearns for us to receive His provision for salvation and abundant living. The Lord Jesus was grieved over Israel's stubborn unbelief when He cried out, *O Jerusalem, Jerusalem, the one who kills the prophets and stones those who are sent to her! How often I wanted to gather your children together, as a hen gathers her chicks under her wings, but you were not willing!* (Matthew

23:37).

Our gracious Savior longs to bless us fully, if we remain yielded and confident in Him.

Dr. John Woodward

Psalms 1-3; Acts 17:1-15   **July 11**

The Blessing of an Ordered Life

Whoever offers praise glorifies Me; And to him who orders his conduct aright I will show the salvation of God. (Psalm 50:23)

When the Israelites left their bondage in Egypt God realized the need for them to have structure in their lives, so He gave them the Law. When a man enters the Colony of Mercy he is leaving the bondage of sin as a form of slavery as well. He, too, needs structure in order to bring his chaotic life into some semblance of order. But we live in a culture that rebels against rules of any kind. "Color Outside the Lines," "No Boundaries" and "Have it Your Way" resound in our ears, as advertising slogans. As a result, we as believers have been taught that ordered living is old-fashioned or, in Christian lingo, legalistic. Did God not tell us to order our prayer life? For example, Daniel lived an incredibly victorious life in extremely adverse conditions. When his enemies sought to trip him up they knew that they could only do so in connection with his ordered prayer life.

While we never want to be obsessive concerning spiritual activities, we do need to be consistent. This is especially true concerning our time of solitude and prayer. A scheduled time alone with our Lord is essential. Some might say I cannot always make time in the morning so I get alone with God some other time of the day. Could you imagine saying to your employer, "I will be into work when I can find some time to do so?" You would be fired immediately. Should we have the audacity to speak to the Supreme Authority with any less respect than we give to human authority?

When our Lord walked on this earth His ministry was far more demanding than anything we will ever know. And yet in the midst of His busiest times He didn't neglect time alone with His Father. *Now in the morning, having risen a long while before daylight, He went out and departed to a solitary place; and there He prayed. And Simon and those who were with Him searched for Him. When they found Him, they said to Him, "Everyone is looking for You"* (Mark 1:35-37).

Lord, forgive me for not sharing your urgency to spend time alone with the Father.

Chaplain Jim Freed

Psalms 4-6; Acts 17:16-34   **July 12**

Who Occupies the Throne?

..."Whoever desires to come after Me, let him deny himself, and take up his cross, and follow Me." (Mark 8:34)

There is only one throne in the Christian life. That throne stands for Lordship. Who sits in the seat and occupies the throne in your life?
There is a cross in each of our lives as a Christian. Many people talk about the cross they bear in life, usually referring to some hardship they are going through that seems to linger on. The cross in our lives, as a Christian, is not a hardship we endure, or an ornament we wear around our necks, or carry in our hands to be seen by others, but a life of self-denial. A person can have crosses on display all through his home and not be born again. You see, there cannot be two Lords in your life; one has to be put down, and that one should be "The Big I." Paul speaks of the flesh in Romans chapter seven. You can take the word "flesh," turn it around and drop the "h" and you have the word "self." Much of what we blame Satan for is none other than "self," that part of us that wants to have its own way.

If I want Christ to rule and reign on the throne of my life, then "self" must be on the cross. Remember, when Jesus died on the cross for your sins, He also died for "self." Jesus died for "sin and self." Leave "self" where it belongs, nailed to the cross.

When I am Spirit-filled, I will want Christ to sit on the throne seat of my life and I will count myself out. I will see my "self" crucified with Christ and no longer a slave to the world, flesh, and devil.

My friend, we do not need to agonize and emotionalize to be filled with the Holy Spirit. He waits to fill us. We need only to confess our sin and take our hands off of our lives and He will take over.

Take the stress out of your life, my friend; surrender "sin and self" to Him. This is what you are looking for; this is the life that is hidden with Christ in God; this is life on the highest plane. So, let go and let the Lord occupy the throne.

Rev. Chris S. Hodges

Psalms 7-9; Acts 18   **July 13**

Christ Himself

For you are all sons of God through faith in Christ Jesus.
(Galatians 3:26)

We all counsel. Whether you have ever stepped foot in a seminary or not, you counsel. Counseling involves teaching, training, encouraging, admonishing, challenging, guiding, sharing, discipling, and coming alongside of another individual. From that view, we all qualify as counselors.

Whether you are chatting with a friend over a steaming cup of tea, or discipling a new or not-so-new believer, or parenting, you are pointing people towards something. What is that something? We are prone to point people to read their Bible, pray, serve, fast, confess their sins, etc. THESE ARE ALL GOOD THINGS, even vital things. However, it is Christ Himself that saves; it is Christ Himself that rescues; it is Christ Himself that heals. He may choose to use any one of the above avenues to accomplish His plan, but in what do we trust? Are we trusting the Person of Jesus Christ or are we trusting in those things we do, helpful things, but activities rooted in ourselves, our abilities, and our faithfulness? Brother and Sister, THESE ARE ALL GOOD THINGS. But our counsel to ourselves and others should point to the person of Jesus Christ. All of those activities are good as tools that point to Christ. Successful counsel results in embracing the One True God rather than doing things in an effort to improve our situation. It is about a Person, not a process.

Philippians 2:13: *for it is God who works in you both to will and to do for His good pleasure.*

1 Thessalonians 5:23-24: *Now may the God of peace Himself sanctify you completely; and may your whole spirit, soul, and body be preserved blameless at the coming of our Lord Jesus Christ. He who calls you is faithful, who also will do it.*

Romans 15:13 (NIV): *May the God of hope fill you with all joy and peace as you trust in him, so that you may overflow with hope by the power of the Holy Spirit.*

Diane Hunt

Psalms 10-12; Acts 19:1-20   **July 14**

The Christian Life is a Practical Life

In this the children of God and the children of the devil are manifest: Whoever does not practice righteousness is not of God, nor is he who does not love his brother. (1 John 3:10)

The Christian life, as presented in the Bible, is a very practical life. When the Bible speaks of *belief,* it speaks of a belief that affects *behavior.* When the Bible speaks of *doctrine,* it speaks of doctrine's effect upon *duty.* In other words, if we say that we believe in the Lord Jesus Christ then there must be some practical expressions of our belief in everyday life. If we say that we embrace the great *doctrines* of the Bible, then we must reveal our adherence to the doctrines in our *duty.*

The apostle John addresses a number of practical aspects of the Christian life in 1 John 3:10-18.

John reminds us that *righteousness* is practical. *Whoever does not practice righteousness is not of God* (v.10). Righteousness is not just a state or standing in the Christian life, it is something that expresses itself. We live in a world that wants things to be gray or neutral. The Christian, however, cannot be neutral. Right is right and wrong is wrong.

John reminds us that *love* is practical. *...nor is he who does not love his brother* (v.10). Love one another is the most basic, elementary aspect of the Christian life. Little children are taught by parents and Sunday School teachers at the earliest age *to love one another.* This is the ABC's of the Christian life. It does not get more practical than this.

John reminds us that *kindness* is practical. *But whoever has this world's goods, and sees his brother in need, and shuts up his heart from him, how does the love of God abide in him?* (v.17). My definition of kindness is *homespun love.* By this I mean that love is expressed in the little, everyday details of life.

The Christian life is practical. It can make its greatest impact in the routine of daily living...right there where you are.

Dr. Roger D. Willmore

Psalms 13-15; Acts 19:21-41 July 15

Keeping Your Guard Up

And the peace of God, which surpasses all comprehension, will guard your hearts and your minds in Christ Jesus. Finally, brethren, whatever is true, whatever is honorable, whatever is right, whatever is pure, whatever is lovely, whatever is of good repute, if there is any excellence, and if anything worthy of praise, dwell on these things. (Philippians 4:7-8 NASB)

On a daily basis I receive a newsletter from a popular TV fitness trainer. This morning I needed to hear what she said. Referring to diet and exercise she wrote, "Just because you are rehabilitated doesn't mean you don't have to be vigilant to guard against a relapse." A few weeks ago I reached my goal weight

(AGAIN!). Since then it has been a battle. Laziness, poor eating, holidays, lack of planning and vacation. All of these excuses have quickly gotten me off track. But the truth is that I made it to my goal weight and I began to relax. That is a dangerous place to be. Feelings of compromise, cheating, I can skip a day, all came flooding in. Pride can easily make one believe that since I have "arrived" nothing can touch me. What a lie!

The same is true in our walk with Jesus. We can get pretty prideful in thinking we have arrived. We have had a wonderful transformation take place in our hearts and lives because of Christ. Then we get to thinking we have arrived or "made it." Before we know it our guard is down. We are not diligent in our study and prayers. We skip prayer meeting and church…just this once… then twice. Read the quote again.

"Just because you are rehabilitated doesn't mean you don't have to be vigilant to guard against a relapse."

No matter what your struggle may have been: alcohol, drugs, food, exercise, devotions, remember that you have been rehabilitated through Jesus Christ. BUT we must always be on guard so that we do not relapse into old ways of thinking and living. Keep your guard up! If you, like me, have let your guard down for a bit, get back to where you need to be! Repent of your prideful thinking that you can go it alone or that you no longer need good disciplines because you have come so far. Remember the battle never ends. Our guard must always be up!

Kathy Withers

Psalms 16-17; Acts 20:1-16　　　　　　　　　　　　　　**July 16**

Health in the Hidden Part

Cause me to hear Your lovingkindness in the morning, For in You do I trust; Cause me to know the way in which I should walk, For I lift up my soul to You. (Psalm 143:8)

One of the most important disciplines of the Christian life is the time of daily personal devotions. This is a time when the inner life of the believer is nourished and strengthened. Some of us give considerable care to factors which would promote good physical health, but we tend to be less concerned about the hidden life of the soul and spirit. Just as proper nutrition is essential to the health of the physical being, systematic feeding is essential to the inner being. Both Peter and Paul comment on the spiritual diet (1 Peter 2:1-2; 1 Corinthians 3:1-3a). Without proper nourishment the spiritual life will lie dormant or retarded in its growth.

I learned this the hard way. I was given a piece of shrubbery for our yard. It came in a container which I thought was tin. On other occasions I had left plants in such containers but had cut slits in the metal to allow the roots to receive nutrients from the surrounding soil. After a short time the tin would rot away. On this occasion I didn't realize that the container was aluminum and not subject to rotting. After a year, the plant began to show signs of ill health and finally died. When I dug it up, I discovered my mistake – the container was still undissolved and the roots had been crowded and starved.

Our spiritual root system needs nurturing and feeding, too. One of the best ways to accomplish this is a daily time of devotion with the Lord. In most cases a morning meeting with the Lord seems to be the most meaningful. Strength for the rest of the day results from this "manna in the morning."

Generally, the devotional time will include two main parts: Bible reading and prayer. The Bible reading is not to be a study time as much as allowing God to speak to us. In prayer we can reflect upon what God has said and then present our petitions.

I have yet to meet a spiritually healthy Christian who does not practice this intimate time with the Lord regularly. Backslidden Christians often admit that the first step away from the Lord was neglecting the Word and prayer.

Rev. William A. Raws

Psalms 18-19; Acts 20:17-38   July 17

Ordering One's Life

My son, give me your heart. (Proverbs 23:26)

Whatever your hand finds to do, do it with all your might. (Ecclesiastes 9:10)

God wants a heart committed to Him. Adoniram Judson, the father of American missionary work, exemplifies that surrender. But he began life in the opposite direction. His strict father sent him to Brown University in Rhode Island. There his best friend led him into deism; this a belief that God created the world and then abandoned it. This denies the biblical revelation about God and Jesus, His Son. Adoniram's father met a brick wall in trying to argue with him; every argument proved too weak.

Adoniram took a steamer from Albany to New York City. The sight of the city made him sick at heart. Returning to Plymouth, MA, by stage coach, he stopped at an inn in Connecticut. He considered death an exit, at best extinction! At worst? "Who knows?"

As he tried to sleep he heard groans and steps coming and going. "I wonder," he said, "would this man be ready for death?" In the morning as he paid his bill he casually asked regarding the young man. The answer: "Dead." One word! Adoniram asked, "Who was he?" "Oh, he was a young man from the university in Rhode Island, name of Eames." "LOST" flashed in his mind.

He began to ponder his whole belief system. Adoniram's doubts began to dissipate gradually. He did not experience a blinding flash on the Damascus Road. However, by December he had completely dedicated his life to Jesus Christ. He asked himself, **"How can I so order my future as best to please God?"**

He finally reached Burma in 1812 and returned for his first furlough thirty-three years later! He met many trying situations in his life, was even imprisoned for seventeen years by the British in Burma. When they buried him in the Bay of Bengal, the Burmese remembered the 7000 members of the Burmese churches, the translation of the Bible into their language and the launching of the Foreign Missionary Enterprise in America.

In giving his heart so completely, he truly ordered his life to please God and make an impact on Burma.

Am I seeking the mind of God and asking that same question: "How can I so order my future as best to please God?" I wonder if I have a focal point of commitment and a willingness to respond to his command: "My son, give me your heart." Will I do this with all of my heart?

Dr. George Kelsey

Psalms 20-22; Acts 21:1-17   **July 18**

Go Deeper

"Put out into deep water, and let down the nets for a catch."
(Luke 5:4 NIV)

In the Gospel of Luke chapter 5:1-11, Jesus gets into Peter's boat and tells him in v. 4 *"Put out into deep water, and let down the nets for a catch."* Can you imagine Peter, an experienced fisherman who had been out all night and had caught nothing, and then came Jesus telling him to go back out there? Peter was exhausted, tired and was cleaning his nets for the next night's work (v. 2). I'm sure Peter was eager to get home and get some sleep before it was time to do it all over again.

Jesus told Peter to go back out, "go deeper," and let down the nets he had just cleaned! These verses are so much more than a "How to Fish" lesson. What was Jesus really asking Peter to do? He was asking Peter to trust Him and obey Him. Peter did have a choice and I'm sure it wasn't just a blind, snap decision for Peter to obey Jesus. I imagine everything inside him wanted to say, "Teacher, I'm tired. I know what I'm doing here. I've been doing this all my life. I'm hungry. I just want to go home." But Jesus was beckoning Peter to *step out of his comfort zone*, to trust Him and "go deeper," to accomplish something greater than he could accomplish without Jesus. Peter did just what Jesus asked of him…and the result? Peter had a catch so huge that the nets and boats could barely contain all the fish!

There are many times Jesus calls us to "go deeper," to take a step of faith and just trust Him even when we are tired or disappointed. Maybe there is something bigger and better that He has planned for us and if we don't trust Him and go deeper we will never experience His blessing.

Perhaps you have just "skimmed" the surface of the calling in your life and the abundant blessing He has for you. Jesus …*is able to do exceedingly abundantly above all that we ask or think, according to the power that works in us* (Ephesians 3:20). I would hate to lose the abundant blessing that He has planned for me because I didn't answer His call to "go deeper."

Is Jesus calling you to take a step out of your comfort zone and "go deeper?" He is right there with you…go ahead, take that step.

Mary Ann Kiernan

Psalms 23-25; Acts 21:18-40　　　　　　　　　　　　**July 19**

The Truth That Sets Us Free

To the Jews who had believed him, Jesus said, "If you hold to my teaching, you are really my disciples. Then you will know the truth, and the truth will set you free." (John 8:31-32 NIV)

Implicit in this passage is an acknowledgement of the reality of knowledge, truth and freedom. Now, to the generation of my grandfather and great-grandfather this would be a rather uninteresting observation. However, these are postmodern times, or so we are told, where these fundamental notions have been called into question. Indeed, we live in a time where truth is thought to be personal or a construction of the accepted standards of one's community. So, there is truth for me and there is truth for you and it is thought to be arrogant of me to impose my truth on you. Indeed, who are we to impose the "truths" of Christianity on anyone who does not share the commitments of our "community"? The problem here is that truth, thought of this way, could not be what Jesus had in mind. In the context of this famous passage, Jesus says such intolerant things as, *if you do not believe that I am the one I claim to be, you will indeed die in your sins* (v. 24) and a bit later says that without being set free by the truth, one is a *slave to sin* (v. 34). The point here seems to be that people are, on their own, inadequate and stand in need of a Savior who brings freedom *through the knowledge of gospel truth*.

It couldn't be the case that Jesus meant that socially-constructed truth brings freedom since societies are not always right. In fact, societies often place value on things that are decidedly wrong and further bondage is the result. (Just ask the most recent celebrity in the grips of scandal!) If I know anything, I know that left on my own, I do not know how to be free from the power of sin. I do not want "my truth" and I definitely don't want the truth of our society. I want His truth, the actual and ultimate truth, that which is truly, well, true. It is this truth that sets us free from the power of sin. How do we find these truths? Jesus gives us the answer in this passage: in the teaching and life of Jesus Himself. This is why Jesus goes on to claim to be the way, THE TRUTH, and the life and that *no one comes to the Father but by Him* (John 14:6).

Travis Dickinson

Psalms 26-28; Acts 22   **July 20**

What Do You Do With the WORD?

But prove yourselves doers of the word, and not merely hearers who delude themselves. For if anyone is a hearer of the word and not a doer, he is like a man who looks at his natural face in the mirror; for once he has looked at himself and gone away, he has immediately forgotten what kind of person he was.
(James 1:22-24 NASB)

As a counselor I see many people who claim to be Christians yet continue to live defeated lives. As a Christian there are times

I struggle with the same syndrome as Paul - doing that which I don't want to do. He says in Romans 7:18b-19 (ESV), *For I have the desire to do what is right, but not the ability to carry it out. For I do not do the good I want, but the evil I do not want is what I keep doing.*

Do you sometimes feel like situations and things are not really going well in your life – so that you are not really experiencing all the blessings and victories you believe God promises? I am going to ask you the same question I myself must face daily – are you truly "doing" the Word? Are you really applying Scripture to your life, or are you just reading and proclaiming it without living it? Maybe you are not even reading it. Without reading and application of the Word, neither you nor I will experience God's working in our lives. Below are some verses that proclaim to us the promises we have from Scripture that if we really believe in them we will find victory. When you read these verses – ask yourself... am I really trusting in or proclaiming these truths in my life?

- God's mercies are NEW every morning – great is Thy faithfulness (Lamentations 3:22-23)
- We are more than conquerors (Romans 8:37-39)
- God is in CONTROL (Jeremiah 31:11)
- We have a Spirit of power and not FEAR (2 Timothy 1:7)
- Our flesh/sin is crucified (Galatians 5:24)
- Our sins are no longer remembered (Isaiah 43:25)
- I forget that which is behind (Philippians 3:15)
- The battle is God's (2 Chronicles 20:15)
- I will fear no evil (Psalm 23:4-6)
- Christians are VICTORIOUS (1 John 5:4-5)

That's just the start – there is so much more.

My prayer is that you (and I) will each day learn how to truly trust in His promises.

Dr. Lynne Jahns

Psalms 29-30; Acts 23:1-15 **July 21**

The Secret of Growing in Grace

But grow in the grace and knowledge of our Lord and Savior Jesus Christ. To Him be the glory both now and forever.
(2 Peter 3:18)

The secret of growing in grace is to grow in the knowledge of the Lord Jesus as we learn how to practice His presence and be continually controlled by His indwelling Holy Spirit. To know more about Him, and to walk along with Him in our everyday life, creates within us a godly desire to be more like Him. It is important not only to know more about God from His Word but to also appropriate what we learn. The world has many Bible scholars but so few who appropriate what they know.

The moment we are baptized into Christ, we are set apart for Him, we are sanctified, and thus we grow more and more like Him. We do not grow into sanctification, but we grow in sanctification. We do not become saints by trying hard to be good, but we want to be good because we are saints in God's eyes. Paul said in 2 Corinthians 3:18, *But we all, with unveiled face, beholding as in a mirror the glory of the Lord, are being transformed into the same image from glory to glory, just as by the Spirit of the Lord.*

Someone has rightly said, *"Wisdom from above brightens a man's face."* The secret of increasing from glory to glory is to behold the glory of the Lord. In other words, when we take time to study His Word and pray and learn of Him, we want to become more and more like Him. This desire for Him to have His way within us leads us into what the saints of old called *"the abiding life."* This *"abiding life"* is the means by which the Holy Spirit conforms us to the image of Jesus. Do people see the beauty of Jesus in you? We become saints by receiving the Savior, but we become saintly by being controlled by the Holy Spirit.

My friend, God not only saves us from the penalty of sin, He is able to save us from the power of sin. This Bible truth becomes experiential as we simply abide in Him Who is our Life!

Walk in this truth, my friend, and people will see the beauty of Jesus in you.

Rev. Chris S. Hodges

Psalms 31-32; Acts 23:16-35   **July 22**

Keeping Silent

Do not move an ancient boundary stone set up by your forefathers. (Proverbs 22:28 NIV)

I have read this verse many times as I read a Proverb a day, but I must admit I haven't taken time to really figure out what the verse means until now.

According to Matthew Henry, commenting on this passage, "We may infer hence that a deference is to be paid, in all civil matters, to usages that have prevailed ...in which it becomes us to acquiesce, lest an attempt to change it, under pretense of changing it for the better, prove of dangerous consequence."

For some, it seems change is always better. Do we have that attitude? I have lived long enough to see many changes in our society, in our churches, and in our personal lives. As I read Scripture, I am impressed with how holy worship was considered to be. When people entered the temple, they were filled with awe. God held a place of authority and sanctity. Today I watch people enter a time of prayer or a worship service with almost an air of casualness or jocularity. *The boundary stone has been moved.* We need to ask ourselves WHY are we moving the boundary stone.

I could mention other obvious changes, but I won't. Let us pray that as we enter a time or place of worship, we will see the need to prepare our hearts to meet *God* Himself. Habakkuk 2:20, *BUT THE LORD IS IN HIS HOLY TEMPLE; LET ALL THE EARTH KEEP SILENCE BEFORE HIM.*

Marilyn Willett Heavilin

Psalms 33-34; Acts 24   **July 23**

Interpreting the Bible

But be doers of the word, and not hearers only, deceiving yourselves. (James 1:22)

Recently I was in a Sunday School class and I left determined not to return. We were looking at the miracle of Jesus walking on the water and how it can relate to us today. There was a fine printed outline and some well-conceived questions. After each question was addressed by various people, one gentleman began to take each word, go into the Greek, look at secondary meanings, go back to the Old Testament history, etc. It was unbelievable.

A friend sent me this story: the Lone Ranger and Tonto stopped in the desert for the night. After they set up their tent, both men fell sound asleep. Some hours later, Tonto woke the Lone Ranger and said, "Kemo Sabe, look toward the sky-what do you see?"

The Lone Ranger replied, "I see a million stars." Tonto said, "What does that tell you?" The Lone Ranger replied, "Astronomically speaking, it tells me there are millions of galaxies and potentially billions of planets. Theologically, it is evident that the Lord is all-powerful, and we are small and insignificant. What does it tell you, Tonto?"

Tonto was silent for a moment and then said, "Kemo Sabe, you are dumber than buffalo. It means someone stole the tent!"

The Bible was written for the common man. Sure, there are thoughts and concepts that need explanation and interpretation, but they are very few. Our problem is not what we don't understand but believing and obeying what we do understand!

It seems the more we plumb the depths the more we come up with our own interpretations. Thus we have various theological camps, denominations, man-made rules and regulations, etc.

2 Peter 1:20-21 (NASB) says, *...no prophecy of Scripture is a matter of one's own interpretation, for no prophecy was ever made by an act of human will, but men moved by the Holy Spirit spoke from God.* 2 Timothy 2:15 (NLT) says, *Work hard so you*

can present yourself to God and receive his approval. Be a good worker, one who does not need to be ashamed and who correctly explains the word of truth.

Deuteronomy 29:29 says, *The secret things belong to the Lord our God, but those things which are revealed belong to us and to our children forever, that we may do all the words of this law.* There are some things theologians have debated for centuries. If they cannot understand them and agree, neither can you or I. But there are a multitude of things that you do understand very clearly. Put them into practice in your life. Leave the rest to God.

Rev. Neil Fichthorn

Psalms 35-36; Acts 25   **July 24**

The Various Positions of Worship

Give unto the LORD the glory due to His name; Worship the LORD in the beauty of holiness. (Psalm 29:2)

Have you ever considered how we approach God's presence, whether corporately or individually? Imagine with me that the Creator, Sustainer, Savior of the universe would desire to have a relationship with the likes of you and me. It is, at times, overwhelming and hard to take in. Our privilege when we know Him as our personal Lord and Savior is to live our lives as living sacrifices, holy and acceptable to Him. 1 Peter 2:9 reminds us that we are *a chosen people, a royal priesthood, a holy nation, a people belonging to God, that you may declare the praises of him who called you out of darkness into his wonderful light* (NIV).

Let's think about sporting events. Crowds cheer in thunderous applause for men and women who have trained and excelled in particular areas. When visiting an art museum, there is a very quiet respectful atmosphere where people reflect, think and take in all that they are observing. Musicians have the ability to move huge crowds of people either in rebellion or respect. Think of Handel's Messiah – the crowd stands to their feet during the Hallelujah Chorus – originally to honor a king – we still stand in honor of the King of Kings and Lord of Lords.

Is there a correct way or position for our worship of God? I love to search through Scriptures to think about how various characters honored and worshipped God. Adam and Eve hid when they knew they had disobeyed God; Moses took his shoes off at the burning bush because the ground was holy; David danced in total abandonment before the Lord; Shadrach, Meshach and Abednego experienced God's presence with them in the fire; Isaiah became aware that he was a man of unclean lips; wise men brought gifts and paid honor; Mary anointed with very costly perfume.

As we think through this topic, I can't help but think that we as believers should be able to worship God with thunderous applause; selflessly give of our time, talents, abilities, resources; quietly, humbly honoring when aware of our sinfulness; a proper display of respect; healthy fear; extreme love and devotion and gratitude.

Is there a proper position? No, not just one. I long for the day when we are in God's presence, our response will be perfect and automatic, without fear of who is around us or may be watching and observing! If we can display respect for our President and various political dignitaries, if we can lose ourselves in support of athletes, or be moved in our emotions by art or music, may I encourage us to really think through how we respond to God Almighty, Who loved us enough to give His only Son, Jesus Christ, for us!

Robert Hayes

Psalms 37-39; Acts 26   **July 25**

Singing and Dancing

The Lord your God is in the midst of you, a Mighty One, a Savior [Who saves]! He will rejoice over you with joy; He will rest [in silent satisfaction] and in His love He will be silent and make no mention [of past sins, or even recall them]; He will exult over you with singing (Zephaniah 3:17, Amplified Bible)

I know some of you grew up in churches that didn't allow dancing. I grew up in an atmosphere where singing and dancing were very much a part of my Ukrainian culture. Whenever family and friends gathered you could bet there would be folk songs sung and couples twirling to polkas. I loved dancing the polka with my Poppa, my brother Adolf and my Uncle Albert. When you polka you can't help but smile and laugh. I recall those times with a bitter sweetness. My brother Adolf died in 1976 and with his death, the polka died, too. My parents no longer danced.

In this past week I've discovered a Scripture through my Grace Walk study by Steve McVey that has opened my eyes in a whole new way. Zephaniah 3:17, *The Lord your God is in the midst of you, a Mighty One, a Savior [Who saves]! He will rejoice over you with joy; He will rest [in silent satisfaction] and in His love He will be silent and make no mention [of past sins, or even recall them]; He will exult over you with singing* (Amplified Bible).

Steve McVey pointed out that the word "exalt" means "to twirl, to dance with enthusiasm. He rejoices over you with shouts of joy." [8] Can you imagine our Father God loving us so much, we who are His children through spiritual rebirth, that He sings and dances...not just dances but twirls (I like to think it's a polka) over us!!! Wow...that's my Abba Father, dancing over me! Me? Can I believe that He would dance over me even though I still mess up? Yes! Yes! Yes! And He dances and sings over you, too! Doesn't that just put a smile on your face?

The polka hasn't died. It's alive and well and today...my God, my Savior is dancing over you and me! May this truth sink deep in your heart and soul. When someone asks why you're smiling...you can tell them, you can't help but smile and rejoice because God is dancing the polka over you today!

MaryAnn Kiernan

---

[8] Grace Walk, Steve McVey. Pg. 185, 2004.

Psalms 40-42; Acts 27:1-26   **July 26**

Run the Race, Win the Prize

Not that I have already attained, or am already perfected; but I press on, that I may lay hold of that for which Christ Jesus has also laid hold of me. Brethren, I do not count myself to have apprehended; but one thing I do, forgetting those things which are behind and reaching forward to those things which are ahead, I press toward the goal for the prize of the upward call of God in Christ Jesus. (Philippians 3:12-14)

    The apostle Paul uses a very descriptive word picture here. He picks up the imagery of the athletic arena where the races are run. He pictures himself as an athlete who is running for the finish line in an effort to win the prize. He also utilizes the picture as a source of exhortation to the Philippian Christians to run the race.

    As we consider the race we run as Christians, let us think about some practical applications of the race.

    Every race has a starting point. Paul informs us that he is in the race and that he is running for the goal and for the prize. However, Paul's starting point in the race is recorded in Acts 9:1-25. His starting point was his encounter with the risen Savior on the road to Damascus. It was here that Paul met Jesus and received Him as his personal Lord and Savior. This was his starting point in the race. Can you remember your starting point? When did you enter the race?

    Every race has a course. This race is not a sprint; it is a marathon. In fact, it is a marathon with an obstacle course. Moses ran this course, Joseph ran this course, Joshua ran this course, Elijah ran this course, Daniel ran this course, Jesus ran this course. Now you run this course. Everyone faces his own personal and unique hurdles and obstacles, but each one has to run and finish the course.

    Every race has a finish line. Paul spoke of his finish line in 2 Timothy 4:6-8, *For I am already being poured out as a drink offering, and the time of my departure is at hand. I have fought a good fight, I have finished the race, I have kept the faith. Finally, there is laid up for me the crown of righteousness, which the Lord, the righteous Judge, will give to me on that Day, and not to me only but also to all who have loved His appearing.*

I admonish you today! Run the race…Win the prize!

Dr. Roger D. Willmore

Psalms 43-45; Acts 27:27-44   **July 27**

Understanding the Things of God

…they are spiritually discerned. (1 Corinthians 2:14b)

The Bible places people in three categories: the natural man, the spiritual man and the carnal Christian. In the setting of our text, the apostle Paul evaluates these according to their capacity to know the truth of God. The caption, "natural man" (person), relates to the unsaved individual whose comprehension is limited to sensual things (things learned through the senses – touching, tasting, smelling, hearing, seeing). He is spiritually dead, separated from the things of the Spirit of God. Since he can't put these things together, they appear to him as foolishness. What will correct this condition? Only through his being born from above (John 3:3,5).

A second category, the carnal Christian, is profiled in 1 Corinthians 3:1-3. He is described as living according to the flesh (the dynamic capacity for sinfulness). His capacity for spiritual things is limited to baby food. His conduct is the expression of envy. It results in strife and divisions. Distinguishing between this person and the natural man is very difficult. Look around among church people and note the fact that there is little discernable difference between the worldly Christian and the unsaved.

Examining the third category, the spiritual man, (1 Corinthians 2:15-16), we recognize a different capacity for understanding the truth of God. The spiritual person is described as "judging all things." Since he is guided by the Spirit, he is able to discern and evaluate both natural and spiritual things. He is said in verse 16 to have the mind of Christ.

How does one move from a flesh-dominated life to a spiritual life? The Holy Spirit stands willing to take over the lordship of the life and control the yielded Christian. This is what is referred to as the Spirit-filled life (Ephesians 5:18).

Each of us fits into one of these categories, but only the Spirit-controlled person can please God. We can recognize the Spirit-filled life by seeing the fruit of the Spirit being displayed in it (Galatians 5:22-23).

Rev. William A. Raws

Psalms 46-48; Acts 28 July 28

Of Him, Through Him and To Him!

For of Him and through Him and to Him are all things, to whom be glory forever. Amen. (Romans 11:36)

The Word of God is very clear, again and again, about the sovereign power of God over all things. We as human beings are totally infected with the sin we have inherited as Adam's descendants. Satan's deception was to tell Eve she would be wise, like God, discerning between good and evil, if she ate from the tree. She was deceived and she ate. Adam joined her, and now the entire human race is deceived. We actually think we are wise enough to make "good" decisions. We generally believe that we, like God, can discern between good and evil and have some power apart from Him. We even believe we have the potential power to change the course of history through our "wise" decisions or our abundant prayers! And we tend to believe we have the right to have our opinions about what God seems to be doing in the realm of world events or in our own personal life.

The second psalm depicts the ultimate display of man's egocentric thinking. *The kings of the earth prepare for battle; the rulers plot together against the LORD and against his anointed one. "Let us break their chains," they cry, "and free ourselves from slavery to God." But the one who rules in heaven laughs.*

The LORD scoffs at them (Psalm 2:2-4 NLT).

Perhaps we need to examine our own belief system in light of biblical truth. The Apostle Paul tells us that *all things* **are** *of Him; all things* **are** *through Him; all things* **are** *to Him, for His glory.* Again Paul tells us that God *worketh* **all things** *after the counsel of his own will* (Ephesians 1:11b KJV, emphasis mine). *And hath put* **all things** *under his feet, and gave him to be the head over* **all things**... (Ephesians 1:22 KJV, emphasis mine).

Our peace and our joy are in direct proportion to our Spirit-given ability to grasp the Lord's sovereign power and to rest in that reality. If we, for a moment, get trapped in the natural man's way of thinking, we will not fully trust God. We will not walk by faith if we have any confidence in our own power to choose wisely or to have wisdom about the nature of God. *But God hath chosen the foolish things of the world to confound the wise... That no flesh should glory in His presence* (1 Corinthians 1:27a, 29 KJV).

We have been called to trust the character of God. "God is love" (I John 4:7). And He is sovereign over *all* things. Thus, all that unfolds in our lives is flowing to us from His heart of love.

Oh Lord, give us grace to release our wonderings and our reasonings and trust Your heart of love in our daily lives.

Glenna Salsbury

Psalm 49-50; Romans 1   **July 29**

Waiting for Answers

God is our refuge and strength, a very present help in trouble... Cease striving and know that I am God. (Psalm 46:1, 10 NASB)

Erwin Lutzer said this regarding God's answers to our prayers, "Sometimes the answer is disguised, sometimes the answer disappoints, sometimes the answer is a disaster and at times the answer is denied." Ouch!

Habakkuk asked God questions like "How long?" and "Why?" In Habakkuk 1:5-11 God gives answers to his questions. "Yes, Habakkuk, I have seen the sin, the trouble and the utter chaos. Yes, I have a plan." Sounds good so far! Then God reveals his plan to use the Chaldeans, a nation more unrighteous than Judah, to rise up and punish the evil of the land. How could that be an answer? I picture Habakkuk with his fingers in his ears at this point, but instead, he listens. In Habakkuk 2:1, he shifts from questioning to being determined to know what God was up to; *I will stand my watch, and set myself on the rampart, and watch to see what He will say to me, and what I will answer when I am corrected.* Habakkuk becomes determined to stand watch and seek God. He gets alone with God to hear His voice. He becomes expectant knowing God has more to say to him. Habakkuk becomes submissive as his will fades and God's will prevails. God was not answering Habakkuk's plea in the way he wanted. The answer was disguised, disappointing, literally a disaster, and Habakkuk's desired answer was denied.

Has your answer come in a disguise? Are you disappointed in the answer God gave you? Are you facing a disaster and you can't imagine how that could be an answer to your prayers? Has your answer been denied for now? This is no time to crumble. Now is the time to stand firm, get alone with God and submit your will to His.

No matter what the answer is or how it will come about, God has a perfect plan!

Kathy Withers

Psalms 51-53; Romans 2 **July 30**

Believing Prayer

...call a sacred assembly. Summon the elders and all who live in the land to the house of the LORD your God, and cry out to the LORD. (Joel 1:14 NIV)

Question: Do we really believe that God hears and answers prayer? Do we want to see the Spirit of God moving in our churches? Then my question is this: What happened to prayer? Prayer meeting in most churches has become obsolete. If there is prayer meeting, much of our praying is praying for Aunt Susie's sisters's cousin's brother who has a hang nail. I am being facetious for sure, but am I really?

When was the last time you experienced the power of God at a prayer meeting? Thankfully there are still churches like the Brooklyn Tabernacle that believe that God still wants to meet with us when we pray.

George Mueller was considered one of the most successful pray-ers in Christian history. Does God only answer Mueller's prayers? Absolutely not. God did amazing things in the book of Acts when people prayed. Mueller wrote in his journal, "God will show up for prayer meetings, if only the people will."

The late Norman Grubb said, "Prayer meetings are dead affairs when they are merely asking sessions. There is adventure, hope and life when they are BELIEVING sessions, and the faith is corporately, practically and deliberately affirmed.

Hey, I am not attacking your PASTOR and your prayer meeting. What I am suggesting is that God wants to do so much more, and He longs to meet us when we pray corporately and cry out to Him with believing faith.

Are we willing enough to be a part of another revival in our day? Are we willing to PUSH – Pray Until Something Happens? Think about it.

Dr. Bill Welte

Psalms 54-56; Romans 3   **July 31**

Who Is Your Prayer Partner?

Therefore He is also able to save to the uttermost those who come to God through Him, since He always lives to make intercession for them. (Hebrew 7:25)

Every once in a while, I am reminded of one of the perks that I am blessed with in my place of employment, which is the number of people who pray for me and my family. I work in the addiction ministry at America's Keswick Colony of Mercy. This ministry has not only existed but produced much fruit, even in the thirteen years that I have been here. I constantly remind folks that we owe it all to the prayers of God's people.

But I must confess that I am not always faithful to pray for everyone who asks. Sometimes I am preoccupied with other matters and sometimes I just forget. I am human. There are some of the saints that I know who are more faithful and diligent than I in prayer. I count it a privilege to be on their prayer lists. But as believers in the Lord Jesus Christ and members of His family by virtue of that belief, we have a prayer partner whose faithfulness in praying for us is without a flaw. He is our Redeemer Jesus Christ.

While on earth, He prayed for His followers. I believe that He was praying for His disciples the night that they got caught in a storm at sea. I know that He prayed for Peter when He knew that Peter was going to fail by denying Him. He even prayed for His enemies who persecuted Him viciously as they hung Him on a cross to die. As a result of Jesus' prayers for His persecutors, a number of them were saved when Peter preached a sermon shortly afterward in Jerusalem.

All of these instances give me hope, because I know that the frequency and fruitfulness of His petitions are not dependent on my performance or perfection. How grateful we must remain that at this very moment we have the Ultimate Prayer Partner in Jesus Christ our Risen Savior.

Therefore He is also able to save to the uttermost those who come to God through Him, since He always lives to make intercession for them (Hebrews 7:25).

Lord, thank you for the prayers that you utter on my behalf to the Father.

Chaplain Jim Freed

Psalms 57-59; Romans 4   **August 1**

Divine Translation

And the Word became flesh and dwelt among us, and we beheld His glory, the glory as of the only begotten of the Father, full of grace and truth. (John 1:14)

    Translation is "the process of rendering from one language into another" (Webster's Collegiate Dictionary). Back in English class we were taught that a word is the basic expression of thought. In the spiritual realm, when God wanted to express His thought to us, He did it by sending His Son into our world in a form which we could understand. In a sense, He was the translation of the mind of God in our terms. All that we need to know about God has been revealed in Christ. This was the answer to the question in Isaiah 40:13 (NCV), *For who has known the mind of the Lord?* Paul adds the statement, *But we have the mind of Christ* (1 Corinthians 2:16. God's mind has been effectively communicated to us in Christ, and He has invested His mind in every believer.

    There is another step in this spiritual translation process. Just as Jesus became the communication of the mind of God toward us, and we have the mind of Christ in us, so we are to become translators of the Word to the world around us. In John's first letter he deals with the principle of the believer's taking the things of Christ and communicating them to the world. In chapter 4:12-17, he speaks of our translating God's love into terms our world can understand. He concludes with the clause, *as He is, so are we in this world.*

    Wycliffe Bible Translators was born through an all-night and extended prayer meeting at Keswick. The focus was on the refusal of Mexico to allow missionaries to enter. As the people prayed, the leaders prepared to approach the president of Mexico with the idea of allowing translators to reduce the tribal languages to writing. When this was agreed upon, translators moved in to begin work in the languages of some of the tribal groups. They used as their medium for translation the Word of

God. Millions have been reached in their own language through translation.

Rev. William A. Raws

Psalms 60-62; Romans 5   **August 2**

Take God at His Word

And Elijah the Tishbite, of the inhabitants of Gilead, said to Ahab, "As the LORD God of Israel lives, before whom I stand, there shall not be dew nor rain these years, except at my word."
(1 Kings 17:1)

The prophet Elijah is one of the most recognized characters in the Old Testament. The Lord used him in great and powerful ways. He is an interesting character because he just suddenly burst onto the scene. We are told nothing about him except that he is a Tishbite. The Bible does not mention his parents, his background or anything else about him. He simply appears on the scene as a courageous prophet of God.

Do you sometimes struggle with the idea that God cannot or may not use your life because you feel that you do not have the proper background, education or connections? As far as we know Elijah had none of these, yet God used him in a supernatural way.

What do we know about Elijah? One of the most important aspects of his life, as revealed in the Scriptures, is that he was a man who took God at His word. Notice in 1 Kings 17:2-5a, *Then the word of the LORD came to him, saying, "Get away from here and turn eastward, and hide by the Brook Cherith, which flows into the Jordan. And it will be that you shall drink from the brook, and I have commanded the ravens to feed you there." So he went and did according to the word of the LORD...*

A second time the word of the Lord came to Elijah. 1 Kings 17:8-10: *Then the word of the LORD came to him saying, "Arise, go to Zarephath, which belongs to Sidon, and dwell there. See, I have commanded a widow there to provide for you." So he arose and went to Zarephath....*

Once again, the Lord spoke to Elijah, 1 Kings 18:1-2a, *And it came to pass after many days that the word of the LORD came to Elijah, in the third year, saying, "Go, present yourself to Ahab, and I will send rain on the earth." So Elijah went to present himself to Ahab...*

The lesson to be learned here is that obedience to the word of the Lord is what qualifies a person to be used by the Lord. It is remarkable that Elijah asked no questions. He put up no arguments. He made no excuses. He simply took God at His word.

Do you take God at His word?

Dr. Roger D. Willmore

Psalms 63-65; Romans 6 **August 3**

Granted

For it has been <u>granted</u> to you on behalf of Christ not only to believe in him, but also to suffer for him. (Philippians 1:29 NIV)

What thoughts come to your mind when you think of the word "granted?" For me it conjures up pleasant thoughts. Something good or pleasant will be "given" to me. Part of the definition of grant[ed] says "to permit as a right, privilege or favor."[9] I like that...a privilege or a favor...now that sounds pretty good. It makes me think, "Wow, I can't wait to see what will be granted to me!"

Recently I was reading and studying Philippians chapter one and I saw something, *really* saw something for the first time, and it stopped me dead in my tracks...

Philippians 1:29: *For it has been <u>granted</u> to you on behalf of Christ not only to believe in him, but also to suffer for him* (emphasis mine).

And then later on in Philippians 3:10 (NIV): *I want to know Christ and the power of his resurrection and the fellowship of sharing in his sufferings, becoming like him in His death.*

---

[9] http://www.m-w.com Retrieved October 24, 2007

Paul indicates that it is a "privilege" or a "favor" that we should suffer for Christ. That seems to go against what I would think would be "favor." But yet it is. Up until this time, here in America, we have not really suffered for Christ. There are countries where people suffer greatly because they are Christians – in China, Sudan, Iraq and Iran (just to name a few). It is heartbreaking to hear testimonies of believers who have suffered greatly because they bear the name of our Lord and Savior. Yet, it is in those persecuted countries that we see more and more people coming to know Jesus as Lord and Savior of their lives no matter what the cost.

The world thinks America is a privileged country. My parents thought so and in 1952 they emigrated here. Yet what is privilege? Who is truly privileged? According to Paul, to suffer for Christ is the greatest privilege.

There may come a day when Christians in America will be "privileged" like those Christians all over the globe. May we rejoice in all things, even suffering, as Paul did 2000 years ago.

Mary Ann Kiernan

Psalms 66-67; Romans 7 **August 4**

Salvation Outweighs Suffering

And my soul shall be joyful in the LORD; It shall rejoice in His salvation. (Psalm 35:9)

No one looks forward to times of suffering, but they way we go through the suffering is a choice we can make today. Habakkuk was pondering about and preparing for the future. *Though the fig tree may not blossom, nor fruit be on the vines; though the labor of the olive may fail, and the fields yield no food; though the flock may be cut off from the fold, and there be no herd in the stalls– Yet I will rejoice in the LORD, I will joy in the God of my salvation* (Habakkuk 3:17-18).

Habakkuk doesn't know for sure that these things will come to pass. If they do he is determined to trust in the sovereignty of God no matter what the circumstances. There may not be any easy answers, quick resolutions or promises that the future will get any better. Of this he is confident: *Yet I will rejoice in the Lord, I will joy in the God of my salvation.* He takes joy in the fact that God is his salvation regardless of what may come.

As you and I face the unknown, do we choose worry or worship? Do we rebel against what has come or do we rejoice? Is our joy in our circumstances or in Jesus Christ who died to save us?

C.J. Mahaney in <u>Living the Cross Centered Life</u> says, "He (Habakkuk) turned his attention away from suffering and fixed it upon the more vital issue of salvation. In your own times of severe distress which are you more aware of - your suffering or your salvation?"

The Puritan Thomas Watson says, "Your sufferings are not so great as your sins. Put these two in the balances and see which weighs heaviest."

The days ahead are unclear. Like Habakkuk, I do not know what may or may not happen. Suffering will certainly come. When it does, will you and I choose to rejoice in the Lord? Will our joy be in the God of our salvation?

Kathy Withers

Psalms 68-69; Romans 8:1-21   **August 5**

Tears

...put thou my tears into thy bottle: are they not in thy book?
(Psalm 56:8b KJV)

Someone once said, "I love walking in the rain, 'cause then no one knows I'm crying." Well, there IS Someone who knows! Did you know that God records our tears? The ancient practice of collecting tears in a bottle is evident in David's above psalm which reminds us that God is keeping record of our pain and suffering and remembers our sorrow. The history of the tear bottle is captivating. Tear bottles were prevalent in ancient Roman times and mourners would cry their tears into little vials and place them in burial tombs out of love and respect for the dead. It is also believed that many would cry their tears throughout their lifetime into their tear bottles and thereby have a continual reminder of all the sufferings they had experienced during their lifetime. These were treasured possessions and it is believed that many were buried with their own tear bottles.

In Luke 7 we read an account of a sinful woman who came to Jesus and knelt at His feet and washed His feet with her tears and dried them with her hair. She then anointed His feet with perfume. Some Bible scholars believe that it is possible she brought her tear bottle and poured out her lifetime of tears at the feet of Jesus and washed His feet with those tears. Her faith while cleansing the feet of Jesus that day brought cleansing to her soul and she was forgiven all her sins. There can be no greater place to bring all of our tears, all of our hurt, all of our suffering, all of our pain, and all of our sin than at the feet of our precious Savior. It is there we will find forgiveness, healing, comfort and joy.

Friend, we then rejoice in knowing that on God's divine calendar, there is coming a day when all tears will be gone! *And God shall wipe away all tears from their eyes; and there shall be no more death, neither sorrow, nor crying, neither shall there be any more pain: for the former things are passed away* (Revelation 21:4 KJV). What a blessed hope!

Bevan Greiner

Psalms 70-71; Romans 8:22-39　　　　　　　　　　**August 6**

Heart Trouble

"The heart is deceitful above all things, and desperately wicked; who can know it?" (Jeremiah 17:9)

For out of the heart proceed evil thoughts, murders, adulteries, fornications, thefts, false witness and blasphemies.
(Matthew 15:19)

Years ago, when I was a young man, I can remember the doctor's reaction when he listened to my heart. On one such occasion the doctor kept listening to my heart for a long time. I asked if there was a problem. He indicated that there was no problem but my heartbeat was so strong that it created an echo. He said I was blessed with a strong heart.

Now that the years have taken their toll, the doctor still listens to my heart for a long time, but now it is because the wear and tear is showing up.

There are many tests that can be administered today to detect the condition of the heart. However, long before such tests came along; the Lord could see and know the condition of a man's heart.

Do you know the spiritual condition of your heart? Is it healthy? Do you have symptoms of spiritual heart problems? Some of the same questions and tests you receive at the doctor's office will help you know the condition of your spiritual heart.

Do you have habits that would threaten the condition of your heart? Are you resting in the Lord, walking daily with the Lord and feeding upon His Word? Proper spiritual rest, exercise and nutrition are important to spiritual health. Of course, the negative of this principle is also true. You cannot neglect things that are vital to spiritual health and remain healthy for long.

What is revealed about your heart when your speech is examined? The words we use say much about the condition of our heart. It always grieves me to hear a Christian use profanity and obscene language. What does your speech say about your heart?

Our desires reveal the condition of our heart. Jesus said, *But seek first the kingdom of God and His righteousness, and all these things shall be added to you* (Matthew 6:33).

Watch your thoughts and motives. These issues are not easily detected. Just like some conditions that exist in the physical heart, they can hide underneath the surface. However, in time these problems manifest themselves and often with great harm.

Dr. Roger D. Willmore

Psalms 72-73; Romans 9:1-15   **August 7**

Is Your Heart Full of Joy?

...the joy of the LORD is your strength. (Nehemiah 8:10b)

I remember one speaker we had at church who asked, "Do you still have a tear in the corner of your eye for the things of the Lord?" Have we become so complacent that we no longer have a tear of joy in the corner of our eye when we see Christ at work? The Bible talks about how Heaven rejoices when one person comes to the Lord (Luke 15:7). Joy is part of the fruit of the spirit (Galatians 5:22). The joy of the Lord is..."Strength" (Nehemiah 8:10).

Growing up you probably heard the acrostic "J.O.Y." - Jesus first, others second and yourself last. If we are truthful with each other, it is all about US most of the time: what we want, what we need, what we desire, our rights and the "why me" concept that we have bought into. We tend to put ourselves first, others second and Jesus last, and we wonder why we do not have joy in our lives anymore.

If we have established our hearts (James 5:8) and focus on putting Christ first, we then will have a heart to serve others and the joy will be in our hearts once again (Mark 10:45).

We are in a unique position today to show joy to others. Life around us is falling apart. The economy is failing, jobs are being lost, children are involved in things we never thought we would see, and there are wars, earthquakes, floods and disasters all around us. And yet we can have the JOY of the Lord in our hearts even though we have experienced some tragedy or disappointment ourselves.

I am sure that you know of someone in your life who you would consider as an example, someone who has real joy. Someone that you like to be around even when the chips are down, because they seem to have a certain something or a certain joy that you want. They might be the same someone that when you have good news to share, you just can't wait to tell them because you know they will be truly excited along with you. We need to be that same example to all who are around us.

The JOY that comes from Him is OUR strength. When we are weak, He is strong. Has the joy left your heart, have your tears dried up? Remind yourself that joy comes from the Lord and He is your strength today. Open your eyes wide and look for the work He is completing in front of you. Get those tears of joy flowing once again. Get the joy deep in your heart.

Lynn A. Wilson

Psalms 74-76; Romans 9:16-33　　　　　　　　　　**August 8**

He's the Lifter of Your Head

But you, O LORD, are a shield around me; you are my glory, the one who holds my head high. I cried out to the LORD, and he answered me from his holy mountain. I lay down and slept, yet I woke up in safety, for the LORD was watching over me.
(Psalm 3:3-5 NLT)

　　Do you remember being told when you were young to keep your head up and don't let your shoulders sag? I am often reminded of that, and understand why it is so important as it reflects our countenance and how we feel about ourselves and our surroundings.

　　I was walking my dog one day as I usually did along the bottom of the lower lake at Keswick between my house and the dam. I usually enjoy looking at the water on the lake and the colors on the trees or whatever flower is blooming wild along the shore, maybe sensing a new fragrance in the air and discovering a new flower I haven't seen before and taking the few moments to enjoy creation. I even keep my eye out for the snake in a tree that my friend Sue Mahoney told me she saw there one day. I was particularly burdened about something and my eyes were on the ground. I wasn't noticing anything, just going through the motions of putting one foot in front of the other, shoulders sagging, feeling very low. I remembered a verse I had read in Psalms that morning. *You are the one who holds my head high.* I felt dejected and run down, not able to hold up my head. I realized I didn't have to operate on my own power; my head raised and I looked around at a beautiful sunshine-filled day. I felt God saying to me, "Hold up your head, I love you." The view of my surroundings was much better when I looked up, I didn't just see dead pine needles dropped from the trees on sand in the Pine Barrens of New Jersey, but rather evidence of life. I started to feel life creep back into me.

My perspective had changed. Peace reigned in me where turmoil had been only moments before.

As you go through your day today, remember to keep looking up! And if you have trouble doing it, ask the Lord; He specializes in lifting heads! Keep Looking UP!

Joyce Hayes

Psalms 77-78; Romans 10   **August 9**

Power Shortage

And He said to me, "My grace is sufficient for you, for My strength is made perfect in weakness..." (2 Corinthians 12:9)

One evening my wife Linda and I were in our living room when we heard a "bang!" The electricity in the neighborhood went out; a while later the electric company fixed the problem and on went the lights. When we lose power it reminds us of the importance of energy!

The apostle Paul's life and ministry were a testimony to God's power. In Galatians 1:15-16, Paul recorded God's calling: *...it pleased God, who separated me from my mother's womb and called me through His grace, to reveal His Son in me, that I might preach Him among the Gentiles...*

The apostles were energized to fulfill God's will. Paul also testified, *He (the Holy Spirit) who worked effectively in Peter for the apostleship to the circumcised also worked effectively in me toward the Gentiles* (Galatians 2:8).

How can we fulfill God's plan for our lives? Selwyn Hughes reminds us of a vital lesson: **God's strength is made perfect in our weakness.** "It is noteworthy that throughout the ages God's greatest servants have made clear that their success was due not to their own efforts but to the grace that God imparted to them ... I have seen Christians suffer a breakdown as a result of trying to live the Christian life in their own strength...On one occasion I was present at a dinner given in honor of a certain bishop. During the after-dinner speeches I heard a layman make a terrible blunder when he declared: 'Bishop, we are both doing God's work; you in your way, and I in His.' Question yourself at this very moment and ask: Am I doing God's work in my own way or in His?... Is this why so many of us fail to go as deeply with God as we ought? We have received Christ but we do not allow Him to diffuse Himself through all our faculties, to animate us with His life and Spirit."

Have you been frustrated by a "power shortage?" Acknowledging your inability is a huge step toward counting on God's strength in and through you.

Dr. John Woodward

Psalms 79-80; Romans 11:1-18   **August 10**

God's Requirements

But Peter and the other apostles answered and said: "We ought to obey God rather than men." (Acts 5:29)

And we are His witnesses to these things, and so also is the Holy Spirit whom God has given to those who obey Him. (Acts 5:32)

If someone asked you which word you considered to be the most important to the Christian life what would you say? Would you say, love? Love is a very necessary part of the Christian testimony. Would you say faith? Faith is certainly a very necessary aspect of the Christian life. Maybe you would say prayer, or giving or witnessing. All of these are very important words. However, I think the most important word is *obedience*. You see, every other word we listed functions in relationship to our obedience.

What does it mean to obey God? We are to obey God in a general way. That is to say, there are biblical principles and truths that apply to all Christians and all Christians should be obedient to those truths.

We are also to obey the Lord specifically and personally. God has a will and purpose for your life that is unique to you. You are to be obedient to His personal, specific will for you.

What inspires and motivates obedience? Love for Jesus should be the main motivation for our obedience. Jesus said, *"If you love Me, keep My commandments"* (John 14:15).

The apostle Paul said, *the love of Christ compels us...*(2 Corinthians 5:14).

Recently I was sitting in my study looking at the shelves of books. I saw books about preaching, books about church growth, books about theology, books about family, and books about famous Christians. There were all kinds of books that instructed me how to get Christians to serve the Lord. I remember thinking, if only Christians would fall in love with Jesus and have a burning, passionate relationship with Him, then they would not need someone pulling on them and pleading with them to serve the Lord.

Do you love the Lord? Is your obedience to the Lord up-to-date?

Dr. Roger D. Willmore

Psalms 81-83; Romans 11:19-36   **August 11**

Practice, Practice, Practice!

But let patience have its perfect work, that you may be perfect and complete, lacking nothing. (James 1:4)

Have you ever found it difficult to maintain a daily quiet time with the Lord? Do you ever experience your mind wandering during your prayer time? Perhaps you start out on January 1st and determine resolutely to be disciplined to maintain your spiritual walk with the Lord, only to miss a day, then two, and your journey becomes a frustration to you because it isn't perfect any longer.

The daily walk with Jesus Christ requires discipline and practice. Athletes, artists, dancers, hobbyists, and musicians practice their skills and abilities over and over until they become a part of them – like breathing. I remember being assigned a 26-page piece of classical music. When I began it seemed an impossible task; however, if I broke it into smaller sections, working on it one segment at a time, it was not so overwhelming. At times I would come into a troublesome three or four measures and if I would practice it over and over, it would become a part of me and I could play it in my sleep.

Our spiritual life is really no different. When we apply discipline to it, we find that it can be a very manageable task. Ultimately we will not find it to be a task; it becomes a part of us, something that we love to do, and an activity we can't live without. Start with small, reachable, attainable goals. This may seem ridiculous, but read one verse and think about it instead of trying to read a whole chapter or book. Try praying for one minute instead of sixty. I think you get the point. Practice this over and over; remember you are on this spiritual journey for the long haul. Remember also that God is a rewarder of those who diligently seek Him (Hebrews 11:6). He will bless your effort and give joy in the journey!

Robert Hayes

Psalms 84-86; Romans 12　　　　　　　　　　　　**August 12**

The Invitation

And He said to them, "Come aside by yourselves to a deserted place and rest a while." For there were many coming and going, and they did not even have time to eat. (Mark 6:31)

I have to smile when I read this. We live in a very connected, hectic society. We are connected by cell phones that never leave our person, Facebook and gmail on our personal laptops, business computers and Blackberries. We have to log our appointments into a datebook just to remember them, and solitude appears to be a lost art. When I picked up my Bible this morning and read Jesus' words, I really had to stop and smile. I know that the message of the Gospel is counter-cultural, but this seems almost unobtainable.

But as always, I read the context to shed more light on the matter. And to my surprise, Jesus and His disciples didn't have much more success in this endeavor than we do. Read on: *So they departed to a deserted place in the boat by themselves. But the multitudes saw them departing, and many knew Him and ran there on foot from all the cities. They arrived before them and came together to Him* (Mark 6:32-33).

When you read on even further, the disciples were confronted with five thousand hungry people! Sometimes ministry is like this, not just formal ministry but ministry to our loved ones. We hear the invitation and we respond, only to have our hopes dashed. But this does not negate the enticing prospect of rest and quiet; it only makes it more alluring. Jesus didn't give up, but IMMEDIATELY after attending to the need separated Himself and His followers from the crowds. *Immediately He made His disciples get into the boat and go before Him to the other side, to Bethsaida, while He sent the multitude away. And when He had sent them away, He departed to the mountain to pray* (Mark 6:45-46).

Jesus was committed to spend time alone with the Father. He was God's own Son but didn't try to live His life without periods of solitude. We must follow in His footsteps and make solitude a priority in our life. Accept His invitation even if you have to work at it. *Come aside by yourselves to a deserted place and rest a while.*

Lord, help me to accept your invitation today.

Chaplain Jim Freed

Psalms 87-88; Romans 13 **August 13**

Ittai's Loyalty

But Ittai answered the king and said, "As the LORD lives, and as my lord the king lives, surely wherever my lord the king may be, whether for death or for life, there also your servant will be."
(2 Samuel 15:21 NASB)

For King David they were the worst of times! Paul's words ring true: *whatever one sows that will he also reap.* King David spoiled Absalom, his son, never apparently rebuking or disciplining him. The son stole the hearts of the king's subjects. He marched to take the throne and destroy the king. David, with many loyal supporters, rushed down the hill into the Kidron Valley. Pausing there, he watched the frightened friends fleeing up the Mt. of Olives.

While those hundreds were scurrying past, David noted that Ittai, the Gittite, was there. "Why do you go with us? Go back and stay with the new king. You are a foreigner and an exile from your home. You only came yesterday!" With a ringing statement of loyalty, Ittai, over the noise of the crowds rushing past, cried out: "Wherever the lord my King lives, wherever he shall be, whether for death or life, there also will your servant be." What a commitment! They continued over the Mt. of Olives and headed for the Jordan River so far below.

David could not claim or expect that level of sacrifice. David's fortunes were never lower. Publicly and solemnly, Ittai committed to do his best for David as a servant. He would stick by his master, come what may. Through thick and thin he would be there even if it meant his death. Ittai was prepared mentally and emotionally to share the arduous conditions that David would experience.

The question for me is: Am I ready to share my journey through life with Jesus? Will I be loyal to Him? Will I determine to go where Jesus wants me to go? The world is increasingly hostile to the followers of Christ. In fact it is upside down! It calls love hate, integrity bigotry and God's revelation fanciful myths. In a world like we live in can we say with Ittai to our

King and Savior, "Where you go I will go?" Jesus spent time with believers, spent time in prayer, spent time teaching, and also spent time healing and comforting. He shared the truth and did what was right, not what was popular.

Jesus was where the action was! It was where fetters needed to be broken, burdens lifted and hearts comforted! It was where people were coming to know and love eternal things over material things. Can Jesus count on your unconditional loyalty and commitment in an antagonistic world? Can He count on mine? Our king is not an earthly king, rather a heavenly King.

Dr. George Kelsey

Psalms 89-90; Romans 14   **August 14**

Out of Gas?

Grace and peace be multiplied to you in the knowledge of God and of Jesus our Lord, as His divine power has given to us all things that pertain to life and godliness, through the knowledge of Him who called us by glory and virtue, by which have been given to us exceedingly great and precious promises...
(2 Peter 1:2-4a)

My husband and I were privileged to minister at a Bible conference on the bay. As we sat on the beach, we constantly observed planes flying back and forth carrying advertisements. Trailing behind the plane would be banners urging the crowd to buy this or that or visit a popular restaurant.

As we were about to eat lunch in the dining hall, a plane carrying a sign flew over the bay, dropped its sign, and headed for an open area on the ground. As it descended it managed to hit the sand and land safely. Very quickly we learned that the plane had run out of gas. After the pilot put fuel in the plane it was soon on its way, but the pilot and those watching on land were given quite a scare.

"How true to life," I thought. As you meet people who claim to know Jesus Christ as personal Savior, (and sometimes advertise that faith) some seem to run out of gas! Perhaps it has been discouragement, a problem or "bump in the road of life" that has caused them to halt in their spiritual journey. I am reminded in God's Word that, in spite of problems or discouragements, and in spite of feelings, I need to constantly be "put in flight." I need to base my life on the Word of God and rely on the power supply of God to keep me going.

The Apostle Paul reminds us in Philippians 1:6, *being confident of this very thing, that He who has begun a good work in you will complete it until the day of Jesus Christ.*

Christian, we have no need to run out of gas spiritually, for there is a limitless supply to God's presence, protection, and provision. Let's trust Him! His grace will keep us going and carry us through.

Carolyn Hibbard

Psalms 91-93; Romans 15:1-13 **August 15**

How to Have Fellowship with God

This is the message which we have heard from Him and declare to you, that God is light and in Him is no darkness at all. If we say that we have fellowship with Him, and we walk in darkness, we lie and do not practice the truth. But if we walk in the light as He is in the light, we have fellowship with one another, and the blood of Jesus Christ His Son cleanses us from all sin.
(1 John 1:5-7)

When we read the words of the apostle John, we read the words of a loving, caring pastor who wants his people to experience the richest, deepest relationship possible with their Savior. He writes as a shepherd directing his sheep into green pastures where the fullness of life can be experienced. He wants His people to know sweet fellowship with the Lord and with one another.

The Christian life is fellowship with God. If we want a clear and practical definition of what a Christian is, it would simply be a person who is in fellowship with God. This point is made very clear in verse three when John writes, *If we say that we have fellowship with Him, and we walk in darkness, we lie and do not practice the truth.* Here John is describing a contradiction in terms. One cannot walk in light and darkness at the same time. He must walk in one or the other.

Fellowship with God is not true just because we say it is true. Fellowship with God has a litmus test. If you say one thing and do another then you have failed the test.

John uses the word *fellowship* four times in this passage. Each time he uses the word it means "to have things in common with God." In order to have fellowship with God we must have something in common with Him.

Light speaks of the glory of God and the holiness of God. When we walk in the light, we walk in the holiness of God to the glory of God.

In some African countries a common greeting among Christians is, "Are you walking in the light, my brother? Are you walking in the light, my sister?"

May I ask you, my friend, are you walking in the light?

Dr. Roger D. Willmore

Psalms 94-96; Romans 15:14-33 August 16

Heavenly Hyperbole

Now to Him who is able to do exceedingly abundantly above all that we ask or think, according to the power that works in us.
(Ephesians 3:20)

When the apostle Paul wrote these words to the Ephesian believers, he used language which could be termed hyperbole or exaggeration. However, under the inspiration of the Holy Spirit, it was fully factual and literal. The verse is a benediction at the conclusion of a prayer that the Ephesian believers might receive the available spiritual resources provided by the Lord.

Examining the verse, we notice how the apostle piles up terms to reveal the all-sufficiency of our God. First, *He is able to do*. This would be an encouraging fact, but that's not the end. Second, He is able to do, literally, "superabundantly" or beyond all measure. There's more. Third, He is able to do *all that we ask*. Answers to our prayers are never limited by any insufficiency on His part. The limitations rest with us alone. There are passages which show the conditions for answered prayer, but none of them point to any lack on God's part. Fourth, even without our asking, He can even do all that we "think" or imagine.

A 17th century English deist met a plain countryman while out walking on a Sunday. The dialogue which followed went like this: "Where are you going?" "To church." "What will you do there?" "Worship God." "Is your God a great or little God?" "He's both, Sir." "How can He be both?" "He's so great that the heaven of heavens cannot contain Him; and so little that He can dwell in my heart." The deist, Anthony Collins, later declared that this simple answer had greater effect on his mind than all the volumes of learned doctors. (Selected)

By faith, let's count upon His total adequacy to meet our needs, no matter how inadequate we feel in ourselves. There's no exaggeration in the statement, "He is able." And there is reality in the truth that the God who is able lives in us.

Rev. William A. Raws

Psalms 97-99; Romans 16　　　　　　　　　　**August 17**

Real Life

Yet indeed I also count all things loss for the excellence of the knowledge of Christ Jesus my Lord, for whom I have suffered the loss of all things, and count them as rubbish, that I may gain Christ. (Philippians 3:8)

The process of Christian maturity requires daily dying. *I have been crucified with Christ; it is no longer I who live, but Christ lives in me; and the life which I now live in the flesh I live by faith in the Son of God, who loved me and gave Himself for me* (Galatians 2:20).

"...it is the secret of my sanctification, for on that cross of Calvary, I, the sinful self, was put to death; and when I lay myself over with Him upon that Cross and reckon myself dead, Christ's risen life passes into me and it is no longer my struggling, my goodness, or my badness, but my Lord who lives in me. Therefore while I abide in Him I am counted even as He, and enabled to walk even as He walked."[10]

Matthew 16:24: *Then Jesus said to His disciples, "If anyone desires to come after Me, let him deny himself, and take up his cross, and follow Me."*

Romans 8:13: *For if you live according to the flesh you will die; but if by the Spirit you put to death the deeds of the body, you will live.*

Jesus' example is unimaginably beyond words. It is breathtaking. There in the garden, deep in anguish, laboring in prayer, the Son pours out His heart to His Father. *He went a little farther and fell on His face, and prayed, saying, O My Father, if it is possible, let this cup pass from Me; nevertheless, not as I will, but as You will* (Matthew 26:13).

Jesus made a choice late that afternoon. Actually, He made the choice long before that day; but that evening in the garden He died to Himself. At many moments along the painful path, Jesus could have said "no" and called down the power of heaven to stop the pain. But He chose instead to say "no" to Himself and "yes" to God the Father. Jesus died to Himself, long before He died the excruciatingly painful death on the cross of Calvary.

We may or may not be called to die for our faith, but we certainly are called daily to die to ourselves. Jesus did not need to deny Himself because of a sinful or selfish desire (like us) but rather because He was about to take onto His sinless self the weight, ugliness, and devastation of the sins of the whole world. *For He made Him who knew no sin to be sin for us...* (2 Corinthians 5:21). *And He Himself is the propitiation for our sins, and not for ours only but also for the whole world* (1 John 2:2).

---

[10] Simpson, A.B. The Christ Life. 1980. Christian Publications, Inc. Harrisburg, PA.

Will we choose our way and our agenda, over and above the path of dying to self, or will we choose to fully embrace life that only comes from God?

Diane Hunt

Psalms 100-102; 1 Corinthians 1**August 18**

I Know My Redeemer Lives

"For I know that my Redeemer lives, and He shall stand at last on the earth; And after my skin is destroyed, this I know, that in my flesh I shall see God, whom I shall see for myself, and my eyes shall behold, and not another. How my heart yearns within me." (Job 19:25-27)

I know my Redeemer lives! These are the words of absolute assurance. There was no doubt in Job's mind that the Lord was indeed alive and that one day he would see Him face to face. Job's words would be quite at home in the Acts of the Apostles or the Epistles of Paul, but that is not where we find them. The book of Job is considered the oldest book in the Bible. How can a man who lived so long before the birth, the death, the burial and the resurrection of the Redeemer be so confident that the Redeemer lives?

Do you want to know that your Redeemer lives? Would you like to have the same confidence Job had that his Redeemer lives and that he would someday see Him face to face? I know the answer to these questions. Every human being longs for assurance and hope. All of us are looking for an anchor that will hold us secure in the storms of life. We all want to know that when the storms of life are over everything is going to be all right.

Look at the depth of Job's assurance. In verses 23 and 24 he wrote, *"Oh, that my words were written! Oh, that they were inscribed in a book! That they were engraved on a rock with an iron pen and lead, forever!"* Job wanted the message of his assurance to be known by the coming generations. (The desire of his heart has been fulfilled.)

How did Job know God? He knew Him through *revelation*. We do not have the details about the times, places and manner in which God revealed Himself to Job, but we know that Job knew God. In Job 1:8, God said of Job, *"...there is none like him on the earth, a blameless and upright man, one who fears God and shuns evil."* Such character can only come from knowing God and walking with God.

Following the great calamity that befell Job, which included the death of his children, we are told that *Job arose and tore his robe, and shaved his head, and fell on the ground and worshiped* (1:20). This worship reflects Job's personal knowledge of God.

Job knew God through *suffering*. The theme message of the Book of Job is the sovereignty of God. Suffering is a great teacher. In suffering we learn much about God.

Do you have assurance that your Redeemer lives? Can you face life and death with confidence? You can know that your Redeemer lives.

Dr. Roger D. Willmore

Psalms 103-104; 1 Corinthians 2   **August 19**

Never Separated

Where shall I go from your Spirit? Or where shall I flee from your presence? If I ascend to heaven, you are there! If I make my bed in Sheol, you are there! If I take the wings of the morning and dwell in the uttermost parts of the sea, even there your hand shall lead me, and your right hand shall hold me.
(Psalm 139:7-10 ESV)

Have you considered the presence of God in your life and how inseparable you are from Him? I love the assurance of Psalm 139 that it is impossible for me to be hidden from His watchful care. No internal fear or external circumstance can remove me from His presence. He leads my way and searches me out. Jesus said that no one can snatch me out of His hand, and the meditation of the psalmist demonstrates His guardianship of me. There is no power than can compete with His might.

I know He is with me, but still, sometimes I feel alone and separated from Him. I can feel like Job when he says, *Behold, I go forward, but he is not there, and backward, but I do not perceive him; on the left hand when he is working, I do not behold him; he turns to the right hand, but I do not see him* (Job 23:8-9 ESV). Despite Job's complaint, the Lord was no more distant from him during his trial than when he was rich and successful. Job said he could not find God. The truth is that despite Job's perceptions, God was near him during every moment of his trial.

When everything's going well, it's so easy to see and to praise God's presence in my life. But, like Job, when I'm in "the valley of the shadow of death," I am tempted to fear evil and to believe that the Lord is not with me. The truth is demonstrated in the full story of Job's life – he was not lost or separated from God for even a moment. The truth is boldly proclaimed in the Word – even in the most forsaken part of the earth, *even there your hand shall lead me, and your right hand shall hold me* (Psalm 139:10 ESV).

The Lord does not idly promise His presence, but He tells us He is with us so that we may be encouraged and strengthened in our faith when trials come. Ponder the comprehensiveness of His assurance: *For I am sure that neither death nor life, nor angels nor rulers, nor things present nor things to come, nor powers, nor height nor depth, nor anything else in all creation, will be able to separate us from the love of God in Christ Jesus our Lord* (Romans 8:38-39 ESV).

Jenn Lawrence

Psalms 105-106; 1 Corinthians 3 **August 20**

Never Alone in More Ways Than One

Are not all angels ministering spirits sent to serve those who will inherit salvation? (Hebrews 1:14 NIV)

When my daughter was two and my wife was putting her to bed, she prayed that God, "would place His angels around her." A friend was downstairs with me when she sat straight up and said, "Chris, I've just seen two angels!" It had to be in her mind but she was visibly shaken. She said that they seemed quite small and that they were yellow. When my wife came down and we told her, she was pleased, but at the same time thought, "Well, I did pray it." The next morning we quizzed my daughter. "Was anyone in your room last night?" "Yes." "Who was it?" "It was angels." "How many were there?" "Two." "What color were they?" "Yellow." "I guess they were pretty big?" "No Mom, they were only little." I was amazed, but to my daughter it was no big deal. I guess if you really believe in something, it's no shock when you see it.

Here is an excerpt from a letter that I once received from a teenager named Jane, "Then you sat down with an 'empty' chair either side of you. But they weren't empty. On your right sat a beautiful angel, the sort I've seen before. Dressed in a white gown with fiery eyes and a brightness that I can only presume comes from being in God's presence. On your left sat an amazing, well, I guess you could say, warrior angel. He was taller than the other, maybe 7 or 8 feet high when standing. He had golden armor. There were times when they both stood with their hands over you while you prayed. Sometimes one would place his hand on your shoulder. I don't know if knowing this will mean anything to you, but I feel that God doesn't show me these things to keep to myself. I feel ever so stupid, an unimportant new member of the church telling the pastor that God wants you to know His protection, but it must feel great to know that this big warrior is with you."

I never felt anything either time, and I've never seen an angel in spirit form. Sometimes I even think that people can be too fascinated by angels. However, I have no reason to doubt what Lynn, Jane, or certainly not my little girl said because what they have told me is consistent with the Word of God. The vision has never made me arrogant. It has brought great humility, even a sense of shame when I have sinned. But it has given me great confidence as well. Some people argue that, "Where was your angel when bad stuff happened, or tragedy struck? Where was he then?" But they're missing the point. Angels can only act in accordance with the will of God. The greatest thing about this whole thing to me is the verse at the top. They are sent to minister to those who will inherit salvation. What does that make me? If you believe the whole Book, and think it through, the angels that have helped you are as real as your salvation. I pray that God will place His angels around you today. And remember that as they watch you, at the same time, they see the face of God.

Rev. Chris Thompson

Psalms 107-109; 1 Corinthians 4　　　　　　　　　　**August 21**

Peace

You will keep him in perfect peace, whose mind is stayed on You, because he trusts in You. Trust in the LORD forever, for in YAH, the LORD, is everlasting strength. (Isaiah 26:3-4)

Have you ever experienced a lack of peace? There have been seasons in my life that I would dub as *times most stressful.* Some have endured for a moment and some for much longer periods of time. In each, my emotions have run the full gamut covering deep sadness, major irritation, concern, sorrow, compassion, resentment, etc.

What I longed for more than anything during those moments is *peace. Peace,* simple quiet peace - in my space, in my mind, in my soul and in my spirit.

What is peace? Webster's online dictionary defines peace as "the absence of war or other hostilities; freedom from quarrels or disagreements; inner contentment; freedom from strife; the absence of mental stress or anxiety." The list could continue, but I'm sure you get the point. When there is no peace, everything in you craves it, wants it, and earnestly desires it!

What caused the stress - whether it's mine or yours - I can assure you, is of little importance in comparison to what our faithful, loving, longsuffering Father will expose in our hearts and lives as we go to Him and cry out for help.

On the surface, I'd say I've learned that most of us don't personally have to be at war with anyone for our sense of peace to be disrupted, destroyed or stolen. A simple glance through recent history bears this out.

How many men, women and children are awakened in the middle of their slumber by guerrilla warriors who press in and take what does not belong to them? Or what about earthquakes! Surely that's enough to destroy peace. Regardless of the situation, the result is the same, and for most, peace is simply gone, replaced by fear and trembling and a plethora of other emotions.

Similarly, we don't need to be full of hostility or anger to have our peace disturbed. Any number of you reading this devotion may live with or know someone who seems to live in a constant state of angst, and whether they're coming or going, they can have an impact on you.

On a deeper level (which brings us to the bottom line) our lack of peace stems from one simple fact: we don't trust in and/or wait patiently on God.

Rest in the LORD and wait patiently for Him...cease from anger and forsake wrath; do not fret – it only causes harm... (Psalm 37:7a, 8).

Stephanie D. Paul

Psalms 110-112; 1 Corinthians 5   **August 22**

Peace – Part 2

Trust in the LORD and do good; dwell in the land and feed on His faithfulness. Delight yourself also in the LORD, and He shall give you the desires of your heart. (Psalm 37:3-4)

So, do you want peace? I know I do. The question is, are we willing to do whatever it takes to get it? *"But those who wait for the LORD shall renew their strength; they shall mount up with wings like eagles, they shall run and not be weary, they shall walk and not faint"* (Isaiah 40:31).

Seeking God sounds like a sure recipe for peace, don't you think? Here is the way The Message Bible paraphrase puts it, beginning with verse 28:

Don't you know anything? Haven't you been listening? God doesn't come and go. God lasts. He's Creator of all you can see or imagine. He doesn't get tired out, doesn't pause to catch His breath. And He knows everything, inside and out. He energizes those who get tired, gives fresh strength to dropouts…but those who wait upon God get fresh strength. They spread their wings and soar like eagles, they run and don't get tired, they walk and don't lag behind.

In conclusion, *we* spread *our* wings, *we* run in *our* strength and, surprise! We get tired and stressed out! Our strength fades and fails and we forget that it is the peace of God that keeps us. Our strength is not sufficient to handle life. **We have to wait on God**! He alone is sufficient.

Together let's praise and rejoice in the fact that **He is enough** and be ever so thankful that He never, ever sleeps or pauses to catch His breath.

Rejoice in the Lord always. Again I will say, rejoice! Let your gentleness be known to all men. The Lord is at hand. Be anxious for nothing, but in everything by prayer and supplication, with thanksgiving, let your requests be made known to God; and the peace of God, which surpasses all understanding, will guard your hearts and minds through Christ Jesus (Philippians 4:4-7).

Let's choose to make time with God an absolute priority today, time above and beyond this simple devotional page. Even if you must secure it by force, do not neglect time with Him. He is the only Peace Giver and it is He alone who can calm the deepest longing our souls have.

Cling to Him. Our lives depend on it.

Stephanie D. Paul

Psalms 113-115; 1 Corinthians 6 **August 23**

Pilate's Stubbornness

Therefore the chief priests of the Jews said to Pilate, "Do not write 'The King of the Jews.'..." Pilate answered, "What I have written, I have written." (John 19:21-22)

Jesus' trial was over. Stubborn Pilate had melted before the priests. He surrendered his responsibilities. But he was also angry, at them and at himself. He seized an opportunity to irritate the priests. In three languages, Greek, Latin and Hebrew, touching on the intellectual, legal and religious realms, this pliable man wrote: "The King of the Jews." Not liking mockery they cried out: "Change it!" This wishy-washy, pliable ruler said, "No!" In essentials he was weak; in non-essentials stubborn.

We can see a deeper meaning. Pilate was giving a commentary on his own life. His deeds made a record. He wrote his record in big, ugly letters for all future generations to read. It could have been a record of glory, courage and honor. Instead, he wrote a record of weakness, injustice and dishonor. He couldn't change what he had written in life.

All of us are writing our record. We start each morning with a blank page. In the evening we can look back at that page and say to ourselves, "What I have written I have written." We're always recording. There is no pause button! We vainly wish we could erase something or that there might be an 18-minute blank on the tape. In airplanes and now cars, black boxes record what is happening. Weather machines continually monitor and record temperatures and other data. Emergencies and problem situations come to us. How will we react? We must react. We can't escape but must write something.

Will your record reveal honor, fidelity, integrity, faith and love? Insignificant, ordinary things you do form habits and mold character. They prepare us for the hour of crisis. Great emergencies are few. Pilate judged Jesus only once. What we did ten years ago through effort or neglect determines what we are today. What we do today will determine what we will be in all future tomorrows. Let's fill our lives with joyful service for Christ and for others. Let's fill them with loving reactions that will lead others to see our Savior is the only one worth worshipping and loving.

Yes, God can forgive, but scars may remain. He can bring good out of evil even as he brought honey from the beast. The one hanging under that writing of Pilate has brought life and hope to us. Is your pen writing a beautiful, honorable and Christ-honoring story today? As Pilate said, *What I have written, I have written.*

Dr. George Kelsey

Psalms 116-118; 1 Corinthians 7:1-19　　　　　　　　**August 24**

Recovery From Spiritual Failure

And the men of Ai struck down about thirty-six men, for they chased them from before the gate as far as Shebarim, and struck them down on the descent; there the hearts of the people melted and became like water. Then Joshua tore his clothes and fell to the earth on his face before the ark of the Lord until evening, both he and the elders of Israel; and they put dust on their heads.
(Joshua 7:5-6)

We all have had times in our lives when prayer came easier, worship was a delight and serving the Lord was a joy. We felt that we were on a spiritual mountaintop and all we could see before us was a life of victory. Then, all of a sudden, victory is gone and we find ourselves upon our faces in failure.

It happens; and it happens even to the best people of God. Joshua had just experienced a supernatural victory in chapter six when he saw the walls of Jericho fall down and victory was his. He saw God give victory where it seemed there could be no victory.

Now, in chapter seven, just a few days later, he is on his face in humiliation and failure.

The cause of their failure is seen in verses three and four. Joshua and his leaders had become self-centered and self-confident. They needed God for the big battle of Jericho, but they felt they did not need Him for the smaller battle of Ai. This arrogant attitude brought about a shameful defeat.

There is never a time in our lives when we do not need God. We may acknowledge our need for Him when we face life's bigger challenges, but we actually need Him in every aspect of life everyday.

Joshua recognized his mistake and took the correct actions to recover his relationship with God. The steps he took are seen in verses 13-21. First, Joshua consecrated himself and the people to God (v.13). He separated himself from the sin that caused the failure. Second, he complied with the Lord. In other words, he did exactly what God told him to do (v.16). Third, Joshua demanded that full confession was made of the sin that had caused the failure (vs.20-21). There you have the way back: consecration, compliance and confession.

Joshua recovered from his failure and went on to be a mighty spiritual leader of the people of Israel. Do not let a spiritual failure keep you down. Confess your sin to God and accept His forgiveness. Then get up and go forward in victory…to the glory of God.

Dr. Roger D. Willmore

Psalm 119: 1-88; 1 Corinthians 7:20-40   **August 25**

The Searching Question

Then the LORD God called to Adam and said to him, "Where are you?" (Genesis 3:9)

The very first question we find in the Old Testament is significant. It is found in Genesis 3:9, where God called to the man He created, *"Where are you?"* "I hid," Adam replied, somewhere out of sight, "because I was afraid."

Never before in his association with his loving Creator had Adam been afraid, so why now? Simple, but tragic, answer: for the first time in his life, Adam had disobeyed God. He knew that to eat the forbidden fruit was wrong, but he did not know the consequences.

Adam and Eve's idyllic life was to drastically change, for they were exiled from their beautiful home – the Garden of Eden. Furthermore, their roles in life were to change. Adam would henceforth have to work hard for his living in a world of weeds and thistles. Moreover, his once-perfect relationship with the beautiful woman God created for him would be damaged. Eve would no longer be his perfect wife. She would no longer be Adam's equal; he was to rule over her now. She was to be submissive to his desires and wishes, and she would "bear children in pain," whatever that meant. Eve would soon know what that meant, when her first baby, Cain, was born. Then she had her second son, Abel.

Consequences of sin can roll on and on, and once again, as Cain and Abel grew into manhood, Adam and Even had to be aware of their sons' times of conflict. Eventually, as the Scripture tells us (Genesis 4:8), out of jealousy Cain killed his brother. What a tragedy! What heartache! That their beloved firstborn would murder his own brother, dearly loved also.

Did Adam and Eve ever think back to their wonderful, peaceful life in Eden? Did they ever discuss the enduring consequences of their sin of disobedience? Did they ever confess their sin to God and receive His gracious forgiveness? I believe they did. Nevertheless, the sin of disobedience always has repercussions, if not immediately, it will in time.

Has God ever called you, "_____, where are you?" Would you hide from Him because of fear of Him? Because of knowing you had sinned against His moral law? Or because you simply do not know Who He is, but instinctively you are afraid?

Or are you one who can be certain that your future lies in His hands? That as a child of His you have assurance that one day you will be transported into His presence and spend eternity with Him?

It is a thought blessed beyond words to be able to answer His question, "Where are you?" with a confident, "Here I am, Lord."

> "I am Thine, O Lord, I have heard Thy voice,
> and it told Thy love to me;
> But I long to rise in the arms of faith
> and be closer drawn to Thee." (Fanny Crosby)

Midge Ruth

Psalm 119:89-176; 1 Corinthians 8   **August 26**

The Freedom of Forgiveness

Be kind and compassionate to one another, forgiving one another, just as in Christ God forgave you.
(Ephesians 4:32 NIV)

One of the most common failures among Christians is the failure to forgive. We are apt to consider an unforgiving spirit to be a "right" in the light of what someone has said or done which has hurt our feelings. When conviction comes to us as the Spirit applies the Scripture to our hearts, we try to argue with the Lord. We say, "That person doesn't deserve to be forgiven after what he did to me."

This kind of reasoning is in direct violation of the imperative of our theme verse. Forgiveness is not optional but obligatory. We are not told to forgive if the offender is repentant. Nor are we provided with a condition, i.e., forgive if there is some evidence of remorse. We are essentially taught that our forgiveness is not to be based on any merit found in the offender. This mandate for mercy is removed from any conditional circumstances but is based on our standing with God – forgiven. Unforgiveness is sin.

What condition in the sinner was sufficient to merit the forgiveness of God? It is strictly the mercy of God which provided the basis of forgiveness. His grace was demonstrated in the sacrifice of Christ on behalf of the sinner. The result – we are forgiven! (Check out Ephesians 1:7, Colossians 2:13-14). The standard for our forgiveness of others is based on His forgiveness of us. This is declared in the pivotal phrase, "just as." Our freedom in Christ makes us free to forgive others.

What happens to the unforgiving Christian? He becomes a slave of the unforgiven. His spirit is in bondage to the one he won't forgive. The conviction of the Holy Spirit presses upon him. By the same token, when forgiveness is granted, the spirit is liberated. There is a tremendous sense of freedom in the heart.

Rev. William A. Raws

Psalms 120-122; 1 Corinthians 9   **August 27**

Fear of Man...

"I, even I, am He who comforts you. Who are you that you should be afraid of a man who will die, And of the son of a man who will be made like grass?" (Isaiah 51:12)

You may be more familiar with the world's term for this very common problem the Bible calls "fear of man." Perhaps you have heard it called "people pleasing" or "co-dependency" or "approval addiction." At its root, it is placing an inordinate value in what other people think about us. Inordinate? How much would be considered inordinate? Well, for sure, if we value what others think more than what our Creator thinks, that would be inordinate. Exactly whom are we listening to? Whose opinion are we valuing?

Here are some ways we fear man:

We pass a person in the hall and they don't say "hi" and we worry about it for 3 days;

We seek the praise of people;

Our world crashes when someone criticizes or questions us;

Our world revolves around another individual, such as our spouse, child or best friend; they are the one we go to to get our world set in order, or to alleviate negative emotions.

There are many other ways. But what they all have in common is that in some way we value what another person thinks or says above what God thinks or says.

"Listen to Me, you who know righteousness, You people in whose heart is My law: Do not fear the reproach of men, Nor be afraid of their insults. For the moth will eat them up like a garment, And the worm will eat them like wool; But My righteousness will be forever, And My salvation from generation to generation" (Isaiah 51:7-8).

"I, even I, am He who comforts you. Who are you that you should be afraid of a man who will die, and of the son of a man who will be made like grass? And you forget the LORD your Maker, who stretched out the heavens and laid the foundations of the earth;..." (Isaiah 51:12-13).

This is a common issue for us. Christians are not exempt. We want to be accepted, we want people to like us, and we want to be well thought of. Whether it is ever true of another living human being or not, it will always be true of God. He accepts us. He not only loves us but He likes us, and He thinks well of us, in fact, He delights in us.

To whom will you listen? The created or the Creator?

Diane Hunt

Psalms 123-125; 1 Corinthians 10:1-18 **August 28**

The King's Offer

...and take your father and your families back to me, and I will give you the best of the land of Egypt, and you can enjoy the fat of the land. ...never mind about your belongings, because the best of all Egypt will be yours.
(Genesis 45:18-20 NIV)

In this wonderful story about Joseph, the king (Pharaoh) has offered Joseph's family a life better than they could have ever imagined. He has invited the entire family to come and enjoy more than they deserved. In fact, they probably deserved a horrible fate based on what they had done to their brother Joseph. The king promises them the best and says forget about your belongings, because what I have for you will be so much better.

The rest of the story comes in Genesis 46:6 (NIV): ... *They also took with them their livestock and the possessions they had acquired in Canaan...*

"What! You have got to be kidding me!" I couldn't believe what I was reading. It made no sense to me. Canaan to Egypt – this is no short trip: there are mountains and deserts and besides there were no U-hauls. The king promised them the best and they were dragging their stuff with them, everything they had acquired in Canaan. I couldn't understand. What they had couldn't have been better than what the king was going to give them. Besides, it was going to be a rough trip trying to take it all with them. Why not wait and enjoy what had already been promised?

I don't think we are much different. Our King promises us when we accept Jesus Christ as our Lord and Savior that we will have eternal treasures and rewards far better than anything we could obtain here on earth. He tells us to come to Him and leave the earthly kingdom behind. He says fix your mind on things above, not on the things of this world. In other words, "never mind about your belongings, because the best of My entire kingdom will be yours."

I think we are missing the boat. We are so busy trying to drag around the possessions we have acquired that we do not experience the fullness of what the King has offered. Are we making the journey to see the King more difficult than it needs to be?

Do not store up for yourselves treasures on earth, where moth and rust destroy, and where thieves break in and steal. But store up for yourselves treasures in heaven, where moth and rust do not destroy, and where thieves do not break in and steal. For where your treasure is, there your heart will be also (Matthew 6:19-21 NIV).

Chaplain Bill Pruitt

Psalms 126-128; 1 Corinthians 10:19-33   **August 29**

Simply Being

Therefore, if anyone is in Christ, he is a new creation; old things have passed away; behold, all things have become new.
(2 Corinthians 5:17)

In August 2008, my friend Larry and I traveled to Whiting, New Jersey where I was scheduled to preach at America's Keswick. One day, as we walked into a restaurant, he stopped me and said, "Chris, look at this huge bee!" Then he asked me this question, "What is the bee doing?"

Well, it was obvious to me, he was collecting pollen, but my friend reminded me that "He's doing what God created him to do; he is simply being a bee." Oh, what a different world we would live in today if only Christians would simply be who they are in Christ.

What does it mean to be who you are *in Christ*? When you became a child of God, the Bible says that you are now *in Christ* and *a new creation.* My friend, you have been born again. God sees you now *in Christ*, and the Holy Spirit is in you. You are right now and forever a new creation!

What does God require of you now? Simply be who you

now are, *in Christ*. I know this brings to your mind the immediate question, "How do I do this?"

Visualize this: I have been placed in Christ, because I have been crucified with Christ. The apostle Paul said in Galatians 2:20, *I have been crucified with Christ.* Therefore, I am now and forever fully accepted by God the Father and completely secure, because I am in Him.

I'm not a sports star nor an entertainer being admired by the world; I am someone far greater: "I am in Christ," and He lives in me. This is my significance. My friend, if this is not how you see yourself, you will look to something else in this world to meet your need for significance.

Sadly, as Christians, we do not see this anymore. It has been lost in all of our busyness trying to be who we are *in Christ* by what we **do**, instead of simply being who we **are**, *in Christ!*

My friend, rest in this absolute and eternal truth that you are, now and forever, **in Christ Jesus, and He is in you** by the Holy Spirit. Now, go and simply be.

Rev. Chris S. Hodges

Psalms 129-131; 1 Corinthians 11:1-16 **August 30**

Triumph in Christ

...thanks be unto God, which always causeth us to triumph in Christ... (2 Corinthians 2:14 KJV)

Our Lord did not plan defeat as an option for those of us "in Christ." We need to keep that in mind. And we need to keep that promise in everything else that is a part of us: our schedules, our thoughts, our relationships, our entertainment, our disciplines, our trials, our tribulations, our frustrations and ... I think you get the idea.

But we must be sure of this. Our God *always* causes us to triumph. Since "always" means *always,* that means there is neither time nor arena left for defeat. That is the way God planned it for us.

We may say that such a promise is radical, that it goes beyond the measure of reasonableness, that it defies the reality of human experience. That may be true, but truer still is that our God "always causes us to triumph in Christ...."

Consider this for the credentials to such a provision:

Christ triumphed on the cross even though everything about it accented the greatest of emotional, physical and spiritual pain.

The servant Paul "always" triumphed in Christ even though he spoke of "much affliction and anguish of heart." *For out of much affliction and anguish of heart I wrote unto you with many tears; not that ye should be grieved, but that ye might know the love which I have more abundantly unto you* (2 Corinthians 2:4).

He always triumphed in Christ even though he spoke of having "no rest" in his spirit (2 Corinthians 2:13).

He triumphed in Christ though he wrote of being *troubled on every side* (2 Corinthians 4:8).

Christ and His missionary servant Paul knew that the presence of triumph did not mean the absence of trials. In fact it means just the opposite. We must understand that there is no such thing as triumph without conflict. For triumph to exist there must be something that is conquered.

Perhaps that is one reason the Bible tells us to *count it all joy when we fall into different temptations* (James 1:2). In such trials our triumph in Christ is manifested and that makes it possible for us to be *unto God a sweet savour of Christ, in them that are saved, and in them that perish:...* And that is always Triumph.

Dr. Robert L. Alderman

Psalms 132-134; 1 Corinthians 11:17-34   **August 31**

Spiritual Reverse Engineering

For sin shall not have dominion over you, for you are not under law but under grace. (Romans 6:14)

Years before a product comes off patent, generic companies are taking that product apart to see what it is made of and how it works. This process is referred to as reverse engineering.

Romans 6:14 is the finished product of Paul's instruction of Romans 6:1-13. Paul's summary statement is that sin does not have control over the believer. But this freedom is not due to the keeping of law and religion but rather an outworking of God's grace! To understand this freedom, let's do some spiritual reverse engineering:

In Romans 6:1 (NASB), Paul raises the objection to the gospel of grace, "If God's grace is greater than sin should we keep on sinning to get more grace?" Paul's immediate response is, *May it never be,* followed by his theological answer, *How shall we who died to sin still live in it?* Paul's response is explained with three facts that we must know:

Fact #1: Verses 3-5 - Every believer should know that they have been baptized into Jesus' death. This is not water baptism. Rather, these verses remind the believer that he or she, at the time of belief, was put into a real spiritual union with Jesus. Living free of sin and law begins when you believe that you are in this union with Jesus.

Fact #2: Verses 6-7 give us a second critical fact to know. Our old man was crucified with Jesus. Because you are in this real and present spiritual union with Jesus (Romans 6:3-5), His death became your death. All that you were before in Adam - guilty, condemned, and alienated from God - was put to death and judged when Jesus died on the cross. That old you, that unregenerate you, died with Christ!

Fact #3: Verses 8-10 - Jesus rose from the dead. He is alive. Due to your union with Jesus (Romans 5:5), you have risen to new life. God sees you as a resurrected person already!

These three facts are the objective basis of Paul's conclusion in Romans 6:14. By grace we are united with Jesus in His death and resurrection. The old you is gone and you are now free.

Pause right now and meditate on the three facts of Romans 6:1-10. Thank the Lord that you are no longer a prisoner to either sin or the law, for you are under grace!

Rev. Jeff Barbieri

Psalms 135-136; 1 Corinthians 12　　　　　　　　**September 1**

Guilty

There is therefore now no condemnation to those who are in Christ Jesus. (Romans 8:1a)

I have found that Satan loves to use guilt in a believer's life to keep him trapped in a prison of condemnation. In Revelation 12:10 the Bible tells us that Satan is our "accuser." He loves it when a believer takes the bait and feels guilty and condemned. His work is done. It's very hard to live in the freedom Christ gives you as a believer if you go into another prison of condemnation. Jesus paid the price for that in full! Jesus has set us free so why do we want to go right back into prison?

What beautiful words! If we feel guilty because of sin there's an answer for it. First ask God for forgiveness, then accept His cleansing love. Christ's perfect sacrifice on the cross set us free! If the great "I Am," the sovereign and holy God of the universe, is not condemning us, why are we? Are we saying that Jesus' sacrifice wasn't sufficient?

In all we do there are consequences; some consequences are life-changing while others may not even be noticeable. Instead of listening to the voice of Satan condemning us, we need to listen to the Holy Spirit of God living in us. Listening to Him will result in conviction of sin (if there is unrepented sin), forgiveness, restoration and freedom. If we listen to the Holy Spirit instead of Satan, we will deal with godly sorrow...but that's a good thing. God can and will take all our junk and use it for His glory if we allow Him to.

If we have sinned against someone, we can ask his forgiveness and then give it to God and be free. We can't change things in the past, but we do have today...the day that God has given us. Allow Christ to live *through* you, and give Him the glory.

Hebrews 10:22 says, *let us draw near with a true heart in full assurance of faith, having our hearts sprinkled from an evil conscience and our bodies washed with pure water.*

Don't continue to fall for the lies of the accuser! In faith believe God; you have been washed with pure water...no longer condemned...the prison door isn't locked...all you have to do is believe and walk through the door and live in the freedom.

Guilt has no place in a believer's life because Christ has already paid the penalty of sin and there is no reason for Him to pay it again! If you feel regret or godly sorrow, it's a perfect opportunity to remember that Jesus has already forgiven you...then thank Him and praise Him for His glorious gift to you!

Mary Ann Kiernan

Psalms 137-139; 1 Corinthians 13   **September 2**

Tears – The Lubricant of Vision

But if we walk in the light as He is in the light, we have fellowship with one another, and the blood of Jesus Christ His Son cleanses us from all sin. (1 John 1:7)

Some of my friends have been afflicted with a medical condition known as dry-eye syndrome. In some cases this has required surgery to open the tear ducts so that the secretion from the lacrimary glands might flow to the eye. Tears have at least two vital physical functions related to good vision. The first is lubrication, and the second is purification.

If the eye is to function normally, it must be lubricated by the secretion from the lacrimary glands through the tear ducts. Any failure of this system results in major discomfort and possible disease.

The second function of tears is purification and cleansing. Foreign particles such as dust are flushed away as the tears flow. Dr. Lewis Sperry Chafer, founder of Dallas Theological Seminary, once visited a coal mining town in Wales to conduct special meetings in a church. The pastor asked Dr. Chafer if he would like to visit the mine and watch the men be lowered into the pit. He readily agreed. Standing there in the dim light of morning, they observed that the men wore clean clothes and carried lunch pails. In groups they entered a cage which lowered them into the darkness of the mine. Late in the afternoon the pastor and Dr. Chafer had occasion to return to the place just as the miners were being hoisted to the surface. A remarkable change had taken place. Faces, hands and clothing were covered with coal dust. However, there was one part of them which was unaffected by the dirt – the eyes. Their whites seemed whiter than before in contrast to their dust-coated faces. What had kept these eyes clean? Tears.

One of the main functions of the shed blood of Christ, according to 1 John 1:7, is to keep cleansing us from sin. The emphasis is on a continuous action like that of the flow of tears.

Earlier in the verse the theme of fellowship was introduced. It appears to be closely related to cleansing. There must be application of the blood of Christ in order for fellowship to exist between ourselves and the Lord and between Christians. This is the means of cleansing and lubricates to prevent friction.

Rev. William A. Raws

Psalm 140-142; 1 Corinthians 14:1-20 September 3

God Calls It Sin

Whoever commits sin also commits lawlessness, and sin is lawlessness. (1 John 3:4)

Whatever became of sin? That seems to be the question today. It seems that we live in the day of the Judges. *In those days there was no king in Israel; everyone did what was right in his own eyes* (Judges 17:6).

Surveys reveal that the larger majority of Christians no longer believe in *Absolute Truth*. Today we say that situations and circumstances determine what is right and wrong. We say that what is sin to one person may not be sin to another person. We have rationalized sin away. However, sin still exists. There is still a holy God in heaven who is offended by our sin.

What is sin? The word *sin* means to miss the mark. It conveys the idea of the archer with bow and arrow. The archer's intended target is the bulls-eye of the target. Yet, he misses and the arrow goes off course. The arrow misses the target. Man has missed God's intended target of holiness, righteousness and Christlikeness.

Sin is *lawlessness* and *transgression*. Traffic lights and no trespassing signs have a purpose. They are designed to protect people and property. When these laws are broken and the lines are crossed bad things can happen. God's laws and boundaries are not intended to hurt His children. They are meant to help and protect His children.

Sin is *rebellion* against God. A classic illustration of *rebellion* is the story of the prodigal son, Luke 15:11-32. The prodigal planned and plotted to leave his father's home, supervision and authority. He wanted to live life his way. He became a rebel. You will note, as you read the story, his decision had disastrous consequences.

Sin is *omission. Therefore, to him who knows to do good and does not do it, to him it is sin* (James 4:17). Sin is not just doing things we should not do. Sin is the failure to do the right thing that we know we should do.

Sin is *unbelief.* Unbelief is the unforgivable sin. Since *belief (faith, trust)* is the only way we can be right with God, not to believe is sin.

God calls it sin. What do you call it? What are you doing about it?

Dr. Roger D. Willmore

Psalms 143-145; 1 Corinthians 14:21-40   September 4

Help My Unbelief

Jesus said to him, "If you can believe, all things are possible to him who believes." (Mark 9:23)

In addressing bondage to life-dominating sin in the lives of men we often come to a "crisis of faith." These situations occur when suddenly we come to a situation where the two alternatives are clearly evident. We can trust God or trust ourselves.

The man in this passage is in a similar situation. We read, *Then one of the crowd answered and said, "Teacher, I brought You my son, who has a mute spirit. And wherever it seizes him, it throws him down; he foams at the mouth, gnashes his teeth, and becomes rigid. So I spoke to Your disciples, that they should cast it out, but they could not." He answered him and said, "O faithless generation, how long shall I be with you? How long shall I bear with you? Bring him to Me." Then they brought him to Him. And when he saw Him, immediately the spirit convulsed him, and he fell on the ground and wallowed, foaming at the mouth. So He asked his father, "How long has this been happening to him?" And he said, "From childhood"* (Mark 9:17-21).

The disciples, being religious novices, had been called upon by this desperate father to cure his son. Unable to do so they, like so many who were watching, were skeptical as to whether anyone could help. The father had moved past skeptical to desperate. Sometimes that is where God has to take us in order to change our lives. It would be nice if He could do it some other way, but we prevent that from happening by our own self-will. As long as we think we can handle it we refuse to put matters into God's hands.

The apostle Paul said, *Yes, we had the sentence of death in ourselves, that we should not trust in ourselves but in God who raises the dead* (2 Corinthians 1:9).

Has God brought you to a place where you are powerless to overcome something that you really desire to overcome? If so, His encouragement to you is *If you can believe, all things are possible to him who believes.*

> Father forgive me, not just for my unbelief, but for my failure to entrust myself fully into Your hands in the midst of it.

Chaplain Jim Freed

Psalms 146-147; 1 Corinthians 15:1-28**September 5**

Snakes and Sin

...How shall we who died to sin live any longer in it?
(Romans 6:2)

It would not be much of a stretch to say I hate snakes. Something inside me recoils in the presence of a snake even if it is neatly tucked inside a tank at the zoo.

One morning I was out walking on a particularly beautiful, spring-like day. I happened to step over a coiled piece of rope that made me take a second glance to make sure it wasn't a small snake. Immediately my mind wandered ...

Dead snakes are somewhat less threatening. I imagined myself handling (with gloves of course) a small dead snake. I thought I'd be somewhat okay with that.

As I continued my walk I recalled a Canadian camping trip as a teen. Someone had struck and killed a VERY LARGE snake. My 35-year memory recalls it to have been about 5 or 6 feet long and about 4 inches in diameter. So I asked myself, would I be willing to handle that LARGE dead snake even with gloves on? I don't think so. No, I know so. I would not be willing to handle a large dead snake. Why? If it's dead, what's the big deal? Because if I were honest, although I could see it is dead, and intellectually believe it is dead, there is something deep within me that fears it springing back to life in my hands. That's when it hit me – the similarity between dead snakes and our sin nature.

...knowing this, that our old man was crucified with Him, that the body of sin might be done away with, that we should no longer be slaves of sin. For he who has died has been freed from sin...Likewise you also, reckon yourselves to be dead indeed to sin, but alive to God in Christ Jesus our Lord (Romans 6:6-7, 11).

I have been crucified with Christ and I no longer live... (Galatians 2:20 NIV).

We are dead to sin. Our old man is dead, dead, dead. We intellectually know it is dead but it seems as if deep down we fear it isn't. That is how many of us live, knowing that our sin nature is dead but keeping our eye on it just in case. In so doing we grant it credence and act as if it has the potential to overpower us. If in the deepest recesses of our heart we fear that it might spring back to life at any moment, then in many subtle ways we will live as if it can.

We are dead to sin; reckon it so. Whether it feels true or not, reckon it so. Fully embrace this truth without fear that somehow we might be mistaken.

Diane Hunt

Psalms 148-150; 1 Corinthians 15:29-58   September 6

Paul's Prayer for the Saints

...that the God of our Lord Jesus Christ, the Father of glory, may give to you the spirit of wisdom and revelation in the knowledge of Him,... (Ephesians 1:17)

Paul's letter to the saints of Ephesus is about the walk of the disciple of Christ. He encourages them to recognize the significance of their calling not only as it pertains to life after death but also as it applies to their everyday walk. As heirs of God who are sealed by His Holy Spirit they need to be reminded of the commitment to Christ that was made at salvation. Keeping this in mind and heart would move them toward the fulfillment of God's purpose in the life of the disciple as one who glorifies God by walking worthy of the calling he has received.

In this process of spiritual transformation Paul prays that they may have ...*the spirit of wisdom and revelation in the knowledge of Him,...* As the disciple grows in this wisdom and revelation he will gain the knowledge of three things:

1) ...*the hope of His calling...* (v. 18). The New Testament word "hope" is always connected to the plan of God. Unlike our English use of the word "hope," this biblical use is of a sure thing that God has and will accomplish. He has called us to both salvation and to sanctification. Spiritual growth is an indicator of true salvation.

2) ...*the riches of the glory of His inheritance*... (v. 18). While the culture around us cries out that we need the wealth of this world, understanding what we have in Christ settles us into that daily crucified life that He has called us to (Luke 9:23). Pursuing anything outside of "...the kingdom of God and His righteousness..." (Matthew 6:33) is idolatry.

3) ...*the exceeding greatness of His power*... (v. 19). This is the source of the overcomer's victorious life. It is the power of God that brought about Christ's resurrection and exaltation (v. 20), a power that is above any and all of our enemies (v. 21).

God has provided us with everything that we need to live the victorious Christian life. Are we ...*increasing in wisdom and revelation in the knowledge of Him*..? This knowledge becomes true wisdom as we live it out in the everyday of life, bringing glory to God and inviting others to do the same.

Dr. Joe Olachea

Ecclesiastes 1-2; 1 Corinthians 16　　　　　　　　September 7

The Excessiveness of God

*Let the wicked forsake his way, and the unrighteous man his thoughts: and let him return unto the L*ORD*, and he will have mercy upon him; and to our God, for he will abundantly pardon.*
(Isaiah 55:7 KJV)

Our LORD has set the pattern for going beyond the ordinary on behalf of His people. Of that we are assured in the excessive, the abundant *pardon* of God.

And that is why the Bible speaks to the wicked with these words, *Let the wicked forsake his way, and the unrighteous man his thoughts: and let him return unto the L*ORD*, and he will have mercy upon him; and to our God, for he will* **abundantly pardon** (Isaiah 55:7KJV, emphasis mine).

We are assured of the excessiveness of God, not only with reference to His *pardon* but also with reference to His *power.*

This excessive nature of our Lord on behalf of His people was illustrated at the Red Sea when His people went through that sea on *dry ground,* not through shallow water and not on wet soil, but on dry ground.

We are assured of the excessiveness of God not only with reference to His pardon and His power, but also with reference to His thoughts. That is why He said, *For as the heavens are higher than the earth, so are my ways higher than your ways, and my thoughts than your thoughts* (Isaiah 55:9 KJV).

We are assured of the excessiveness of God not only with reference to His pardon, His power, and His thoughts, but also with reference to His provision of *more abundant life* (John 10:10). That is why He said, *I am come that they might have life, and that they might have it more abundantly* (John 10:10).

But there is more, and this is perhaps the ultimate excessiveness. It is the reality of deliverance and of exaltation in the two-fold excessiveness of God.

Our LORD has not only *delivered us from the power of darkness* but He has also *translated us into the kingdom of his dear Son...* (Colossians 1:13).

The same excessive nature of God appears again in Revelation 5:9-10 when the redeemed sing not only of their redemption but of their being made unto God kings and priests.

That is a brief look at the excessiveness of our Lord. It is enough to let us know that we should never fear of falling short of His provision for our victory in Christ.

Dr. Robert L. Alderman

Ecclesiastes 3-4; 2 Corinthians 1   **September 8**

What Did It Take to Convince You?

...the Helper ... will convict the world of sin, and of righteousness, and of judgment: of sin, because they do not believe in Me; of righteousness, because I go to My Father and

you see Me no more; of judgment, because the ruler of this world is judged. (John 16:7-11)

Jesus was preparing His disciples for the time of His departure. He made the surprising statement that it would be to their advantage for Him to go away (v. 7). They must have questioned this assertion. "How in the world could it be to our advantage for Him to go away?" Jesus continued with an explanation that if He did not depart the Helper (the Holy Spirit) would not come to them. How could He provide an advantage? During His earthly ministry, Jesus was physically present in one location at a time. If He were in Galilee, He was not in Judea. If He were in Galilee, He might not be in Nazareth. The promised Helper, the Holy Spirit, would not be limited geographically. He could be fully and personally present everywhere. He would be not merely with them but in them (14:20).

As Jesus continued His amplification of this truth, He provided a job description of the kind of help the Holy Spirit would give in the performance of the impossible task he was about to give them. They could be encouraged by the promised enabling of the Helper. His role would be to convict the world of three realities: sin, righteousness and judgment. The word translated convict was used in legal proceedings of the prosecutor bringing conviction through his cross-examination. The Spirit examines the heart, exposing the basic need and revealing God's provision to meet that need. Unbelief is the primary obstacle to salvation, and the facts to be believed include the finished work of the cross satisfying God's righteousness and the final judgment of the ruler of this world.

It is not the responsibility of present day believers to bring conviction to the unsaved or even to the sinning Christian. This is the role of the Holy Spirit – the Divine Helper.

Rev. William A. Raws

Ecclesiastes 5-6; 2 Corinthians 2   **September 9**

Take the Test

These things I have written to you who believe in the name of the Son of God, that you may know that you have eternal life, and that you may continue to believe in the name of the Son of God.
(1 John 5:13)

The apostle John wrote his first letter for the express purpose of enabling Christians to have assurance of their salvation. John knew that the Christians of his day were tempted to doubt the validity of their salvation. Today many Christians struggle with doubts about their salvation. John's letter contains some helpful tests that will help a person know the condition of their standing with Jesus Christ.

Test One: No habitual sinning. *Whoever has been born of God does not sin, for His seed remains in him; and he cannot sin, because he has been born of God* (3:9).

Test Two: Believe in Jesus Christ. *Whoever believes that Jesus is the Christ is born of God, and everyone who loves Him who begot also loves him who is begotten of Him* (5:1).

Test Three: Do righteousness. *If you know that He is righteous, you know that everyone who practices righteousness is born of Him* (2:29).

Test Four: Love others. *We know that we have passed from death to life, because we love the brethren. He who does not love his brother abides in death* (3:14).

Test Five: Overcome the world. *For whatever is born of God overcomes the world. And this is the victory that has overcome the world—our faith* (5:4).

Test Six: Purity. *We know that whoever is born of God does not sin; but he who has been born of God keeps himself, and the wicked one does not touch him* (5:18).

How did you do? Are you passing the tests? You have before you the evidences of genuine salvation.

Dr. Roger D. Willmore

Ecclesiastes 7-8; 2 Corinthians 3 **September 10**

Even Now

"Lord," Martha said to Jesus, "If you had been here, my brother would not have died. But I know that even now God will give you whatever you ask." (John 11:21-22 NIV)

Because He's an "even now" kind of God, we can have an even now kind of faith. Say what you want about Martha, when her brother was four days dead and her sister wouldn't even come out of the house, when she was feeling very let down by God, Martha still looked at Jesus and said, "even now." I find this kind of stuff throughout the Bible. With the enemy closing in, and nothing but the sea in front of them, Moses raises his staff. He acts in faith and, "even now." Hezekiah spreads a hate letter before the Lord and, "even now." Daniel is to be eaten alive because he won't give up his quiet time, and "even now." On and on the list goes.

We see it through history. A monk trapped in the system gets fed up with his lack of joy, nails his convictions to a door, and "even now," the re-birth of the church. Nazis decide to rid the earth of Jews. The world finally steps in, and in 1948, the nation that God loves is re-born. Can a nation be reborn in a day? It can when people act in faith to our "even now" God. An ex-drunk named William Raws decides to build a rehab in the pinelands of New Jersey so that men like himself can live worthwhile lives and, at the end of them, make it to heaven. He digs in his pockets, comes up with $1.87 and goes for it because he knows really well what our "even now" God can do. I've seen this very clearly in my own life. I lost my family, my house, my career, my health, and my dignity through cocaine addiction. Now, I have the best wife, the two greatest kids, and the best job in the world. I'm healthy and haven't done drugs in twenty years. Two words, even now. I got asked to pastor a church of fifteen people in spiritually crippled England. We now have a hundred and twenty adults and a hundred children and teens coming every week to worship their new Savior. Even now.

I wonder what you're facing today. Has a doctor told you what you never wanted to hear? Or are you going through divorce? God hates it but it still happens; and just when you think that everything is over, God thinks, even now. Loved one in prison? Gay child? No work? Alone? Depressed? Sexual failure? Feeling worthless? Two words for you: Even now. And when the whole world was going to hell because we told God to "shove off, we'll do what we want," that was when God sent His Son to the cross. Because He's never going to quit at loving you, He did the ultimate even now.

Martha was a special lady. She looked past everything else, into the eyes of Jesus, and said, even now. You're a special person as well. Deep inside, you know that Jesus is the same yesterday, today and forever. So come out to meet Him. Spill your guts if you need to, but know that God will always give Jesus whatever He asks for. Even today. Even now.

Rev. Chris Thompson

Ecclesiastes 9-10; 2 Corinthians 4 **September 11**

Is God Shorthanded?

...Is My hand shortened at all that it cannot redeem? Or have I no power to deliver?... (Isaiah 50:2)

Usually the term *shorthanded* communicates a numerical deficiency such as might occur in business or the military. However, in our theme verse it is used by God in a rhetorical question concerning His ability to reach the sinner. He draws the picture of someone reaching out to rescue another but coming short of grasping the subject. The anticipated answer to the above question would be, "No." God can reach to the lowest and to the farthest to redeem and to deliver.

In Isaiah 59:1 there is an emphatic statement made which reinforces the implied answer of the above passage. *Behold, the Lord's hand is not shortened, that it cannot save; nor His ear heavy, that it cannot hear.* What a provision for rescue! But verse 2 gives a sad picture of the failure of God's people and the separation from their rescuer. The ability of the Lord did not change, but there had been a barrier set up in their hearts which interfered with His rescue work. In a sense, we can resist the delivering hand of God, making it appear that His hand is shortened.

One of the most feared things in making a water rescue of a drowning person is the victim's struggle to grab hold of the rescuer. In some cases this interference has resulted in the loss of both.

There is a sense in which we might say that God is shorthanded. That is in the area of willing servants. Most missions report that there is a much greater need than can be met by the present number of candidates. The Lord has extended His call, but potential candidates face the daunting task of raising the required amount of support. Often, they turn to secular employment and the work of God suffers shortages.

When God promised Moses that the people would be given meat sufficient for a whole month, Moses calculated that this would require the slaughter of their livestock and the catching of tons of fish (Numbers 11:22). But God replied, *"Has the Lord's arm been shortened? Now you shall see whether what I say will happen to you or not"* (v. 23). We must believe His Word despite the appearance that our situation is beyond His reach.

Rev. William A. Raws

Ecclesiastes 11-12; 2 Corinthians 5　　　　　　　**September 12**

God Is Unchanging

Jesus Christ is the same yesterday, today, and forever.
(Hebrews 13:8)

As we gathered together as a staff we were asked, "On a scale of 1-10, how well do you handle change?" We were then asked to form a line according to the number we gave ourselves. I think I handle change fairly well so I gave myself an 8-9. How about you? Whether you handle change well or change seems to overwhelm you, aren't you glad that God does not change one bit?

We can always count on change. We can also count on God's consistency. We will never wake one morning to find that He is no longer there. A day will not come when He is not gracious, loving, kind, patient and faithful. He will still make a way to bring you through the Red Sea that stands before you. The same God who provided manna is the same One who will supply your need today.

Let me rephrase the original question. On a scale of 1-10, how well do you handle change? What happens when change is not about what is happening around you but it is what God desires to do in you? Outward change is one thing but a change of heart and mind is another. The habit, attitude or sin seems to never change. We feel helpless and defeated. Yet the same power that was used to raise Jesus Christ from the dead is the same power offered to us this very day. No matter what God may be changing the answer is the same. We can always count on knowing that He will never change.

Kathy Withers

Song of Solomon 1-2; 2 Corinthians 6 **September 13**

Your Heart is Like a Room in Your Life...

...man looks at the outward appearance, but the LORD looks at the heart. (1 Samuel 16:7b)

If the Lord came today and decided to visit one of the rooms in your life, what would He find? What have your hands touched? Where have your feet walked? What did your mouth taste? What did you ponder in your mind? Where is your heart today? What would He find in all of these areas?

Do you remember that tract where it talks about the Lord coming to your house? It goes on to say that if He were to come to your home today what would He find? Would you need to dust off your Bible? Would you have to close a door? Would you have to change the TV or music station?

I don't like it when company comes and I do not have a clean house. My human side feels like I am not a good housekeeper and I wonder what they will think of me. How often am I concerned about the condition of my life and the rooms in it?

When friends do drop in, I tell them that my house might not be clean but the coffee pot is always on and I always have time to spend with them. We should consider the same with the Lord. If He decided to drop in today to visit ... you might have dusty feet, a cluttered mind, and your hands might be full of things, but your heart can be open to Him and willing to spend time with Him. He can clean up what needs to be cleaned better then you ever could. We need to make sure our heart is in the right place first (James 5:8).

In the book of Philippians, we are encouraged to think on things such as truth, things that are noble, things that are right and pure and lovely. Is this where our heart is today?

There are days when my heart is filled with joy, other days sadness, and other days (I hate to admit it) a critical spirit or judgment against another believer. Let's "'fess up" together. We all have these days. Why do we? I think it goes back to James 5:8, where it tells us to establish our hearts. It goes back to putting Jesus first, others second and ourselves last.

When we leave the Lord out of our hearts and lives for any length of time, we find our lives are in disarray, messy and unclean. Our thoughts are not clear, our focus is gone, our joy is depleted, and what is pure, true, noble and right (Philippians 4:8) is not what we are thinking about.

Just as if our home is messy for company and a good cleaning needs to be done, so must our hearts be cleaned before the Lord. He already knows what is in your heart, but it is our job to confess it to Him and allow Him to clean it up.

Do you have a dirty room in your life today? How is your heart established? Can any visitor come and visit with you today and find joy, pure thoughts, noble and right things in it?

Lynn A. Wilson

Song of Solomon 3-4; 2 Corinthians 7 September 14

Prayer Maturity

The prayer of a righteous man is powerful and effective.
(James 5:16b, NIV)

As Christians we cannot attain a higher spiritual life than our prayer life. Everything we are and everything we do for the Lord depends on prayer. Unfortunately most of us would rather work than pray.

What a difference it would make in our personal lives, our homes, our church and our world if we really learned to pray and actually prayed daily in earnest. Here is a quote from Warren Wiersbe's book, <u>Window on the Parables</u>: "If we had the privilege of asking the Lord for one specific blessing would we ask, teach me to pray, Lord, or would it be teach me how to make more money, or how to teach or preach? The wisest request would be *teach me how to pray,* because every other blessing in the Christian life depends on our ability to pray." From Charles Stanley's book, <u>Handle with Prayer</u>, comes this quote, "Unfortunately many Christians are top–notch worriers and mediocre prayers. Prayer is a soul exercise that takes daily practice. It's a matter of waiting."

There are several elements for learning how to pray maturely found in Luke 11:1-13.

1) We must learn that we must pray. It is not an option. Jesus prayed, John the Baptist prayed, the disciples asked Jesus to teach them how to pray. Prayer is not a luxury, it is a necessity.

2) We must pray in God's will. In 1 John 5:14-15, we have His three-fold promise: a) He is listening when we pray according to His will; b) we know that He hears the petitions we desire; c) we already possess what we have asked for. These two verses deal with our ability to approach God openly, freely, confidently and boldly with assurance that He will hear and grant our request according to His will for us. 3) We must pray as children coming to a father. In the parable in Luke 11:5-13, we see that the neighbor was not able to get a positive response from his sleeping friend. Our Father in heaven never sleeps. We do not

have to beat down His door to get His attention. He knows our needs before we do. He loves us and is willingly waiting to meet our every need. But He does require us to bring to Him, in prayer, those requests. Persistence in prayer does not mean that we must twist God's arm to get what we want. It means keeping in close communion with Him. We must never be afraid of answered prayer that is in the will of God.

God will not put things into our hands until He first prepares our hearts. The greatest blessing of prayer is not in receiving the answer but in being the kind of person God can trust with the answer. The most important part of our lives is the part that only God sees and knows. The hidden life of prayer is the secret of an open life of victory.

Chaplain Stan Marsh

Song of Solomon 5-6; 2 Corinthians 8   **September 15**

Cry Out

I cry out to the LORD with my voice; With my voice to the LORD I make my supplication. I pour out my complaint before Him; I declare before Him my trouble. (Psalm 142:1-2)

Do you struggle with praying out loud? For years I did. I was always afraid I wouldn't say the right words, or sound "spiritual enough." What that really boils down to is fear of people – and the only One who should command our fear is God. After all, He is the one to Whom we're speaking anyway. When we pray out loud, we're inviting others to join in with us as we pray, but we aren't really talking to them.

I've recently been reading a little book by Bill Gothard titled The Power of Crying Out. While I've somewhat conquered my fears of praying out loud in groups of people, I had never thought about praying out loud when I'm by myself. After all, God knows my thoughts, right? Psalm 139:2b says, *You understand my thought afar off.* So when I'm praying in my heart and my mind and my spirit, God hears me. But the Scripture is full of verses indicating we are to cry out to God with our voice.

So, I've started praying out loud. It was really weird at first. Kind of makes me feel like I'm talking to myself. My dad says only little old ladies with money talk to themselves – and I'm neither! But the truth is, I'm not talking to myself – I'm talking to my Father, and I know He hears me. *I cry out with my whole heart; Hear me, O LORD! I will keep Your statutes* (Psalm 119:145).

I was sharing with a friend about this "new" concept and she reminded me that, while God can hear my prayers whether silent or spoken out loud, Satan can only hear what I speak with my voice. So when I pray out loud, I'm also letting him know what I'm asking God to do – and he knows I have the power of God on my side.

Is there a burden on your heart that you've been praying about? Cry out loud to God – He will hear!

Ruth Schmidt

Song of Solomon 7-8; 2 Corinthians 9   **September 16**

Prayer and Abiding

I am the vine, you are the branches. He who abides in Me, and I in him, bears much fruit; for without Me you can do nothing.
(John 15:5)

Since abiding in Christ is the essence of abundant living, we must understand its implications. To abide in Christ involves trusting Him as life, not depending on our own resources. One way we express this dependence on Christ is through prayer. In the same context of the vine and branches metaphor, our Savior teaches, *If you abide in Me, and My words abide in you, you will ask what you desire, and it shall be done for you* (John 15:7).

George Müller has inspired countless believers concerning God's faithfulness in responding to prayer. Müller described the role that prayer should have in our lives: "Our very weakness gives opportunity for the power of the Lord Jesus Christ to be manifested. That Blessed One never leaves and never forsakes us. The greater the weakness, the nearer He is to manifest His strength; the greater our necessities, the more ground we have to rely on Him, that He will prove Himself our Friend. This has been my experience for more than seventy years; the greater the trial, the greater the difficulty, the nearer the Lord's help. Often the appearance was as if I must be overwhelmed, but it never came to it, and never will. More prayer, more faith, more exercise of patience, will bring the blessing. Therefore our business is just to pour out our hearts before Him; and help in His own time and way is sure to come."

After exhorting us to put on the armor of God, the apostle Paul emphasized the need of prayer: *praying always with all prayer and supplication in the Spirit, being watchful to this end with all perseverance and supplication for all the saints* (Ephesians 6:18).

May we daily abide in Christ through the fellowship of prayer, thus relying on the sustaining power of the Holy Spirit.

Dr. John Woodward

Isaiah 1-2; 2 Corinthians 10　　　　　　　　**September 17**

Walking in the Will of God

And let the peace of God rule in your hearts, to which also you were called in one body; and be thankful. Let the word of Christ dwell in you richly in all wisdom, teaching and admonishing one another in psalms and hymns and spiritual songs, singing with grace in your hearts to the Lord. And whatever you do in word or deed, do all in the name of the Lord Jesus, giving thanks to God the Father through Him. (Colossians 3:15-17)

I can remember the early days of my Christian life. I seriously sought the will of God for my life. It was important to me to be in the center of His will. I still remember the frustration I experienced in my attempts to know God's will. Many told me that God had a will and purpose for my life, but no one told me the way to know His will.

As time went by, I came upon this passage and saw that Paul's words to the Colossians contain some important guidelines for knowing the will of God.

First, we must let the *peace of God rule in our hearts.* The word peace means soul harmony. It is a sense of well being. The word rule is a word which carries the idea of umpire. In other words, Paul is saying let the peace of God umpire your life. Here is how that works. When you are in bounds and playing by God's rules, when you are walking in obedience to Him, there is a sense of peace in your heart. However, the moment you step out of bounds or break a rule, the peace of God makes itself visibly and noticeably absent from your life. There is a sudden sense that something is wrong. It is the absence of God's peace.

Second, we *let the Word of Christ dwell in us richly.* For someone to truly know the will of God he must spend time in the Word of God, the Bible. He cannot depend on the "lucky dip" method where he just randomly selects passages of Scriptures in an effort to get a word from God. No, this is not what it means for the Word of Christ to dwell in us. We must spend time in His Word daily.

Lastly, *whatever we do in word or deed, do all in the name of the Lord.* This means that we must have the Lord's endorsement. Can He put His name on our actions? Can He sign off on it?

God has a wonderful will and purpose for your life. Find it…follow it…fulfill it!

Dr. Roger D. Willmore

Isaiah 3-4; 2 Corinthians 11:1-15   **September 18**

Pilot, Co-Pilot or Navigator?

Jesus saith unto him, "I am the way, the truth, and the life: no man comes unto the Father, but by me." (John 14:6 KJV)

I am sure you all remember those bumper stickers that state: GOD is my CO-PILOT. There was a time I thought, "How nice that they have a relationship with God." Now, as my Christian faith has grown, I have come to understand that the bumper sticker is not in line with what the Bible says about my relationship with God.

The bumper sticker implies that I am basically in control of my life and direction, but that when times get tough or for some reason I am put out of commission that God will step in and take the controls. In Jeremiah 7:23, God speaks and tells the people, *"Obey My voice, and I will be your God, and you shall be My people. And walk in all the ways that I have commanded you, that it will be well with you."* In Psalm 32:8, God says, *I will instruct you and teach you in the way you should go; I will guide you with My eye.* In Proverbs 14:12 and 16:25 we are also told that there is a way that seems right to a man, but it leads us to destruction or death.

The more I read of Scripture, the more I believe that I may have my hands on the wheel, but God asks me to let him do the navigating. Scripture is filled with verses that teach us to walk in "HIS WAY." I have not counted them all, but they number into the hundreds.

1 Kings 8:58 (NIV): *May he turn our hearts to him, to walk in all his **ways** and keep the commands, decrees and regulations he gave our fathers.*

1 Kings 3:14 (NIV): *And if you walk in my **ways** and obey my statutes and commands as David your father did, I will give you a long life.*

Psalm 142:3a (NIV): *When my spirit grows faint within me, it is you who know my **way**.*

Isaiah 28:26 (NIV): *His God instructs him and teaches him the right **way**.*

Isaiah 30:21 (NIV): *Whether you turn to the right or to the left, your ears will hear a voice behind you, saying, "This is the **way**; walk in it."*

Not only are we to follow His ways instead of our own ways as we go about our daily lives, but Scripture also reminds us that eternity with God is only found by following Christ. Are you following Christ - or your own way?

Dr. Lynne Jahns

Isaiah 5-6; 2 Corinthians 11:16-33   September 19

Do You Want To Be Well?

When Jesus saw him lying there, and knew that he already had been in that condition a long time, He said to him, "Do you want to be made well?" (John 5:6)

Asking a man who has been sick for thirty-eight years if he wants to be well may seem a bit unusual to you and me. However, Jesus wanted to hear the man's answer. He wanted to hear the desire of his heart expressed.

The crowd of sick people around the Pool of Bethesda is a picture of the spiritual condition of many people today. They have lost their health, they have no one to help them and they have lost hope. This is a sad picture. It may be a picture of your life.

Are you struggling with a spiritual health malady? Is there some chronic spiritual illness that just keeps on lingering, sapping vitality out of you?

Jesus is the great Physician; He can diagnose your sickness, and He can heal your sin sickness.

Jesus knows your spiritual sickness. He does not ask you if you want to be made well in order that He may know; He asks you if you want to be made well so you will have to face your malady and express your desire to be free of it.

The man at the Pool of Bethesda did not have **health, help, or hope**. He had no resource within himself to make himself better. He was totally dependent upon someone else helping him. Are you willing to admit that you do not have what it takes to cure yourself? You also need someone else. You need a Savior.

Jesus can deliver you from your spiritual sickness. Notice His authoritative word in verse 8, *Rise, take up your bed and walk*. Before us, we see a man who had been sick and helpless for thirty-eight years now taking up his bed and walking. In the miracle of a moment, he is free from his infirmity.

Is anything too hard for the Lord? No! Jesus can deliver you, too! Look beyond your circumstances to the One who has the power to set you free.

Jesus can give you an entire new life. In verse 14, Jesus said to the man who had been healed, *See, you have been made well, sin no more*...A glorious future lay before him.

Do you want to be spiritually well? Then come to Jesus.

Dr. Roger D. Willmore

Isaiah 7-8; 2 Corinthians 12 September 20

Overcoming Fear

Oh, taste and see that the LORD is good; Blessed is the man who trusts in Him. (Psalm 34:8)

The historical background may be found in 1 Samuel 21. Because of King Saul's intense jealousy of David, David fled southward from the court of Saul and went to Philistia where he was captured. The Philistines recognized David as the one who had killed their champion, Goliath. So David was brought before King Achish.

Fearing for his life, David used the strategy of acting as though he were insane. He fell down, groveled in the dirt, drooled down his beard, and gave every indication of being mad. King Achish commanded David to leave his court so David went to the wilderness where he took refuge in the cave of Adullam waiting for his key comrades to join him.

It was during this period of time when David was confronted with fear, frustration, uncertainty, and discouragement that he composed this psalm. David's song certainly has spoken to the hearts of the Lord's people down through the years.

No matter how the twists and turns of life may have gone, the believer knows that God is good. A key verse is verse 8: *The LORD is good.*

But what does "good" mean in this context? It does not mean that God always smoothes the way, or always gives good health, or always provides wealth. No...rather the "goodness" of God means that God always acts on behalf of the believer in ways which are consistent with His own purposes for the ultimate spiritual blessing of the believer in order that God's goal for the believer's life might be realized.

Psalm 34:4 was the favorite verse which President Lincoln claimed during the dark days of the Civil War. The ink on the verse in his Bible was blurred due to the many times his finger followed the words, *I sought the LORD, and He heard me, and delivered me from all my fears.*

In the midst of a very difficult time, David praised the Lord and was delivered from his fear. He could say, *Oh, taste and see that the LORD is good; Blessed is the man who trusts in Him* (Psalm 34:8).

Joy Hubbard

Isaiah 9-10; 2 Corinthians 13   **September 21**

Source of Joy

...My heart leaps for joy and I will give thanks to Him in song.
(Psalm 28:7b NIV)

Webster defines joy as "the emotion evoked by well-being, success, good fortune or by the prospect of possessing what one desires: a source or cause of delight." So, by Webster's definition, we find joy from a source or a cause. If you were to ask any group of people on the street, "What brings you joy?" the answers would be as varied and diverse as the people you asked. They may say money, power, fame, a nice house, car or boat...or perhaps you would receive less materialistic answers like a good meal, a great round of golf or a great relationship. The list could go on forever because a measure of joy can come from an infinite number of sources. But the most important question we could ask is this: Do these sources in our lives provide consistent, lasting, abiding joy? The earthly blessings in this life are gifts extended to us by God's grace and are to be stewarded and enjoyed for His glory, but they offer only temporal joy. Is that enough?

Friend, it is imperative first and foremost that we allow God Himself to be our source of true, abiding joy. This deep joy must first be founded, secured and rooted in our eternal God and Savior, Jesus Christ, by delighting in Him! If we get that right, everything else is simply stacked on top...joy upon joy. Joy found in Christ is a reliable, unbroken constant. It can always be there, ever-present for all days, all circumstances and situations. No external sources deliver like that! The Psalmist understood where his source of joy was when he said, *Satisfy us in the morning with your unfailing love, that we may sing for joy and be glad all our days* (Psalm 90:14). It is only the unfailing love of God that can ensure satisfaction and joy...every day!

Dear one, have you made the discovery of being satisfied in, delighting in and enjoying God? Once you have, you will find joy unspeakable!

These things I have spoken to you, that My joy may remain in you, and that your joy may be full (John 15:11).

Bevan Greiner

Isaiah 11-12; Galatians 1　　　　　　　　　　　**September 22**

Step Aside and Trust God

Answer me quickly, O LORD! My spirit fails! Hide not your face from me, lest I be like those who go down to the pit. Let me hear in the morning of your steadfast love, for in you I trust. Make me know the way I should go, for to you I lift up my soul. (Psalm 143:7-8 ESV)

As the mother of two adult children, I sort of unconsciously figured that parenting would be a whole lot easier at this stage of life. I'm usually not a worrier or a fretter. At least I didn't think I was. In the past few years, many nights of sleep have been lost. I can't seem to shut my brain down. More thoughts than I can handle stumble and tumble through my head and an upset stomach is what I get for my aimless "what if" wandering.

Through all the horrible life scenarios that my kids could wind up in, the constant true thing in all of it is lack of trust in the One Who is in control.

In the phase commonly referred to as "the terrible twos," I had a blast with my children! Two-year-olds are so funny! They also don't yet know that you don't know everything. Nor have they had years of exposure to all your mistakes. You are the one with limitless hugs, a holding lap or "pot hole," as my kids called it. You are the "booboo" kisser and fixer. You're the one who cracks up at all their silly antics and jokes - no matter how often they occur. They know and believe you love them. You are *"Mommy!"*

Today my children are 25 and 23 and I'm no longer Mommy, I'm Mom to one and Ma to the other. They've seen me mess up so often (sometimes at their expense) that they are convinced I need serious therapy or I'm just plain crazy. (The jury is still out on that one.) My hugs are still given and received. My lap is still available for holding. I don't laugh at all their jokes anymore, because I don't get them. It takes so long to explain their jokes, they simply don't bother.

More often than not, their antics drive me to my knees in prayer. They still know and believe I love them, at least I hope so. More important than that or anything else, I hope that my children know and believe that God loves them.

Today, my heavenly Father is teaching me ever so painfully that I must let go; I must stop clinging, and that other "c" word, <u>controlling</u>, step back and let Him lead. Over and over, Father is gently - sometimes not so gently - reminding me of the obvious. There is a God... and it isn't me! The other words He lovingly, repeatedly speaks to me are, "Step aside, my beloved one. Let Me be the One who draws them and woos them. After all, Honey, it isn't about you, now is it?"

Stephanie D. Paul

Isaiah 13-14; Galatians 2 **September 23**

The Great Discovery

Dear friends, let us love one another, for love comes from God. Everyone who loves has been born of God and knows God. Whoever does not love does not know God, because God is love. This is how God showed his love among us: He sent his one and only Son into the world that we might live through him. This is love: not that we loved God, but that he loved us and sent his Son as an atoning sacrifice for our sins. Dear friends, since God so loved us, we also ought to love one another... We love because he first loved us. (1 John 4:7-11, 19 NIV)

God may be the most misunderstood person in the universe! Some don't even believe He exists. Others see Him as an oppressive, overbearing killjoy who only wants to whack us when we "cross the line." Still others view Him as a kindly grandfather-type who is so kind and gracious that He will let us get by with anything.

Not even one of us had a perfect father. Any understanding of God the Father that is based on our earthly fathers will miss the mark. When our view of God is skewed, we lose sight of who we are and how we relate to the Creator of all we know. That is why the biblical revelation of God is so important to us.

The apostle John tells us about God in his first epistle. He even defines God for us by telling us "God is love." His very essence—the distinctive quality of His life—is love. Everything else flows from that. We know He has other attributes and qualities of personality, but John says His defining quality is love. Think back to Jesus' story of the prodigal son, a story that may be more about the father than the son. In that story, the defining quality of the prodigal's father is his great love for his son.

The apostle tells us more about the God who is love. We discover that God proved His loving nature by sending His Son into our world to become the payment for our sin (v. 10). He also tells us that God loved us first (v. 19). What a concept! When you and I were completely unlovely, God loved us! When we were doing our best prodigal imitation, God loved us! Go back as far as you want; it will always be true that God loved you and me first.

We also learn that our gracious God expects us to love one another just like He loves us (vs. 11). Perhaps the key to grasping how to love one another is found in discovering how much God loves us, in discovering that He IS love. The church of Jesus Christ and individuals in that church desperately need to come back to "The Great Discovery." God is love – self-sacrificing, unconditional, initiating love!

Rev. John Strain

Isaiah 15-16; Galatians 3 September 24

In the Formative Stage

My little children, for whom I labor in birth again until Christ is formed in you. (Galatians 4:19)

The apostle Paul often took a parental attitude toward those who had come to Christ under his ministry, either directly or indirectly. In writing to the Galatians, he scolded them for their doctrinal compromise in trying to combine works with faith. He also revealed a parent's heart when he addressed the Galatians as "My little children." The term of address is that of a young child of a trainable age. Paul declares that he is experiencing the spiritual equivalent of maternal labor pains on behalf of the Galatians. He says that the birth pains have recurred, but this time they relate to the formation of Christ-likeness in them.

How could this result be achieved? It is the role of the Holy Spirit to communicate the truth of Jesus Christ to the hearts of believers (John 16:12-14). In doing so, He forms the very character of Christ in the yielded Christian. Remember that the term "Christian" literally means "a Christ one." The Spirit of God not only indwells the believer, but wants to infill us. This means that He desires to control our lives. Paul instructed the Ephesians, *Do not be drunk with wine, in which is dissipation; but be filled (or be getting filled) with the Spirit* (Ephesians

5:18). Just as wine has the capacity to control both the mind and body of a person, so the Spirit can control the life of a believer to make him Christ-like. In our theme verse, the root of the word "formed" is translated elsewhere as "transform" or "transfigure." It means essentially "to take on the form of." Therefore, it is the job of the Holy Spirit to enable us to take on the form of Christ.

What would be evidence of His being formed in us? His character traits will be produced in us by the Spirit. Galatians 5:22,23 give us a verbal portrait of Christ's character – "the fruit of the Spirit."

Rev. William A. Raws

Isaiah 17-18; Galatians 4   **September 25**

Significant Family Living

You shall teach them diligently to your children, and shall talk of them when you sit in your house, when you walk by the way, when you lie down, and when you rise up.
(Deuteronomy 6:7)

Train up a child in the way he should go, and when he is old he will not depart from it. (Proverbs 22:16)

Today our society is watching the disintegration of the family unit as it has been known. Christian families find themselves at great risk in the present cultural environment.

It is basic to the Christian family to establish spiritual priorities. What are priorities? Webster defines a priority as an "order of preference based on urgency, importance, or merit." It is that which is foremost in our judgment; indeed, it is where we place our values.

God holds the parents responsible for the development of the right priorities in the household. Children imitate their parents...and copy their concepts, attitudes and actions. That is why Moses put such great emphasis on this in Deuteronomy 6:7.

Here are some practical helps for us as parents to encourage our children in receiving loving training and life experiences.

1. Seek the Lord daily in prayer for His strength and wisdom.

2. Study your children well – their likes and dislikes, their personalities, their spiritual gifts and their passions.

3. Set the standards and draw the line biblically and sensibly, not culturally or conveniently.

4. Spend time together in family devotions.

5. Start by example and leading the way.

6. Stand together and support each other as mom and dad - "united we stand, divided we fall."

7. Standards that are set should be followed firmly and freely.

Martin Luther realized that training was the right mixture of discipline and love when he said, "Punish if you must but let the sugar plum go with the correction."

The father of the righteous will greatly rejoice, and he who begets a wise child will delight in him (Proverbs 23:24) *...But a child left to himself brings shame to his mother* (Proverbs 29:15b).

Give your children lots of hugs…hugs don't have to be dusted!

Joy Hubbard

Isaiah 19-20; Galatians 5　　　　　　　　**September 26**

What's in a Name?

…I have inscribed you on the palms of My hands. (Isaiah 49:16)

Is there anything more personal than your name? Once born, you are given a name, which then legally must be registered. From that point on, you are known by that very name. Of course, you were too young, too new to this world, to be aware of the significance of having acquired a particular identity by which you will henceforth be known.

As the years go by, you may choose to change your name, for whatever reason. You don't like the sound of it; you don't like the spelling of it; you would like to have the same name as someone you admire; you have embraced a new religion, and therefore you want a name that will identify you as a follower.

Of eternal importance is not by what name you are known, but whether your name is written in the "Lamb's Book of Life" (Revelation 21:27). It is if you are a Christian, and with that knowledge comes your security in Him. You have been adopted into His family. Powerful thought! You belong to Him and your name is written in the "Lamb's Book of Life."

Isaiah wrote, "My name is engraved in the palms of your hands." I can imagine Isaiah rejoicing in believing that and realizing that no one, nothing, could erase his name from that most sacred place!

There is a beautiful song in which are the following words:

> "Oh, to see my name
> Written in the wounds,
> For through Your suffering I am free."
> "The Power of the Cross"
> Words and Music by Keith Getty & Stuart Townsend
> Copyright © 2005 Thankyou Music

Think about those words. Meditate on the love expressed!

Do not be like the unnamed rich man in Luke 16:19-31, who lost the opportunity to have his name registered in the "Lamb's Book of Life." In this world he had everything material a man of wealth could wish for, but he lacked an identity as a man who loved God. In time he died and was separated from God forever.

On the other hand, in the same story, a poor man was starving, and he had to scramble for food at the very door of the rich man. He was worth nothing materially, but he was rich spiritually. He knew God and he trusted Him. In time he too died, but he was taken into heaven with his name intact – Lazarus. His name had been written on the palm of his faithful, loving God.

Is your name written there? Is your security found in God's faithfulness?

Midge Ruth

Isaiah 21-22; Galatians 6 **September 27**

The Ministry of a Hug

..."Love the Lord your God with all your heart with all your soul and with all your mind. This is the first and greatest commandment." And the second is like it: "Love your neighbor as yourself." (Matthew 22:37-39 NIV)

During the 2006 summer conference season, an elderly woman came into my office and asked for counsel. After meeting with her and praying with her, my heart was deeply impacted by the pain this women carried. When our session ended I felt the Lord prompting me to ask her if I could give her a hug. She said "yes," and I gave her a hug that indicated to her that I cared about her and what she was going through. To my amazement she said this was the first time in 10 years that she had received a hug! I just had to give her a second hug. I couldn't imagine not having that personal touch in such a long time.

Have you ever thought that a hug could be a ministry? I've been thinking seriously about this very idea. Sometimes a listening ear is enough and sometimes it isn't, and although a hug is not appropriate in all circumstances, there are times when a hug is very much what the person needs. It conveys so much to the person receiving a hug. It expresses our Christ-like love for one another and our compassion. It can convey to a hurting person so much more than words ever could.

Have you ever been so deep in a pit that you couldn't imagine anyone caring about you? Or have you ever been so full of despair and pain that you felt unworthy of a hug? Maybe it's been a long time since someone gave you a hug or even a gentle touch of a hand. Perhaps there's someone you know who is going through a very difficult time, or illness, or is grieving over the loss of a loved one. Maybe you've sat with a friend, or a stranger, and have listened to them share their heart with you. You prayed with them and felt God prompting you to give them a hug. Ask permission and then give them their hug from God. I haven't met anyone who has turned a hug down or told me they didn't need a hug. Ephesians 4:2 (NIV): *Be completely humble and gentle; be patient, bearing with one another in love.*

> *"Lord, when I learn that someone is hurting,*
> *Help me to know what to do and say;*
> *Speak to my heart and give me compassion;*
> *Let your great love flow through me today."*
> Kurt De Haan

Mary Ann Kiernan

Isaiah 23-24; Ephesians 1   **September 28**

Nice Touch

But Jesus came and touched them… (Matthew 17:7 NIV)

I suppose Jesus could have just said, "Fear not." He did that a lot. But this was the mount of transfiguration. They had just been taken beyond what any person might usually have to cope with. And so to show that He was, after all, still human (He is the Son of Man), Jesus must have felt that a human touch was needed. So He touched them. Maybe then they would know that both He and His love for them were real. Jesus did a lot of touching. A guy had lost his ear and when Jesus "touched it," it just grew back. He touched eyes, and after He did, they could see. He touched the lepers that no one else would. One time when He wanted to bring a dead boy back to life and couldn't quite get at him, He just "touched" the coffin. And the gospel writers are careful to tell us that "all who touched Him were healed." There must be something to this "touching" stuff.

I once spent five weeks smuggling Bibles to the underground church in China. It was an amazing experience, but I must say, it was very hard work. After all of the pressure of border crossings, customs officers, and police, you still had to travel over a vast land where you couldn't speak the language and only hoped that the "drop" went well. Sometimes you'd be on the same train for a couple of days. I once went into the "sink" car to brush my teeth. It was crowded, but this Chinese guy went out of his way to show me that I was welcome, and that I could have a sink. When I was finished, I wanted to thank him and so I smiled, and patted him on his shoulders. I know this is going to sound a bit weird, but when I patted him on his shoulders I felt a surge of love come over me that almost made me cry. That's when I realized that away from my family, serving in another culture, and on a team where I was the only man, that except for the hostile elbows that come from millions of people living in the same space, it had been a very long time since I had actually touched anyone.

I've got a friend who lives in Belarus working to love orphaned children and to help find foster parents who will do it out of love, and not for the revenue it might bring them. He told me about an orphanage that they go to where all they do is hold babies. The babies are changed and fed once a day by the caretakers. It's just a process that keeps most of them alive. It takes a few minutes. Other than that they are left alone. So some loving people go in to just hold babies. People need to know what love is. No wonder Jesus was always touching people. He knew that they needed it. And I guess I'm going out on a limb here, but my guess is that He needed it, too. He was, after all, made human. Scripture tells us that one day God is going to wipe every tear from our eyes. It doesn't take a lot of thinking to figure out that to do that He's going to need to touch us. That's how it works. Personally, I can't wait to look into His eyes and to feel the loving arms that I have always believed in actually wrapped around me, and the hands that spread the universe holding my face.

So who are you going to touch today?

Rev. Chris Thompson

Isaiah 25-26; Ephesians 2   **September 29**

The Joy of Mentoring

You therefore, my son, be strong in the grace that is in Christ Jesus. And the things that you have heard from me among many witnesses, commit these to faithful men who will be able to teach others also. You therefore must endure hardship as a good soldier of Jesus Christ. No one engaged in warfare entangles himself with the affairs of this life, that he may please him who enlisted him as a soldier. And also if anyone competes in athletics, he is not crowned unless he competes according to the rules. The hardworking farmer must be first to partake of the crops. Consider what I say, and may the Lord give you understanding in all things. (2 Timothy 2:1-7)

    In 2 Timothy 2:2, Paul admonishes Timothy to pour his life into the lives of others. One of the greatest joys in life is just to do that, to pour or invest our lives into others. When I was a preteen, I had a Sunday School teacher named Russ Harrison. Mr. Harrison worked at the Holly Ravine Dairy Farm and on Saturdays would often take me and others in the class to the farm. Watching him work there, we were taught just by observing his lifestyle. He deeply enriched my life and the life of my brother. Today, my brother and I are both in ministry and often we have shared with one another how much this mild-mannered, quiet, reserved man made such an impact on us.

    You don't have to be a unique person, just an available one. As you study the Scriptures, you see that Jesus had influence over a group called the "seventy," those whom He sent out to minister two-by-two. There also were His twelve disciples that "...He had with Him." Then we have Peter, James, and John, the three closest to Jesus, and within the three, His "beloved disciple" John. Paul was mentored by Barnabas. Barnabas and Peter mentored John Mark. Paul mentored Timothy and Titus among others. And on it goes – nurturing, making disciples and pouring our lives into the lives of others.

    I could give many more examples of those who nurtured me, men like Dr. Robert Dawson, Dr. Charles Ryrie and many others.

Paul admonished Timothy to teach others so that they in turn could teach others. This is such a rich and rewarding experience. I have sought throughout my ministry to mentor others. Try it, you'll like (love!) it. Reproducing yourself is rewarding!

Dr. George L. Nichols, Jr.

Isaiah 27-28; Ephesians 3 September 30

Stake Your Claim

But thanks be to God, who gives us the victory through our Lord Jesus Christ. (1 Corinthians 15:57)

From the very beginning, the emphasis of America's Keswick's conference and addiction recovery ministries has been on a life of fullness and victory through Jesus Christ. The earlier title given to the conferences was Victorious Life Conferences. During the 2007 season a slogan was adopted – <u>Think Victory</u>. Each of the speakers was encouraged to build into his messages some aspects of the biblical truth of the victorious life.

It is proper and helpful to consider the subject of victory, not just at the Keswick conferences but continuously. But thinking about this theme does not automatically produce the experience of victory over sin in the daily life. Being informed concerning God's provision of it does not automatically result in our personal appropriation of it. Defeated Christians may be well-taught concerning the fact that victory is available, but their lives have not been changed. Availability does not equal actuality. Provision must be accompanied by appropriation.

Our theme verse declares that victory is a gift. The purchase of it was the work of Jesus Christ on the cross. It was included in His cry, "It is finished." When a gift is offered to us, we may momentarily study the package and think about the motive which prompted it and conclude that it is fully acceptable. However, it is not truly ours until we receive it. This principle is basic to our salvation. The gift of Jesus Christ must be received, and this requires transactional faith. The same is true in the matter of the victorious life. It is a gift to be received through our Lord Jesus

Christ. However, in contrast to the one-time acceptance of Christ as Savior, the life of victory requires continuing appropriation.

Perhaps it would help us to think of an additional level to the motto, <u>Think Victory</u>. By faith we should be prompted to <u>Claim Victory</u>. It's a gift!

Rev. William A. Raws

Isaiah 29-30; Ephesians 4　　　　　　　　　　　　　　**October 1**

Interpreting the Bible

But be doers of the word, and not hearers only, deceiving yourselves. (James 1:22)

Recently I was in a Sunday School class and I left determined not to return. We were looking at the miracle of Jesus walking on the water and how it can relate to us today. There was a fine printed outline and some well-conceived questions. After each question was addressed by various people, one gentleman began to take each word, go into the Greek, look at secondary meanings, go back to the Old Testament history, etc. It was unbelievable.

A friend sent me this story: the Lone Ranger and Tonto stopped in the desert for the night. After they set up their tent, both men fell sound asleep. Some hours later, Tonto woke the Lone Ranger and said, "Kemo Sabe, look toward the sky. What do you see?"

The Lone Ranger replied, "I see a million stars." Tonto said, "What does that tell you?" The Lone Ranger replied, "Astronomically speaking, it tells me there are millions of galaxies and potentially billions of planets. Theologically, it is evident that the Lord is all-powerful, and we are small and insignificant. What does it tell you, Tonto?"

Tonto was silent for a moment and then said, "Kemo Sabe, you are dumber than buffalo. It means someone stole the tent!"

The Bible was written for the common man. Sure, there are thoughts and concepts that need explanation and interpretation, but they are very few. Our problem is not what we don't understand but believing and obeying what we do understand!

It seems the more we plumb the depths the more we come up with our own interpretations. Thus we have various theological camps, denominations, man-made rules and regulations, etc.

2 Peter 1:20-21 (NASB) says, *...no prophecy of Scripture is a matter of one's own interpretation, for no prophecy was ever made by an act of human will, but men moved by the Holy Spirit spoke from God.* 2 Timothy 2:15 (NLT) says, *Work hard so you can present yourself to God and receive his approval. Be a good worker, one who does not need to be ashamed and who correctly explains the word of truth.*

Deuteronomy 29:29 says, *The secret things belong to the Lord our God, but those things which are revealed belong to us and to our children forever, that we may do all the words of this law.* There are some things theologians have debated for centuries. If they cannot understand them and agree, neither can you or I. But there are a multitude of things that you can understand very clearly. Put them into practice in your life. Leave the rest to God.

Rev. Neil Fichthorn

Isaiah 31-32; Ephesians 5:1-16 October 2

"…watch…"

Watch, stand fast in the faith, be brave, be strong.
(1 Corinthians 16:13)

That simple word was written to a troubled church and to troubled people. Among the various meanings of the word are other words such as wake, be vigilant, and be cautious. There is also a warning in the word that unless we *watch* we may become indolent and overtaken by "some destructive calamity" (Strong's Enhanced Lexicon).

In essence, that simple instruction is telling us to wise up - to be aware and to be alert, to exercise wise disciplines. This is a responsibility assigned to those of us who desire to experience victory in Christ. To be sure, the victory we have in Christ is in fact *in Christ*. We cannot afford to overlook that. Neither can we afford to overlook our human responsibility in the opportunity of such victory.

Therefore we must *watch*. We must be informed by God's Word about the crucial issues of life. And one of the first things for which we must *watch* is that we do not gain our knowledge of evil and danger by receiving our information from that which is evil and dangerous. We just simply cannot go there.

The Bible tells us that we are to be *...wise in that which is good, and simple* (unmixed with evil) *concerning evil* (Romans 16:19).

Watch is a clear instruction. We are to be aware of all our Lord has provided for our spiritual enrichment. We are to be aware of where we may find what He has provided and how we may attain that which He has provided. We must *watch* in order to find that which is good and to avoid that which is evil. Our *watch* must be active - not passive. It must be guarded - not careless.

Victory is often lost when one chooses to carelessly explore rather than carefully *watch*. Watching involves prayer, Bible study, worship, proper fellowship, being in the proper places, avoiding the places of evil enticement. You get the idea.

Watching means knowing what to turn to as well as what to turn from. Now for the question: have you taken an inventory lately of the matters influencing your spiritual victory - or lack of it? Have you *watched* lately? Do you *watch* constantly? Are you being honest with what you are finding? Do you deal quickly and adequately with what you find?

Watch. It is a serious part of our victory in Christ.

Dr. Robert L. Alderman

Isaiah 33-34; Ephesians 5:17-33   October 3

"...stand fast..."

Watch, stand fast in the faith, be brave, be strong.
(1 Corinthians 16:13)

We hear much and experience the sadness of "believers" who "fall away" and "slide backward" or "run from" their confession of faith and devotion to Christ.

Little wonder then that our Lord's Word tells us to "stand fast." Keep in mind that the instruction to do so is one of several such instructions in 1 Corinthians. The need was apparent in the church and is no less so today among our Christian ranks.

Christian believers in every generation have struggled with victory in faithfulness. That struggle is not God's fault. He has given clear instructions and made available the spiritual power for our victory. That is our message and provision.

Stand fast is not a complicated instruction. It is so simple we do not even need to explain the Greek language. We do not need extra instructions or complicated counsel or super tricks to obey such an instruction. We just need to know that where we are standing in Christ is the proper place to stand and that we do not need to move from that standing - for any reason or in response to any pressure.

There is wisdom in being reminded that to *stand fast* is our responsibility and protection. Perhaps that is why 1 Corinthians 15:58 tells us to

be steadfast, unmovable, always abounding...

and then again so quickly tells us to *...stand fast... (16:13)*.

We should soon get the idea that to *stand fast* is not only possible - but expected. Maybe that is why all of those good instructions in Ephesians 4 are aimed at us being

...no more children, tossed to and fro, carried about with every wind of doctrine, by the sleight of men, ...and cunning craftiness... (v. 14 KJV).

And maybe that is why we are also told to *grow up...* (v.15).

Standing fast must begin with the understanding that we are standing in the proper place and with the proper One. It must continue with the firm understanding that options to attract us and pressures to move us are not worthy of any of our attention. *Standing fast* means that we do not move in the least in the direction of such enemies of the soul and enemies of our Lord.

Have you checked your *standing* lately?

Dr. Robert L. Alderman

Isaiah 35-36; Ephesians 6　　　　　　　　　　　　　　October 4

Be Brave

...quit you like men ... (1 Corinthians 16:13 KJV)

Here is a simple and straight instruction for victory in the Christian life. Be brave. Act like men. Putting this with the other instructions given in the context of 1 Corinthians 16, we must draw the conclusion that the men we are to act like are the men who are really proper men. Not the wimps - but the brave. Not the insolent - but the honorable and respected. Not the slothful – but the industrious. Not the confused - but the properly directed.

A person like this has taken time to know what is significant in life. He has searched, examined and appraised worthy those matters in life that are worthy of his devotion. If he has not done so he will never know that for which he must be brave. He will never be brave for he has not cared enough to find a reason for bravery. He will never know what it is in life that is worth standing for.

To act like a man in the proper sense not only means that we take time to learn that which is significant but that we also affirm our incorruptible commitment to it. It means that there is no "for sale" price on our faith, virtue and value. We determine in advance that our walk with Christ cannot be detoured, that our moral virtue cannot be auctioned, that our stand with Christ cannot be shaken.

To act like a man in the proper sense not only means that we take time to learn that which is significant and that we affirm our incorruptible commitment to it, it also means that we have unshakable confidence in the foundation upon which we stand. If our virtues and values are founded upon changing cultures, upon the whims of human philosophies, upon fleshly appetites that change with the seasons and the surroundings, then it is highly unlikely that we are going to act with bravery in clinging to those virtues and values.

In attempting to "act like a man" we must be careful about the foundation upon which we stand. We have no reason to act like a man if the foundation on which we stand is not Christ Himself. History has proven that in Christ we have a sure foundation for the exercise of bravery in the manifestation of truth and virtue. So why not stand and "act like men"?

Dr. Robert L. Alderman

Isaiah 37-38; Philippians 1   **October 5**

...be strong....

Watch, stand fast in the faith, be brave, be strong.
(1 Corinthians 16:13)

The Bible does not "beat around the bush" when the issue is teaching us how to live victoriously in our Christian journey. Again I say that such victory is neither a secret nor a mystery. That victory is openly revealed in the Scripture and it is done in a very simple and easy to understand way.

The instructions of 1 Corinthians 16:13 (and following verses) illustrate the point. We look today at the instruction to *be strong*. In our walk with Christ we are to eliminate the idea of crippling and defeating weakness. *Be strong* is a simple order. It is not a suggestion.

To be sure, we are all naturally weak people. That is why our Bible reminds us that ...*God hath chosen the weak things of the world to confound the things which are mighty...* (1 Corinthians 1:27b, KJV).

So we are chosen as *weak things* and then ordered to *be strong*. That may not make sense at first glance. It may even sound contradictory and cruel. Think again. It makes perfect sense - as God's Word always does.

To be chosen as *weak things* and then ordered to *be strong* lets us know that the strength needed for victory is not a natural possession but rather a supernatural provision. Victory is not ours because we are able. Victory is ours because God is able and He has provided.

We must rest and rejoice in this: Our Lord has not ordered us to *be strong* without providing the necessities for such strength. We must then conclude that no follower of Christ is overlooked in the provision of strength for the victorious Christian life.

Now we must look beyond the provision to our corresponding responsibility to properly use the strength we are given. Strength for strength's sake is not a good attitude. Strength is provided for a purpose and that purpose is a portion of our victory in Christ. That order to *be strong* and that provision of strength must now be applied to the struggles that would defeat us. Such an application is our responsibility. We have neither reason nor excuse for defeat. *Be strong.*

Dr. Robert L. Alderman

Isaiah 39-40; Philippians 2 October 6

Be Active

Let all that you do be done... (1 Corinthians 16:14 KJV)

For this devotional thought I have lifted a phrase from its broader context without violating a clear and unmistakable truth of Christian discipleship. It is the simple truth that truth is do-able and should be done. There are so many examples in both Testaments. We are to "be kind - to go and teach - to encourage - to pray - to serve." I think you get the idea.

In speaking to the troubled and discouraging church at Corinth, the Bible has some pointed instructions for such proper action. Several of these are the subjects of this collection of devotional thoughts and you may want to take time to meditate on them in the order they appear in 1 Corinthians 16.

Now for the one for today - Be Active.

Activity so often sounds like an interference with spirituality. Often it is - but not in this context, and not in the proper context of developing spiritual vitality. Truth without action is a stimulant to spiritual mortification. Truth with action is spiritual victory.

That we are to be active and properly aggressive in the exercise of Christian truth is a given. It is a non-negotiable. Passivity toward the things of Christ is not an option. We learn and in doing so it becomes incumbent that we do. Marching orders are not given in order that we may live a passive life.

Note again the instruction, *Let all that you do be done...*

Consider the word "Let." That means that something is to be "brought to pass."

Now consider "...*all your things....*" As a disciple of Christ there is nothing in my possession that escapes the oversight and management of His Lordship. I am not allowed to exempt anything under my stewardship from His Lordship. The little word all is big enough to include everything.

Then there is that simple instruction "*be done.*" This is action. In simple terms it means doing. But it is doing with a goal in sight. There is to be completeness in sight. Nothing is left pending. All must be accomplished - it must be done.

Victory is realized when the doing is done - on His part and on ours.

Dr. Robert L. Alderman

Isaiah 41-42; Philippians 3   **October 7**

Be Loving

Let all your things be done with charity.
(1 Corinthians 16:14 KJV)

Please recall that one of the instructions to the troubled church at Corinth was to "be active" - *Let all your things be done.* To make that opportunity more exciting and properly demanding, the Bible then requires that such action be done "in love."

That may sound exciting but all things so ordered are not necessarily the kind of things we are excited about doing *in love.* Love, by its very nature, has its restraints and its imperatives. It prohibits me from acting in a selfish or haughty manner. It requires that I be patient and kind. It requires that I not get upset when better things come to others than those that come to me. It requires that I not do things designed to exalt myself. It even requires that I behave in an acceptable way. It even requires that I think no evil.

Those are some of the clear instructions for the way I am to take care of my responsibilities - my "all things" as mentioned in the verse.

Often we are tempted to console ourselves with the doing part of Christian living as long as we will not be held responsible for the loving part. You know the process. It may go like this: "Lord, I will forgive, just do not expect me to do so with love."

To put this "love" into perspective we may consider our attitude toward Christ. Would our attitude be the same if one of His last words from the cross had been, "Father, I hate this idea of dying for these sinners." Of course He came no where near such an attitude of hate. Instead, *we love Him, because He first loved us* (1 John 4:19).

It should be rather simple for us to understand that our victory in Christ is clearly related to our doing all things in love. To do so advances the attack against the disruptive nature of our broken relationships. To do so goes even further. It reminds us of how Christ did all things on our behalf - in love.

This devotional thought must not end with a casual reading. It must proceed to our understanding of our "all things" and of our responsibility to do them and to do them in love.

Dr. Robert L. Alderman

Isaiah 43-44; Philippians 4   **October 8**

Be Addicted

...they have addicted themselves to the ministry of the saints...
(1 Corinthians 16:15 KJV)

We should look first at the historical background of this triumphant testimony. The reference is to a family known as the "house of Stephanas." The story of their baptism is given in 1 Corinthians 1:16. By the time we get to chapter 16 we learn that they had become "addicted" to ministering to others who were followers of Christ.

This story is even more remarkable when we consider the church with which this family was associated. Unfortunately the church at Corinth was a troubled church. Disagreements were abundant and personal and church behavior was questionable.

We are practically forced to raise the question concerning whether or not any good could possibly come from such a confused and confusing local church. Often churches of that style do not produce faithful followers of Christ. In fact such churches often assist in the major discouragement of proper belief and behavior.

It is in this setting that we get at least two major lessons with reference to the Bible, the church, and to personal responsibility.

First is that of the integrity of the Bible. It makes no attempt to cover the sins of the church. If the church sins such should not be denied. Confession is the order - not concealment. Dealing with the problem is the action - not denying the sinful situation. We all need to learn that.

The second lesson deals with obvious opportunities that often prevail in a bad situation. Stephanas and his family did not use the problems in the church as an excuse to fail their Lord or their fellow believers. Instead they "addicted" (KJV) themselves to the ministry of the saints. They kept their focus on faithful ministry, not on the failures of others. And they grew stronger through the experience.

Think on that one. We may not be able to control the confusion around us but we can surely be responsible for not allowing the confusion to control us. That is how Stephanas trained his family and that is how his family lived and served and became a blessing of victory to others. And that is a great lesson for those of us who would prefer to experience victory in Christ rather than sinful defeat.

Dr. Robert L. Alderman

Isaiah 45-46; Colossians 1   **October 9**

Be Teachable

...submit yourselves unto such... (1 Corinthians 16:16a KJV)

This call for a submission of the church is for the church to submit to those who *have addicted themselves to the ministry of the saints* (v. 15). The ones to whom the church is to submit are the ones who have proper credentials for ministry. They had an excellent recommendation from a trusted servant.

The church in every day must be careful at this point of submission. There are many false teachers. False teachers have an ability to deceive with reference to their own authority. They even have the ability to deceive themselves. We must all be careful at this point.

Once the issue of proper authority for teaching and spiritual assistance is settled we are then instructed to be *submissive*. The path to Christian victory is paved with proper teaching and responsive obedience. That is no secret.

It is only proper then that the instruction to submit to proven and faithful servants is of significant interest to those who honor our Lord, bless His servants and experience His victory.

Submission to such servants involves the proper learning of truth. The proper learning of truth involves our protection for life, liberty and faithfulness. The word used here for *submission* is sometimes referenced with military terminology. That reference yields itself to the understanding of a chain of command, a strict and personal discipline and a dependence on others for personal protection. It goes further and encompasses our preparation for the training and protection of others.

The process and desirability of being teachable is found throughout the Bible and throughout history. The pinnacle of such is clearly stated in such revelation as Psalm 32:8. Our Lord said, *I will instruct you and teach you in the way you should go...*

This same Lord has also made it possible for His people to be taught, protected and served by those who are capable and devoted to doing so. It should come as no surprise that for a church or an individual that has experienced conflict in belief and behavior, our Bible instructs us to be submissive to proper teaching. It is a major step on the road of victory.

Dr. Robert L. Alderman

Isaiah 47-48; Colossians 2   October 10

Be Cooperative

I am glad of the coming of Stephanas and Fortunatus and Achaicus: for that which was lacking on your part they have supplied. (1 Corinthians 16:17 KJV)

Imagine that – believers in the same church actually supporting each other and working together. If we ever see a breakdown of oneness in Christ by His supposed followers it may be helpful to refer to this brief and simple statement of historical and biblical fact. Here is a key to our victory in Christ. Here is a key to victory in the church.

To be sure, there is a caution here. Obviously this complimentary observation by the missionary servant is not intended to cross the line of inappropriate cooperation. There are areas of improper cooperation. Those areas may be in the realms of theology, social practices, entertainment, divisive argumentation - well, you get the idea.

Stephanas, Fortunatus and Achaicus set the proper example. They came to help and help they did. All of the Corinthians may not have appreciated that assistance. Some Corinthians may have thought these three were encroaching on their personal domain or revealing their personal weaknesses. That attitude has been known to exist even among some who profess to be followers of our Lord.

The plaudit given in the Word of God may well have been to silence and softly rebuke any such resentment.

Now we should concentrate on the positive. With reference to the ministry there is much to be done. And there is great need in the process of getting it done. We should all know that. There is always the need of prayer, personnel and planning. There will be the need of encouragement, inspiration and insight. You have probably already added in your thoughts that prevailing concept and need of money.

A major portion of our victory in Christ is when we understand and experience the joy of the spirit and devotion accented in this simple truth. Such a positive statement charts the path for our behavior and availability in relationships. It charts the path for expanded victory in our service. It provides the biblical incentive for us to build the bridges that were built by Stephanas, Fortunatus and Achaicus. It reminds us that there are others who need our assistance in life, in love and in service. It reminds us that we may also have that need.

Dr. Robert L. Alderman

Isaiah 49; Colossians 3   **October 11**

Be Refreshing

...they have refreshed my spirit and yours:...
(1 Corinthians 16:18 KJV)

We should all confess that such a statement is a nice thing to have said about us. We know the value of those who refresh the spirit of others.

Members of a troubled church are often in an emergency need to have their spirit refreshed. That is the case here. Even the missionary Paul admitted that his spirit had been refreshed by those who had the ability, the desire and the discipline to refresh others. He was obviously thankful for that and took advantage of the opportunity to acknowledge those who had provided the refreshing.

This need of a refreshed spirit is not confined to life within the church. Have you ever known a family that needed a refreshed spirit – a wife, a husband, a child, a parent? How about a friend, an employee or employer? Perhaps a deacon, an elder, a pastor, a teacher? This list could get so long it may even give us some ideas of another concept of living victoriously in Christ. After all, being a spirit refresher is a biblical thing to be.

Please do not look at such an opportunity as an exercise of religious psychology. If we do that we may have a tendency to think that our task is to simply produce a feel-good experience. This is a matter of the spirit, not the psyche. We must not lose sight of the spiritual need and the need of spiritual victory.

Having a need for a spiritual refreshing must deal with spiritual matters. Often it must deal with a sin problem. That may get a little touchy - or even nasty. But if the need is there, either in our life or in the life of one we seek to refresh, we must deal with removing the dirt. Simply to cover the dirt or decorate it with cute paint will not really work.

A refreshed spirit may be stopped or hindered by a failure to *grow in the grace and knowledge of our Lord and Savior Jesus Christ* (2 Peter 3:18). When that is the case a simple religious pat on the back will not do. Somebody needs help on how to grow in grace and knowledge.

You get the idea. To be a spirit refresher is not always easy. It is always needed.

Dr. Robert L. Alderman

Isaiah 50-51; Colossians 4   October 12

Be Expressive

All the brethren greet you... (1 Corinthians 16:20 KJV)

Christians do not have the right to be silent when it comes to the matter of being courteous and friendly. Yet such silence and evasiveness is often found in the church as well as on the street. The biblical model for courteous friendship is frequently presented in such expressions as this one given to the troubled church in the city of Corinth. Look at the broader text to get the message.

The churches of Asia salute you. Aquila and Priscilla salute you much in the Lord, with the church that is in their house. All the brethren greet you. Greet ye one another with an holy kiss (v. 19-20).

The missionary servant knew that Christians needed to learn to speak to each other in an encouraging way. Be courteous. Be friendly. Be respectful. It is right to do even if others do not approve. *(Caution: Make sure you understand the cultural significance and necessary restraints of the holy kiss before exercising it.)*

I like to illustrate this friendship matter with a little thing I did in a church I visited some years ago. Amelia and I were in a distant city on Sunday morning and we had no particular responsibility at the hour of morning worship. We decided to worship in one of the city's historical churches. As we passed through the entrance hall to the worship center we were casually handed a copy of the Sunday bulletin. No one greeted or spoke. We sat alone in a pew for several minutes. As others were entering I noticed that the silent treatment continued. Encouraging greetings were just not taking place.

About five minutes before the service was scheduled to begin I left my seat and told Amelia I would return shortly. I made my way to the entrance foyer, picked up a stack of bulletins and began to welcome those who were entering. I thanked them for their presence and attempted to share an encouraging statement. I had a great time doing so. No one enquired of my identity. No one checked my credentials to determine if I was an authorized greeter. No one checked my committee assignment. No one greeted me.

As I left my post to return to my seat I overheard one usher asking another, "Who is that man?" He could have replied, "He must be one of those fellows who believes the brethren should greet each other."

Dr. Robert L. Alderman

Isaiah 52-53; 1 Thessalonians 1   **October 13**

Be Personal

The salutation ... with mine own hand.
(1 Corinthians 16:21 KJV)

For my personal enrichment I have made it a practice to carefully notice what may often be overlooked in Scripture as a routine statement couched in proper literary style. In such cases I have found many simple yet significant matters that help shape some of the finer disciplines of life.

My objective has not been to brush up on some form of social etiquette. Rather it has been to explore and develop the encouraging and meaningful practices that enhance the beauty and effectiveness of the larger Christian message.

For that reason I like the statement made by the apostle as he emphasized his personal involvement with that which he had written. *"I wrote it with my own hand."* In some way, perhaps in many ways, that statement moves us into the arena of the significant.

Personal greetings, hand written or spoken, drive home several messages, not just the message of the words being communicated.

They let us know of the personal interest being taken by the communicator. It is not a quick and easy way of fulfilling a responsibility. It is a way of communicating personal interest and compassionate concern. It accents the involvement of the heart with interest. Personal greetings go far beyond the mere communication of knowledge or information. That may not be true in every case but it does give a hint to that effect.

Personal greetings indicate a sacrifice of time on behalf of the one receiving the message. This is becoming more and more evident with the advent of rapid publication and electronic mail. Not that I am critical of such ways but they do cause me to question the value of a communication that merely required a computer click or a postal stamp, and little or nothing else.

By now you should see the value of the biblical method, *I wrote this with my own hand.* I took time to do this. I care for you. This is important enough for me to let you know that in addition to what I share in written or spoken form I have a heart to share with you also.

The de-personalization of a culture is a major step into barbarism. Jesus personalized His love for us. We should do the same for each other.

Dr. Robert L. Alderman

Isaiah 54-55; 1 Thessalonians 2 October 14

Be Honest

If any man love not the Lord Jesus Christ,...
(1 Corinthians 16:22 KJV)

We know even with a casual reading of the biblical text and history that these people and this church at Corinth were troubled over many issues. God's Word clearly speaks to these issues.

Bad beliefs and bad behavior have been rebuked. Instruction has been given. Correction has been sought.

But there is one other foundational issue that is now presented with preciseness and firmness. It confronts the issue that the conflicts in churches and among Christians may be traced to the frightening absence of love for Christ.

If bad doctrine and bad behavior are not settled with proper teaching and true repentance, then the issue must be an absence of love for Christ. Such *badness* in the church and in the lives of those who profess to love Christ but show no evidence of such love are now confronted with the terrifying words, *Let him be Anathema (accursed)*. That is serious business. It is serious business because it deals with a serious crime.

The crime is simply this - Hypocrisy in the church, hypocrisy in the lives of those who say they love Christ but obviously love their own ways to the exclusion of loving Christ in any way. But our Lord sees the hypocrisy. He knows who loves Him. He knows how those who love Him behave. He knows what they desire. He knows what they believe. And He knows who it is that does not love Him.

He knows what such hypocrisy does to destroy integrity and blessing in the church. He knows how such hypocrisy confuses the message of victory in Christ for those who are young in faith and even for the more mature.

Do not consider it alarming that the missionary servant, speaking the Word of God, would say to such a situation, "Let him (the one who fakes a love for Christ) be accursed." We should not think that such is a stiff response. We should not think that such firmness and finality violates the love of Christ or the course of the church. To the contrary, such firmness accents our Lord's love in every way. It accents His love for the fake "lover," for His church, and for the unbeliever who is examining the integrity of the church. It accents the seriousness of loving Him.

Dr. Robert L. Alderman

Isaiah 56; 1 Thessalonians 3　　　　　　　　　　**October 15**

Warning and Hope

Maranatha. (1 Corinthians 16:22 KJV)

We should make sure that we have a proper understanding of this significant word - *Maranatha*. Linguists and commentators have presented to us different views of its proper translation. The two most acceptable translations are: "Our Lord comes" or "Our Lord has come." Please note that though there are various translations, all views deal with the reality of our Lord's presence. No rendering of the word avoids that fact.

Maranatha is in the context both a word of warning and a word of hope. It is both to a church and to a people who are in conflict with belief and behavior. Such belief and behavior should not be. A firm warning to that belief and behavior had gone before: *If any man love not the Lord Jesus Christ, let him be Anathema* (accursed) (v. 22).

But we must not overlook the reality that our Lord's presence, our *Maranatha*, is also a word of hope. Here is an affirmation that the prophets have been correct. Here is an affirmation that the apostles in their continuing ministry affirmed the pre-crucifixion and post-resurrection promises of our Lord. Here is an affirmation that the waywardness of the church would have a confrontation with the ultimate Authority of belief and behavior.

For some that is a frightening reality. For the faithful it is an exciting word of peace and victorious anticipation. For the church it must be an incentive for purity and faithfulness. For the redeemed it is a further affirmation of victory in Jesus. For the Scripture it accents the consistency of its message.

Maranatha is now applied to the crucified One, who spoke of His body and said, *"Destroy this temple. and in three days I will raise it up"* (John 2:19). It is applied to the One who said, *I will come again...* (John 14:3). It is applied to the One of whom the two men ...in white apparel said as they watched Him ascend into Heaven: *This same Jesus, which was taken up from you into heaven, will so come in like manner as you saw Him go into heaven* (Acts 1:12).

This is our *Maranatha*. This is one of our great incentives for love and faithfulness and for our obedience and hope. This is our ultimate victory and it is clearly our victory in Jesus.

Dr. Robert L. Alderman

Isaiah 57-58; 1 Thessalonians 4   **October 16**

Do You Have a Servant's Heart?

for even the Son of Man did not come to be served, but to serve...
(Mark 10:45a)

    I used to work with a woman who walked about almost so heavenly-minded that she was no earthly good ... as they say. Many of the staff would laugh or make fun of her. Needless to say that her work ethics were not the best; she tried hard but seemed unfocused and ended up making more work for the rest of us.

    On one hot summer day, I was reminded how she had a better insight into what was really important than the rest of us did. It was one of those days where the minute you stepped outside you would faint from the heat. The UPS man came into our office that day with several bundles of boxes and he looked very weary. He was a man of few words and what he did say never seemed very friendly. My friend and co-worker jumped up while he was delivering his last load and ran and got him a glass of cold water (Mark 9:41). She then asked him to sit and rest for a minute before returning to his work. He took one look at this tiny, JOY-filled woman, smiled and then sat down. She made some small talk with him and then shared the gospel message. It brings tears to my eyes to realize that her heart was really in a better place than mine. She had established her heart for the service of Christ (James 5:8). She seemed to have this concept in place in her life and it became an example to me even though it has been ten years since I worked with her.

    While on this earth, Jesus served others. He seemed to reach out and have a heart for those whom we would consider less fortunate. He had a heart for the widows and orphans. Has God blessed you with the insight to see the needs of others? Do you reach out with a cup of cold water and compassion to others? You should fulfill the needs of others with no strings attached or a debt to be paid back. When was the last time that you reached out to someone just because they needed it?

When Jesus was on this earth He touched lives. Are you touching lives for Him with outstretched arms and the heart of a servant? God is calling each and every one of us to serve in a way unique to us. Pay attention when God calls you to serve others. There is much work to be done.

Lynn A. Wilson

Isaiah 59-60; 1 Thessalonians 5   **October 17**

Having Been Warned in a Dream…

Surely the arm of the LORD is not too short to save, nor his ear too dull to hear. (Isaiah 59:1 NIV)

There's a guy in our church named Andy who was greatly abused by a foster father when he was a little boy. He used to run away often. He'd live in people's sheds until caught. He was often in trouble with the police for fighting, or stealing, or drugs. His whole life has been sort of a train wreck. Three marriages, three divorces. Five children, but none of them in relationship with him. Then his health declined. He's diabetic, narcoleptic, and has a tumor on his pituitary gland that has further ruined his life. Ten years ago he was about to become homeless and was in great despair when he said toward heaven, "Somebody, help me please."

God accepted that as a prayer because that night Andy had a dream. An old man with white hair and a white beard approached him outside a hardware store and said, "Seek the Lord, young man, before it's too late." So the following Sunday Andy came to our church. There are four churches in our town but on this winter night, ours was the only one open. Andy sat down in the back by himself. Then Ted came in and sat next to him. Ted's in glory now but at the time was in his mid-nineties. This godly man had eleven children. All of them are walking with God. He was a walking Bible. And he had a full head of pure white hair with a large white beard to match. He was the man in the dream, and the first words he spoke to Andy were,

"Do you know the Lord, young man?" Andy knew instantly that God was real, and that God was reaching into his own broken life. He very quickly became a Christian and ten years later is still a treasured part of our church.

As the body of Christ on earth, we minister to people. We love people. We help people. We meet their needs. We share with people in various ways how they can know Jesus and be assured of a place in heaven. Lots of us were involved in Andy's salvation, and lots of us are still involved with helping him in life. We know that God uses us, but thinking back on how Andy actually came to know God, it's very clear that God Himself responded to the prayer of the destitute, as He says in His Word that He will, and that God Himself spoke to him through the dream that opened the door of his heart. God made this whole thing happen. I think that we should take great comfort in this.

We need to share the gospel with as many as we can, but can we really reach everybody? Our arms are just too short. And our ears are just too dull, even to hear their cries. But God's aren't. Let's rejoice in the greatness of our God. His love endures forever. He responds to the prayer of the destitute. Always has and always will. His keen ears hear their cry, and His strong arms reach down to save. He's a great God and He will find some way to bring all of His children home.

Rev. Chris Thompson

Isaiah 61-62; 2 Thessalonians 1 October 18

Indwelling Life

I have been crucified with Christ; it is no longer I who live, but Christ lives in me; and the life which I now live in the flesh I live by faith in the Son of God, who loved me and gave Himself for me. (Galatians 2:20)

God sustains all life. God is creator and sustainer of every created thing. He is the only self-existent One. He orchestrates the heavens, the stars, all the galaxies, every molecule in the entire universe. *...he himself gives all men life and breath and everything else* (Acts 17:25).

God's sustaining life is not the same as Christ's life IN his children. God sustains all life, but not everyone has Christ living in them. *...the Spirit of truth whom the world cannot receive, because it neither sees Him nor knows Him; but you know Him, for He dwells with you and will be in you* (John 14:17).

At the moment of conversion, the instant the dead spirit is regenerated, made alive by the power of the Holy Spirit, the very Spirit of God indwells, resides in, lives in that individual.

Romans 8:11: *But if the Spirit of Him who raised Jesus from the dead dwells in you, He who raised Christ from the dead will also give life to your mortal bodies through His Spirit who dwells in you.*

1 Corinthians 3:16: *Do you not know that you are the temple of God and that the Spirit of God dwells in you?*

2 Corinthians 6:16: *For you are the temple of the living God. As God has said: "I will dwell in them and walk among them. I will be their God, and they shall be My people."*

Ephesians 3:17: *...that Christ may dwell in your hearts through faith...*

Colossians 1:27: *To them God willed to make known what are the riches of the glory of this mystery among the Gentiles: which is Christ in you, the hope of glory.*

Jesus Christ desires to live His life through you. By faith He will love others through you. He will forgive others through you. He will be kind, gracious, compassionate and gentle through you.

Diane Hunt

Isaiah 63-64; 2 Thessalonians 2   **October 19**

The Glory of God

Blessed be the God and Father of our Lord Jesus Christ, who has blessed us with every spiritual blessing in the heavenly places in Christ, just as He chose us in Him before the foundation of the world, that we should be holy and without blame before Him in love, having predestined us to adoption as sons by Jesus Christ to Himself, according to the good pleasure of His will, to the praise of the glory of His grace, by which He made us accepted in the Beloved. (Ephesians 1:3-6)

    Jonathan Edwards, that prince of preachers from New England, once described God's glory as "the end for which God created the world." Author and preacher John Piper, in describing worship, suggested it is "to behold and display His glory for the enjoyment of His redeemed people from every person, language, and nation." The glory of God is a subject that is overwhelming.

    In Ephesians 1, the apostle Paul is addressing the glory of God as he teaches the Ephesians that God chose us and predestined us for His glory (v. 5). God created people for His glory (v.6). We are called to be the exhibits of His glory (v.6). Just as Paul the apostle reminded the Ephesians about the glory of God, we are to be reminded that we are on the earth to bring honor and glory to God.

    The obvious question then needs to be, "What does it mean to bring glory to God?" Does it mean that we are in some way to increase Him? It would be beyond imagination to think that we can somehow make God more than who He is. Perhaps a good way to understand this proposition would be to recognize that we are to display His glory, not increase His glory. For how can we increase the greatness and majesty of God? We are unable to do it.

    The issue then becomes the need to increase His glory which is already available to all of us. The psalmist proclaims, *The heavens declare the glory of God and the firmament shows His handiwork* (Psalm 19:1). As we look to the universe and recognize the majesty of God, we are reminded of the words of theologian R.C. Sproul, "Men are never duly touched and impressed with a conviction of their insignificance, until they have contrasted themselves with the majesty of God." This is where God's glory is best seen.

When Jesus wanted to provide an illustration about worship, He did not choose a person who would appear to be one of the greatest intellects nor a person of high moral standing. Rather He chose a woman who previously had five husbands and was living with a man who was not her husband. They began to discuss worship and the topic became one of location of worship. This woman, known simply as the Samaritan woman at the well (John 4), desired to know why her people worshipped on Mt. Gerizim and the Jews worshipped in Jerusalem. Jesus quickly changed the tone of the conversation and said ...*They that worship Him must worship Him in spirit and in truth; for the Father seeks such to worship Him* (John 4: 23, 24). Powerful words from the One we are to glorify! This woman then went and told the people in her village that she, a woman with a deplorable past, had found the Messiah!

It is the purpose of each Christian to understand that we are on the earth to make Him known. The glory of God is best seen through lives that have been changed by the One who is to be glorified. Take time today and consider the importance of making much of Jesus through your life. We need to be the Jesus they see.

Spend some time today thinking through various ways Jesus can be known through your life. God is pleased with this as it brings glory to Him.

Dr. Dino Pedrone

Isaiah 65-66; 2 Thessalonians 3   **October 20**

Waiting on Him

...Their strength is to sit still. (Isaiah 30:7b KJV)

Just recently I had someone hang up on me, without even telling me why they were upset! My first thought was, "I'll call him back and tell him exactly how I feel." However, my mind went to the verse I had read that morning: *Their strength is to sit still* (Isaiah 30:7b KJV). So I sat still! Ugh. "But Lord," I thought, "the phone is just over there. All I have to do is walk just a couple of steps, pick up the phone, dial it, and give that man a piece of my mind." But then another verse popped into my thoughts: *Be still, and know that I am God* (Psalm 46:10). My first thought was, "Now aren't you glad you memorized THAT verse!" So first I was given the instruction to sit still and then God told me I was to be quiet. Such simple instructions and yet they are so hard to follow.

Who or what is bugging you today? Can you say that your strength is to sit still? When we wait upon the Lord and sit still, we give Him a chance to work in us and in the situation. When we sit still, God can change us because we have willingly given Him time to work on us.

How about you? When you read my experience, did a person or a situation come to your mind? Are you willing to sit and be still? Tell the Lord how you are feeling…impetuous, defensive, angry. Confess your wrong feelings and let Him know if you are willing to let God improve your ability to sit still and be quiet as you wait on Him.

Marilyn Willett Heavilin

Jeremiah 1-2; 1 Timothy 1   **October 21**

Facing the Door

Turn to me and be gracious to me, as is your way with those who love your name. (Psalm 119:132 ESV)

You can probably recall a time when you entered a room and felt out of place, like you didn't belong. No one turned to welcome you, making you feel very awkward.

My sister-in-law told me about a seminar she went to that talked about "facing the door" at your church. Too many times we huddle with those we know and when a new person comes in he/she feels like an outsider. The challenge given was to "face the door" of your church so that you can make others feel welcome. I've thought of this so often, as I've been a visitor; I scan the room to look for a friendly face to see if I'll be welcomed or if anyone cares that I am there. My husband and I once visited a church where no one said a thing to us the entire time we were there. Even when they had people stand and turn and shake hands, no one even said hello. After the service, we looked at each other and simply turned and walked out. We've often laughed about that day. We never went back. It has also helped me to remember how important it is to "face the door" and make sure no one goes away feeling unwelcome.

The next time you feel alone, or unwanted, remember that your heavenly Father turns toward you and is gracious to you.

Joyce Hayes

Jeremiah 3-4; 1 Timothy 2   **October 22**

The Lonely Soul

How long, O LORD? Will You forget me forever? How long will You hide Your face from me? (Psalm 13:1)

Have you ever felt that God was far away and had forgotten you? Thankfully, these are only human feelings that can come upon us. But the truth is, God never leaves us nor forsakes us. When there is distance between God and the Christian, it is not God Who moved.

Joseph Parker said that this psalm begins with winter and ends with summer. It is a hymn of a lonely soul.

Notice as David sings his way out of loneliness into the presence of God.

It is a horrible thing to lose the sense of God's presence. It happens to everyone to varying degrees and for different reasons. The psalmist felt void of God's presence, God's purpose and God's power. Nevertheless, in his loneliness he cried out to God.

Consider and hear me, O LORD my God; enlighten my eyes... (Psalm 13:3). What is David asking? He is asking God to show him the way back lest he die and give victory to the enemy. David pleaded with God and God heard him.

I have trusted in your mercy... (Psalm 13:5). David cast himself upon the mercy of God and from that point he began to sing *...My heart shall rejoice in your salvation. I will sing to the LORD, because He has dealt bountifully with me* (Psalm 13:5b-6).

If you are feeling lonely today, try singing praises to the Lord. The Lord inhabits the praises of His people. If you feel that God has forgotten you then ask the Lord to reveal if there is anything in your heart that may have disrupted your fellowship with Him. Repent of any sin that may be hindering your fellowship with God.

David's spiritual winter was turned into a spiritual summer. The same can happen for you.

Dr. Roger D. Willmore

Jeremiah 5-6; 1 Timothy 3   **October 23**

Singing in the Wilderness, Part 1

But I will sing of Your power; Yes, I will sing aloud of Your mercy in the morning; For You have been my defense And refuge in the day of my trouble. (Psalm 59:16)

    I think about how wonderful it would be if life were picture perfect. You have an uneventful birth, grow up in a Christian home with godly Christian parents, get a great education and college degree, have wonderful friends, enjoy various activities such as sports and music, meet and marry someone with a similar background, enjoy a great job with a good salary, benefits, pension, etc…, have healthy kids, retire and die uneventfully. Do you know anyone like this? It seems to me that real life is more like a rollercoaster – up and down, twisting and turning, always catching you unaware!

    We tend to be afraid of what God allows to come our way in life. While I may not enjoy various events and circumstances, do I believe that God can use them for good and to bring glory to Himself? I would like to remember some of the individuals who have faced adversity and how it has enhanced their usefulness for service to the Lord.

    Joni Eareckson Tada became a quadriplegic following a diving accident as a teenager. Despite depression and the difficulty of her new life situation, she chose to pursue her relationship with Jesus Christ and reach out rather than focusing inwardly. Joni is a writer, artist and singer! God has given her amazing opportunities to encourage people who are hurting because of her experience. Who can better relate to issues facing disabled people and their families than Joni?

    How about Jim Elliot? Jim was a missionary to Ecuador who, along with four others, was killed while attempting to evangelize the Waodani people. Their sacrifice included giving their lives, but as a result, think of the souls who have come to Jesus Christ.

    Steven Curtis and Mary Beth Chapman lost their little girl Maria Sue Chunxi Chapman in a car accident that should never have taken place. One result from this tragedy is the beginning of Maria's Big House of Hope, which is "dedicated to saving the lives of special needs orphans in China by providing surgeries and medical attention. This home will offer the highest level of care, enabling the children to thrive, and greatly increasing their chances of being adopted."

While these stories are of people with whom we are very familiar, I know that these stories could be duplicated millions of times over. How do we handle adversity in our life? Does it render us ineffective or can we sing in the wilderness?

Robert Hayes

Jeremiah 7-8; 1 Timothy 4　　　　　　　　　　　　**October 24**

Singing in the Wilderness, Part 2

And we know that all things work together for good to those who love God, to those who are the called according to His purpose.
(Romans 8:28)

In thinking through this topic of singing in the wilderness – let's take a look at some hymn writers and circumstances God used in their lives to bring them to write as they did.

Fanny Crosby wrote over 8,000 hymns despite being blind since infancy. At eight years of age, she wrote this about her condition,

> "Oh what a happy soul I am,
> although I cannot see;
> I am resolved that in this world
> contented I will be.
> How many blessings I enjoy
> that other people don't,
> to weep and sigh because I'm blind,
> I cannot, and I won't."

"It seemed intended by the blessed providence of God that I should be blind all my life, and I thank him for the dispensation. If perfect sight were offered me tomorrow I would not accept it. I might not have sung hymns to the praise of God if I had been distracted by the beautiful and interesting things about me.

When I get to heaven, the first face that shall ever gladden my sight will be that of my Savior."

Horatio Spafford, a prominent Chicago lawyer, owned a great deal of real estate that was destroyed by the Chicago fire of 1871. Two years later, delayed on business, he sent his wife and four daughters to Europe for a holiday. While crossing the Atlantic, their ship collided with another and sank. Anna Spafford was the only surviving member of the family. As Horatio sped to join his wife, he wrote the words to "It Is Well With My Soul."

Joseph Scrivin planned to marry his Irish sweetheart and start a business. The day before their marriage, his bride-to-be drowned. The shock of this never left him. He moved to Canada and helped the less fortunate. Years later after learning that his mother was experiencing a difficult time, he penned a poem he called "A Friend Who Understands." Today we know this poem as "What A Friend We Have In Jesus."

I am grateful that countless men and women who have encountered various tragedies and difficulties in their lives have turned to their relationship with the Lord Jesus Christ to find their hope, strength, peace and oasis in the midst of their desert. We know that Romans 8:28 is true; God does want to work things together for good, but ultimately it is to conform us to His image and to bring glory to Himself.

Robert Hayes

Jeremiah 9-10; 1 Timothy 5 October 25

What Are You Doing Here?

And there he went into a cave, and spent the night in that place; and behold the word of the LORD came to him, and He said to him, "What are you doing here, Elijah?" (1 Kings 19:9)

Do you remember how Elijah started his ministerial career as a prophet and preacher? Well, he was noted for his unquestionable obedience to God. When God spoke, Elijah obeyed. He learned the principle of <u>thereness</u>. Wherever God told him to go, wherever God told him to be, that is where you would find Elijah.

Because of his obedience, God used him in supernatural ways. However, we now find the great prophet hiding in a cave. God finds him there and asks the sobering and penetrating question, *What are you doing here, Elijah?*

Are you in a place in your life that would prompt that question from God? Are you running, hiding and trying to get away from God? Are you in a cave of disobedience to God? Why are you there? What has driven you there?

From time to time we need to turn this question around and ask ourselves, "What am I doing here?"

This question certainly needs to be asked if we are in a place of rebellion or disobedience. However, it is also a question that should be asked even of our places of service and worship and Christian fellowship. For example, we should ask ourselves these questions, "What am I doing in the place of corporate worship as I sit with my brothers and sisters on a Sunday morning? What am I doing in the prayer meeting? What am I doing in the board or committee meeting?" Sometimes I can hear the voice of God, when I am in these legitimate places of service and worship, asking me, *What are you doing here?* We should not assume that we are where He wants us to be simply because we think we are where we are supposed to be. Are we where He wants us to be?

What is your answer to Him when He asks of you, *What are you doing here?*

Whatever has driven you to your cave, be aware that God is not through with you yet. Come out of your cave, experience the restoring touch of God, and get back into the game.

Dr. Roger D. Willmore

Jeremiah 11-12; 1 Timothy 6 October 26

The God of a Second Chance

Now the word of the Lord came to Jonah the son of Amittai, saying, "Arise, go to Nineveh, that great city, and cry out against it; for their wickedness has come up before me." (Jonah 1:1-2)

Now the word of the Lord came to Jonah the second time, saying, "Arise, go to Nineveh, that great city, and preach to it the message that I tell you." (Jonah 3:1-2)

Jonah was the reluctant evangelist. For various reasons, none of which were complimentary to Jonah, he chose to run the opposite way from Ninevah. He was not only the reluctant evangelist, he was the disobedient evangelist. The preacher who was commissioned to preach the message of the God of a second chance is about to encounter the God of a second chance.

Jonah was a remarkable man created by God for a special and specific purpose. He was God's choice servant to take the message of repentance and salvation to the Gentile people of Nineveh, Assyria. God did not intend to keep His love, grace and mercy for the Israelites alone. No, He intended that all people of every culture and country have the opportunity to know His love and forgiveness. Jesus preached a global gospel. Peter preached a global gospel. Paul preached a global gospel. The Church today preaches a global gospel. However, reluctant Jonah did not want to preach a global gospel.

Jonah planned his escape from God's orders. He decided to take a trip to Tarshish. Chapter one of Jonah tells us that he paid his own fare to board a ship bound to Tarshish. This ship sailed into a storm on its way to Tarshish. Jonah was asleep and unaware of the danger; the sailors onboard the ship were all in danger of perishing. Every step Jonah took in disobedience to God took him down, down, down. Disobedience is always a one-way street…down.

Jonah was captured and changed by God. The Lord prepared a great fish to provide Jonah transportation to Nineveh. After Jonah arrived in Nineveh God came to him a second time and re-commissioned him to preach to Nineveh.

Whenever you are reluctant to give another person a second chance, remember, you are a recipient of a second chance. God is a God of a second chance.

Dr. Roger D. Willmore

Jeremiah 13-14; 2 Timothy 1   October 27

Never Lose Hope

Now may the God of hope fill you with all joy and peace in believing, that you may abound in hope by the power of the Holy Spirit. (Romans 15:13)

Sometimes it is difficult to imagine that things will ever be different than they are right now. Perhaps circumstance, or a person, has caused a heavy burden upon your heart and it seems as if it has become a part of who you are. Life looks endlessly the same. It is times like these that we tend to slip into praying, not believing that change will happen. Oh, sure, we know it is possible but we don't actually believe it. How can we? Our prayers have made little difference thus far, or so it seems. The hope we once had has dwindled to merely a thimbleful or has long since disappeared completely.

Hope. *Now may the God of hope fill you with all joy and peace in believing, that you may abound in hope by the power of the Holy Spirit* (Romans 15:13).

If we do not have hope, then how are we different than our unsaved neighbor or friend? What difference is Jesus making in our life?

Be encouraged by Manasseh. You may read his entire story in 2 Chronicles 33, but here are some excerpts: (v.1-2) *Manasseh was twelve years old when he became king, and he reigned fifty-five years in Jerusalem. But he did evil in the sight of the LORD, according to the abominations of the nations whom the LORD had cast out before the children of Israel...(v. 6) ...he caused his sons to pass through the fire in the Valley of the Son of Hinnom; he practiced soothsaying, used witchcraft and sorcery, and consulted mediums and spiritists. He did much evil in the sight of the LORD, to provoke Him to anger. (v. 9-13) So Manasseh seduced Judah and the inhabitants of Jerusalem to do more evil than the nations whom the LORD had destroyed before the children of Israel. And the LORD spoke to Manasseh and his people, but they would not listen. Therefore the LORD brought upon them the captains of the army of the king of Assyria, who took Manasseh with hooks, bound him with bronze fetters, and carried him off to Babylon. Now when he was in affliction, he implored the LORD his God, and humbled himself greatly before the God of his fathers, and prayed to Him; and He received his entreaty, heard his supplication, and brought him back to Jerusalem into his kingdom. Then Manasseh knew that the LORD was God.*

Manasseh did evil - he rebuilt the high places, raised up altars to false gods, worshiped the host of heaven, sacrificed his sons, practiced soothsaying, witchcraft and sorcery; he did much evil in the sight of God. Imagine his mother's or wife's perspective watching him do much evil. It appeared hopeless and yet the Lord spoke to him and change happened.

God stepped in.

Never lose hope, because at any moment God can step in. God can change circumstances and hearts, even if it's your own.

Diane Hunt

Jeremiah 15-17; 2 Timothy 2 October 28

The Lord Gives Victory

So Joshua did as Moses said to him, and fought with Amalek. And Moses, Aaron, and Hur went up to the top of the hill. And so it was, when Moses held up his hand, that Israel prevailed; and when he let down his hand, Amalek prevailed. But Moses' hands became heavy; so they took a stone and put it under him, and he sat on it. And Aaron and Hur supported his hands, one on one side, and the other on the other side; and his hands were steady until the going down of the sun. (Exodus 17:10-12)

There are a number of things in these three verses that immediately catch my attention.
- There is a serious battle raging.
- Moses depended on the Lord.
- With his hands lifted up Moses prays, prays, prays, prays.
- Moses' hands got tired.
- Moses had two faithful friends who supported his weary hands until the sun went down and the battle was won.

Wow! I have a lump in my throat even now as I think about that last point. The very idea, the thought, of someone standing in the gap with you until...

Are you at a place in life where you are weary and wondering how, oh how, you are going to get through? Is there a battle raging in your home, heart or life that threatens to undo you? And lest we be too self-focused, I must also ask you to consider the people in your sphere of influence. Is there one among them whose hands are tired and needs your support?

Dear friend, there are two things I encourage you to do and see:

To do:
- Pray! Pray! Pray and ask for help! Don't allow pride or any other thing rob your strength for another second!
- I urge you not to be slow in offering that place to sit and rest.

To see:
- See that not a single one of us can get through life without help. See that the main thing, the most important thing written in verse 15 (CEV) is: *Moses built an altar and named it, "The Lord Gives Me Victory."*

No one experiences victory in his own strength, power or might. We have a faithful God who draws near and delivers us in our times of distress.

Moses explains, *This is because I depended on the LORD...* Our bottom line, now and always - we don't get through on our own. We must press in and remember that God is our banner and shield and it is He alone who sustains us.

Stephanie D. Paul

Jeremiah 18-19; 2 Timothy 3   **October 29**

The Indwelling Christ

Now if anyone does not have the Spirit of Christ, he is not His.
(Romans 8:9b)

It is very important for every child of God to know the essential truth that Christ dwells in every believer. I want you to understand that Christ, Himself, is in heaven but also that He lives in us by the Holy Spirit.

So, what does the Holy Spirit do for us? He makes Christ real to us. He causes us to know that His Spirit is in us. The Holy Spirit is the Christian life. He lives the Christian life through us because it is impossible for us to do so in the flesh.

The ministry of the Holy Spirit is to make Christ as real to us as He was to His disciples. Yet Christ is not real to many Christians. Many say this, *"I believe the Bible, I pray, I go to church, but Christ is not real to me."* Why is this so?

First, we need to point out that there are those who think they are Christians, but they have never been born again. Christ is not real to them because they do not belong to Him and the Holy Spirit does not indwell them.

Another reason Christ is not real to people, even when they are truly born again, is because they are grieving the Holy Spirit. When we grieve the Holy Spirit, He no longer manifests Christ to us, and we lose our daily communion with Him. Christ never leaves us, yet He does not seem real to us because we have grieved His Spirit. It is important for us to understand the difference between our relationship and our fellowship, or communion, with God. As a believer you can never lose your relationship with God; you are eternally sealed in Christ

(Ephesians 1:13). But you can be out of fellowship with Him, and in that state, my friend, you will wonder if you are truly saved. It is unwise to live in sin and grieve the Holy Spirit. We restore our fellowship with God by confessing our sins, and at that moment the Holy Spirit will make Christ real to us again.

My friend, will you choose this day to confess and repent of all your sins, and stay close and clean with your heavenly Father? This is how to make Christ real to you as you rest in His indwelling life.

Rev. Chris S. Hodges

Jeremiah 20-21; 2 Timothy 4　　　　　　　　　　**October 30**

Spirit-Filled Craftsmen

There are different kinds of spiritual gifts, but the same Spirit is the source of them all. There are different kinds of service, but we serve the same Lord. God works in different ways, but it is the same God who does the work in all of us.
(1 Corinthians 12:4-6 NLT)

How many people do you know who feel they have nothing special, no gift, they can offer the Lord?

In Exodus 31:1-6 there is a description of the special people, gifted of God and filled with the Spirit, who did "menial" tasks in the building of the tabernacle. In 1 Peter 4:10a (NLT) we're told, *God has given each of you a gift from his great variety of spiritual gifts.* Specifically mentioned is the gift of helps.

Helps? That doesn't sound very spiritual! But preaching...or teaching...or worship leading...or singing, playing an instrument...or being involved in drama...or administration (heading a ministry of the church)...or ???? They're great. No, we're talking about helps!

If the English language means anything at all, those verses mean that people who do regular things, not just "ministry" things, have a *spiritual* gift from God. That means *you* can *minister* with your *talent*.

How I thank God for people who have the gift of helps. Where would our churches and para-church ministries be today if we didn't have volunteers who love to serve Jesus with their abilities, talents, gifts?

In my experience I have seen people who have built buildings, worked full-time in food service, repaired all manner of electrical products, re-wired an entire camp, kept major large pieces of equipment running, headed a volunteer organization, etc., etc., etc., all as volunteers.

You have heard, "time is money." Think of the money saved by Christian ministries because of the volunteerism they have experienced. But perhaps of even greater value is the spiritual fulfillment of the volunteer who fully realizes that he/she has used the gift God gave to honor Him and further His cause.

Some say that 80% of the ministry is perpetuated by 20% of the people. Let's change those statistics and get involved.

What is it that you can do? Which church or Christian ministry can you serve? God has placed something inside of you that you do well. Do it for Jesus. If you have never known the joy of serving, why not begin now?

> A volunteer for Jesus, a soldier true.
> Others have enlisted, why not you?
> Jesus is the captain, we will never fear.
> Will you be enlisted as a volunteer.

Rev. Neil Fichthorn

Jeremiah 22-23; Titus 1   **October 31**

Faces

At Halloween, we enter into the tradition of putting on costumes and false faces. I never particularly enjoyed doing this as a kid but did it because everyone else was doing it. But I discovered that I play Halloween throughout the whole year – by wearing different faces – many of which were not so false. How about you? See if you ever wear any of the following, even suggested by the Scriptures:

Fear - Many times we are fearful of things and our faces show it. *The Lord is my light and my salvation – whom shall I fear? Though an army besiege me, my heart will not fear; though war break out against me, even then will I be confident.* (Psalm 27: 1, 3 NIV) But there is a proper fear– reverential trust. *Fear the Lord, you His saints, for those who fear Him lack nothing* (Psalm 34:9 NIV). Which face do you wear?

Sadness - After the Lord's prayer, Jesus corrected the hypocrites. *"When you fast, do not look somber* (sad) *as the hypocrites do, for they disfigure their faces to show men they were fasting"* (Matthew 6:16 NIV). Instead of a sad face, you can wear a face of joy.

Joy – In John 15:10-11 (NIV), Jesus is speaking: *If you obey my commands, you will remain in my love, just as I have obeyed my Father's commands and remain in his love. I have told you this so that my joy may be in you and that your joy may be complete.* When you wear this face, let it be genuine and not a false face.

Anger - Today I see many people who are angry, but read what Jesus says about anger. *But I tell you that anyone who is angry with his brother will be subject to judgment...* (Matthew 5:22 NIV). To combat our society of anger we should overwhelm it with faces of...

Love - Now Jesus is teaching the most important commandment to the Pharisees. *"The most important one.... 'Love the Lord your God with all your heart and... soul and...mind and...strength.' The second is this: 'Love your* *neighbor as yourself.' There is no commandment greater than these"* (Mark 12:29-31 NIV). Not loving God is like being asleep.

Sleepiness - This is the face I wear when I am lazy and don't want to be involved. How about you? This is why the apostle Paul quotes Isaiah in Ephesians 5:14 (NVI) when he says, *Wake up, O sleeper, rise from the dead, and Christ will shine on you.* And wear this next face.

Seriousness - Jesus asks the Pharisees, *What do you think about the Christ?* (Matthew 22:42 NIV). Quite the opposite of being sleepy – being one who is thoughtfully serious about Jesus.

Finally, brothers and sisters, whatever is true, ... noble, ... right, ... pure, ... lovely, ... admirable—if anything is excellent or praiseworthy—think about such things (Philippians 4:8 NIV) - seriously!

Let these Scriptures remind you to wear faces each day that will bring glory to Him.

Jack Noel

Jeremiah 24-26; Titus 2　　　　　　　　　　　**November 1**

Signs? What Signs?

Then Jesus said to him, "Unless you people see signs and wonders, you will by no means believe." (John 4:48)

When I was a kid growing up around an Italian household some everyday occurrences were taken as a "sign." A fork would fall to the floor and my grandmother would say "Co'pany's coming and they will be hungry. I better get something cooking." Well, who could it be? I had some pretty cool aunts and uncles at one time, so like a puppy dog my ears would perk up and I would start to look out the window. And wait. And wait. Then dinner would be ready and my grandmother would try and have us eat everything in one shot. The only problem was it was for the company. Where were they to help us eat all this food? Oh, well. More for us I guess?

I also could never understand the meaning of when the right hand would itch. It was taken as a sign that you would be receiving money. Well, my hand still itches and I am no Donald Trump. Praise the Lord!!

My point here is that there were signs that had been interpreted to mean something but nothing would happen. But I believed they would happen.

Not too long ago I ignored the sign that said 25mph. But when I got pulled over I had to believe that I was travelling well beyond what the sign said. It was a little sign surrounded by branches but I, well, just disobeyed. Oops. Lost some money but earned some points for that. (Just for the record, my wife was not as visibly angry at me as I was at me.)

Now how many of you reading this are looking for a sign so you can believe? You're in a spot in your life where you have been praying for Jesus to give you a sign or some sort of signal that He acknowledges you. I have been there saying my occasional "foxhole prayer" as well. You know what...the only sign to see is the cross. And at times I fail to see it...or dare I say...just not look to it. It's not a little sign hidden by branches, so what's my excuse? There is none.

As I travel through the everyday I am bombarded by signs. None of them have the depth or the power of the cross. The cross does not encourage me to buy something nor does it tell me how fast to go. It does not blink or change its color. It does, however, give me direction and wisdom. But most importantly it tells me to yield. Just like He yielded. That's the sign. For me. What about you? What does it say to you?

Chris Hughes

Jeremiah 27-29; Titus 3   **November 2**

The Good Life

I beseech you therefore, brethren, by the mercies of God, that you present your bodies a living sacrifice, holy, acceptable to God, which is your reasonable service. And do not be conformed to this world, but be transformed by the renewing of your mind, that you may prove what is that good and acceptable and perfect will of God. (Romans 12:1-2)

    I have been attempting to read Proverbs on a daily basis, and I admit that I am fluctuating in my faithfulness to that task. My goal is to read daily the Proverb that matches the day of the month. Each time I read one of the Proverbs I am challenged in a new way. It would be great if I could do this to the point that I actually had them memorized. Having to admit my lack of discipline at times, I doubt that I can get to that place. So, I just continue to challenge myself to read them and receive my lesson for the day from Solomon. Let me share some thoughts from Proverbs 19 with you today.

    Today, the media and Hollywood regularly attempt to define the good life philosophy and push it on each of us. Scripture has a whole different approach to living the good life. Solomon had it all, but that's not what he attributed to the good life.

Proverbs 19

- Listen to instruction (vs. 16, 20, 27).
- Be kind to those less fortunate (v. 17).
- Discipline your children – help them stay on the right path (v. 18).
- Don't hang around with those that have no personal discipline in their lives (v. 19).
- Follow in God's ways, contrary to the view of finding your own path and making your own destiny (v. 21).
- Kindness and honesty are to be the norm in our lives rather than the exception (v. 22).

- Walking in the "fear of the Lord" leads to the "good life" and keeps us from evil (v. 23).
- Be diligent in all you do (vs. 15, 24).

Are you experiencing the good life? Often we think or believe that the good life should just come to us, yet that is not what Scripture says… it tells us basically if you do this… then you will know the good life. Many of us are well acquainted with the verse in Romans 12, but repetition is good for us… it constantly reminds us that if we want to know what is good then we need to not follow the way of the world, but follow the ways of God.

Dr. Lynne Jahns

Jeremiah 30-31; Philemon　　　　　　　　　　　November 3

The Price of Holiness

By faith, Moses, when he became of age, refused to be called the son of Pharaoh's daughter, choosing rather to suffer affliction with the people of God than to enjoy the passing pleasures of sin… (Hebrews 11: 24-25)

　　I am impressed each time I read the eleventh chapter of Hebrews by the collection of remarkable saints of God. The chapter is appropriately called, *God's Hall of Fame.* The common thread that ties together this unique group of people is *Faith.*

　　Moses, the great man of God who was used to liberate God's people from Egyptian bondage, was the adopted son of Pharaoh's daughter. Moses was in line to the most powerful throne in the world. Great wealth was at his disposal. Yet, he gave it all up.

　　Commitment to God and His purposes in the world do not come without a price. Many are not willing to pay that price. Moses rises as a shining example of one who paid the price to be pleasing to God and to be used by God. The price he paid included the things he had to give up and the things he had to accept.

He gave up *greatness* (v. 24). He surrendered his rights as adopted son of Pharaoh's daughter and adopted grandson of Pharaoh.

He gave up *pleasure* (v. 25). He surrendered all of the comforts and luxuries of the King's palace.

He gave up *riches* (v. 26). He surrendered his access to the wealth of Pharaoh's coffers.

The price one pays in serving God involves letting go of some things, but it also involves embracing some things. We have seen what Moses gave up. Now let us see what Moses chose.

He chose *suffering and affliction* (v. 25). He left a life of comfort and ease to live a life of discomfort and pain.

He chose *to identify with the people of God* (v. 25).

He chose *reproach* (v. 26). He knew that he would be scorned and laughed at.

You and I must give up certain things and embrace other things before we can be holy people of God.

Dr. Roger D. Willmore

Jeremiah 32-33; Hebrews 1   **November 4**

Stripping to Avoid Tripping

...let us lay aside every weight, and the sin which so easily ensnares us, and let us run with endurance the race that is set before us. (Hebrews 12:1b)

The writer to the Hebrews draws from the sports arena of his day to illustrate some essential principles of Christian living. In chapter 12 he pictures a multi-tiered stadium filled with people. Special recognition is given to those who have competed previously and endured by faith (see chapter 11). Their example is then applied to the readers, and a set of instructions is given for their participation in the spiritual race.

The first preparatory requirement is to lay aside every weight. The term for this action is used in other portions for stripping off old, sinful garments. (See Colossians 3:8 for samples of the discarded clothing.) Runners in the Greek games shed essentially all of their clothing in order to have freedom of motion. Even today the warm-up suit is laid aside before the start of a race. In our text the item to be laid aside is called a weight. The idea naturally includes excess physical pounds which strictly limit the potential for victorious testimony. But the word is broad enough in its meaning to refer to every encumbrance which handicaps, such as doubt, pride, laziness, unforgiveness, anger and the like. This process amounts to disciplined spiritual training.

An additional instruction requires that sin be laid aside. It is described as the sin which so easily besets us (trips us up). Certain types of sin especially ensnare us, causing us to stumble repeatedly. The expression can be applied to the danger for a runner of catching his spikes in the leg of his warm-up suit. There may be things in our lives which are apt to lead us into a spiritual fall. They may be subtle influences which need to be avoided. For further consideration, check out 1 Corinthians 10:12 and Jude 25. Are we taking the proper steps to prevent these sins? Are we depending on the One who can keep us from falling?

Rev. William A. Raws

Jeremiah 34-36; Hebrews 2   **November 5**

Finishing Well

I have fought the good fight, I have finished the race, I have kept the faith. (2 Timothy 4:7)

My aunt went through two major surgeries at the age of 87. I was with her when she awoke from the second surgery. Her first comment was that she didn't think she would be here much longer. I knew in my heart that was probably the case. She then continued her thought by quoting a familiar hymn: "This is my story; this is my song, praising my Savior all the day long." A life spent pondering on the things of God now flowed through her mind. Now, coming to the end of her life, her desire was to see Jesus and praise Him all day long. Watching her struggle physically in the end was difficult. Seeing her finish well was a privilege.

I am challenged to consider how I want to finish. Will Jesus continue to be the desire of my heart? Will my love for Him be as strong when I am 87? I want to finish well. Finishing well in the end begins with the choices we make each day. What choices do you and I have today that will lead us to the finish line strong?

Let these words be our hope and goal today: *Therefore we also, since we are surrounded by so great a cloud of witnesses, let us lay aside every weight, and the sin which so easily ensnares us, and let us run with endurance the race that is set before us, looking unto Jesus, the author and finisher of our faith, who for the joy that was set before Him endured the cross, despising the shame, and has sat down at the right hand of the throne of God* (Hebrews 12:1-2).

Kathy Withers

Jeremiah 37-39; Hebrews 3   November 6

The Power of Forgiveness

... Father forgive them, for they do not know what they do…
(Luke 23:34)

One of life's most powerful statements is "I forgive you." Jesus is on the cross. He has been mocked. He is hanging limp before the observers. His few garments are now the property of the soldiers. The One who claimed to be God was dying. He says, *Father forgive...* The word is a verb denoting action, meaning to remit and pardon. It is occasionally a noun referring to "a release." There are 109 forms of the word in the New Testament.

The beautiful language of the deaf, perhaps like no other, illustrates the meaning of forgiveness. With a clenched fist next to one's chest they spread the arm out with an open palm depicting a release. Forgiveness is releasing someone from a harm they have done. Here Jesus is forgiving those who have cruelly treated Him. But the forgiveness goes beyond those that are there. God forgives us of all our sins when we accept the Lord Jesus as our one and only Savior. Jesus is the one and only Savior. The reason is He died for our sins and rose again from the grave.

When God the Father looks at someone, He sees his sin. When Jesus Christ is seen between the person and the heavenly Father, there is righteousness based on the finished work of Jesus Christ through His blood. Herbert Lockyer, the English cleric, said it so well, "The Son of God became the Son of man that sons of men could become the sons of God."

Throughout this day keep in mind that God has forgiven you in Christ. There is not one sin held to your account, for Jesus Christ provides the forgiveness of your sins. Regardless of the situation you may be going through in life, when one recognizes that sins are forgiven, it brings a new dimension to life and an understanding that Jesus is what we need now and He is sufficient forever. Songwriter Andre Crouch reminds us "Through it all, I've learned to trust in Jesus, I've learned to trust in God. Through it all, through it all, I've learned to depend upon His Word."

Dr. Dino Pedrone

Jeremiah 40-42; Hebrews 4   November 7

You Matter to God

O LORD, thou hast searched me, and known me. (Psalm 139:1)

The sovereign Creator of the universe cares about you! Just take a moment and try to wrap your mind around that fact. It's easy to lose sight of Him in the busyness of the day. His Word tells us that:

- <u>He created you in His image</u> (Genesis 1:27). Of all the created beings on the earth, humans are the only ones created in His image.
- <u>He loved you when you were His enemy</u> (Romans 5:10). His perfect love allowed Him to love us even when we hated Him. How much more does He love us as His children?
- <u>He sent His only Son to be your perfect sacrifice for sin</u> (John 3:16). His law called for perfection, only Jesus was perfect and was the only suitable sacrifice to provide atonement for sin.
- <u>He knows your every movement</u> (Psalm 139:2). Not in a "puppet master" way, but because He loves you NOTHING escapes His attention.
- <u>He knew you before the foundation of the world</u> (Psalm 139:15). He knew who you would be even before you were a glimmer in your parents' eyes.
- <u>He knows the number of hairs on your head</u> (Matthew 10:30). I don't know about you, but that is a fact I cannot even comprehend.
- <u>He thinks about you so many times in a day that you can't even number them</u> (Psalm 139:17-18). At any given moment there over 6 billion people on this planet, and the Creator of the entire universe thinks about you, His child, individually and personally.
- <u>He hears and answers every prayer</u> (Psalm 86:6-7). In the commotion of life, He hears your individual voice. He knows exactly what is going on in your life, and knows how best to respond to that prayer.
- <u>He provides for your every need</u> (Philippians 4:19). Only a perfect God knows how to meet your needs perfectly, every time.
- <u>He knows your needs even before you do</u> (Matthew 6:28-30). He knows the master plan of your life. We can only see the day-to-day details, but He sees the overview.
- <u>He collects your tears in His bottle</u> (Psalm 56:8). In His infinite mercy, He has compassion on you. His heart

breaks whenever a child of His is sad, struggling or lonely.

Any time you are feeling unloved or alone, I would encourage you to take some time and meditate on these things. Pray that God will help you understand and accept them more fully. It will truly change your outlook on everyday life!

Donna Connors

Jeremiah 43-45; Hebrews 5   **November 8**

The Power of His Presence

I am with you to deliver you, says the LORD. (Jeremiah 1:8)

When God places you and me in dangerous or difficult circumstances, He does not abandon us to face the challenge alone. He knows that we are incompetent to deal with them and takes note of our personal inadequacies. When we receive an assignment from Him which we consider to be beyond our capacity, we often have reactions which could be described by the expressions: "Who, me?" "You've got to be kidding." "I can't." "That's not fair." etc. We need to consciously consider several things in responding to His assignment.

1. Remember His person, i.e., Who it is assigning us. It is the LORD, the sovereign, self-existent One. He declares Himself as the almighty, unchanging God.

2. Recognize His power as revealed in His Word and demonstrated in the lives of His people. History bears witness to His taking supposedly inadequate people, humanly speaking, and placing them in supposedly impossible situations (i.e., Moses, Gideon, D. L. Moody, etc.).

3. Rely on His presence. Along with His presence comes the enablement to meet the challenge of the assignment. We see this in the statement to Jeremiah in our text. He was being called by God to a most difficult and unpopular assignment. His reaction was that he was not mature enough to handle the task. He was fearful of the anticipated opposition. God's answer was in terms of His divine presence and His promise – deliverance.

In commissioning His disciples, our Lord combined the statement of their responsibilities with the facts of His authoritative power and His assured presence (Matthew 28:18-20). They faced a task for which they in themselves were entirely inadequate.

The writer of Hebrews relates these facts to his readers and to us when he quotes the words of the Lord, *I will never leave you nor forsake you* (Hebrews 13:5b). In verse 8 he declares that *Jesus Christ is the same yesterday, today and forever.*

Rev. William A. Raws

Jeremiah 46-47; Hebrews 6 November 9

We Cry Abba, Father

Therefore, brethren, we are debtors—not to the flesh, to live according to the flesh. For if you live according to the flesh you will die; but if by the Spirit you put to death the deeds of the body, you will live. For as many as are led by the Spirit of God, these are sons of God. For you did not receive the spirit of bondage again to fear, but you received the Spirit of adoption by whom we cry out, "Abba, Father." The Spirit Himself bears witness with our spirit that we are children of God, and if children, then heirs—heirs of God and joint heirs with Christ, if indeed we suffer with Him, that we may also be glorified together. (Romans 8:12-17)

"Father," what a wonderful word! How privileged we are to call God our Father. When I pastored in Western Pennsylvania, I had the privilege of speaking at the Peoples' Church in Spanish Wells, Bahamas. In fact, I was going to Spanish Wells every other year to minister. One Thursday, I received a telephone call from the leader at Spanish Wells asking me if I could come and speak at the Bible Conference the following week. At the last minute, because of illness, one of the scheduled speakers could not come. This was my "off year" so I called the Chairman of our Board of Deacons to ask his thoughts about my going. We had a missionary speaker scheduled for the weekend I would be away so our Chairman thought it would be no problem.

My son, Steve, nine years old at the time, was home from school because of a heavy snow storm. My wife, Diane, suggested that I surprise Steve and take him with me. Actually, I was already thinking about taking him so I began to kid with him. I asked if he would like to have some fish. His answer, "Are we going to Long John Silvers?" I said no, then asked him if he would like to see Uncle Willie. He asked if Willie Pender from Spanish Wells, Uncle Willie to him, was in Pittsburgh. I said no and Steve then knew right away that I was talking about going to Spanish Wells! He immediately began calling all of his snow-bound friends sharing that he was going to the Bahamas.

We had a wonderful time although I was very busy speaking throughout the week. I did have one day off and on that day Steve and I were riding on a motorcycle. While riding Steve leaned over and touched me on the shoulder. He then said to me, "Dad, I really am enjoying this trip but I think that I am enjoying today more than any other day." Why this day? It was because of the father and son time, the "he" and "I" time that we were enjoying together. The lesson to learn is that there is no richer time than that time alone with the Father spent in His presence. Remembering that "Abba" is the Hebrew word for Father, we need that time to cry "Abba, Father." Take some time to be in the presence of the Father and allow Him to be your Father!

Dr. George L. Nichols, Jr.

Jeremiah 48-49; Hebrews 7 November 10
When We Feel Forsaken

And about the ninth hour Jesus cried out with a loud voice, saying, "ELI, ELI, LAMA SABACHTHANI?" that is, "MY GOD, MY GOD, WHY HAVE YOU FORSAKEN ME?"
(Matthew 27:46)

Thinking about Jesus' last spoken words moments before his death can be quite startling. It is not clear exactly what was going on, theologically speaking, at this moment between the Father and the Son to prompt Jesus' questioning cry. However, I think it is safe to assume that Jesus *felt* forsaken. Jesus felt the way we feel when, despite our best efforts, our lives spin out of control and we wonder where God is and why He has allowed our current circumstances. We feel, well, forsaken. This kind of struggle has, at times, led some to reject God in one way or another. Reflective Christians have offered many logically astute reasons why a good God may allow evil and suffering but when one finds oneself in the midst of the suffering, the rational argumentation is often dry and without effect. I want to focus us on the fact that Jesus knows precisely how we feel (see Hebrews 2:18). On the biblical view, God specifically <u>entered into the human predicament.</u> Jesus, no doubt, understood rationally that evil and suffering does not impugn the power and goodness of God. However, in that moment, He experienced the results of existence outside the moral bounds of God. Though He was perfectly and completely innocent, He saw the world as one upon whose shoulders laid "the curse of the law" (Galatians 3:13).

There would perhaps be no more tragic story ever told except that we know the end of the story. We all will face moments of forsakenness. Take a deep breath and hear afresh the future that awaits:

[The apostle John speaking] And I saw the holy city, new Jerusalem, coming down out of heaven from God, made ready as a bride adorned for her husband. And I heard a loud voice from the throne, saying, "Behold, the dwelling place of God is among men, and He will dwell among them, and they shall be His people, and God Himself will be among them, and He will wipe away every tear from their eyes; and there will no longer be any death; there will no longer be any mourning, or crying, or pain; the first things have passed away." And He who sits on the throne said, "Behold, I am making all things new" (Revelation 21:2-5a NASB).

Travis Dickinson

Jeremiah 50; Hebrews 8   **November 11**

Unseen Protection

*And the Angel of God, who went before the camp of Israel, moved and went behind them; and the pillar of cloud went from **before them and stood behind them. So it came between** the camp of the Egyptians and the camp of Israel. Thus it was **a cloud and darkness** to the one, and **it gave light by night** to the other, so that the one did not come near the other all that night.*
(Exodus 14:19-20, emphasis mine)

    The Israelites were trusting God to deliver them from bondage in Egypt. Every time Moses had been obedient to God and confronted Pharaoh things appeared to get worse instead of better. Now it appeared that they were finally out of Egypt and on their way to the Promised Land. But God did something unexpected and illogical in their eyes. He led them in an indirect route.

    Then it came to pass, when Pharaoh had let the people go, that God did not lead them by way of the land of the Philistines, although that was near; for God said, "Lest perhaps the people change their minds when they see war, and return to Egypt." So God led the people around by way of the wilderness of the Red Sea. And the children of Israel went up in orderly ranks out of the land of Egypt (Exodus 13:17-18).

    Often God acts on our behalf and we are clueless as to why. I smile when an unbeliever says that if there were really a God He wouldn't do this or that. As if we mortals could comprehend the working of the mind of God! The Bible assures us that His thoughts are higher than our thoughts and His ways higher than ours. I have long since my conversion quit trying to figure out His ways according to my logic. What I do know is that God hedges me in from in front and behind. This was evident in the case of His people. His intention was to destroy the entire Egyptian army once and for all. And to protect His people He put a wall of darkness between their enemies and themselves. I have to ask myself this question, "How many times has the Lord protected my life when I could not possibly see or understand?"

Father, I ask forgiveness for ever being afraid, and thank You for Your unseen protection.

Chaplain Jim Freed

Jeremiah 51-52; Hebrews 9   **November 12**

Expressions of a Sinful Heart

And not many days after, the younger son gathered all together, journeyed to a far country, and there wasted his possessions with prodigal living. (Luke 15:13)

This is one of the first messages I preached at America's Keswick. I still have clear memories of what God did in the lives of some people that night and that week. Each time I turn to the story of the prodigal I remember that night at Keswick.

When we look at the prodigal, we see where sin begins. The ultimate outcome of his life that left him broken down in a pigpen had its roots in his heart. The journey to the far country began as a dream, a thought, a wish. He conceived the idea, then he planned it, then he announced it and then he pursued it. However, it all started in the private recesses of his heart.

When we investigate what we know about the prodigal's heart we see that his sin actually began there and grew and grew until it had full control of him.

We notice first his attitude of greed (v.12). He wanted his part of his inheritance even before his father was dead. His attitude really reflects his wish that his father was dead. At this point in his life, his heart is filled with dreams of money, materialism and pleasure. He thought only of himself.

We also see pride in his heart (v.12-13). He wanted to be away from his father's authority, rules and requirements. In his pride, he rebelled against authority. Pride is the root of all sin and is fundamentally rebellion against the sovereign authority of God.

We see carelessness in his heart (v.13-14). He wasted his life. He threw away his money and his morals. He was blinded by his obsession to live in sin. Many today are blinded by sin and do not see that it is destroying their lives.

Last of all, we see how lonely he is (v.15-16). There he is, a Jewish boy in a pigpen. Lonely and alone. Sin does this to a person. It takes him further than he wants to go, costs him more than he wants to pay and keeps him longer than he wants to stay.

What is going on in your heart today? Jesus said, *For out of the heart proceed evil thoughts, murders, adulteries, fornications, thefts, false witness, blasphemies* (Matthew 15:19).

Dr. Roger D. Willmore

Lamentations 1-2; Hebrews 10:1-18 November 13

The God of One More Chance

He also spoke this parable: "A certain man had a fig tree planted in his vineyard, and he came seeking fruit on it and found none. Then he said to the keeper of his vineyard, 'Look, for three years I have come seeking fruit on this fig tree and find none. Cut it down; why does it use up the ground?' But he answered and said to him, 'Sir, let it alone this year also, until I dig around it and fertilize it. And if it bears fruit, well. But if not, after that you can cut it down.'" (Luke 13:6-9)

Pay close attention to this parable. It contains a plea for a second chance. Whatever else this text teaches us, it teaches that God is a God of a second chance.

The owner of the vineyard had a right to expect the trees of his vineyard to produce fruit. They were his trees. They were his purchased possessions. The trees were planted for the purpose of bearing fruit. The owner of the vineyard had the right to expect fruit. The owner of the vineyard had the right to inspect for fruit. The owner of the vineyard had the right to demand the barren tree be taken down and out of the vineyard.

God has a right to expect you and me to produce fruit. We are His purchased possession. He saved us for a purpose. He has the right to expect us to bear fruit and He has the right to inspect our lives for fruit. He has the right to set us aside if we are not producing fruit.

Cut it down; why does it use up the ground? These are sobering words. But thank God, He is a God of a second chance. The keeper of the vineyard pleaded with his master for one more chance.

God gives second chances and third chances. He is a patient and loving God.

Do you need one more chance? Ask Him. However, when it is granted get busy digging and fertilizing your life. Do what is necessary to become a fruit-bearing Christian.

Dr. Roger D. Willmore

Lamentations 3-5; Hebrews 10:19-39 November 14

Practice Makes…

Little children, let no one deceive you. He who practices righteousness is righteous, just as He is righteous. (1 John 3:17)

Everybody knows the expression "practice makes perfect." I was told that over and over as a child taking piano lessons. The need to practice was essential.

However, the expression really is somewhat false. Practice does not make perfect, it just makes permanent. If you practice correctly, whatever it is you practice, then yes, it makes perfect the execution of what we are learning. But if we practice incorrectly, or the wrong way, then that pattern becomes ingrained in us and is very hard to break. Practice something the wrong way and you will always tend to do it the wrong way.

Maybe you've also heard this: "Sow a thought and you reap an action; sow an act and you reap a habit; sow a habit and you reap a character; sow a character and you reap a destiny."
~Ralph Waldo Emerson

What we practice spiritually also becomes our habit, our character. What are our daily "practices" as we walk with God? Do we spend time with Him? Do we seek His face daily, in every circumstance? When difficulties come, is it our practice to run to Him? Do we worry, fret, try to figure out how to deal with things – or do we make it a practice to give it to Him?

These are things that I am learning, and working on practicing correctly so that practice truly does make "perfect."

*But what things were gain to me, these I have counted loss for Christ. Yet indeed I also count all things loss for the excellence of the knowledge of Christ Jesus my Lord, for whom I have suffered the loss of all things, and count them as rubbish, that I may gain Christ and be found in Him, not having my own righteousness, which is from the law, but that which is through faith in Christ, the righteousness which is from God by faith; that I may know Him and the power of His resurrection, and the fellowship of His sufferings, being conformed to His death, if, by any means, I may attain to the resurrection from the dead. Not that I have already attained, or am already **perfected**; but I **press on**, that I may lay hold of that for which Christ Jesus has also laid hold of me. Brethren, I do not count myself to have apprehended; but one thing I do, forgetting those things which are behind and reaching forward to those things which are ahead, I **press toward** the goal for the prize of the upward call of God in Christ Jesus.* (Philippians 3:7-14 emphasis mine)

May we press on as we practice becoming perfect in Him!

Ruth Schmidt

Ezekiel 1-2; Hebrews 11:1-19   **November 15**

True Wisdom

Who is wise and understanding among you? Let him show it by his good life, by deeds done in the humility that comes from wisdom. (James 3:13 NIV)

    You don't have to look very far to find opinionated people. Talk show hosts seem to be the most extreme examples, but as uncomfortable as it may be for many of us, our closest examples are within our own skin. It seems we often need the proverbial admonition to "not be wise in [our] own eyes."

    Wisdom seems to grow out of the fertile soil of knowledge and experience. Since experience is the best teacher, wise people tend to have a few gray hairs. But not all those who have great experience have great wisdom. Sadly, there are many adults whose decision-making ability even now flounders at a child's level. Yet, what strikes me in this passage is not what it includes, but what it leaves out.

    Wise people according to James probably won't win on Jeopardy. They may not remember their calculus, or what a covalent bond is. They may not have traveled to the other side of the world either. All of these make a person wise in the world's eyes. However, those who want wisdom are not left to merely speculate. We are told that walking with the wise is the path to becoming wise ourselves (Proverbs 13:30). And who shall be our model?

    If we would truly be wise we would look to Jesus as our example ahead of all the poets and philosophers. Even Solomon's wisdom, which proved a double-edged sword, pales in comparison. Jesus fits James' definition of wisdom so well that it seems that he had Jesus in mind when he wrote verse thirteen. Indeed, like an archer who paints a circle around an arrow he's already shot into the side of a barn, James looks to Jesus and then tells us what wisdom is.

    Jesus was good, although He deflected such praise from men (Matthew 19:17). His humility was unparalleled (Philippians 2:5-11). His wise words were always for the benefit of others, not His own glorification. He used His vast knowledge to heal the sick, give hope to the hopeless, a voice to the oppressed, strength to the weak, and understanding to the seekers. Appropriately, His only harsh words were reserved for the worldly wise. These are the characteristics of wisdom.

Let us end with a warning and a word of hope. The warning goes to those who think they are wise. Are you wise? Answering in the affirmative may be the first sign you are not! Beware of pride, and remember that knowledge puffs up (1 Corinthians 8:1), and puffed up people aren't wise. Conversely, if you despair of ever gaining wisdom, take heart! The Lord is the source of heavenly wisdom and He loves to teach those who seek it (James 1:5). All the wisdom you'll ever need is at your fingertips. Faithfully apply the Scriptures to your life and you will find yourself on the unfailing path to wisdom.

Rev. Jason R. Walsh

Ezekiel 3-4; Hebrews 11:20-40　　　　　　　　　November 16

I'm a Marked Man

And do not grieve the Holy Spirit of God, by whom you were sealed for the day of redemption. (Ephesians 4:30)

In the political and commercial world of the apostle Paul's day the seal played an important role. The word was used to indicate a mark of ownership, a classified document or an official decree. Kings or other officers used a wax seal which bore the impression of a signet ring or other identifying stamp to make a document official and authoritative. John in Revelation 5 and 6 speaks of a seven-sealed scroll which was unrolled and unsealed by the Lamb. In that case the seal denoted divine authority.

A seal indicated ownership. It could take the form of an identifying mark other than a waxen signature seal. Such a mark was used in the logging industry. When logs were cut in the forests of Asia Minor, they were hauled to the sea to be added to a flotilla of other logs to be moved along the coast to the saw mills located toward the south. Each log was marked (sealed) to identify its owner. It was almost unheard of for anyone but the owner to take the log. It had been sealed to identify its owner.

Our theme verse indicates that one of the ministries of the Holy Spirit is to seal the believer. This is the basis of our security. Notice that the sealed person does not do anything to secure himself; it is all done for him on the basis of his belonging to Jesus Christ. If the sealed person should harbor any of the sins listed in the context of verse 30, the Spirit of God would be grieved or caused sorrow.

Since the Spirit has placed His mark upon me and dwells within, I am eternally secure. However, when sin occurs in my life I'll be out of fellowship until confession and cleansing is accomplished (1 John 1:9). Bearing His mark also places upon me the responsibility of a consistent testimony of life and lip because I am identified as belonging to Him.

Following the day of redemption when we are delivered from the very presence of sin, we shall need no identifying mark. In the meanwhile, I am a marked person.

Rev. William A. Raws

Ezekiel 5-7; Hebrews 12   **November 17**

Road Noise - Life Noise

Watch, stand fast in the faith, be brave, be strong.
(1 Corinthians 16:13)

Hovering around the speed limit of 65, on a warm and sunny day, the radio keeping me company, windows open, singing at the top of my lungs, all was well with my world. One of my favorite Christian songs came on and I sang along.

The traffic on Route 287 can get heavy at times especially when the trucks go whizzing by. With my car windows open the road noise periodically drowned out my voice so I couldn't even hear myself. Undeterred, I kept singing. Soon the traffic subsided and once again I could hear my voice. The traffic ebbed and flowed through the duration of the song; I just kept singing.

Sometimes I could hear the song, other times I could not. I kept singing.

I couldn't help but ponder how much like life road noise is. Sometimes life-noise around us is so intense we can barely hear ourselves think, yet at other times it quiets and we regain awareness of our voice.

What is important is not whether we can hear our voice or not, but rather that our heart continually sings and that it sings truth.

Are you singing truth to yourself, steadfast and immovable, whether you can hear your voice or not? Are you singing God's song as life-noise ebbs and flows, drowning out your voice yet knowing that even when you can't hear it, it is still there strong and vibrant?

Stand firm, and sing your heart out whether you can hear it through the noise or not.

He has put a new song in my mouth—Praise to our God; Many will see it and fear, And will trust in the LORD (Psalm 40:3).

Diane Hunt

Ezekiel 8-10; Hebrews 13   **November 18**

What Is Important to You?

But seek first the kingdom of God and His righteousness, and all these things shall be added to you. (Matthew 6:33)

I love to see passionate people. It does not take long to discover what is important to a passionate person. The thing that is most important to him is the source of his passion.

What is important to you? What is the primary driving force in your life? If you are a Christian, you should be driven by a passion for the things of God. The Apostle Paul is a wonderful example of a passion-driven person. In his letter to the Philippians (3:13-14), he wrote, *Brethren, I do not count myself to have apprehended; but one thing I do, forgetting those things which are behind and reaching forward to those things which are ahead, I press toward the goal for the prize of the upward call of God in Christ Jesus.*

What is important to you is a matter of choice. A person chooses what is most important to him. Allow me to use some simple illustrations to clarify this point. A child in a candy store who has just been given a dollar bill can decide to spend the dollar on candy or keep the dollar bill, but he cannot do both. What is most important to the child will be revealed in his decision. When faced with a temptation to tell a lie the person will make a decision that reflects what is most important to him. A man cannot go in two directions at the same time. He must make a choice and his choice will reflect what is most important to him.

In every person's life something is most important. In every person's life there is one primary affection to which all other affections are subordinate.

Jesus admonished His followers to seek the kingdom of God. The word *seek* means to strive after, to strongly desire, to have a strong affection for and to yearn after. Are you striving for and yearning for the things of God?

There is a promise found in verse 33; please do not miss it. Jesus said, *all these things shall be added to you.* If Jesus Christ and His kingdom is the most important pursuit of our lives then everything else we need for life, happiness and holiness will be given to us.

Make the right choice today and pursue Jesus Christ with your whole heart.

Dr. Roger D. Willmore

Ezekiel 11-13; James 1　　　　　　　　　　　**November 19**

Spiritual Deposits

...committed to Him...committed to you...commit to faithful men... (2 Timothy 1:12, 14; 2:2)

One of Paul's repeated words used in 2 Timothy is translated in most versions as *committed* or *commit.* Literally, the word in the original means "place aside." Another word that would fit the translation is *deposit* or *deposited*. If we adopt the latter word for our translation, we recognize three spiritual deposits in the first and second chapters of the book.

The first deposit occurs in 1:12. This we could label as a security deposit. The apostle Paul declares his confidence in God's ability to keep that which he has deposited with Him. He holds no fear of his deposit being lost or stolen. Those who make a savings deposit in a bank which is insured by the FDIC can enjoy a measure of confidence that when they want to withdraw their money it will be there. It follows, however, that only that which is deposited is insured. In the Christian life there is a danger of our loss of spiritual blessing and victory due to our making only partial commitment of our lives to the Lord.

Closely associated with the idea of a security deposit is a safety deposit. In the material world this would relate to preserving certain valuables and documents in a safety deposit box. Paul urges Timothy to preserve the sound words of the Gospel as a sacred deposit. He doesn't say to hide them in an obscure place but to receive them as a valued deposit and to guard them (v. 14). This was necessary because there were false teachers who were seeking to rob or corrupt the truth.

The third type of deposit is found in verse 2 of chapter 2. We might call this a shared deposit. The treasured truth referred to earlier which was to be kept in security and safety is to be invested in the lives of faithful persons. These would, in turn, make a commitment of it to others through their teaching. There is no better investment that we can make than sharing the truth of Jesus Christ with others in a discipling relationship (Matthew 28:19). Let's look for opportunities today to transfer our deposit to the lives of others.

Rev. William A. Raws

Ezekiel 14-15; James 2   **November 20**

An Attitude of Gratitude

Whoever has will be given more; whoever does not have, even what he has will be taken from him. (Mark 4:25 NIV)

When I read this verse I was sure that Jesus had said that "the rich get richer and the poor get poorer." That, of course, is not the meaning of His words. He was teaching our need to be grateful.

As soon as I was able to write, my mother made me write a "thank you" note to my aunt for the new underwear that she gave me for Christmas. How I hated that! It seemed like I was being untruthful. How glad I am now that she taught me this valuable lesson.

When we are thankful for what others do for us they are happy to do more; conversely when we are unthankful they want to take away what they have just given.

How could anyone take away what we have when we have just said that we have nothing? Is it not our Father's will that we learn to value what we have? Truly grateful people are happy. Much of our unhappiness comes from ingratitude.

Two centuries ago a London pastor stopped by, on his way home for supper, to check on an old widow, who lived in a basement apartment. He found her sitting at a table with only a crust of bread and glass of water. "Oh pastor," she said, "will you ask God's blessing on my meal. Think of it, I have all of this **and Jesus!**"

I thought how true it is that if we have the whole world but have not Jesus, we have nothing; but just a crust of bread with Jesus is everything! May God give us an attitude of gratitude.

<pre>
      Dear Jesus teach me while I may have little
              With you I have so much
           May I value most that I have you
              And may I value your touch!
</pre>

Dr. H. G. VanSandt

Ezekiel 16-17; James 3   **November 21**

What Does God Want from Me?

For you know the grace of our Lord Jesus Christ, that though He was rich, yet for your sakes He became poor, so that you through His poverty might become rich. (2 Corinthians 8:9)

    There are a few questions about tithing that seem to continually seek an answer. The most common question is: "How much does God expect me to give?" This question then branches off into several side issues: "Is ten percent a goal or a starting point?" or "Do I tithe on gross income or net income?" The New Testament never gives a direct answer to any of these questions but a careful study will open our hearts to principles that should settle these questions in our minds.

    In 2 Corinthians 8:9 Paul tells us that *Jesus was rich, but for [our sake] He became poor, that through His poverty we might become rich.* Not only did we become rich through Jesus, but we gained equality with Him in God's eyes. Since Jesus was willing to give all He had for us, we need to follow His example and give all we have for Him to use as He wills. This is not limited to finances but includes our time, talents and possessions as well.

    How much we give is not as important to God as the attitude with which we give. *Each one must give as he has decided in his heart, not reluctantly or under compulsion, for God loves a cheerful giver* (2 Corinthians 9:7 ESV). The churches of Macedonia were poor but they found great joy in giving. Paul says: *For they gave according to their means, as I can testify, and beyond their means, of their own accord, begging us earnestly for the favor of taking part in the relief of the saints* (2 Corinthians 8:3-4 ESV).

    Giving is more than meeting needs; it is an indication of where our heart is. God blesses those who give with a willing and cheerful heart. *You will be enriched in every way to be generous in every way, which through us will produce thanksgiving to God. For the ministry of this service is not only supplying the needs of the saints but is also overflowing in many thanksgivings to God* (2 Corinthians 9:11-12 ESV). The joy of our salvation and the gratefulness we have toward Jesus in recognition of all He has done for us is demonstrated in the way we reach out to help others in their need.

Allen E. Beltle

Ezekiel 18-19; James 4   **November 22**

Worry and Worship?

Oh, worship the LORD in the beauty of holiness!
Tremble before Him, all the earth. (Psalm 96:9)

    One of the privileges of living and working at America's Keswick is the opportunity of spending time with the men at the Colony of Mercy. When a man who is beaten and broken down by sin comes into the Colony, meets Jesus Christ as his Lord and Savior and as the only means of overcoming the sin of addiction, we watch a transformation take place. When they then begin learning about worship, their response is so amazing. They don't know about all the traditions and do's and don'ts that man has come up with and they freely worship with no fear of what others might think.

    Growing up in a very conservative, traditional church background, our style of worship in a typical service was very controlled. We dressed a certain way, smiled and said all the right things; I guess I would say that we just knew the "unwritten" rules that governed our behavior while we were in the church building. Kids would enjoy singing songs with motions and energy in "children's church" and then when they got to "big church," something happened. I don't remember anything being said, you just knew that your behavior needed to be more reserved.

    Julie Andrews said this, "I've learned things about myself through singing. I used to have a certain dislike of the audience, not as individual people, but as a giant body who was judging me. Of course, it wasn't them judging me. It was me judging me. Once I got past that fear, it freed me up, not just when I was performing but in other parts of my life."

I am prone to fear of people, worrying about my image, my behavior, what I say, what I wear, my performance as a person, how my kids behave, etc… This can be very draining and wearing on a person. This past summer a friend posted a quote on Facebook, "If you displease God, it doesn't matter who you please. If you please God, it doesn't matter who you displease." (Pastor Richard Allen Duncan)

When it comes to worship as a way of life seven days a week, it is time to stop worrying about the people around you and time to be concerned with what pleases God. Other people's opinions are just that, opinions. Let's focus on total abandonment to God and develop that love relationship with Him that is far beyond what we can ask, think or imagine. Remember, if God is for us, who can be against us (Romans 8:31b)? Remember that God will never throw past failures back in our faces. Remember that God loves you unconditionally!

Robert Hayes

Ezekiel 20-21; James 5   **November 23**

The Importance of Worship

…A certain woman named Martha welcomed Him into her house. And she had a sister called Mary, who also sat at Jesus' feet and heard His word… And Jesus answered and said to her, "Martha, Martha, you are worried and troubled about many things. But one thing is needed, and Mary has chosen that good part, which will not be taken away from her." (Luke 10:38-42)

We are going to visit the home of Martha, Mary and Lazarus to learn an important lesson about worship. This family lived in Bethany, just outside Jerusalem. Martha seemed intent on working; Lazarus seemed occupied with waiting; Mary seemed absorbed in worshipping.

On one occasion, while Jesus taught others, Martha worked in the kitchen while Mary sat at Jesus' feet. All of this apparently irritated Martha. Here was a potential for discord in a home over a spiritual issue. Martha was making a fundamental mistake that so many believers make. She was substituting activity (good activity, necessary activity at other times, to be sure) for time spent in the Lord's presence. Yet it was Mary who took the time to listen to the Lord.

Preparing food is important but there are some things that come before that. Here is a great lesson that worship is something we do for God, not what God does for us. Mary chose to worship. Love always wants to be near the one loved. Thus, Mary becomes a "silent witness" because she only says one thing in all of the passages in which her name appears, but her testimony is outstanding.

When my husband and I were in Russia, we observed that there were no chairs in many Orthodox churches. I asked "Why?" and was told that in worshipping God "standing was part of the sacrifice."

God does not specify any definite physical posture (sitting, kneeling, bowing, standing, etc.) by which to worship Him. The important thing is we are always in a "position" of worship in our heart attitudes and thoughts. Are we worshiping followers of Jesus? Are our thoughts toward Him or are we "in the kitchen" grumbling about others?

Joy Hubbard

Ezekiel 22-23; 1 Peter 1   **November 24**

Prayer of Thanksgiving

Offer to God thanksgiving, And pay your vows to the Most High.
(Psalm 50:14)

Christian gratitude is produced when we think of how dependent we are, how unworthy we are, and how favored we are.

First, how dependent we are! It is not by accident that Thanksgiving comes after harvest. Thanksgiving is offered after the toil and labor, after the plowed fields, after the golden harvest. It teaches us that we, as creatures of the earth, are dependent upon the divine promise found in Genesis 8:22 (KJV), *While the earth remaineth, seedtime and harvest, and cold and heat, and summer and winter, and day and night shall not cease.* Sad to say that some people work the year 'round with no consideration of the fact that season by season, day by day, they are dependent upon God's promise and power.

Secondly, how unworthy we are! As rebels in God's world, we have broken His law, defied His authority and sought to make God like us. Why should the Sovereign of the universe bear with the human race any longer? Why should He not wipe out the earth in judgment?

Third, how favored we are! God has not only patiently stayed with us, but He also offers us pardon and peace. He appeals to mankind to be reconciled to Him through Jesus Christ. So, in addition to the blessings in the natural world, we are recipients of His justifying grace and His pardoning mercy. Truly we can say with Jacob of old, *I am not worthy the least of all the mercies, and of all the truth, which Thou has showed Thy servant...* (Genesis 32:10 KJV).

You and I are approaching another Thanksgiving season. Much of the thanksgiving will be on the surface, even superficial. May ours be sincere and spiritual! May we offer the sacrifices of thanksgiving in sincerity and in truth. May we pray, "Lord, Thou hast given us so much; give us one more thing – a thankful heart!"

Rev. John Hibbard

Ezekiel 24-26; 1 Peter 2   **November 25**

Loved and Never Alone

For God so loved the world that He gave His only begotten Son, that whoever believes in Him should not perish but have everlasting life. (John 3:16)

Since the beginning God has been calling us and wooing us with one desire. That we would fall so in love with Him that loving Him would be enough to satisfy every longing, every craving, <u>every</u> everything.

And you shall love the Lord your God with all your heart, and with all your soul, with all your mind, and with all your strength... (Mark 12:30).

Dare we remember the price paid to ransom us? He took Himself and came down to earth to dwell among men. He hung on a cross. Bled. Died. Rose again.

Before He left for good, He appeared to a few and made a promise to us all that we would not be left alone, comfortless. He sent His Holy Spirit to dwell in us.

Therefore we are never alone. Never! As alone as we may <u>feel</u>, we can trust God. He is there and He is here, for us and not against us.

Most, if not all of us, have experienced some sort of bondage, oppression and torment, sickness or disease. In the midst, our enemy Satan, the father of all lies, the enemy of our soul, has deceived us into believing that we have no value or worth and that we can't possibly be loved by God.

Who shall separate us from the love of Christ? Shall tribulation, or distress, or persecution, or famine, or nakedness, or peril, or sword? As it is written: "For Your sake we are killed all day long; we are accounted as sheep for the slaughter." Yet in all these things we are more than conquerors through Him who loved us. For I am persuaded that neither death nor life, nor angels nor principalities nor powers, nor things present nor things to come, nor height nor depth, nor any other created thing, shall be able to separate us from the love of God which is in Christ Jesus our Lord. (Romans 8:35-39)

Do you know, that you know, that you know that you are loved by God? Do you believe it?

Stephanie D. Paul

Ezekiel 27-29; 1 Peter 3   **November 26**

Faithfulness – His and Ours

He who calls you is faithful, who also will do it.
(1 Thessalonians 5:24)

    In this age of infidelity and dishonesty, who can we trust? We constantly read of political corruption, corporate deception, cheating in schools, violation of marriage commitment, etc. All of this is a confirmation of Jeremiah 17:9, *The heart is deceitful above all things, and desperately wicked; Who can know it?* Where do we believers look for integrity?

    The Bible points to this as an essential characteristic of God. His faithfulness is basic to His own nature and forms the foundation for all of His words and works. This, combined with His unchangeableness, becomes the basis of faith for His children. He can be trusted.

    What does this word "faithfulness" mean? Through examining the Old and New Testament words translated "faithfulness" we are able to form a definition: Faithfulness is the god-like characteristic of complete trustworthiness and dependability which expresses itself in word and action.

    God's faithfulness does not depend on mankind's faith. The unbelief of the unsaved does not alter His faithfulness (Romans 3:3) nor does the doubting of believers change Him (2 Timothy 2:13). Our endorsement of His revealed character does not contribute to it, but makes a major difference in us. Our responsibility is to count on His faithfulness and act accordingly.

    The fact that God is faithful calls for our continual trust. When circumstances might indicate that He has deserted us – He is faithful. When problems seem to overwhelm us – He is faithful. When temptations press in on us – He is faithful.

    What is the relationship between His faithfulness and mine? Can I be depended on to speak the truth and act with integrity? The answer is found in the divine indwelling and infilling of the Holy Spirit. He imparts to me characteristics which are not native. Galatians 5:22-23 lists the ninefold fruit of the Spirit. Included in them is faithfulness. Through the controlling ministry of the Holy Spirit, this quality of God's character becomes operational in me. I do not produce it, but I can appropriate it by faith.

Rev. William A. Raws

Ezekiel 30-32; 1 Peter 4   **November 27**

Watching Our Words

Let no unwholesome word proceed from your mouth, but only such a word as is good for edification according to the need of the moment, so that it will give grace to those who hear.
(Ephesians 4:29 NASB)

When I first became truly aware of the words in this verse, about twenty some years ago, it brought tears to my eyes. Now I wasn't one to use "bad language," swear words, or even a lot of "slang" words, but the Lord used something about this verse to speak to me in a very deep way that day. I will address that more further along, but first some other issues about our words and the application of this verse. Other Scripture translations read "corrupt communication" (KJV), "corrupt word" (NKJV), "unwholesome talk" (NIV), "foul language" (HCSB).

Perhaps you are like me and never have considered your words to be "unwholesome," "corrupt" or "rotten," but how often are there some words we might use in place of those that we seek to never let pass over our lips. Such as "darn," "dang" or "drats," "heck" or "gads," "gees" or "fudge," and others, expressed with the same intent. They are a habitual response that tends to come out of our mouth when we are frustrated or irritated or angry. Perhaps there have been other times when we have muttered them under our breath, not really aloud for anyone to hear! I was convicted of this even more years ago by these verses from the book of James, chapter 3:9–10, addressing the use of the tongue: *With the tongue we praise our Lord and*

Father, and with it we curse men...Out of the same mouth come praise and cursing. My brothers, this should not be (NIV).

Another thing that I've become more and more aware of in recent years is the use of God's name by those in the Christian community in an exclamatory way: "God!" or "My, God!" or "Oh, my God!" While teaching the Ten Commandments to my kindergarten class (also a number of years ago), and wanting to impress on them what was meant by, *You shall not take the name of the LORD your God in vain...*(Exodus 20:7a), we talked about how we would use God's name "in vain." Understanding "in vain" to mean "misuse" or "for no reason," we concluded that God's name should not be used just casually or at anytime other than in praying to Him or praising Him. The Israelites considered God's name too holy to even speak it. "Yahweh is the promised name of God. This name of God which (by Jewish tradition) is too holy to voice, is actually spelled 'YHWH' without vowels....During the third century A.D., the Jewish people stopped saying this name in fear of contravening the commandment. *Thou shalt not take the name of the LORD thy God in vain.*" (www.blueletterbiblestudy.org/study).

DeEtta Marsh

Ezekiel 33-34; 1 Peter 5   November 28
Watching Our Words

Let no unwholesome word proceed from your mouth, but only such a word as is good for edification according to the need of the moment, so that it will give grace to those who hear.
(Ephesians 4:29 NASB)

Next let's consider the words, *...only such a word as is good for edification according to the need of the moment...*

How often are my words those that "edify" or build up others? It's so easy to criticize, be judgmental, or speak with a negative attitude; to gossip or discourage someone by what I say. Those words would then be considered to be "unwholesome," "corrupt," and even "rotten." But here we are instructed to be using our words for the good of those around us, to build them up in the Lord, edifying them *according to the need of the moment*. As we observe those we meet along the way each day, how can this Scripture be applied in our home, at our workplace, in the grocery store, at the post office, in our neighborhood, at the doctor's office, or while shopping at the mall? I need to ask myself, "Am I aware of *'the need of the moment'* of those around me, or is my focus just on myself, and the things that I have to do?"

An encouraging word, an act of kindness, a smile, a word of affirmation can express the love, joy, and peace of the Lord to someone who may be having a difficult day. The Lord has been teaching me to be resting in Him in the details of my life, trusting Him for His timing and direction moment by moment. Perhaps this is so that I can observe "the needs of the moment" in the lives of those with whom I come in contact and share Jesus' caring love with them. Philippians 4:4–8 *Rejoice in the Lord always, I will say it again: Rejoice! Let your graciousness be known to everyone. The Lord is near. Don't worry about anything, but in everything through prayer and petition with thanksgiving, let your requests be made known to God. And the peace of God which surpasses every thought will guard your hearts and your minds in Christ Jesus. Finally brothers, whatever is true, whatever is honorable, whatever is just, whatever is pure, whatever is lovely, whatever is commendable – if there is any moral excellence and if there is any praise – dwell on these things* (HCSB).

DeEtta Marsh

Ezekiel 35-36; 2 Peter 1   **November 29**

Watching Our Words

Let no unwholesome word proceed from your mouth, but only such a word as is good for edification according to the need of the moment, so that it will give grace to those who hear.
(Ephesians 4:29 NASB)

Then there's the last phrase, *...so that it will give grace to those who hear.* This is what the Lord used to really impact me that day many years ago concerning my speech and the use of my words. And I'm often reminded of this verse again and cautioned.

As I read those words, the Holy Spirit gave me the mental picture of being in conversation with someone about another person, and not only using my words but also the inflection of my voice, the body language, the rolling of my eyes, and facial expression to get my point across. Not only was I gossiping, but also slandering the person, and claiming that I was the one who was right in the situation. I was convicted not only of these unwholesome words, but of the fact that they would not be edifying to the person I was speaking to or anyone else passing by who heard me speak; nor did they in any way express grace to every one of those people who observed my tone as well as my words. Thus, tears came to my eyes and confession to my lips; repenting, I asked God's forgiveness.

How easy it is to be deceived into not "watching our words," then falling into sin by not using our words to bring glory and praise to the Lord. Let us be diligent about honoring Him with every word that comes from our mouths, so that the motive and intent of our words might be pure and edifying to all who hear.

As we continue the practice of watching our words, I trust that the following Scriptures will be helpful:

Proverbs 4:23 (NIV) *Above all else, guard your heart, for it is the wellspring of life.*
Matthew 12:34b (NIV) *For out of the overflow of the heart the mouth speaks.*

Psalm 141:3 (NIV) *Set a guard over my mouth, O LORD; keep a watch over the door of my lips.*
Proverbs 13:3 (NIV) *He who guards his lips guards his life, but he who speaks rashly will come to ruin.*
Proverbs 21:23 (NIV) *He who guards his mouth and his tongue keeps himself from calamity.*
Psalm 19:14 (NIV) *May the words of my mouth and the meditation of my heart be pleasing in your sight, O LORD, my Rock, and my Redeemer.*

Let's pray that others will be drawn to the Lord by the expression of the fruit of His Spirit evidenced in our lives as we are prayerfully "watching our words."

But the fruit of the Spirit is love, joy, peace, patience, kindness, goodness, faithfulness, gentleness and self-control. Against such things there is no law. Galatians 5:22-23 (NIV)

DeEtta Marsh

Ezekiel 37-39; 2 Peter 2   **November 30**

Lord, Wash My Mouth!

But the things that come out of a person's mouth come from the heart. (Matthew 15:18a NIV)

I saw a framed picture a few years ago that I wanted to have if I ever renovated my bathroom. The picture was a black and white still life of a water basin and pitcher in front of a window with flowing white sheer panel curtains. A small cut out in the matting read "Wash me and I will be whiter than snow." The picture seemed so gentle and relaxing. One day, after having words with my daughter, I thought of how those words came out of my mouth. The tongue is a small muscle but it can be a mighty weapon. Often the tongue is used without thinking, aimed at others and let loose. I knew that my mouth needed to be washed out. Washed from words that were hurtful and cutting. Words that were not spoken in love. Words that rang with an unspoken, "One day I may remind you that I have told you so." As I thought about what had come from my mouth the Lord showed me that my heart was even uglier. If my heart had been right those words would not have left my lips. In my heart fear and anger reigned rather than peace and trust. Self-righteousness and pride took over and made it impossible to show the compassion, mercy and grace that was needed. Clearly my mouth was not the only thing that would benefit from a cake of soap and a basin of water. I have never literally had my mouth washed out with soap but the thought of that picture did not come to mind as Jesus revealed the condition of my heart. When confronted with the ugliness of what lurked beneath my words I knew I needed to be washed.

James 3 tells us what a struggle you and I have with our untamable tongues. Verse 2 says *For we all stumble in many things. If anyone does not stumble in word, he is a perfect man, able also to bridle the whole body.* The word perfect also translates mature. I know I will not attain perfection but I can strive to be mature. Maturing our words is a process and we will stumble. Part of the process is knowing that when we stumble, you and I need to come to the basin to be washed again and again.

Kathy Withers

Ezekiel 40-41; 2 Peter 3　　　　　　　　　　　**December 1**

The Proud Tongue

May the LORD cut off all flattering lips, And the tongue that speaks proud things, Who have said, "With our tongue we will prevail; Our lips are our own; Who is lord over us?"
(Psalm 12:3-4)

When we think of a proud tongue we tend to think of the arrogant person who blatantly exhibits self-importance and a superior attitude toward others. Sure that kind of person is easy to spot and typically we do what we can to avoid such a one because he is draining to be around. Most likely, we do not identify ourselves to be that kind of person, and hopefully we are not. But just because we are not blatantly arrogant doesn't mean we don't have a proud tongue.

How many times do we try to get in the last word or keep saying the same thing over and over perhaps with a little different twist? We may feel like we just need to make our point (because we know we are right) or we're "just telling it like it is," or "just telling the truth." When we do this we are simply "prevailing" with our tongue. Right? In reality what we've done is claimed our lips as our own to be used for our purposes. We are refusing the Lordship of Christ over our tongues because we are set on accomplishing our own agendas rather than God's.

And do not present your members as instruments of unrighteousness to sin, but present yourselves to God as being alive from the dead, and your members as instruments of righteousness to God (Romans 6:13).

Each time we choose to use our tongue as an instrument of unrighteousness we are advancing Satan's agenda. When we clench our tongue as part of the silent treatment, are sarcastic or deceptive, when we nag, gossip or entertain coarse jesting, or when we grumble and complain we are prevailing with our tongue, being "lord" of our own tongue. All of which are forms of a proud tongue.

Putting off a proud tongue is not as simple as being silent but requires putting on a humble tongue, one that purposes to advance God's agenda. We walk in victory every time we yield to Jesus' spirit of humility in us to speak truth, encourage, edify, bless, instruct, exhort, admonish, rebuke and comfort, all forms of righteous speech.

What will you choose? Will you claim your tongue and prevail with your agenda or will you yield to the Spirit of Jesus Christ and walk in victory today?

Diane Hunt

Ezekiel 42-44; 1 John 1   **December 2**

Shine

Multitudes who sleep in the dust of the earth will awake: some to everlasting life, others to shame and everlasting contempt. Those who are wise will shine like the brightness of the heavens, and those who lead many to righteousness, like the stars for ever and ever. (Daniel 12:2-3 NIV)

    I've done a few Christmases now, and apart from a place in heaven through Jesus, I think my favorite thing is the fairy lights that go on the tree. Maybe I'm a little weary of Santa. When my son was four, about the eighth Santa we'd seen one day kind of attacked him. When my son looked him dead in the eye, and told him that Santa wasn't real, I wasn't sure what was about to happen. Santa looked embarrassed, but at the same time, a bit like someone about to hit a kid. So anyway, I'm sticking with the fairy lights. One year, I got so in love with fairy lights that when Christmas was over, instead of boxing them up, I hung them around our bedroom window. We kept them up for a whole year. Every night, we went to bed to the fairy lights. Perhaps the best year of our marriage!

    But some people just get frustrated by the things. After all, they do get tangled. They get stepped on. And if one is missing, the whole strand isn't right until you fix that one. But maybe these are the very reasons that I love them. Because people get tangled. Do you ever feel like, "Who's going to fix this mess?" Do you ever wonder if life could actually be all that you dreamed of as a kid? Can all that's gone wrong ever really be fixed? And people get stepped on. All the time. I'll bet that you've sometimes felt like you just don't matter. You've felt the crunch of someone's foot and they didn't even know that you were there. Or even worse, they did. We've all felt like the one left out.

    The truth is, though, that you're far more loved than you'll ever know. Remember the whole point? A place in heaven through Jesus? And so God himself got tangled. Thirty-three years of it. Made in human likeness. And then He got stepped on. Big time. He died to pay the penalty for sin. OK, let's get personal, your sin. And so you can rip up your list of how great you are, and why God should let you into heaven one day, and just do this thing God's way. You can receive forgiveness. We all can. We can all just lay down our pride, bundle up our problems and bring ourselves to God. All of us.

Which takes us back to the fairy lights. Remember what happens if even one is missing? But how beautiful it is when it all comes together? I know that in the build-up to Christmas, there are a million things to think about, but in the end there's only one thing that really matters. Only one thing that's going to matter a million years from now. That we know Jesus. That we make it to heaven. And that we have given our lives to bringing along as many people as we can. Are there people that you love that it just wouldn't be a perfect heaven without? We're all in this together. And one day, when it all comes together, we're going to shine!

Rev. Chris Thompson

Ezekiel 45-46; 1 John 2   **December 3**

My Workout Program

...work out your own salvation with fear and trembling; for it is God who works in you both to will and do of His good pleasure.
(Philippians 2:12c, 13)

We should be fully aware that our beings are complex but thoroughly integrated. We are more than a body, and more than a soul, and more than a spirit. These are united in one person (1 Thessalonians 5:23). Since God made us, He has a deep interest in all aspects of our being. Our body is to be maintained systematically through proper nutrition and physical exercise. He wants us to be mentally healthy to the degree that we can control and develop our minds. Of course, He is vitally concerned about our spiritual growth.

In our theme passage we have a spiritual mandate to work <u>out</u> our salvation. Notice that it does not suggest that we could possibly work <u>for</u> it. I have to possess it in order to work it out. In some mathematical exercises, a problem is given accompanied by the answer. The student is expected to show how the answer is arrived at through a series of steps. The idea in the Greek verb is "to work out to the finish."

Our salvation is treated in Scripture in three time aspects: past, present and future. In each God provides deliverance from an aspect of sin: its penalty, its power and its very presence. Our passage deals with the present process called sanctification. It is this that is to be worked out. God's gracious gift of salvation comes with a user's guide – the Holy Spirit and the Word.

Verse 13 declares the means for our fulfilling the mandate. God works in you to prompt your desires and enables your doing of His good pleasure. This eliminates external demands such as those found in the law. It rather presents the motive and the means for doing God's will as promoted from within by the Holy Spirit.

We are therefore responsible to <u>work out</u> what God <u>works in</u>.

Rev. William A. Raws

Ezekiel 47-48; 1 John 3   **December 4**

Those Interruptions!

Then they went into Capernaum, and immediately on the Sabbath He entered the synagogue and taught...Now there was a man in their synagogue with an unclean spirit. And he cried out, saying, "Let us alone! What have we to do with You, Jesus of Nazareth? Did You come to destroy us? I know who You are--the Holy One of God!" (Mark 1:21-24)

Interruptions! Those unanticipated and unplanned circumstances have a way of confronting our daily routines and wreaking havoc even with the most carefully laid plans.

We are probably the most managed society in history. Now the management of time is important. Few would really question that. But that is not the issue for us in this moment. The issue has to do with the interruptions we all confront every day. Do you think Jesus would have used a day planner had one been available to Him? Jesus and a day planner...what a provocative thought! Did interruptions happen to Jesus? Many times! How did He handle them? Let's take a look at one of them.

Jesus had gone to the synagogue in Capernaum and was invited to bring the reading and the comments, that is, to preach and teach the townsmen who had gathered there. But in the house of worship that morning there was a man with some demons within him. The devil was in that house of worship. In any church service, the devil can always be found there.

As Jesus preached, the man became more and more restless under the sound of the truth. Finally, he interrupted the Lord's sermon by shouting, *Let us alone! What have we to do with You, Jesus of Nazareth? Did You come to destroy us? I know who You are--the Holy One of God!*

Jesus used the interruption to rebuke the unclean spirit and those demons within the man were forced to leave him. As they did so, they tore the man in some kind of physical way that the other worshippers could see. The power of God was evident. This filled all of them with a sense of wonder and awe, and Jesus became more famous. Interruptions may prove to be the pathways to blessings.

Dr. Donald R. Hubbard

Daniel 1-2; 1 John 4   **December 5**

The Joy of the Lord

...For the joy of the Lord is your strength. (Nehemiah 8:10)
The fruit of the Spirit is love, joy... (Galatians 5:22)

Often Jesus is viewed by many as a "kill joy" but really He is a joy giver.

There is a difference between happiness and joy. Happiness is dependent upon favorable external circumstances. In contrast, joy comes from within independent of outward circumstances. One can have joy even though outward circumstances may be difficult.

God gives us something superior to happiness and that is His joy. His joy is not only superior but supernatural. Supernatural joy is a result of inviting Jesus into our lives as our Savior, trusting Him alone for the forgiveness of our sins and giving us eternal life and entrance into heaven to be forever with Him.

The Lord brings joy into our lives by transforming us. In John 16:21, Jesus used the illustration of a woman giving birth to a child. The point Jesus makes is that the baby born not only causes pain but also brings joy. The mother does not focus on the pain of the childbirth but on her new baby (a different way of looking at the experience transforming the circumstance into one of joy).

When the Holy Spirit saves and transforms our lives, He gives us His joy…therefore, joy is a fruit of the Holy Spirit (Galatians 5:22). There is a close connection between love and joy. A life lacking joy is a life lacking love, and a life lacking love is a life lacking joy.

Joy is a great power in the life of the believer in the Lord Jesus Christ. We can choose to activate God's joy in our lives, or we can choose to have "a pity party," feeling sorry for ourselves, moping around making ourselves and others miserable. Have you ever tried to use a power tool without it being plugged into the source of power? As Christians we are "connected" to Jesus…so let His joy flow through our lives! *...For the joy of the Lord is your strength.* (Nehemiah 8:10)

It takes less muscles to smile than to frown, so smile more often and give your face a rest and a "faith lift"!

Joy Hubbard

Daniel 3-4; 1 John 5 **December 6**

The Battlefield of the Mind

Set your mind on things above, not on things on the earth.
(Colossians 3:2)

War is raging on the battlefield of our minds. It seems as if there are times our thoughts are on a runaway train that we can't keep on the track let alone stop.

Because we live in a fallen, sin-sick world, our mind is much more likely to dwell on fleshly things than things of the Spirit. Have you ever noticed that when you want to sit and mediate on the Word that your mind flits hither and yon to everything BUT the Word? Yet, when you try not to think about something it seems as if that is all you can think about!!

Sometimes it feels impossible to tear our thoughts away from the negative, fearful, worrisome, angry, bitter thoughts. How do we "Set our mind?"

1. Know God's truth and promises
2. Be ready for battle
3. Persevere

We need to <u>know God's truth and promises</u> or else we will have no ammunition in our arsenal. *For the weapons of our warfare are not carnal but mighty in God for pulling down strongholds, casting down arguments and every high thing that exalts itself against the knowledge of God, bringing every thought into captivity to the obedience of Christ* (2 Corinthians 10:4-5).

We need to <u>be ready for battle</u> or else we will be easily overcome and discouraged. If we are not suited up and ready for battle we will be caught unaware and unprepared. Knowing we are in a battle will give us the attitude necessary to fight. *Put on the whole armor of God, that you may be able to stand against the wiles of the devil. For we do not wrestle against flesh and blood, but against principalities, against powers, against the rulers of the darkness of this age, against spiritual hosts of wickedness in the heavenly places. Therefore take up the whole armor of God, that you may be able to withstand in the evil day, and having done all, to stand.* (Ephesians 6:11-13)

We need to <u>persevere</u>. When those unwanted thoughts press in they feel powerful and overwhelming but don't believe it… not for a moment. Our thoughts only have power if we give in to them. Our propensity is to "try" battle but surrender as soon as we realize our enemy is not going to give up easily. We must persevere. The battle was not won on our behalf without a fight. Jesus had to persevere through the first slash of the whip, the first stroke of the hammer, to the very end when He surrendered His Spirit into the Father's Hands. Yet, the victory came when He rose again - conquering sin and death. Because He rose, you can persevere. Don't give up. Don't give up. Don't ever give up.

Diane Hunt

Daniel 5-7; 2 John   **December 7**

The Beauty of the Lord

And let the beauty of the LORD our God be upon us, and establish the work of our hands for us; Yes, establish the work of our hands. (Psalm 90:17)

Have you ever seen the beauty of the Lord? Pause for a moment and think about the beauty of a sunrise or a sunset. Think about the beautiful colors of autumn or the brilliant colors of spring. Think about a starlit night. The beauty of the Lord is seen all around us.

The beauty of the Lord should not be limited to nature. The beauty of the Lord should abide upon Christians. Have you asked the Lord to bestow His beauty upon you? That was the prayer of the Psalmist, *And let the beauty of the LORD our God be upon us…* In Psalm 149:4 the Psalmist writes, *For the LORD takes pleasure in His people; He will beautify the humble with salvation.*

Today what is perceived as beauty is actually a collection of artificial adornments. Much like the Christmas tree with its lights and tinsel, we now decorate our Christianity with big and beautiful buildings and professional music and entertaining preachers and call it beautiful. Where is the beauty of the Lord?

The beauty of the Lord should be sought. The Psalmist asked the Lord to bestow His beauty upon him. May He bestow upon us the beauty of compassion, the beauty of purity and the beauty of His grace, mercy and kindness. May He bestow upon us the beauty of His presence.

The beauty of the Lord can be lost. The Psalmist reminds us that we can lose the beauty the Lord bestows on us. He writes, *When with rebukes You correct man for iniquity, You make his beauty melt away like a moth; Surely every man is vapor* (Psalm 39:11).

Guard against the sin that saps the beauty of the Lord from your life. Make it your daily passion to seek the beauty of the Lord and your constant prayer that the beauty of the Lord would abide upon you.

Dr. Roger D. Willmore

Daniel 8-10; 3 John December 8

Prostrate Trouble

Humble yourselves in the sight of the Lord, and He will lift you up. (James 4:10)

The song leader announced the next hymn by repeating the first line. He said, "Let's all stand and sing, 'All hail the power of Jesus' name, Let angels *prostate* fall'." The twist of his tongue might have been traceable to the fact that several of his friends were being treated for prostate trouble. Most people in the large audience did not react to the slip-up, but a few found it difficult to sing the first stanza. Afterwards, I remembered recently hearing several people speak seriously of having *prostrate* trouble.

Spiritually speaking, many Christians suffer from prostrate trouble by failing to humble themselves and bowing in adoration and submission before the incomparable majesty and holiness of God. In the heavenly scene described by the apostle John in

Revelation 4:9-10, we observe that the heavenly hosts are delivered from prostrate trouble. Responding to the glory of the Lord, *...the twenty-four elders fall down before Him who sits on the throne and worship Him Who lives forever and ever...*

Lack of awe and adoration seems to characterize some of our style of worship. This tends to be especially true in our personal devotional practices. We rush into the presence of the Lord to satisfy our sense of obligation. We read the calendar-assigned Scripture and offer hurried prayer, but we fail to cultivate heart humility before the Almighty One.

I am not suggesting a form of physical posturing but an exercise of the heart bowing before the Lord of lords. In preparation for our entering the heavenly scene, it would be well for us to practice heart prostration on a regular basis.

Rev. William A. Raws

Daniel 11-12; Jude   **December 9**

Were Rules Really Made to Be Broken?

For I am the Lord, I do not change... (Malachi 3:6a)

While browsing a local gift store a sign caught my eye. It read, "If you always follow the rules you never have any fun." Today we see so many believers in Jesus Christ willingly compromise the commands of Scripture. In Malachi's day this was true as well. In chapter 2:10-16, God said, *Do not intermarry*, but they did. God said, *Do not follow after foreign gods*, but they did. God said, *Do not divorce* but they did so for no reason. We live in a time when people want to update Jesus and give Him a new look. They want to take His words and put them into a new context and compromise the rules. Some are challenging what God really meant by some of His rules. We hear little *thus saith the Lord*. Malachi 3:6 says, *I am the Lord, and I do not change.* The rules don't change because God doesn't change.

So, how will we know the rules? By reading the Bible and taking God at His Word. This is not a lesson in legalism, which kills, but in obedience, which brings life. The Bible, Bible helps and sound biblical materials are easily accessible. We have no excuse for not knowing God's expectations for us.

How can we keep the rules? Malachi 2:16 says ...*therefore take heed to your spirit.* Heed also means "to guard." We are usually prone to compromise when our guard is down and we are distracted from living in obedience.

What do you do if you have broken the rules? Recognize your sin. Repent of your sin. Remove the sin. Restore your relationship with Jesus.

I am the Lord, I do not change... The rules don't change because God doesn't change.

Kathy Withers

Hosea 1-4; Revelation 1   **December 10**

Unclean!

Now the leper on whom the sore is, his clothes shall be torn and his head bare; and he shall cover his mustache, and cry, "Unclean! Unclean!" (Leviticus 13:45)

According to levitical law, a person with leprosy was condemned to be an outcast not only by the world but by all his or her friends and family. Never to be touched or included in any family or social activity. They were outcasts from the temple as well...never able to worship God as was commanded. Wherever they went they were under the levitical law and had to cry out "Unclean!" as a warning to all. There was no way to hide it or disguise it. People would look upon them with fear, disgust and loathing. How heartbreaking.....

Jesus never shied away from anyone. He loved spending time with outcasts, sinners or those who were labeled "unclean." Jesus loved them, spent time with them, touched them and taught them. But He never turned His back on them.

And it happened when He [Jesus] was in a certain city, that behold, a man who was full of leprosy saw Jesus; and he fell on his face and implored Him, saying, "Lord, if You are willing, You can make me clean." Then He put out His hand and touched him, saying, "I am willing; be cleansed." Immediately the leprosy left him (Luke 5:12-13).

The "unclean" were Jesus' favorite people to hang out with and He received a lot of condemnation for it from the Pharisees, Sadducees and religious leaders. *And the Pharisees and scribes complained, saying, "This Man receives sinners and eats with them"* (Luke 15:2).

Jesus saw beyond the illness, the sin and the ugliness. He loved them and offered Himself to them through His love, His touch, His healing and His forgiveness. He was never too busy, too freaked out by what He saw or too disgusted by the sins that held them captive.

Who are the "unclean" in our society today? The addict? The sex offender? The thief? The adulterer? The murderer? They are no longer under the obligation to cry out "Unclean!" yet don't we still treat them in the same manner as in biblical times? If the "unclean" walk into our church, do we go to the opposite side of the church? Do we ignore them, shun them or turn up our noses at them?

What if we put on biblical glasses and saw them through the eyes of our Savior Jesus? How different would they look? How would we minister to them? Would we love them with the love of Jesus? Would we embrace them and introduce them to Jesus?

What a different world this would be….want to try on a new pair of glasses?

MaryAnn Kiernan

Hosea 5-8; Revelation 2   December 11

Redemption

...being justified freely by His grace through the redemption that is in Christ Jesus, (Romans 3:24)

When we think of redemption we immediately think of our salvation and God's saving grace that has rescued us from well-earned, well-deserved eternal damnation.

Yet there are so many other works of redemption in our daily lives that we need to stop and take notice of. Redemption is "to buy back, to get or win back, to free from what distresses or harms, to change for the better; to offset the bad effect of; to make worthwhile."[11]

When we consider this definition it is easier to see how what we consider bad actually can have redemptive value.

For example, suffering, in which God's purposes are accomplished by further conforming us to the image of Jesus Christ, "offsets the bad effect and makes the 'suffering' worthwhile." Being pushed beyond our personal limit can be redemptive when it causes us to cease trying and start trusting God. Not being able to see the big picture can be redemptive when it causes us to walk by faith rather than sight. Sharing our story of struggle and sin can be redemptive when it provides us the opportunity to share with others the transforming grace of God in our lives. Our own history of pain and hurt can be redemptive when we share God's comfort and encouragement which we experienced with others that are hurting. Conflict can be redemptive when it causes us to look at the sinfulness of our own hearts and compels us to run to the cross.

There is nothing beyond the redemptive power of Jesus Christ. ABSOLUTELY NOTHING. So no matter how desperate your situation looks today, you are not without hope because God is a God of redemption.

Diane Hunt

---

[11] www.merriamwebster.com

Hosea 9-11; Revelation 3   **December 12**

What's the Gospel All About?

For God so loved the world that He gave His only begotten Son, that whosoever believes in Him should not perish but have everlasting life. (John 3:16)

Here are two lists of words:
1. sin, rebellion, guilt, condemnation, eternal punishment, hell
2. emptiness, loneliness, fear, frustration

With which list is the Gospel chiefly concerned? This is not a trick question. In evangelistic preaching today, the impression is often given that the Gospel is primarily concerned with the personal needs of man: that is, satisfaction, fulfillment, guidance and hope.

The Bible, to me, touches on this to some degree in John 4 where the Lord Jesus appealed to human need as He addressed the woman's thirst.

But in the light of the total teaching of the Bible, this emphasis is definitely unbalanced. Such teaching can lead to misrepresentation of the Gospel.

There is another set of words that must be employed and I refer to the first list – sin, guilt, and hell. Because of sin man is dissatisfied, directionless, hopeless. But these conditions are the results of man's sin against God. Therefore, the Gospel gets to the root of man's problem – his rebellion against God.

It is certainly more popular to preach about man being disoriented and searching for identity rather than to declare that man is a rebel, unclean by nature, incurring the wrath of a sin-hating God.

What is your conception of the nature of the Gospel remedy? If we look upon man merely as a being needing guidance or fulfillment, the Gospel will become like a mere Band-aid© on our hands or like a pill we take for temporary relief. But if we look upon man as being sinful, proud in his rebellion, deserving the eternal wrath of God, the Gospel will become the most glorious message ever heard. It will bring deliverance from sin and its consequences.

Rev. John Hibbard

Hosea 12-14; Revelation 4   **December 13**

Your Word Is Truth

Sanctify them by Your truth. Your word is truth. (John 17:17)

Jesus' words in our verse today remind us that sanctification comes by God's Word.
Sanctify - Greek: Hagiazo 1) to render or acknowledge, or to be venerable or hallow. 2) to separate from profane things and dedicate to God. 2A) consecrate things to God. 2B) dedicate people to God. 3) to purify. 3A) to cleanse externally. 3B) to purify by expiation: free from the guilt of sin. 3C) to purify internally by renewing of the soul. (Enhanced Strong's Lexicon)[12]

Ephesians 5:25-27, *...as Christ also loved the church and gave Himself for her, that He might sanctify and cleanse her with the washing of water by the word, that He might present her to Himself a glorious church, not having spot or wrinkle or any such thing, but that she should be holy and without blemish.*

The Word of God is a vital component in the life of any child of God for growth, purification and sanctification. It is the means by which God changes us. It is one of His chosen tools to accomplish His goal in our lives to conform us to the image of Jesus Christ.

Romans 8:29, *For whom He foreknew, He also predestined to be conformed to the image of His Son...*

---

[12] Strong, J. 1996. The exhaustive concordance of the Bible: Showing every word of the text of the common English version of the canonical books, and every occurrence of each word in regular order. (electronic ed.) . Woodside Bible Fellowship.: Ontario

Oh, brothers and sisters, embrace the Word. Ask God to give you a passion for His Word. Savor it as you would a delightful morsel. Let it engulf your entire being. Don't render it to your "to do" list; rather put it on your "can't wait" list.

If this is a discipline you have yet to develop or it is something you do out of duty, be encouraged. Ask God to enlighten your mind, impact your heart, show you Himself. Keep at it until the duty becomes your delight.

Diane Hunt

Joel; Revelation 5 December 14

Powerful and Sharp

For the word of God is living and powerful, and sharper than any two-edged sword, piercing even to the division of soul and spirit, and of joints and marrow, and is a discerner of the thoughts and intents of the heart. (Hebrews 4:12)

In other words, according to The Message paraphrase, *God means what he says. What he says goes. His powerful Word is sharper than a surgeon's scalpel, cutting through everything, whether doubt or defense, laying us open to listen and obey...*

The thought of being cut by something so powerful and sharp is frightening! To have my thought-life laid open to reveal all its secret places is something I simultaneously dread and long for. Yet, in order for me to come to the place of obedience, I know that I must choose exposure *to* and saturation *by* the living and powerful Word of God Then, and only then, will any desire I have to "speak the truth in love" be marked by the sincere desire for what is best for the other person, rather than a desire to just "speak my mind."

As the writer of Hebrews says, only God's Word has the power to reveal the thoughts and attitudes of my heart or yours. That means I must be slow, very slow, to speak and pray what the writer of Psalm 12:3-4 so rightly penned, *May the Lord cut off all flattering lips and the tongue that speaks proud things, who have said, "With our tongues we will prevail; Our lips are our own, who is lord over us?"*

Simply put, I do not own **me** – my lips or my heart! God owns all of me! He is Lord over me and He would have my words be seasoned with grace and thus an instrument for His righteous purpose…not mine.

My question for you: Are the words that you speak to others seasoned with grace and love?

Stephanie D. Paul

Amos 1-3; Revelation 6 **December 15**

Will You Be Salt and Light Today?

When Jesus spoke again to the people, he said, "I am the light of the world. Whoever follows me will never walk in darkness, but will have the light of life." (John 8:12 NIV)

Is your testimony for Jesus in your circle of influence sprinkling salt & radiating light? In Matthew 5:13, we read: *"You are the salt of the earth…"* And in vs. 14, *"You are the light of the world…* Then in vs. 16 … *let your light so shine before men, that they may see your good deeds and praise your Father in heaven"* (NIV).

What does it mean to be the salt of the earth? To influence others for God, to be an example for God, and to share the love of God.

If you fill a pitcher with water and put an egg in it, the egg will settle in the bottom of the pitcher. Now remove the egg and add a lot of kosher salt to the same water in the pitcher. Place the egg in the water seasoned with salt. The egg will now float. Is that the way your life and my life are on a daily basis when it comes to being salt for Jesus? Do we come to the top? Is our testimony alive for Christ? Do we stand out for Him? Our love for Jesus is the salt that will cause us to rise to the top for Him.

Do you remember the chorus, "This little light of mine, I'm going to let it shine"? How brightly do our lights shine in our circle of influence? Are there bushels that we hide our light under so that no one really knows that we have Jesus in our hearts and lives? In John 12:36, we read, *"Put your trust in the light while you have it so that you may become sons of light..."* (NIV). In Ephesians 5:8 ... *but now you are light in the Lord. Live as children of light...* In verse 11, our instructions are, *Have nothing to do with the fruitless deeds of darkness, but rather expose them.*

We must be the children of light as Jesus is the Light of the world because we are His followers, God's children. Our light (witness) must continue to glow for all to see that we have become children of God by trusting in Jesus' blood shed on the cross for our redemption.

Have you lost your saltiness and glow for God? Ask Him to forgive you and restore the salt and light. Victory in Jesus will once again replace defeat.

Chaplain Stan Marsh

Amos 4-6; Revelation 7 **December 16**

Our Giving Father

Every good and perfect gift is from above, coming down from the Father of the heavenly lights, who does not change like shifting shadows. (James 1:17 NIV)

There is something delightful about watching someone open a gift—especially an unexpected one. We've all experienced growing excitement as a present loses its wrapping paper veil. Some people tear through in a flash while others can be painfully deliberate. They seem to treat this covering as a mandatorily preservable treasure. But once the gift is unveiled the giver watches the face of the recipient to see their reaction. It only takes a few seconds to tell whether the sacrifice has been worth the effort.

Have you ever stopped to think about our Heavenly Father as a giver? He's not just any giver either. James tells us that all of the good and perfect gifts we've been given have ultimately come from His hand of blessing. This truth has powerful implications for us whether we are giving or receiving. When we *receive* good gifts from others we should thank them for their consideration. Not only so, we should thank the Lord as the ultimate provider of all blessings, whether material or immaterial. Remember that the Lord longs to give us good things. Jesus said, *Ask, and it will be given to you; seek, and you will find; knock, and it will be opened to you. For everyone who asks receives, and he who seeks finds, and to him who knocks it will be opened. Or what man is there among you who, if his son asks for bread, will give him a stone? Or if he asks for a fish, will he give him a serpent? If you then, being evil, know how to give good gifts to your children, how much more will your Father who is in heaven give good things to those who ask Him!* (Matthew 7:7-11)

When it comes to *giving* gifts, they should emerge from seeds of gratitude and affection—not barren obligation. Additionally, we shouldn't forget that when we give well, we are ultimately acting as an instrument in the hands of God—the greatest giver of all. Therefore, we should seek the mind of the Lord in our gift giving. Let's consider what gifts matter most to Him, and allow Him to use us as a conduit through which His good and perfect gifts flow freely to others.

Rev. Jason Walsh

Amos 7-9; Revelation 8   **December 17**

Ready for Christmas?

Now the birth of Jesus Christ was as follows… (Matthew 1:18)

Are you ready for Christmas? Usually that question means…do you have a Christmas tree…are all the presents bought…is all the baking done…did we mail the cards?

But there are other ways, more important ways, in which we should get ready for Christmas. Let me give you a few suggestions. Perhaps they will help you get ready.

1. Re-read the Christmas story. Familiar though it may be, the accounts in Matthew and Luke contain hidden treasures that will enrich us with insight and inspiration. Read them over as if you never read them before. I know you will be rewarded!
2. Re-think the meaning of Christmas. Christmas teaches us that God is a giving God. John 3:16 states, *For God so loved the world that He gave His only begotten Son, that whoever believes in Him should not perish but have everlasting life.* And if we are going to be like Him, we too must be giving. That becomes visible at the point where we give ourselves for others.
3. Re-dedicate yourself to God. How? By seeking Him to open your mouth in praise. It is not by accident that Christmas has always been associated with song and music. On the night of our Savior's birth, the heavens rang out with angelic chorus praising God and glorifying His name.

Christmas calls for each one of us who knows Christ as our personal Savior to commit our lives to God – all that we have and all that we are – in order that He, in turn, may use us for His glory.

There are many ways to get ready for Christmas. This year let each of us prepare ourselves for God's rich blessing. Let us determine not to get lost in the trivia and tinsel of Christmas, preventing us from experiencing all God wants to give at this beautiful season of the year.

Rev. John Hibbard

Obadiah; Revelation 9   **December 18**

The Fullness of Time

But when the fullness of the time had come, God sent forth His Son, born of a woman, born under the law, to redeem those who were under the law, that we might receive the adoption as sons.
(Galatians 4:4-5)

    One of the most sweeping theological statements dealing with the first advent of Jesus Christ is found in Galatians 4:4-5. The context is important. Paul's letter to the Galatians is a severe letter, for some of the Galatians were in danger of moving from salvation by grace alone in the Person of Jesus Christ to that which had been taught among them by the Judaizers who were composed of those who insisted that a person must be obedient to the Law of Moses in order to be saved.

    Such a view proclaimed by the Judaizers is "another gospel" and is, therefore, soundly condemned by Paul. But that view was affecting a number of the Galatian believers. In Chapter 4 of Galatians, Paul illustrates the difference between the freedom we have in Christ and the bondage which the Law effects. Minor children, though they are heirs, are under guardians. Their position within the household differs little from the slaves of the household. Children who had reached maturity enjoyed the freedom which the inheritance brought, and were no longer under teachers, guardians and trustees. Jesus Christ makes the difference.

    In Galatians 4:4, the "But...God" marks the distinction Paul emphasizes: God brought both hope as well as freedom to all mankind in His Son. The coming of Christ was God making provision for spiritual sonship for all who believe.

    Christmas is full of wonder. The text tells us that at the right time (*fullness of [the] time*) God sent the right Person (*sent forth His Son*) in the right way (*born of a woman*) by the right requirement (*born under the Law*) for the right purpose (*to redeem them that were under the Law that we might receive the adoption as sons*). We should remember Christmas in this way.

Dr. Donald R. Hubbard

Jonah; Revelation 10 **December 19**

When It Makes No Sense

...the just shall live by his faith. (Habakkuk 2:4b)

There are times when our view of circumstances around us would seem to indicate that God is unjust or unfair. The culture of unrighteousness seems to flourish while the people of God appear to suffer disproportionately. These perceptions raise some very real questions. Why do the promoters of wickedness seem so successful? Why does God seem so silent? When God responds, why does He use wicked instruments to purify His own people? These were major questions in the mind of the prophet Habakkuk. He lamented over the condition of God's people and the seeming unresponsiveness of God. When God answered, Habakkuk considered the answer to be unjust. The agent of purification seemed to be more wicked than God's own sinning people.

After considering these supposed injustices, the prophet came to a proper resolution (2:1). Essentially, it was to watch, wait and see. One of the difficult lessons we must learn is that of waiting on God. In our impatience we assume that God is negligent or tardy, but He is prompt according to His eternal purpose.

When God's response was given, it included instruction for recording the events that will reveal His scheduled plan (v. 2-3). Two contrasting facts are given by the Lord (v. 4). The first has to do with the peril of pride. In contrast is the principle of faith. With just a few words, the Lord declares an essential life principle for His people. *The just shall live by his faith* is quoted three times in the New Testament, revealing the scope of its meaning. Galatians 3:11 speaks of initial faith, the basis of righteousness. Hebrews 10:38 speaks of continuing faith, the basis of security. Romans 1:17 seems to combine these when it speaks of moving from initial faith to progressive faith.

One further thing: when the principle of living by faith is presented, there is a possible alternate translation – *the just shall live by* <u>His faithfulness</u>. Aren't you glad that it's His faithfulness rather than ours? We are prone to doubt and disobedience; He is unchanging.

Rev. William A. Raws

Micah 1-3; Revelation 11   **December 20**

Not Bad, Just Not Good Enough

The Lord rewards every man for his righteousness and faithfulness, (1 Samuel 26:23 ESV)

Righteous means to be free from all guilt or wrong. So I'm going to be judged for being free from all guilt and wrong? That scares me! I'm a good person. I attend church regularly, I tithe, I am active in serving the Lord, I keep good friends and avoid bad ones, I pray, I visit sick people in the hospital, and I do a whole lot more that God should give me credit for.

Even worse, all of my righteousnesses are as filthy rags (Isaiah 64:6). That's bad news. Lexus has as its purpose statement, "The relentless pursuit of perfection." That's mine too. But I don't get credit for it. Not fair.

Well, if 99.9% were good enough, then:

...107 incorrect medical procedures would be performed today.

...880,000 credit cards in circulation will turn out to have incorrect cardholder information on their magnetic strips.

...12 babies will be given to the wrong parents each day.

...22,000 checks will be deducted from the wrong bank account in the next 60 minutes.

...and there are dozens more illustrations that would shock you.

So 99.9% isn't good enough for God either. Only perfection will do.

I can do all manner of good works and receive praise from men, but that doesn't make me more righteous. I can be a member in good standing of the best service club, social organization and church in town, but that doesn't make me more righteous.

But wait. I can be a liar and be accepted by God; Abraham was. I can be an adulterer and murderer and be accepted by God; David was. I can deny Christ and be accepted by God; Peter did.

This doesn't make sense.

Now God has me right where He wants me! There isn't anything I can do to earn salvation; it's a free gift (Ephesians 2:8-9). He wants me to understand that believing in Him to do what He promised to do causes Him to reckon the righteousness of Jesus to my account. (Romans 4:3,22). Therefore God seeing me through Jesus sees a perfectly righteous person and I am good enough because of Jesus.

That changes the whole picture. Now instead of being scared of God's demand, I am grateful for His provision. Now instead of working to be accepted, I work to please. Now instead of striving for perfection, I strive to exalt Him.

Rev. Neil Fichthorn

Micah 4-5; Revelation 12　　　　　　　　**December 21**

Total Preservation

... may your whole spirit, soul, and body be preserved blameless at the coming of our Lord Jesus Christ. (1 Thessalonians 5:23b)

One of the most encouraging teachings of the Bible is that of the security of the believer. Theologians speak of the *perseverance of the saints.* Our theme verse deals with the *preservation* of the saints. My perseverance is fully dependant on the preserving work of the God of peace. A more common translation of the word "preserve" is *kept*. It includes the thought of being guarded.

Jesus spoke of the shepherd and the sheep to illustrate His keeping or guarding provision (John 1:28-29). He said that we, His sheep, are secure in His hand. No one is able to snatch us from it. Not only are His sheep secure in His hand, but they are also held in the Father's hand. What a secure position! Doubly protected.

Now we may be sure of our eternal security, but what about the latter portion of the verse, *blameless at the coming of the Lord?* Is God able to preserve me blameless at the coming of our Lord Jesus Christ? This is the prayerful desire of the apostle Paul for the believers in Thessalonica (and for us). He relates blamelessness to the sanctifying work of the God of peace Himself. Only by His divine work of setting us apart unto Himself could He accomplish the end result of our being without blame at His coming.

Does His preserving and guarding work apply only to the immaterial part of our beings? No, God has set apart unto Himself our spirit, soul and body. This sanctification is to be complete in every part of our being. Founded upon our position in Christ (Hebrews 10:10), it is progressive, as the truth of God works in us (John 17:17), and it will be perfected at His coming (1 John 3:2).

Our part in this is in submitting to His keeping hand. When our children were just beginning to have confidence in their ability to walk, we would on occasion foresee a hazard which could cause them to stumble. We would extend our parental hand to guide them over or around the situation. On some occasions our help would be rejected, with the result that a tumble would bring a tearful submission. Let us not refuse His powerful, protective, and perfective hand.

Rev. William A. Raws

Micah 6-7; Revelation 13   **December 22**

A Whale of a Tail…

How many are your works, O LORD! In wisdom you made them all; the earth is full of your creatures. There is the sea, vast and spacious, teeming with creatures beyond number – living things both large and small. (Psalm 104:24-25 NIV)

When I was in Cape Cod on vacation I was able to go out on a whale watch. It wasn't my first trip out, and it probably will not be my last time to go whale watching. I was again not disappointed as the whales played and waved their tails at us like they were showing off. This time as we were coming up on different whales the guide would begin to name it or them. I looked at the lady next to me and almost in unison we said... "How do they know their names?" As if the guide heard us he then preceded to tell us that whales are most commonly identified by their tails, (the coloration of the ventral surface of their flukes.) You see whales have different tail patterns ranging from all white to all black. A whale's tail patterns are like human fingerprints - no whale has the exact same pattern, just like no human has the exact same fingerprint as another human. Each one is unique to the individual. All I could think of as I listened and observed each whale I was taking pictures of was – that's just like our God Who created them! How can we not believe in a God when we learn that even non-humans were each created different and unique? In Genesis we learn the animals were named... I figured that meant - that's a whale, that's a raccoon, that's a deer, etc... but now, I'm thinking they were actually named. Creation screams there is a GOD!

For since the creation of the world God's invisible qualities – his eternal power and divine nature – have been clearly seen, being understood from what has been made, so that men are without excuse (Romans 1:20 NIV).

If God took so much effort to make whales different and know them by name... How exciting it is to know that that same God tells me that he knows me by name. There is nothing that escapes God's knowledge and ability to pick me out from the rest. God doesn't miss what is going on in my life... I am clearly identified by Him, my Creator. That is the kind of God I have looking out for me. My Creator has given me an identity from all others. Not just whales, but humans... we are each fearfully and wonderfully made. That is the same God who is looking out and watching over you.

Scientists can follow whales as they migrate and swim the vast seas. God watches over us no matter where we are or what is going on in our lives. Because He made us, designed us and marked us... there is no place where we are hidden from Him. I don't know about you, but to me that is fantastic news and news that allows me to rest in Him. I am never alone...

If I take the wings of the morning, and dwell in the uttermost parts of the sea; even there Your hand shall lead me, and Your right hand shall hold me (Psalm 139:9-10).

Dr. Lynne Jahns

Nahum; Revelation 14   **December 23**

Last of All, He Sent His Son

Within your temple, O God, we meditate on your unfailing love.
(Psalm 48:9 NIV)

When my son was born there were complications. His head was out, but the rest of him was stuck. After quite a struggle, the midwife in charge said that she was going to push a button and that a team of doctors would be present in a matter of seconds to take over. The room was instantly full, and the doctor in charge took a look and then said one word, "Scissors." Several midwives held my wife down while he cut. Then with all of his strength he pulled my son into the world. My son had been without oxygen for several minutes. He was blue and lifeless. He wasn't breathing, and he had no heartbeat. The cord was quickly cut and he was raced away in the arms of another doctor. One team revived him, while another team tended to my wife.

Both were, and are, fine. My son has no lasting damage, but for about an hour we didn't know if he would live, and if so, what he would be like. The experience had a tremendous impact on me. For the first couple months of my son's life I couldn't hold him without crying. And so when we were in public, I just wouldn't hold him, because I knew what would happen next. But as soon as we were home, I couldn't wait to hold him, and to cry all over him. He's entering his teens now and I love him with all of my heart.

In 1990, when I became a missionary, I thought that I would end up in an Islamic or developing country. And if that were the case then I knew that at some point my own life could be in danger. I decided that if I were ever in any situation where I had to choose between my own life and someone else's, that I would give mine. I remember telling God that. And sharing it with loved ones so that if anything ever happened, everyone would know. Twenty years later, I still feel the same. However, there is one thing that I would not be prepared to do. If, by some bizarre circumstance, I had to choose between someone else's life, and the life of my son, then they'd have to die. I'm still not prepared to give the life of my son. Sorry, I'm just not there yet.

But that's what God did. He so loved the world that He gave His Son. He gave His Son. He actually gave His Son. He traded His own son. If you ever feel that you are not loved, think again. At some point in eternity God had your life in one hand, and the life of his own son in the other, and He chose that you would live. We all know what it's like to love another person. You must know how that feels. So get this. God loves you. It's something that He feels. His only Son has the scars to prove it. So find yourself a temple today where you can meditate on His unfailing love. Let Him hold you in His arms and let Him cry all over you.

Rev. Chris Thompson

Habakkuk; Revelation 15   **December 24**

When Love Came Down

Behold what manner of love the Father has bestowed upon us, that we should be called children of God! (1 John 3:1a)

Our God is a loving God. He is a seeking God. He came down from heaven in the person of His Son, the Lord Jesus Christ, in order to deliver us from our sins, clean up the mess we had made and restore us to a right relationship with Himself.

John begins the verse with the word *Behold*. This word is a challenge to pay close attention. He does not want his reader to be daydreaming. He wants them to see the wonder, the glory and the seriousness of what he is saying.

John uses the *manner* to describe God's love. He said, *Behold what manner of love the Father has bestowed upon us.* The word *manner* does not mean <u>what kind of love</u>. It means <u>where this love came from</u>. John is saying that the love of God is not a natural, earthly kind of love. It is a love that came from somewhere else. Indeed, it did come from somewhere else. It came from heaven above.

God bestowed His love upon us. He came down to us. When did He come to us? Where were we and what was our condition when He bestowed His love upon us? Paul answers this question in Romans 5:6-8, *For when we were still without strength, in due time Christ died for the ungodly. For scarcely for a righteous man will one die; yet perhaps for a good man someone would even dare to die. But God demonstrates His love toward us, in that while we were yet sinners Christ died for us.*

Think about this, He came to us when we were rebellious sinners, rejecting and scorning Him. How remarkable.

John then reminds us that after God came down to us He picked us up, put us into His family, and made us children of God. Now we are children of God.

Behold what manner of love the Father has bestowed upon us and give Him thanks, praise and adoration for His life-changing love.

Dr. Roger D. Willmore

Zephaniah; Revelation 16   **December 25**

A Life Transformed

"Where is He who has been born King of the Jews?..."
(Matthew 2:2)

The very first question in the New Testament is asked by the magi who had traveled a great distance looking for Someone. The three men from the East had apparently met one time to discuss a premonition each had had that something extraordinary either had happened or was going to happen, and they decided to travel together in their quest to faraway Jerusalem. Their decision was based partly on the awesome sighting of a brilliant star that appeared to be moving westward, as though it was deliberately leading the way which, as we know from Matthew 2:2 and 9, was the case.

Details regarding the background of the magi are slight. We know they were friends and educated. We know they were wealthy, evidenced by the treasured gifts they carried with them – gold, frankincense and myrrh. We wish we knew further details about what they discussed day after day as they traveled. When did they first hear that a special Baby had been born in a far-off land? How did they get their news in the first place?

"Where is He who has been born King of the Jews?" That was their question. When King Herod heard what three obviously important strangers from the East were asking, he called his priests to ask what they knew. Their reply included words from Micah 5:2: *out of you shall come a Ruler Who will shepherd My people Israel.* Herod was enraged. He was king! No baby, no child, was going to usurp his throne!

Masking his ire and thinking to trick the magi, Herod sent for them and requested that when they found the One they were seeking they return and tell him so that he, too, could visit Him and worship Him. Devious Herod!

In order to ensure that no little one would be able to dethrone him, he ordered that all boys under two years of age be killed. What anguish in so many households!

Once the magi found "the King of the Jews," called Jesus, they intuitively recognized the divine in Him. They worshipped Him and laid at His feet the wondrous gifts they had carried from afar. I believe they questioned Mary and Joseph about this Child and listened carefully to their story, including what was promised regarding His future.

God asked Adam, "Where are you?" and Adam was afraid. The magi asked Herod, *"where is He who has been born King of the Jews?"* and Herod was afraid.

Do you think the magi returned home unchanged? I think that special encounter with the Christ Child changed them forever. I believe God first led the magi, then worked a miracle of transformation. I believe they returned home rejoicing.

That is what a personal encounter with Christ does. He transforms lives.

Midge Ruth

Haggai; Revelation 17   **December 26**

After Christmas What?

And she brought forth her firstborn Son, and wrapped Him in swaddling cloths, and laid Him in a manger, because there was no room for them in the inn. (Luke 2:7)

So what happens in our homes after Christmas? It is well to remember that in the Bible the story of Christmas did not end with the narrative of the birth of Jesus. It continued afterward in dramatic ways. What happened after Jesus was born?

I. In the Temple – what gratitude…Luke 2:21-38. When Joseph and Mary brought the infant Jesus to the Temple to do for Him what the law required, there were two witnesses: the aged Simeon and Anna. Led by the Spirit to enter the Temple, Simeon gave his testimony…he could now die in peace because he had seen the Lord's Messiah. How he blessed God. And aged Anna joined them in giving thanks to God. What wondrous words were these to Mary and Joseph! There were those who were looking for Him!

II. In the palace – what godlessness…Matthew 2:3-7. It is difficult to believe, yet it is true...here were men who spent their lives in the study of the Scripture yet they ignored the truth they knew. The Scribes and Pharisees were professional students of the Old Testament. They knew well the prophecies of the Old Testament. But they did not have God in their hearts or in their minds. They did not act on the light they had. It is incredible to think that these religious professionals showed absolutely no interest whatsoever in discovering whether or not the Messiah had indeed been born.

III. In the house – what gifts…Matthew 2:9-12. Mary, Joseph and the infant Jesus moved into a house in Bethlehem where later they would receive the Wise Men. The Wise Men were the first Gentiles to bow their knees to the Lord Jesus with many to follow. They arrived at the doorstep of Joseph's home to worship the Christ child. The gifts they presented to Jesus were God's provision for the family. What they gave were not trinkets for an infant but gifts for a king. Without realizing it, their gifts would finance the holy family's quick trip to Egypt to escape Herod's murderous scheme.

How long after Christmas will we continue the spirit of gratitude and giving about our Savior?

Dr. Donald R. Hubbard

Zechariah 1-4; Revelation 18   **December 27**

You're Closer Than You Think

"As you go, preach this message: 'The Kingdom of heaven is near.'" (Matthew 10:7 NIV)

We used to sing this song that said that "somewhere in outer space, God has prepared a place…" It was fun but a bit confusing. Was heaven really in outer space? Like, go to Pluto, turn left, then go a million light years? Was my grandpa in some other galaxy? Why did Jesus call it "near?" The center of the universe is the throne of God, and it's nearer than we think. When the Bible speaks of "heaven" it can mean the atmosphere and beyond, as in, *The heavens declare the glory of God* (Psalms 19:1) Or it can mean the spirit world, as in our struggles being *against the spiritual forces of evil in the heavenly realms* (Ephesians 6:12 NIV). Or it can mean the very abode of God, as in *Our God is in heaven; He does whatever pleases him* (Psalm 115:3 NIV) …where Jesus called "paradise" and has gone to prepare our place. This is the "third heaven" that Paul couldn't describe. I believe in it entirely. I just see no biblical reason to believe it's in outer space. Jesus ascended, but only until "a cloud hid Him from their sight." Then what?

We're told to pray to our Father who is "in heaven" and promised over and over again that God hears our prayers "from heaven." God's Spirit is everywhere so He perceives all things but it's more than that. It's a child talking to his father who is right there. And the Bible says that we hear God "from heaven." God had something to say to Elijah but His voice wasn't in the wind or the quake or the fire; it was in the whisper. God whispered from heaven and Elijah heard every word. How close is that? Jesus told us that we had better be careful how we treat children because "their angels in heaven always see the face of my Father in heaven." So their angels are in heaven, looking at the face of God, and at that same moment watching a little child at his school desk, or on her bike, or better yet, sound asleep. Don't get me wrong. I'm not trying to say that this is heaven or anything as foolish as that. I'm just saying that it's closer than we've been trained to think.

As a minister, I have the privilege, at times, of being with Christians as they die. There's this moment when the spirit and the soul leave the body; and to be absent from the body is to be present with the Lord. Just like that. And so when I look into the eyes of a person who is so very soon going to be with Jesus, there is this incredible feeling of just how close heaven really is. Oh, I cry along with everybody else. I'll never get used to the pain of separation. But on the way home I usually think, "Wow, an hour ago they were with me. Now they are in heaven." How close was I to heaven? As you go about your day today, I pray that you will have an amazing sense of how close you are to God and all His glory even now. And that the distance between you and the loved ones that you have lost is not as vast as you once imagined. And that the time that you have here before you go to heaven is really not all that much. The kingdom of heaven is nearer than you think.

Rev. Chris Thompson

Zechariah 5-8; Revelation 19   **December 28**

Yearning For God

How lovely is Your tabernacle, O LORD of hosts! My soul longs, yes, even faints for the courts of the LORD. My heart and my flesh cry out for the living God. (Psalm 84:1-2)

Charles Spurgeon called this psalm, "One of the choicest of the collection."

Spurgeon said, "If the 23rd Psalm be the most popular, the 103rd the most joyful, the 119th the most deeply experimental, the 51st the most plaintive, this one is the most sweet of the Psalms of Peace."

W. Graham Scroggie said, "This psalm must have been written at a time when the temple and its services were established and when pilgrimages thereto were an established part of national life." He said, "This psalm fairly throbs with expectation and delight; the opening lines are the outburst of long pent up feelings."

Whatever else this psalm is about, it is certainly about a heart that longs for God.

The word "yearn" is a word we do not use much anymore. The New International Version translation uses the word. It is a good word. It means to desire something earnestly. It implies strong emotional longing.

Desire is a very important part of our Christian pilgrimage. Do you have a burning desire, a yearning for God?

A person can fake or counterfeit his words. He can learn to speak the words of Zion without knowing God. A person can fake or counterfeit actions. He can act like a Christian even though he is not one. A person can wear a façade or a mask and pretend to be something he is not. However, you cannot fake desire. Desire emerges from the heart. Your desire reflects the true nature of your heart.

I once heard Stuart Briscoe say, "God meets man on the level of his desire. Man can have as much of God as he wants."

Are you yearning for God?

Dr. Roger D. Willmore

Zechariah 9-12; Revelation 20　　　　　　　**December 29**

Zippity Do Dah!

Make a joyful shout to God, all the earth! (Psalm 66:1)

Do you remember that song? It has become rather famous over the years. The great thing about that song is that it is very hard to sing it with a frown on your face. It is all about enjoying life and celebrating all those beautiful things in our lives. In the 80s there was a song called "Celebrate" - not so profound and it only talked about the good times.

Did you know that God asks us to have Zippity Do Dah days every day? He calls us to celebration and joy. Not just in the good times, but at all times. Philippians 4:4: *Rejoice in the Lord always. Again I say, rejoice!* Here is my question... Do we really apply that verse or just quote it? It is one of those easier-said-than-done type of verses. I know personally it can be a real struggle to call life joyful when it can be rather difficult. Here is where God comes in to our everyday. One of the great things about God is that He knows all about our days and how difficult they can be, so He tells us that it is HIS joy that can be our joy when we need it. *The joy of the Lord is our strength* (Nehemiah 8:10b).

St. Augustine wrote: "A Christian should be an alleluia from head to foot."

Check out these verses:

Our mouths were filled with laughter, and our tongues with shouts of joy. (Psalm 126:2a NIV)

...continually offer up a sacrifice of praise to God, that is, the fruit of lips that acknowledge his name.
(Hebrews 13:15 ESV)

These things I have spoken to you... that your joy may be full.
(John 15:11)

Are you filled with joy? Do people know that you have the joy of the Lord, or are you so strung out from life's pressures that you struggle to experience such joy? In Christ, we have so much to be joyful about in the midst of our daily walk. Remember that nothing happens today that God is not in control of and that nothing compares with the eternity we will spend with Him if Christ is our Lord and Savior.

Dr. Lynne Jahns

Zechariah 13-14; Revelation 21   December 30

You Only Live Once!

You have made known to me the ways of life; You will make me full of joy in Your presence. (Acts 2:28)

Some time ago I heard an ad on the radio. It ended with the statement, "You only live once!" – obviously appealing to the listener to purchase their product now before it's too late. I thought about that – I will only live this one time. So what does it mean to live? For some it means "hurry, worry & bury." But Jesus said, *I am come that they might have life.* So today, let's see some things to help us live. To "live" is to....

L = Love (Luke 10:27-28) To live is to love: to love God and to love your neighbor. When we love someone we want to be near them, want to serve them, want to make them happy. Love is the secret to life. *Whoever finds Me finds life* (Proverbs 8:35). *God is love* (1 John 4:8). Our lives influence others; are you influencing them with love?

I = Individual To live is individual; it is a personal matter. The Apostle Paul put it very personally in Galatians 2:20, *For me to live...* I cannot live your life, nor can you live mine. In Luke 12:15-23 we read the parable of the rich fool who made an individual decision about his riches which led to his personal disaster. Are you living your individual life for God?

V = Value Life has value – it is short, but valuable. James 4:14 says it is *but a mist*. The definition of life is "that which is fresh, new, an active existence." Romans 6 is a chapter concerned with Christian conduct. 2 Corinthians 5:17 tells us that any man in Christ is a new creature – if not new, then no life equals no value! Think about this: If your life should end today, would the Lord's work suffer any? Your life is of great value!

E = Eternal (John 11:25-26) Whoever lives in Christ will never die. Your life today is eternal. Spiritually you will live forever if you have received Christ. Even those without Christ will never die as Revelation 20:10 & 15 reveal an eternity in torment. So, you can begin this day to live now according to the words of the hymn that says, "With eternity's values in view, Lord." God needs people who are willing to live for Him.

Remember: You only live once!

"Only one life, 'twill soon be past, only what's done for Christ will last."

Jack Noel

Malachi, Revelation 22   **December 31**

Don't Stop Making New Year's Resolutions!

"Tomorrow, Tomorrow, Tomorrow,"
The poet did say.
As if each new tomorrow
Was just like yesterday.

Well, a new tomorrow is coming
That will put an end to it all
For at the stroke of midnight
(And the dropping of the ball)

It will be not just a new day
But the starting of a year.
As we begin each decade
One might face it with fear.

Or one may have hope and confidence
As the year is newly born,
And greet each new tomorrow
As God's blessed morn.

Some say they'll make no resolution
As in the days of yore
Because they have kept none of them
That they had made before.

One need not make a resolution
If one has reached perfection.
Nor if in despair they find life
Only worthy of rejection.

But if you find life worth living,
Possessed of some great hope
Then a New Year's resolution
Will help you be able to cope.

So pledge that each new tomorrow
You will endeavor to improve,
Until God calls you into His presence
As from this life you move.

Then should you miss your mark
And not make it to perfection,
You will still be much better off
For moving in that direction.

So don't give up on God
Nor on yourself and others,
But try again to improve relations
Between your sisters and brothers.

If "entropy" teaches us that
Everything tends to run down
Then not to put up a struggle will
Simply mean you will drown.

Thus, your New Year's resolutions
Will mean that you are alive
And against the evil within or without
You will continue to strive.

Make a New Year's resolution
Trusting in strength from above,
And know that success or failure
You are still safe in God's love.

You see, it is good to set a goal,
And to start to pack your grip
Should you fail to reach your destination
You can still enjoy the trip.

Dr. H. G. VanSandt

For more information about the ministries of
America's Keswick, please visit our website:

www.americaskeswick.org

or contact us at:
America's Keswick
601 Route 530
Whiting, NJ 08759
732-350-1187 or 1-800-453-7942